EUROPEAN MEDIEVAL DRAMA
AN ANNUAL JOURNAL DEVOTED TO THE STUDY OF THE DRAMA OF THE
EUROPEAN MIDDLE AGES, PUBLISHED IN ASSOCIATION WITH THE
SOCIÉTÉ INTERNATIONALE POUR L'ÉTUDE DU THÉÂTRE MÉDIÉVAL

EUROPEAN MEDIEVAL DRAMA

Editorial Board
Cora Dietl, *Justus-Liebig Universität Gießen*
Lenke Kovács, *Universitat de les Illes Balears (Mallorca)*
Martin Bažil, *Univerzita Karlova*
Eliška Kubartová, *Univerzita Palackého*

Advisory Board
Marie Bouhaïk-Gironès, *Sorbonne Université*
Mark Chambers, *University of Durham*
Elisabeth Dutton, *University of Fribourg*
Glenn Ehrstine, *University of Iowa*
Max Harris, *University of Wisconsin-Madison*
Alexandra Johnston, *University of Toronto*
Pamela King, *University of Glasgow*
Gordon Kipling, *UCLA*
Jelle Koopmans, *University of Amsterdam*
Mario Longtin, *University of Western Ontario*
Nerida Newbigin, *University of Sydney*
Bart Ramakers, *Rijksuniversiteit Groningen*
Leif Søndergaard, *Syddansk Universitet*
Charlotte Steenbrugge, *University of Sheffield*
Elsa Strietman, *University of Cambridge*
Meg Twycross, *Lancaster University*

European Medieval Drama

27 (2023)

BREPOLS

Material for publication in EMD should be addressed to the General Editor:
Cora Dietl (cora.dietl@germanistik.uni-giessen.de).

Members of the Société Internationale pour l'étude du Théâtre Médiéval (SITM) are entitled to subscribe to EMD at a members' rate. For further information about membership of the SITM and addresses of the national secretaries, please contact the SITM General Secretary, Eliška Kubartová; contact details available from the SITM website: http://www.sitm.info/summary/officers/.

For information about subscriptions and orders, please contact periodicals@brepols.net.

© 2023, Brepols Publishers n.v., Turnhout, Belgium.

All rights reserved. No part of this publication may be reproduced, stored in a retrieval system, or transmitted, in any form or by any means, electronic, mechanical, photocopying, recording, or otherwise without the prior permission of the publisher.

D/2023/0095/341
ISBN 978-2-503-60364-3
DOI 10.1484/J.EMD.5.137639
ISSN 1378-2274
eISSN 2031-0064

Printed in the EU on acid-free paper.

Contents

List of Illustrations   7

The Spiritual Dimension of the Majorcan Play Texts. MS 1139, Biblioteca de Catalunya
Lenke KOVÁCS   9

'Reality Effect' in Religious Performances of the Passion. *Depositio Crucis, Planctus Mariae, St Vitus Passion Play* **from Bohemia**
Eliška KUBARTOVÁ   41

Singen und Wiegen. Das Weihnachtslied 'Ecce mundi gaudia' im *Wienhäuser Liederbuch*
Clara STRIJBOSCH   71

Gesang auf dem Sinai. Dynamische Räume und Signale der Transgression im *Mühlhäuser (thüringischen) Katharinenspiel*
Angelika KEMPER   105

Du Moyen Âge à aujourd'hui. Sainte Barbe en scène
Susanna SCAVELLO   131

Catechism and Miracles as Arguments in Religious Debate. Hanns Wagner's *Play of St Ursus*
Cora DIETL   161

George Buchanan, Dramatic Strategies, and Polemics in the Scottish Reformation
Pamela M. KING   189

Staging Enmity. Performance Strategies in Wartime
Susannah CROWDER   215

6 CONTENTS

**MS Bodley 175, William Bedford's 1604 Copy and the
Antiquarian Afterlife of the Chester Plays**
Theodore K. LERUD   235

Reviews   259

List of Illustrations

Eliška Kubartová

Figure 2.1. Crucifixus Dolorosus from Jihlava ('Přemyslid Crucifix'); first third of the fourteenth century. The Royal Canonry of Premonstratensians at Strahov. Photo: NoJin, Wikimedia Commons.   52

Figure 2.2. Crucifixus Dolorosus from Drasty (previously Hradčany); around 1350. Carmel of St Joseph in Prague. Photo: Petr Uličný.   54

Figure 2.3. *Arma Christi, Passional of Abbess Kunigunde*, Prague, National Library of the Czech Republic, MS XIV A 17, fol. 3^r. Photo: National Library of the Czech Republic.   63

Figure 2.4. *Arma Christi, Passional of Abbess Kunigunde*, Prague, National Library of the Czech Republic, MS XIV A 17, fol. 10^r. Photo: National Library of the Czech Republic.   64

Clara Strijbosch

Figure 3.1. Fragment eines Andachtsbilds aus Kloster Wienhausen. Photo: Kloster Wienhausen.   83

Figure 3.2. Florenz, Biblioteca Medicea-Laurenziana. Ms Plut. 29.1, fol. 428^r. Photo: Biblioteca Medicea-Laurenziana.   85

Cora Dietl

Figure 6.1. Franz Graff, Reconstruction of the old minster of St Ursus before 1763 (copper engraving, 1855). Photo: City Archive of Solothurn.   162

Figure 6.2. Hanns Wagner, *Tragoedia Ursina*, 1581, Solothurn, Central Library, ZBS S I 120, p. 34. Photo: Cora Dietl.   181

Figure 6.3. Hanns Wagner, *Sant Vrsen Spiel*, 1575, Solothurn: Central Library, S I 81, p. 58. Photo: Cora Dietl.   183

Theodore K. Lerud

Table 9.1.	Post-Reformation copying of the Chester Whitsun plays: Five substantially complete manuscripts.	236
Figure 9.1.	Chester Midsummer Watch 2019. Photo: Theodore K. Lerud.	238
Figure 9.2.	Chester Midsummer Watch 2019: Hellmouth with other figures. Photo: Theodore K. Lerud.	239
Figure 9.3.	Chester Midsummer Watch 2019: The giants. Photo: Theodore K. Lerud.	240
Figure 9.4.	Chester's weir, just above the Dee Bridge. Photo: Theodore K. Lerud.	242
Figure 9.5.	A characteristic page of William Bedford's manuscript of the Chester Whitsun Plays. Oxford, Bodleian Library, MS Bodley 175, fol. 48ᵛ. Photo: Theodore K. Lerud.	245
Figure 9.6.	William Bedford's manuscript of the Chester Whitsun Plays, Oxford, Bodleian Library, MS Bodley 175, first page. Note partial restoration at top. Photo: Theodore K. Lerud.	246
Table 9.2.	The Five Versions of David Rogers' *Breviary*.	250
Figure 9.7.	*Arma Civitatis*, Arms of Chester, David Roger's *Breviary* (1609), Cheshire Archives and Local Studies (CALS) ZCX 3, fol. 89ʳ. Photo: Theodore K. Lerud.	251
Figure 9.8.	Coat of arms of Richard Lupus, David Roger's *Breviary* (1609), Cheshire Archives and Local Studies (CALS) ZCX 3, fol. 52ʳ. Photo: Theodore K. Lerud.	251

LENKE KOVÁCS

The Spiritual Dimension of the Majorcan Play Texts

MS 1139, Biblioteca de Catalunya*

▼ **ABSTRACT** In our analysis of the spiritual dimension of the Majorcan play manuscript (MS 1139, Catalan National Library, Barcelona), we focus our attention on the image of God and the faithful that these texts convey and on how these plays aim at enhancing the audience's disposition and the longing to be transformed by participating in the religious experience imparted by the church. We show how as a whole the late medieval plays, objects of our study, were conceived as media intended to increase the spiritual progress of the members of the community who created and witnessed throughout the liturgical year the scenic representation of the main subjects of the history of the Salvation.

▼ **KEYWORDS:** community drama, religious plays, spirituality, Catalan Late Medieval Drama, manuscript studies

---

* I am grateful to Glenn Ehrstine (University of Iowa) for his helpful revision of this text. Needless to say, for the flaws that remain I am solely responsible.

Lenke Kovács (lenke.kovacs@uib.cat) is a tenure-track contract lecturer with a PhD in the Department of Catalan Philology and General Linguistics at the University of the Balearic Islands. Her main field of research is medieval and early modern religious Catalan drama. She belongs to the Institut d'Estudis Hispànics en la Modernitat, unit associated to the CSIC. Since December 2022, she has been part of the family of Benedictine Oblates of Montserrat.

European Medieval Drama, 27 (2023), 9–40
BREPOLS ❦ PUBLISHERS
10.1484/J.EMD.5.137676

> Dedicated to the memory of Dom Josep Massot i
> Muntaner, OSB (3 November 1941–24 April 2022)

The Majorcan Play Texts as a Devotional Medium

Some historians of Catalan medieval and early modern religious drama acknowledge the importance of the spiritual dimension in this play tradition. Thus, Ferran Huerta,[1] in his edition of late medieval Catalan Old Testament plays, refers to sacred drama as 'veritable suport i aliment de la pietat medieval' ('true support and nourishment for medieval piety'), and Guillermina Cenoz,[2] in the introductory section of her unpublished doctoral dissertation on late medieval Catalan Christmas plays, emphasizes the need to analyse these pieces as testimonies of faith, rather than as artistic creations. Francesc Massip[3] shows how the use of aerial devices to stage supernatural situations or acts — such as apparitions, disappearances, or miracles — illustrate the importance of transcendental reality in Catalan medieval and early modern religious drama. For his part, Josep Romeu i Figueras[4] identifies 'la captació de la meravella i el misteri' ('the capture of the wonderful and the mysterious') as one of the centres of interest in this play tradition.

To date, Catalan medieval and early modern religious plays have not yet been analysed in-depth as an expression of spirituality and as a manifestation of Christian faith.[5] Neither have they been related to other aural and visual media — such as vernacular homilies, treaties, prayer books, devotional objects, and iconographic motifs — nor to any form of preliminary or ensuing individual or communitarian practices — such as the completion of devotional exercises or the participation in processions, vigils, and pilgrimages — that form the spiritual context and the reception framework of these plays.

A fruitful line of research concerns the plays' reception by the audience members to whom these performances were addressed. Thus, for example, the theatrical representation of the torments inflicted on Christ in the Passion plays, as well as the explicit visualization of the martyrdom in medieval hagiographic theatre, are justified by their soteriological meaning, that is, in the light of what the patristic tradition calls the 'economy of Salvation' or the 'economy of the Word Incarnate'. Inserted in the

---

1 *Teatre bíblic*, ed. by Huerta, p. 6.

2 Cenoz, *'Teatro navideño'*, p. 10.

3 Massip, *La Festa d'Elx*; Massip, *La ilusión*, and Massip, 'Le vol scénique'.

4 Romeu, *Teatre català*, vol. i, p. 39.

5 For an analysis of the Marian devotion in medieval and early modern Majorca, and its relation to iconography and drama, see Llompart, 'La devoció mariana'.

context of redemption, the spectators perceived the bloody and poignant scenes as edifying and uplifting in illustrating a part of the history of Salvation. To understand the spiritual benefit that the public hoped to gain from these scenes, one must keep in mind the faith that motivates and sustains religious theatre. In short, we consider the plays' 'function as a devotional medium',[6] an aspect worthy of consideration by theatre historians interested in the Majorcan play texts when it comes to approaching the initiators' aims, the performers' roles, and the spectators' viewing experience.

The first step we propose to take in this direction is the analysis of the portrayal of the characters in the Majorcan play texts, a core feature of the performance designed to contribute to the devotional reception by the audience. Further studies may envision other aspects we have mentioned as elements for future analysis towards reaching a better understanding of this play tradition.

The Majorcan Play Manuscript

The famous codex of late medieval plays from Majorca, known as the Llabrés Manuscript, was copied at the end of the sixteenth century in the Majorcan village of Búger and contains forty-nine plays, all in Catalan except for five plays in Spanish, excluded from the present analysis.[7]

The first aspect to be considered is the fact that all but one[8] of the plays in the codex deal with topics related to the Salvation of mankind, ranging from the Binding of Isaac to the Last Judgement. The manuscript further includes examples of the four different dramatic models that, according to Joan Mas,[9] coexist in Catalan late medieval drama. The first category includes works that respond to a traditional scheme, reduced to a minimum

---

6 Ehrstine, 'Passion Spectatorship', p. 304.

7 We focus in our study on the autochthonous tradition of religious drama, i.e. the plays in Catalan, all of which anonymous, except for no. 10, written by Fra Cardils. In contrast, four of the five Castilian plays in the codex are works available in sixteenth- and seventeenth-century editions: the piece no. 3 (*Obra del sanctíssimo Nacimiento*, which is a version of *Obra del pecador* a Nativity play by Bartolomé Aparicio), published in 1616, and the pieces no. 23 (*Obra llamada la Pastorella*), no. 24 (*Aucto del Nacimiento*), and no. 25 (*Descendimiento de la Cruz*) by Joan Timoneda, published in 1558. For a study on these plays, see Shoemaker, 'The Llabrés Manuscript'. The fifth Castilian play stands out from the rest for being the only profane piece in the codex.

8 The exception is the profane play entitled *Doctor y batxiller* (no. 4), which consists of 110 lines and is written in Spanish and Macaroni Latin. The two characters mentioned in the title dialogue, show off their supposed wisdom and allude to a series of authorities, such as Cato (ll. 35 and 54), Solomon (l. 36), Seneca (l. 37), Galen (l. 41), Averroes (l. 43) and Avicenna (l. 43).

9 Mas, 'El teatre religiós', pp. 30–32.

of elements, for example, the *Play of the Samaritan Woman* (no. 15) or the *First Play of the Raising of Lazarus* (no. 17). A second category includes plays with greater dramatic complexity, such as the *Play of the Nativity of Christ* (no. 6), the *Play of Susanna and the Elders* (no. 16), the *Play of Saint George* (no. 30), the *Play of King Ahasuerus* (no. 35), the *Play of Saints Crispin and Crispinian* (no. 45), and the *Play of Judith* (no. 47). In these plays, the traditional model with its basic structure is enriched by religious or profane materials (carols, virelais, pre-existing dramatic monologues, spiritual *contrafacta* of profane songs, etc.), featuring actions, characters, and intrigues, some of a highly spectacular nature. A third category includes plays with some allegorical elements, and more discursive characters, presenting a verse pattern and original features that denote the personal style of an author. Examples of this category are *the Play of the Temptation of Christ* (no. 10), *the Play of the Last Judgement* (no. 11), *the Play of Death* (no. 36), the *Play of the Glorious Saint George* (no. 31), the *Play of the Glorious Saint Christopher* (no. 32) and the *Play of the Seven Sacraments* (no. 40). A fourth category includes the pieces that exhibit a transition to the humanistic Renaissance, with laconic rubrics and pious and ascetic meditations. They include the *Play for Christmas Eve* (no. 37) and three hagiographic plays structured in acts or 'passos' ('steps'): the *Play of the Life of Saint Francis* (no. 29), the *Play of the Conversion and Life of Saint Matthew* (no. 44) and the *Play of the Conversion of Saint Paul* (no. 48).

The Majorcan Plays as Communitarian Worship

Several rubrics in the Llabrés Manuscript indicate that the plays contained therein were performed in the cathedral of Majorca and other churches. In the first sixty lines of the fragmentarily preserved *Shepherds' Play* (no. 5), for example, five prophets make their entry from different areas of the cathedral: the first from behind the high altar, the second from the chapel of the Rosebush, the third from the chapel of Saint Lucy, the fourth from the chapel of Saint James and the fifth from below the choir. According to the initial rubric of the *Second Play of the Temptation* (no. 10), Saint John makes his entry from the sacristy ('És mester que [sant Joan] vinga de la sacrestia').[10] The initial stage direction in the *Play of the Last Judgement* (no. 11) mentions a chapel located in the central part of the church ('Per recitar la present consueta, se farà un cadefal, gran quan porà, en la capella més el mig de la iglésia, algun tant enfora, y detràs d'ell se'n farà un

---

10 According to another stage direction in the same play, Jesus is to walk up the aisle of the church: 'Ara és menester que Jesús vinga per la sglésia amunt' (no. 10, l. 58a).

altre junt an el mateix').[11] In the *Play of Susanna and the Elders* (no. 16, l. 312a), the bailiff meets the protagonist's lascivious accusers in the aisle ('L'algutzir encontre los vells en lo coredor').[12] According to the final stage direction of the *Second Play of the Raising of Lazarus* (no. 17, l. 250a), the characters of the Jews leave the church before all the others sing a song of thanksgiving to God ('Los jueus ixen de la sglésia, y, après, tots los altres canteran fent gràsias a consert'). In the *First Play of the Descent from the Cross* (no. 21, l. 84a), the characters of the Virgin Mary, Saint John, Nicodemus and Joseph of Arimathea meet in the transept of the church ('en lo creuer dels bancs'). A rubric in the *First Play of Maundy Thursday* (no. 27, l. 36a) mentions the altar of repose, referred to as 'casa sancta' (holy house), which is to be situated in the mayor's pew ('la casa sancta, la qual sterà en el banch del bal·le').[13] In the *Play of King Ahasuerus* (no. 35) the initial stage direction mentions four scaffolds to be erected in different places of the church, with the one for the main character's residence being located next to the mayor's pew.[14] In the *Second Play of Good Friday* (no. 38, l. 554a), Saint John and the Virgin Mary meet at the head of the pews ('al cap dels banchs'). In the *Play of the Seven Sacraments* (no. 40, l. 17a), the Law of Grace walks through the pews of a church building which is not further specified ('La Ley de gràtia, cami[n]ant per los banchs').

As for the plays' frequency of staging, the initial rubric of the *First Play of the Descent from the Cross* (no. 21) indicates that it took place every year in the cathedral of Majorca. Apart from the four Passion plays included in the Majorcan play codex, containing one play of Maundy Thursday and one play of Good Friday each, three plays of the Descent from the Cross and one play of the Resurrection, each to be staged on the corresponding day of the Holy Week, we know from the initial rubric that the *Play of Susanna and the Elders* (no. 16) was staged on the fourth Sunday of Lent.

To capture the ambience of communitarian worship created by those who participated in the staging of the Majorcan plays, it is important to point out that these pieces are practically entirely sung to the tunes of liturgical chants, using the technique of *contrafactum*. The choice of these tunes confers a high degree of solemnity to the plays, and, remarkably, the

---

11 The rubric after line 36 in the same play reads: 'Are faran fosque la iglesi tant com poran' ('Now they darken the church as best they can').

12 Two more plays in which an aisle is mentioned are the *Third Play of Maundy Thursday* ('Ara romanga Maria enmig del corridor per fer-se encontradissa amb lo Iesús', no. 38, l. 588a) and the *Third Play of Good Friday* ('Ara ve la Maria y lo Ioan y Magdelena y Marta. Y diu la Maria, encontrant-se ab las tres donas qui steran an el corridor', no. 39, l. 48a).

13 According to the initial stage direction, at the beginning of the play there are three prophets in a chapel ('Primer ý haurà tres prophetas qui steran dins una capella').

14 The stage direction reads: 'Per representar la present consueta és menester quatre cadefals; asò és, dos a cade part de la església. Sia lo primer junt en lo banch del bal·le'.

use of liturgical chants in these plays is not limited to exemplary characters but can also be found in wicked ones, such as Mortal Sin (no. 1), Venial Sin (no. 1), Original Sin (no. 1), Lucifer (no. 10), Superbia (no. 11), Luxury (no. 11), Beelzebub ('Bersabuch', no. 11), Envy (no. 11), Potiphar's Wife (no. 12), the Prodigal Son (no. 13 and no. 14), Vanity (no. 13), Judas (no. 19), Pilate (no. 21 and no. 41), Annas (no. 27), the Lycian king Degra[15] and his entourage (no. 33), the Assyrian king Sennacherib (no. 34), Ahasuerus, king of Persia and Media, with his counsellors and servants (no. 34), Longinus (no. 40) and the Babylonian king Nebuchadnezzar (no. 47).

Another aspect to be considered in order to understand the nature of the Majorcan plays as an enactment of Christian spirituality is that many of these plays end with a chant of thanksgiving and praise. This can be found, for example, at the end of the *Second Play of the Prodigal Son* (no. 14, ll. 580–91), the *Play of the Samaritan Woman* (no. 15, ll. 201–04), the *Play of Susanna and the Elders* (no. 16, ll. 399–14), the two plays of the *Raising of Lazarus* (no. 17, ll. 251–66 and no. 18, ll. 420–27), the *Play of the Resurrection* (no. 22, ll. 329–40), the *Play of Abraham* (no. 26, ll. 207–18),[16] the two plays of *Saint George* (no. 30, ll. 387–98 and no. 31, ll. 487–98), the two plays of *Saint Christopher* (no. 32, ll. 250–53 and no. 33, ll. 414–29) and the *Play of Tobies* (no. 34, ll. 588–91). Whereas in all these cases the closing prayer is in the vernacular, the *Second Play of the Temptation* (no. 10) culminates with the chanting of the hymn 'Te Deum laudamus',[17]

---

15 In the *Golden Legend*, the king's name is Dagnus. Jacobus, *Legenda aurea*, ed. by Häuptli, vol. II, p. 1302, l. 3.

16 The blessing contains a formula that is used in the *Play of Saint Agatha* in her profession of faith before she suffers the martyrdom ordered by emperor Quintian. The protagonist refers to the Creator saying: 'Sirventa só d'aquell sol Déu | qui cel, terra y la mar feu' ('I am a servant of that one and only God, who made Heaven, the earth and the sea', ll. 395–96), using a formula which comes from the Decalogue (Exodus 20. 11), and which can also be found in other biblical passages (Psalm 146. 6; Acts 14. 15; Revelation 17. 7). These words recall the profession of faith of Saint Fructuosus of Tarragona: 'I worship the only God, who has made heaven, earth, sea, and all that they contain', a formula that is also found in other acts of martyrdom of ancient times (*Actes del martiri*, ed. by Serra, p. 11, n. 10). Another reference to God as the creator of Heaven, the earth and the sea is to be found in no. 47, ll. 179–80.

17 Castro specifies that the *Te Deum*, according to the medieval allegorical interpretation, was the hymn that marked liturgically the moment when Christ resurrects. *Teatre medieval*, ed. by Castro, p. 38. According to Dominguez: 'De façon traditionnelle, les pièces s'achèvent sur un *Te Deum laudamus*, où les acteurs et les spectateurs réunis rendent hommage à leur Dieu. [...] Plutôt qu'une "atmosphère de componction", on imagine des applaudissements enthousiastes, équivalents d'une danse collective qui diraient la joie de voir se terminer le spectacle sur la confirmation du salut. Le *Te Deum*, c'est d'une certaine façon le générique du spectacle favori des chrétiens: la Passion dramatique de Jésus, qui atténue l'angoisse profonde du paradis à jadis perdu.' Dominguez, *La scène*, p. 249. However, rather than 'alleviating the deep anguish of a paradise lost forever', we believe that what the Christian

accompanied by a group of musicians. The *Shepherds' Play* (no. 6, ll. 195–296) contains a sequence of fifteen stanzas sung by different characters, each of which ends with the line 'God be praised!'.

Some of the plays also include a doxology, a characteristic shared with the Eucharistic Prayers, the Liturgy of the Hours, and devotional practices such as novenas and the Rosary Prayer. Thus, for example, in the *Play of the Resurrection* (no. 22, ll. 129–40), the Forefathers praise Christ before the Harrowing of Hell; in the *First Play of Maundy Thursday* (no. 27, ll. 71–74), the boy whom Christ has freed from the evil spirit praises him for his goodness; in the *Play of Christmas Eve* (no. 37, ll. 330–37), Abraham praises 'the eternal God' and in the *Play of the Conversion and Life of Saint Matthew* (no. 44, ll. 441–45), the protagonist praises the 'eternal God and Lord who created the world'. The Trinitarian doxology 'Gloria in excelsis' can be found in the *Second Play of Christmas Eve* (no. 2, l. 135a), sung by angels.

Another common element in the Majorcan plays is the giving of blessings. For instance, the *Play of Saint Francis* (no. 29, ll. 668–77) ends with the Trinitarian blessing that the founder of the order, immediately before his death, bestows on his brothers in faith who are prostrate on the ground. In the *Second Play of the Raising of Lazarus* (no. 18, l. 42), Jesus gives Lazarus the blessing he asked for. According to the final stage direction in the *Play of the Conversion of Saint Paul* (no. 48), after his final speech, the main character gives his blessing before he takes leave.

The Trinitarian formula, 'in the name of the Father, and of the Son, and of the Holy Spirit', is used twice by Jesus in the third play of Maundy Thursday at the institution of the Lord's Supper (no. 38, ll. 244–45 and ll. 250–51). Likewise, the Virgin Mary in the *Play of the Three Magi* asks for the blessing of the Christ Child, whom she refers to as:

Pare, Fill, Sanct Sperit,
tres persones en trinitat
e en divina unitat (no. 7, ll. 217–19)

> (Father, Son and Holy Spirit, three persons in Trinity and in divine unity).

Stage characters making the sign of the cross are Jesus healing a paralytic in the *First Play of the Raising of Lazarus* (no. 18, l. 24a), the king in the *Second Play of Saint Christopher* when he hears the devil's name (no. 32, l. 119a), and the Hermit in the *Play of Saint Crispin and Saint Crispinian* (no. 45, l. 316a).

---

community does in representing the Passion is to celebrate its faith in salvation and its hope in the resurrection. On the singing of the *Te Deum* in the old Catalan theatre, see also Santandreu, *Teatre*, p. 54.

However, it should be noted that the gesture of blessing is not always explicitly mentioned in the play texts. Instead, in the scene of the Last Supper in the *Second Play of Maundy Thursday*, there is a cross in front of the stage direction that indicates that Jesus is blessing the table (no. 27, l. 188a). The sign is repeated before the consecration of the bread (no. 27, l. 243a) and the chalice (no. 27, l. 249a), and before the final blessing of the table (no. 27, l. 327a). We consider that these signs do not refer to another passage in the manuscript, as supposed by Mas,[18] but that they are rather stage directions that indicate the gesture of blessing.

The Majorcan Plays as a School of Prayer

Watching and listening to the different characters in the Majorcan plays pray was likely to function as a means of spiritual guidance for the audience. Throughout the plays, the spectators were observing the characters in an attitude of reverence and receptiveness carefully created as helpful models for their response to God's call to serve Him, acknowledging and accepting the gifts that have been bestowed on them. Thus, the attendees were not expected to consume the religious content provided by the plays or to be entertained by what was put on stage, but to obtain a spiritual benefit from the communitarian exposure to reenactments of episodes from the Holy Scriptures, from the lives of the saints and other subjects related to the Salvation of mankind.

Through typological exegesis, Old Testament characters such as Adam, David, or Susanna appear as devout members of the faith, whose prayers express the hope for redemption through Christ. Thus, in the *First Play of Christmas Eve*, Adam on his knees begs God by his great mercy to send to the world the One who, as he has promised, will free them from the great harm he has caused.[19] He brings forth this prayer intoning the melody of the hymn 'Christe qui lux',[20] a chant he has already used in his previous interventions. In the same play (no. 1, ll. 306–09), David exhorts all present to kneel devoutly to give thanks to the Almighty for the good news of the announcement of the Saviour's birth, which Isaiah has just foretold. In the *Play of Susanna and the Elders* (no. 16, ll. 216–17), the innocently convicted protagonist, who is bound to the sound of trumpets

---

18 Mas, 'Tipologies de les passions catalanes', p. 270.

19 'O Senyor, per te gran mercè | aquell en lo món vulles dar, | que prometeres per desliurar | de tan gran dany que comès he', no. 1, ll. 74–77.

20 Hymn of the first Sunday of Lent: https://cantusindex.org/id/830070 (accessed: 4 February 2024). This hymn is also used in the plays no. 1, ll. 45a and 61a, no. 5, l. 12a, no. 12, ll. 394a, 466a, 522a, 598a, and 670a, no. 32, l. 67a, no. 34, ll. 131a, 211a, 299a, and 467a, no. 40, ll. 232a and 360a.

THE SPIRITUAL DIMENSION OF THE MAJORCAN PLAY TEXTS 17

and is about to be led outside the city to be executed, begs Christ for help, addressing him as 'Christ, Déu, Senyor, | Sperança de Ysrael!' ('Christ, God and Lord, the hope of Israel'), in allusion to Jeremiah 14. 8 and 17. 13.

Kneeling is a common gesture with which the stage characters in the Majorcan plays accompany prayer to God. Thus, in the *Play of the Binding of Isaac* (no. 26, l. 32a), Abraham kneels to ask God where he wants him to sacrifice his son. Likewise, in their nuptial chamber, Tobies and Sara kneel and pray that God may bless their union (no. 34, l. 467a). Another example is that of Saint Christopher who after his imprisonment kneels and, like Adam intoning the hymn 'Christe qui lux', asks the Lord to save him in his great goodness from sin so that he can serve Him until his death.[21]

Interestingly, kneeling appears in two different ways in the third and the fourth Maundy Thursday plays in the apocryphal scene in which Jesus takes leave of his mother before the Last Supper. Whereas in the third play Jesus exhorts the Virgin Mary, after she has fainted, to raise from her knelt position to give him her benediction once he has given her his (no. 38, l. 164), in the fourth play it is Jesus who kneels before receiving his mother's benediction (no. 42, l. 379a).

Apart from kneeling, another gesture related to prayer used in the Majorcan plays is placing one's hand on one's chest. This is the way how the Christian slave prays in the *Play of Saint Crispin and Saint Crispinian* (no. 45, l. 53a). For his part, in the *First Play of the Raising of Lazarus* (no. 17, l. 152a), Jesus says a prayer with folded hands, and in the second play on the same subject, he looks up to heaven (no. 18, l. 389a). In the *Play of Tobies*, the spouses, after having knelt, also pray with folded hands (no. 34, l. 467a). The same prayer position is adopted by the main character in the *Play of the Conversion of Saint Paul* (no. 48, l. 171a), after having miraculously recovered his eyesight. As already mentioned, in the *Play of Saint Francis* (no. 29, l. 667a), the friars prostrate on the ground to receive his benediction.

The fact that the audience was familiar with these gestures from their own individual or communitarian prayer practice is likely to have favoured the identification of those present with the actions depicted in the plays. By the inclusion of these gestures in the texts, the spectators were invited to both recognize and mirror the faithful attitude and behaviour of the stage characters who exercised an exemplary function for the community.

Regarding the reception of the plays, it might be helpful to remember that, according to Ronald E. Surtz, 'the most important function of the prologue is that of serving as a bridge between the reality of the audience and the reality of the play'.[22] The concern for an adequate reception of

---

21 'O Senyor, per te gran bondat, | io·s prech ma guardau de peccat, | perquè sempre puga servir | a vós, Senyor, fins el morir!', no. 33, ll. 217–20.
22 Surtz, *Teatro medieval*, p. 130.

the performance is prevalent in the prologue of the *Second Play of Saint George* (no. 31). In the opening sequence, the Prologue speaker pays scant attention to the content of the play. Knowing that his audience is perfectly familiar with the narrative, there is no need for him to go into detail.[23] He limits himself to stating that what is going to be seen is the martyrdom of the glorious Saint George, adding that this saint is highly venerated in the village that hosts the staging (ll. 9–10). Whereas the conventional summary is missing in the preliminary part, there are several other conventional elements such as the plea for silence (l. 2) and for the ceasing of laughter and humour (l. 6), the apology for any shortcomings (l. 15), the claim of telling nothing but the truth (l. 16), the assurance of the spiritual profit to be obtained from the performance (l. 18), and the wish not to lengthen the prologue unnecessarily (l. 28). More than in any other of the Majorcan plays the prologue speaker stresses the communal character of the event (ll. 19–20) and reminds his audience that peace and concord should reign among those who are Christians (l. 21). He exhorts them to refrain from stupidity both in words and in actions (l. 23) and to make room for each other in a fraternal way (l. 24), so that these human efforts may serve God to increase people's virtue and goodness (ll. 25–26). The importance of unity and cohesion is also manifest in the final exit when all the actors sing together praising the Almighty and asking for the protection of Saint George, their patron (ll. 486–98).

Another prologue, which focusses mainly on the audience, is the one that opens the first Majorcan play of Saint Christopher (no. 32). Of its 55 lines, which represent approximately twenty percent of the whole play, fourty lines refer to the spectators and fifteen summarise the content. In this play, it is a character designated as 'the Author' who addresses the spectators, asking them to sit down (l. 3), concentrate (l. 4), and pay attention (l. 5). He expects the play to stir the spirits conveniently (ll. 11–13) if the audience is not distracted (l. 19). Once he has outlined the basic action (ll. 21–35), the Author insists on the importance of the spectators' attitude and behaviour. He promises them to obtain pleasure from watching the performance if they listen attentively and keep quiet (ll. 36–45). The last two stanzas of the prologue are identical to the final part of the prologue of the Majorcan *Play of Death* (no. 36), a coincidence,

---

23 An important feature of the audience in medieval theatre is their familiarity with what is seen as stageworthy material. In his comment on the prologue of the *Mystère de sainte Barbe en deux journées*, Mario Longtin draws our attention to this circumstance: '[…] the story has already been told. Barbara was known to the Christian audience, and her prior story emerged in the memory of each spectator, in a form of knowledge that preceded the stage version of the story. The characters of this story have stories that have been told and will be told again and again by "personnages" (characters) with the help of actors. The name of Barbara bears a story, and the utterance of the name invokes that story'. Longtin, 'Prompting', p. 195.

which has been pointed out by Josep Romeu i Figueras, the editor of these plays.[24] First, the audience is once again reminded of the need to pay attention, if they want the play to contribute to their salvation (ll. 46–50), and finally, the Author expresses his hope to be successful in awakening the spirits of the audience (ll. 51–55).

In the *Play of Death* (no. 36), the prologue seems particularly aimed at trying to prevent the spectators from getting upset by what is being staged. The audience is asked to keep calm and watch with the utmost attention, when Death enters the stage (ll. 6–10). The spectators' emotional distress should not lead to confusion, but to a reflexive and diligent attitude oriented towards salvation (ll. 11–20). Another concern expressed in the opening speech is the fear that the performance might not be received as a serious matter but as something risible (ll. 21–23). The prologue in the Majorcan *Play of Death* has the function to avoid two extreme reactions among the audience. Neither should the spectators express their fear of Death by making noise and upsetting each other, nor should they adopt an attitude of mockery and contempt for what is being staged (ll. 21–30). The prologue exerts thus the function of trying to control the response of the audience.

Whereas in the *Play of Death* the prologue is clearly focused on the audience, the opening sequence in the *Second Play of the Descent from the Cross* (no. 41, ll. 1–42) stands out for being centred on the contemplation of the Saviour and the cruelty of his death on the Cross. Reference to the spectators is made indirectly by reminding them of their condition as creatures in need of redemption. The Prologue character, clad in a tunic and black mourning cloak, and wearing a black wig crowned by a diadem, sings his role to the melody of the hymn 'Pange lingua gloriosi'. Together, the character's attire, the text, and the *contrafactum* of a liturgical composition contribute to creating an ambience of worship in which the boundary between performance and service is clearly blurred.

The Christology of the Majorcan Play Texts

A key element in determining the specificity of the Majorcan play texts is the analysis of the figure of Christ, as presented to the spectators who witnessed the performance of these plays. Through textual analysis, we propose to point out the main features that characterize Jesus as a stage character in this play tradition.

To define the Christological profile prevalent in the Majorcan plays, first, we examine the direct characterization of the stage character, by word

---

24 Romeu i Figueras, *Teatre català antic*, vol. III, p. 46.

and gesture. Then, while aspiring to achieve an even more complete view, we focus our attention on indirect characterization, i.e., on the characterization that derives from the interaction of the figure of Christ with the rest of the characters who appear in the Majorcan plays.

Our study of the Christology of the Majorcan plays has a precedent in Guy Borgnet's[25] analysis of the *Short Passion of Benediktbeuren* — also known as *Ludus breviter de Passione* — which is part of the famous *Carmina Burana* collection. This short Latin drama, copied between the second half and the end of the thirteenth century, consists almost exclusively of verses from the Vulgate, for which reason Karl Young considers it devoid of any literary originality.[26] Borgnet, on the other hand, illustrates that what at first glance may seem like a mere montage of stories of the Passion of the four Gospels, is the work of an adapter who chooses those pericopes that show how Christ dominates the situation that leads him to the Cross with the authority that his divine nature confers on him.[27]

In the *Ludus breviter*, the most prominent feature is sovereignty as a manifestation of the divinity of Christ. The Majorcan plays, in turn, invite the viewer to contemplate how God reveals himself to mortals in the exemplary humanity of Jesus of Nazareth. This is not just common practice in the texts which form the four Passion plays, but also in those which belong to the public life of Jesus,[28] that is, the two plays of the Temptation

---

25 Borgnet, 'Structure'.

26 Young, *The Drama*, I, p. 516.

27 Borgnet observes that in addition to selecting those passages from the Gospel narrative of the Passion that show Christ in his sovereignty, the adapter removes from the chosen pericopes everything related to suffering and humiliation. Thus, for example, in the scene of Jesus's agony and prayer in the Garden of Gethsemane, he only retains the reference to the traitor who is about to arrive ('ecce appropinquabit qui me tradet', Matthew 26. 46). Borgnet, 'Structure', pp. 67–68. The adapter also leaves out the trial before the Sanhedrin and keeps Christ in absolute silence throughout Pilate's interrogation. There is also no mockery, no flogging, no coronation of thorns, and both the Way of Calvary and the Crucifixion show how Jesus, in the words of Borgnet, 's'avance dignement vers une mort qu'il a choisie et qui représente l'aboutissement de sa mission'. Borgnet, 'Structure', p. 69.

28 Romeu i Figueras indicates that there are five texts in this group, which are those published in *Teatre sobre la vida adulta*, ed. by Santandreu. *Teatre català*, ed. by Romeu i Figueras, vol. I, p. 41. We consider that the two plays of the Parable of the Prodigal Son, as they belong to the preaching of Jesus, could be included in the group of pieces of his public life. Santandreu opts to use the term 'adult life', arguing that the retreat to the desert of Jesus predates his public ministry. *Teatre sobre la vida adulta*, ed. by Santandreu, p. 13. Jesus indeed began his preaching in Galilee after the temptations in the wilderness. But before that, when Jesus is baptized by John, the Holy Spirit descends on him and the voice of the Father is heard: 'You are my beloved Son, with you I am well pleased.' (Mark 1. 11; Matthew 3. 17; Luke 1. 22) This baptism is a public act of great importance for the Church because according to the Gospel account it is here that it is manifested that Jesus, in addition to being a man among men, is the Son begotten by the Father, in the fullness of the Holy Spirit. In the light of the theophany before the temptations, the forty days that Jesus spent fasting in the wilderness are part of his public mission, as well as all the other times when he retires, from

THE SPIRITUAL DIMENSION OF THE MAJORCAN PLAY TEXTS 21

(nos 9 and 10), the Play of the Samaritan woman (no. 15) and the two plays of the Raising of Lazarus (nos 17 and 18).

The scenic character of Jesus, we find in the Majorcan plays, is based, on the one hand, on the scriptural and ecclesiastical tradition and, on the other, on the updating of this legacy within the community that brings it to life and perpetuates its practice. In other words, the protagonist of these pieces is constructed, not only from sources of diverse origin (biblical, apocryphal, homiletic, liturgical, devotional, iconographic, etc.) and statements of teaching, agreed and transmitted throughout the history of the Church, but the characterization of the stage character also responds to the concrete reality of the Christian community involved in the staging of this theatre.

An important stage moment in defining the Christological profile of the Majorcan plays is the first appearance of Jesus in each of the plays that interest us here. The main character's entry into action captures the attention of the audience and is likely to please them to the extent that it meets the expectations of the audience's familiarity with what is being staged.

This first appearance of the protagonist on stage is almost always preceded by the intervention of other characters, although in some cases it is the character of Jesus who is the one to pronounce the first lines of the play. When other characters take part in the play before the protagonist, they usually refer to certain traits that characterize him and anticipate some details about the stage development. Prolepsis, i.e. the advance of the plot before the performance, is a common practice in medieval theatre, widely documented throughout Europe, and often performed by a character called the 'Prologue'.[29]

Looking at the protagonist's first stage appearance, we ask ourselves: What is the Majorcan Jesus like? How is he presented? What does he say about himself? What does he say to others? How does he relate to God the Father, to men, and the world? — From these questions, which reflect the expectant presence of the audience, we try a first approach to the character.

---

his retreat following the beheading of the Baptist (Matthew 14. 13) until his prayer in the Garden of Gethsemane (Matthew 26. 36–46; Mark 14. 32–42; Luke 22. 39–46). Unless stated otherwise, we quote from the English Standard Version Anglicised, available online: https://www.biblegateway.com/.

29 In the Llabrés manuscript, the character of the Prologue appears in the *Play of Saint Francis* (no. 29, ll. 1–64), in the *Play of the Glorious Saint George* (no. 31, ll. 1–31), in the *Play of Death* (no. 36, ll. 1–40), in the *Second Play of the Descent from the Cross* (no. 41, ll. 1–36), in the *Play of the Conversion and Life of Saint Matthew* (no. 44, ll. 1–60) and in the *Representation of the Life of Saint Peter* (no. 46, ll. 1–35). In the *Play of the Glorious Saint Christopher*, the role of the prologue writer corresponds to the character of the Author (no. 32, ll. 1–55).

This initial characterization will be completed later with what the dramatic action and other characters add to this characterization.

We start from the hypothesis that the pieces analysed here revolve around the centre of the Christian faith and aim to illustrate who Jesus of Nazareth is, what he has come to do, what this coming means for humanity, and what he reveals about God the Father. Based on what we can identify as the main topics that make up the epicentre of this theatre, we propose the following classification of the words with which the Jesus of the Majorcan play texts is presented: a) revelations about his identity, b) statements about his mission, and c) statements about the situation — past and present — of mankind and its attitude towards God.

At this point, it is evident that the nature of our object of study forces us to cross the frontier of philology to enter the fields of Christology, soteriology, Christian anthropology, and eschatology, guided by the authorized voices in these disciplines. We understand our task as an attempt to interpret the texts in the view of the faith that inspires them. This step can only be taken from a knowledge of the plays' theological, ecclesial, and cultural background. However, it is important to note that we are only trying to outline these issues. Further study should be carried out by specialists in the relevant subjects.

Our initial focus is on the words with which Jesus on stage is introduced to the audience. The aspects that we identify here will allow us to begin to trace the predominant Christological profile in the Majorcan plays. Given that we are dealing with texts that reflect a stage use inside a church our goal is to try to identify the pastoral intention that inspires and justifies them.

First, we should look at what the character reveals about his identity. We see that Jesus begins his stage appearance in the *First Play of Maundy Thursday*, addressing his disciples by calling them 'mos fills' ('my sons', no. 19, l. 1). This expression, which is frequently used throughout the pieces we study here (no. 17, ll. 77 and 87; no. 19, ll. 41 and 175; no. 27, ll. 151, 155, 209, 247 and 339; no. 38, ll. 1, 5 and 416),[30] is of special interest because it is not found in the Gospel accounts, from which the passages in question are inspired,[31] but belongs to the ecclesial tradition.

---

30 In contrast, in the *Fourth Play of Maundy Thursday*, Jesus refers to the Twelve as 'Dexebles y apòstols meus' ('My disciples and apostles'; no. 42, l. 463), 'Dexebles meus' ('my disciples', no. 42, ll. 105, 110, 140, 578, 588, 638 and 698; see also no. 38, ll. 219, 344 and 368), 'Dexebles meus molt amats' ('my beloved disciples', no. 42, ll. 458, 518 and 553), 'Dexebles molt amats' ('beloved disciples', no. 42, l. 405), or simply 'Dexebles' ('disciples', no. 42, l. 694). In the *Play of the Samaritan Woman*, Jesus calls his disciples 'Apòstols meus' ('my apostles', no. 15, ll. 95 and 171), following Luke 6. 13: 'And when day came, he called his disciples and chose from them twelve, whom he named apostles'.

31 The pericopes of reference include the announcement of the fulfilment of the prophecies (Luke 18. 31 / no. 27, l. 151), the preparations for the celebration of the Passover supper,

For Jesus in the Gospels, the disciples are his brothers (Matthew 12. 49; Mark 3. 34) and his friends (John 15. 13–15). Significantly, the only time he calls them 'sons' (John 13. 33), they lack the possessive.[32] Thus, the word acquires a generic meaning and is not properly kinship. Noteworthy, in the Majorcan play texts, the use of the expression 'my sons' has a clear Trinitarian connotation: God, the Father, and Jesus, his only begotten Son, are in the unity of the Holy Spirit 'Of the same nature' (*homoousion*), as defined by the Council of Nicaea (325).[33]

The Majorcan Jesus can address his disciples by calling them 'my sons' because the Church recognizes and confesses the inseparability of Father and Son.[34] Spectators have in front of them the stage character who evokes the One who, according to the fourth Gospel, said: 'Whoever has seen me has seen the Father' (John 14. 9) and 'If you had known me, you would have known my Father also. From now on you do know him and have seen him.' (John 14. 7). Jesus Christ and the Father are one, as Thomas professes once he has thrust his finger into the side of the risen Christ by saying: 'My Lord and my God' (John 20. 28).

In the light of Thomas's words, it is understandable that the characters in the Majorcan plays can address Jesus as 'God'. Examples are found in the roles of Peter, who calls him 'mon Déu i Senyor' ('my God and Lord', no. 38, l. 233, no. 42, l. 868), 'mon Déu i Creador' ('my God and Creator', no. 38, l. 453), 'mon Déu i mon Senyor' ('my God and my Lord', no. 42, l. 577), 'ver Déu infinit' ('true infinite God', no. 42, l. 855); the Angel, who addresses him as 'Rey, Iesús, Déu, Redemptor' ('King, Jesus, God, Redeemer', no. 27, l. 359); John, for whom he is 'Senyor, y Déu infinit' ('Lord, and infinite God', no. 42, l. 126), Magdalene, who praises him as

---

and the sending of the disciples to Jerusalem (Luke 22. 8 / no. 19, l. 1; no. 27, ll. 151 and 155; no. 38, ll. 1 and 5), the ablution (John 13. 4 / no. 27, l. 209), the announcement of the betrayal (Matthew 26. 21, Mark 14. 17, John 13. 21 / no. 27, l. 247), the request to watch during the prayer in Gethsemane (Matthew 26. 38 and Mark 14. 34 / no. 27, l. 339), and the rebuke of the sleeping disciples (Matthew 26. 40 / no. 19, l. 175; no. 38, l. 416).

32 Note that this is also the generic form, without the possessive adjective, with which Jesus encourages the hemorrhagic woman after healing her: 'Filla, la teva fe t'ha salvat!' ('Daughter, your faith has saved you', see Matthew 9. 22; Mark 5. 34; Luke 8. 48). Another example is the healing of the paralyzed blind man to whom Jesus says, 'Fill, et són perdonats els pecats!' ('Son, your sins are forgiven', see Matthew 9. 2; Mark 2. 5). We see that this is a generic use of the word 'son' because the same passage in the Gospel of Luke 5. 20 reads: 'Man, your sins are forgiven.'

33 The Jesus in the performance praises the one who faithfully embraces the mystery of the Trinity: 'Lo qui creurà en mi en bon punt és nat | que en mi és la Trinitat | — Pare y Fill, Sant Sperit —, | per la qual és en mi tot unit' ('Wellborn [literally: "Born at the right moment"] is the one who will believe that in me is the Trinity — Father and Son, Holy Spirit —, which is all united in me', no. 18, ll. 379–82).

34 It is this unity to which the Majorcan Jesus refers, when before resurrecting Lazarus he gives thanks to God, calling him 'Pare, Senyor, en mi unit' ('Father, Lord, in me united', no. 18, l. 405).

'Déu, tot ple de caritat' ('God, full of charity', no. 42, l. 361), and the Virgin Mary, who calls him 'Déu meu y Creador' ('my God and Creator', no. 42, l. 385) and 'mon Déu increat' ('my uncreated God', no. 42, l. 389).

For the Church, Christ is the beginning of the new humanity, which has the authority to address God as '*Abba*, Father' (Romans 8. 15; Galatians 4. 6). This trusting treatment is possible because, in Pauline language, 'all who are led by the Spirit of God are the sons of God' (Romans 8. 14). Putting the extra-biblical expression 'mos fills' ('my sons') in the mouth of the Majorcan Jesus seems to reflect the desire to emphasize the grace of the filial condition, established between God and men in Jesus Christ, which the Church recognizes as 'the new Adam' (Romans 5. 12–21; 1 Corinthians 15. 21–22, 45).

The Majorcan Jesus revealed at the baptismal scene as the Son of God[35] addresses his disciples as children, and teaches them the nature of this sonship, making them partakers of his life, death, and resurrection. The fact that the Jesus of the Gospels is defined above all by his relationship with God the Father is widely reflected in the Majorcan play texts.

Thus, the Jesus as portrayed in the Majorcan plays, retired to the desert, invokes God with the words: 'O, Pare meu omnipotent' ('O my Father Almighty', no. 10, l. 261).[36] When he takes leave of his mother, in a scene not recorded in the canonical scriptures, he announces to her:

Mare mia, vos no dupteu
que d'equest modo se deu fer
y puis a mon Pare és plasent;
io li vull ser obedient (no. 38, ll. 139–42)

(My mother, do not doubt that in this way it must be done and then my Father is pleased; I want to be obedient to him).

As mentioned above, during the Last Supper, Jesus blesses the table, the bread, the wine, and again the table, beginning each of the blessings with

---

35 The baptism of Jesus appears in the second of the two plays about the Temptation. Referring to the culmination of the theophany, it is specified: 'És menester que Déu lo Pare stiga a un cadefal ab sos àngels, los que el voldrà, y trameta una coloma, feta ab un artifici, que vinga sobre lo cap de Jesús, com se ferà lo baptisme; y dirà Déu lo Pare ab to de *Veni creator*: "Aquest és lo meu fill amat, | ab lo qual jo·m só alegrat; | obeïu a son manament | per a viure eternalment."' ('God the Father shall stand on a scaffold with his angels, those who will love him, and send a dove, made with a device, to come upon the head of Jesus, as baptism will take place; and God the Father will say, using the tune of *Veni creator*: "This is my beloved Son, in whom I am well pleased; obey his commandment to live forever."', no. 10, ll. 85–88).

36 The Gospels do not include the words of the prayer in the wilderness. They merely recount that Jesus spent forty days there fasting, tempted by the devil (Matthew 4. 1–11; Mark 1. 12–13; Luke 4. 1–13) and served by angels (Matthew 4. 11; Mark 1. 13).

the phrase 'En nom del Pare infinit' ('In the name of the infinite Father', no. 38, ll. 189, 244, 250 and 328).[37]

Before praying in the Garden of Gethsemane, he warns his disciples, saying, 'Stau un poch, io pregaré | lo meu Pare per vostron bé' ('Wait here, and I will pray my Father for your sake', no. 19, l. 152) or 'apartar-m'é per pregar | mon Pare celestial' ('I have to step aside to pray to my heavenly Father', no. 42, ll. 601–02).[38] At the time of the affliction, he addresses God, calling him 'Pare, Senyor Omnipotent' ('Father, Lord Almighty', no. 19, l. 157), 'Pare etern' ('Eternal Father', no. 27, l. 338), 'Aternal Pare y Senyor' ('Eternal Father and Lord', no. 27, l. 343), 'mon Pare' ('my Father', no. 38, l. 356), 'Eternal Pare, inmens Déu' ('Eternal Father, immense God', no. 38, l. 364), 'Pare celestial' ('Heavenly Father', no. 42, l. 603), 'Pare, Senyor' ('Father, Lord', no. 42, l. 621), 'Clementíssim Pare meu' ('My most Merciful Father', no. 42, l. 633), 'Pare, Déu eternal' ('Father, Eternal God', no. 42, l. 643), or simply 'Pare' ('Father', no. 27, ll. 245 and 351; no. 38, ll. 346 and 372; no. 42, l. 637).[39]

When Pilate asks him to comment on the accusations made against him, Jesus responds from the consciousness of being the instrument of the will of God the Father: 'de mi se à de fer | segons del Pare lo voler' ('It shall be done to me according to my Father's will', no. 20, ll. 103–04).[40] He also heals the paralytic with an invocation of the Father: 'En nom del Pare infinit, | lo teu mal sia prest guarit' ('In the name of the infinite Father, your evil is soon healed', no. 18, ll. 25–26),[41] and when he heals the demon-possessed mute, he says he does it 'en nom del Pare eternal' ('in the name of the Eternal Father', no. 27, l. 61). In the *First Play of the Temptation*, Satan says of Jesus:

---

37 The Synoptics mention the blessing (Matthew 26. 26, Mark 14. 22) and the thanksgiving (Luke 22. 19) during the Last Supper without reproducing Jesus's words.

38 However, the corresponding Gospel text does not contain the reference to the Father ('Sit here while pray', Mark 14. 32; 'Sit here, while I go over there and pray', Matthew 26. 36).

39 The corresponding pericopes read: 'Abba, Father, all things are possible for you. Remove this cup from me.' (Mark 14. 36); 'My Father, if it be possible, let this cup pass from me' (Matthew 26. 39); 'Father, if you are willing, remove this cup from me' (Luke 22. 42) and 'And what shall I say? Father, save me from this hour? But for this purpose I have come to this hour.' (John 12. 27).

40 In the corresponding pericope, Jesus, when asked by Pilate if he was king of the Jews, merely answers, 'You have said so.' (Matthew 27. 11, Mark 15. 2, Luke 23. 3) or 'You say that I am a king.' (John 18. 37). The reference to the coming of Christ to fulfil the will of the Father is found, for instance, in the Epistle to the Hebrews: 'Then I said, "Behold, I have come to do your will, O God, as is written of me in the scroll of the book".' (Hebrews 10. 7).

41 Santandreu points out that verses 1–32 of the *Second Play of the Raising of Lazarus* which contain the episode of healing may correspond to several biblical passages (Matthew 4. 23–24; 8–9 or John 5. 1–9). He adds that whereas in the Gospel of John, Jesus heals the paralytic in Jerusalem, in the Majorcan play Jesus is not in Judea, i.e. away from Jerusalem, according to verse 332 ('en Judea vull tornar', 'I want to return to Judea') *Teatre sobre la vida adulta*, ed. by Santandreu, p. 116, n. 102.

En nom dele Pare increate,
tenant ten gran potestat,
fa de aygua tornar vi (no. 9, ll. 219–21).[42]

> (In the name of the uncreated Father, having great power, he turns water into wine).

He thereby alludes to the miracle performed during the wedding of Cana (John 2. 1–12).[43] All these extraordinary events, as well as the raising of Lazarus, are set in the context of the manifestation of the glory of God the Father. The Jesus of the Majorcan plays expresses it by saying:

l'infirmitat
en què Làtzer stà posat
no serà ara per la mort
[…]
ans serà per glorificar
Déu, mon Pare, qui·m fa obrar (no. 17, ll. 43–44).[44]

> (the infirmity in which Lazarus is placed will not be mortal […] it will be for glorification of God, my Father, who makes me work).

From the cross, the Jesus of the third play of Good Friday — in accordance with the Jesus of the Gospels — intercedes for his executioners when he asks:

O mon Pare, vull vos pregar
vullau a esta gent perdonar,
e bé que lur peccat és gran
però no saben lo que fan (no. 39, ll. 324–27).[45]

> (O my Father, I want to pray to you forgive these people, and their sin is great but they do not know what they are doing).

---

42 This reference to God the Father is lacking in the corresponding Gospel accounts (Matthew 17. 14–20; Mark 9. 14–29, and Luke 9. 37–43).

43 The evangelist does not say that Jesus performed the miracle 'in the name of the uncreated Father', but he says that with that first miracle in Cana of Galilee he 'manifested his glory. And his disciples believed in him' (John 2. 11).

44 Here the work paraphrases the corresponding pericope: 'This illness does not lead to death. It is for the glory of God, so that the Son of God may be glorified through it.' (John 11. 4).

45 The reference to the Father is also found in the Gospel text: 'And Jesus said, "Father, forgive them, for they know not what they do."' (Luke 23. 34).

THE SPIRITUAL DIMENSION OF THE MAJORCAN PLAY TEXTS 27

Before he expires, he says, 'O mon Pare, Déu infinit, | a vós coman mon sperit!' ('O my Father, Infinite God, to you I commit my spirit!', no. 39, ll. 346–47).[46]

Another characteristic feature of the Majorcan Jesus is the bond of friendship that binds him to his disciples, as evidenced in particular by the fourth Gospel.[47] This friendly treatment is found, for example, at the beginning of the *Play of the Samaritan Woman*: 'Amichs, jo só molt fadigat | del gran camí qu·é caminat' ('Friends, I am very tired of the long way that I have walked', no. 15, ll. 1–2),[48] in the *Second Play of the Raising of Lazarus*: 'Amich, jo·s vull denunciar, | com en Judea vull tornar' ('Friends, I want to announce you that I want to return to Judea', no. 18, ll. 333–34), or in the *Second Play of Maundy Thursday*:

Pere y Ioan, y vós amich,
a vosaltres tots vós ó dich:
Aneu-vos-na a la ciutat (no. 27, ll. 161–63)[49]

(Peter and John, and my friend, to all of you I say: Go to the city!).

Finally, Jesus says: 'Amich Ioan, no stigas trist' ('My friend John, don't be sad', no. 27, l. 267).[50]

Yet, in fact, Jesus does not limit this friendship to the circle of disciples but extends it to those who come to meet him.[51] For example, Jesus responds to the Samaritan woman and her husband by saying, 'Amichs,

---

46 Here, the play follows the pericope of the Gospel of Luke: 'Then Jesus, calling out with a loud voice, said, "Father, into your hands, I commit my spirit!"' (Luke 23. 46). The *First* and *Fourth Play of Good Friday* do not contain this passage, as they resolve the scene of the crucifixion by substituting the actor for 'a Christ', that is, for the image of the crucified Christ (see no. 20, l. 161a and no. 43, l. 265a). The *Second Play of Good Friday*, fragmentarily preserved, does not contain this passage either, because the text ends during the interrogation before Pilate. Given the coincidence of the last ten lines of this play (no. 28, ll. 230–39) with ll. 274–83 of play no. 39, both plays might have had a similar ending.

47 According to this Gospel, Jesus told his disciples: 'Greater love has no one than this, that someone lay down his life for his friends. You are my friends if you do what I command you. No longer do I call you servants, for the servant does not know what his master is doing; but I have called you friends, for all that I have heard from my Father I have made known to you.' (John 15. 13–15).

48 The Gospel account does not convey the words addressed to the disciples, but limits itself to saying: 'Jesus, wearied as he was from his journey, was sitting beside the well' (John 4. 6).

49 In the pericope in question, we read: 'Then after this [Jesus] said to the disciples: "Let us go to Judea again."' (John 11. 7).

50 The Gospel text reads: 'One of his disciples, whom Jesus loved, was reclining at table at Jesus's side', and in the following dialogue the word 'friend' does not appear (John 13. 23–36).

51 In none of the Gospel accounts corresponding to this passage, Jesus uses the word 'friends' when sending the disciples to make preparations for the Passover (Matthew 26. 17; Mark 14. 13; Luke 22. 7).

tots quants en mi creureu | obeyreu lo pare meu' ('Friends, all of you who believe in me and obey my Father', no. 15, ll. 146–47) and later, having called them once again 'Amichs' ('Friends', no. 15, l. 159),[52] refers to them as 'Germans' ('Brothers', no. 15, l. 167).[53] When the blind man implores him, he says, 'Amich, què vols que jo façe?' ('Friend, what do you want me to do?', no. 15, l. 191).[54] The innkeeper of the place where Jesus celebrates the Passover is greeted as an 'onrat amic' ('honourable friend', no. 19, l. 59), and in Gethsemane, the traitor is greeted with the words, 'Amich Iudas, què vas a sercar?' ('Friend Judas, what are you looking for?', no. 38, l. 420).[55]

Summarizing what we have seen so far, from the words of the Majorcan Jesus we can deduce three main traits that define the character: firstly, he highlights his status as a Father, in accordance with the faith of the Church in the Trinitarian God. Secondly, he highlights his awareness of being the Son of God, as the Scriptures testify. And thirdly, his friendly and fraternal relationship is important not only with the disciples, but also with the people who address him either by faith, as in the case of the blind man or the Samaritan couple, or from distrust, as in the case of Judas.

Having traced out what the stage Jesus reveals about his identity — Father, Son of God, friend and brother of men — let us now turn to his statements about his mission. First of all, the Jesus of the Majorcan plays — in line with the Gospels — expresses his awareness of having been sent[56] by God the Father to redeem and save humanity,[57] as prophesied.[58]

---

52 In this context, it is worth remembering that one of the accusations against Jesus was that of being a 'friend of publicans and sinners' (Luke 7. 35; Matthew 11. 19). In this case, we quote from the King James Bible, which gives the word 'publicans' — parallel to 'publicans y peccadors', no. 44, l. 175 — instead of 'tax collectors', the translation given in the English Standard Version Anglicised.

53 In the fourth Gospel — the only one that tells the episode of the Samaritan woman —, the woman appears alone, and is addressed by Jesus without any qualifier (John 4. 1–42).

54 The passage in the Gospel is: '[…] Jesus said to him: What do you want me to do for you?' (Mark 10. 51).

55 The pericope in question reads: 'Jesus said to him: Friend, do what you have to do.' (Matthew 26. 50).

56 According to the fourth Gospel, 'Jesus answered them, "My teaching is not mine, but his who sent me."' (John 7. 16); 'Jesus said to them, […] I came from God and I am here. I came not of my own account, but he sent me.' (John 8. 42) and 'Jesus said to them, "My food is to do the will of him who sent me and to accomplish his work"' (John 4. 34).

57 Thus, we read, for example, that Jesus said: '[…] For even the Son of Man came not to served, but to serve, and to give his life as a ransom for many' (Mark 10. 45; cf. also Matthew 20. 28) and '[…] for this is my blood of the covenant, which is poured out for many for the forgiveness of sins' (Matthew 26. 28).

58 According to the Gospel of Luke (22. 37), Jesus alludes to the figure of the Servant of God, prophesied by Isaiah (53. 12), saying: 'For I tell you that this Scripture must be fulfilled in me: "And he was numbered with the transgressors." For what is written about me has its fulfilment'.

THE SPIRITUAL DIMENSION OF THE MAJORCAN PLAY TEXTS   29

This is the central idea with which the character presents himself, for example, in his first stage appearance in the *Second Play of the Temptation*:

> Puis per redemir lo peccat
> Déu eternal me à·nviat,
> cossa convenient serà
> faça lo que manat me ha.
> O, quin camí tant traballós,
> tant ple de sospirs y de plors,
> que entre·ls hòmens he de passar
> per lo linatge humà salvar (no. 10, ll. 59–66).[59]

> > (For to redeem from sin the eternal God sent me; it will be convenient to do what He has commanded me to do. O, what a laborious path, so full of sighs and tears, that I must pass between men to save the human lineage).

The promise of salvation is also found in the *Play of the Samaritan Woman* when Jesus says, 'Vinch el món per dar salvament' ('I have come to the world to bring salvation!', no. 15, l. 82).[60] In the *Second Play of the Raising of Lazarus* we read the message announcing the deliverance: '[…] só tremès per lo rescat | y per donar-vos sanitat' ('I've been sent to rescue you and to make you whole', no. 17, ll. 19–20). Finally, in the prayer in the Garden of Gethsemane, Jesus, comforted by the angel, expresses his commitment to humanity: 'De bon cor vull io morir | y paradís a tots obrir' ('With all my heart I want to die and to open paradise for all', no. 19, ll. 173–74).

The most detailed reference to the fulfilment of the prophecies is included in the *Play of the Samaritan Woman*, where Jesus addresses the Twelve, saying:

> Apòstols meus, jo u[s] diré
> lo que tots tems selat vos é:
> que tots nosaltres anirem
> en Hierusalem pujarem.
> E aqui serà acabat
> tot lo qu·està prophetitzat:
> traït seré, y escarnit,
> en la care m'escupiran
> tots los jueus en gran scarn.
> E quan tot asò fet auran

---

59 According to Mark 8. 31 and Luke 9. 22, on the other hand, Jesus announces his Passion in a more sober language, saying: 'The Son of Man must suffer many things.'

60 In these words of the stage Jesus is reflected the recognition of the Samaritans who testify 'we know that this is indeed the Saviour of the world.' (John 4. 42).

e greu mor ma condemnaran;
el terç [jorn] resuscitaré (no. 15, ll. 171–82).[61]

(My apostles, I will tell you what I have always hidden from you:
that we will all go up to Jerusalem. And there will be accomplished
all that is prophesied: I will be betrayed, and mocked, all the Jews
will spit in my face with great scorn. And when all this is done, they
will condemn me to grave death; the third [day] I will rise.)

In addition to presenting himself as God's messenger, fulfilling his redemptive mission, the Jesus of the plays announces that he has come to proclaim
the gospel message: 'Jo am tinch de humiliar | y lo avangeli predicar.' ('I
have to humble myself and preach the gospel', no. 10, ll. 75–76).[62] In
the *Play of the Samaritan Woman*, he says that he wants to give 'bons
ensenyaments' ('good teachings', no. 15, l. 64) and teach his 'doctrina'
('doctrine', no. 15, l. 16). In front of the disciples, Jesus shows himself as
the 'Mestre vertader' ('true Master', no. 19, l. 15),[63] who illustrates to them
with his own life the virtue of humility (no. 19, ll. 42 and 47).[64]

---

61 On the other hand, the reference Gospel passage of these verses does not connect the
announcement of the passion with the prophecies: 'See, we are going up to Jerusalem, and
the Son of Man will be delivered over to the chief priests and the scribes, and they will
condemn him to death and deliver him over to the Gentiles. And they will mock him and
spit on him, and flog him and kill him. And after three days he will rise.' (Mark 10. 33–34).

62 See 'Jesus came into Galilee, proclaiming the gospel of God, and saying, "The time is
fulfilled, and the kingdom of God is at hand; repent and believe in the gospel."' (Mark
1. 14–15).

63 According to the Synoptics, Jesus speaks of himself as 'Master' (Matthew 26. 18, Mark
14. 14, and Luke 22. 11). Here, we also quote from the King James Bible, as in the English
Standard Version Anglicised, the translation is 'Teacher'.

64 It is necessary to differentiate the evangelical meaning of the word 'humility' from its
use, sometimes distorted, in everyday language. According to Cassià Just, 'El mateix mot
d'humilitat evoca actualment una certa actitud i sovint un complex, les components
psicològiques del qual serien la modèstia, la credulitat, la manca de confiança en si mateix,
la desvaloració de les pròpies accions, la propensió a sobrevalorar els altres [...], en fi,
un conjunt de connotacions més o menys ambigües. I escorcollant un xic més, encara
trobo aspectes clarament negatius: unes ressonàncies d'afectació exterior que pot encobrir
un fariseisme, un centrament refinat sobre si mateix i una manca d'interès i de coratge
envers els altres [...]. Per a sant Benet, en canvi, la humilitat té un contingut molt diferent,
profundament evangèlic. Tanmateix, convé tenir presents les ressonàncies negatives que
acabem d'evocar a fi que no ens bloquegin per a una comprensió viscuda i creadora d'aquest
punt fonamental.' ('The very word humility currently evokes a certain attitude and often
a complex, the psychological components of which would be modesty, credulity, lack of
confidence in oneself, the devaluation of one's own actions, the propensity to overvalue
others [...] in short, a set of more or less ambiguous connotations. And searching a little
more, I still find clearly negative aspects: resonances of external affectation that can cover
up a pharisaism, a refined focus on oneself and a lack of interest and courage towards
others [...]. For St Benedict, on the other hand, humility has a very different, deeply
evangelical content. However, it is appropriate to bear in mind the negative resonances that

Analysing the message of the Majorcan Jesus, we can distinguish, on the one hand, his statements about the situation — past and present — of man and his attitude towards God and, on the other, his teachings on the divine will and God's relationship with creation.

The Jesus of the Majorcan plays acts from the will to restore the original communion between God and men. He puts it this way, for example, in the prayer of thanksgiving that precedes the raising of Lazarus:

> Pare etern, grà[c]ias fas
> a tu, [qui sempre oït me às].
> Sé que [sempre] me [ous y veus];
> mas [vull creguen estos jueus]
> que [tu ets lo qui m'as tramès]
> per salvar lo qui perdut és (no 17, ll. 153–58).

> > (Eternal Father, I thank you, who always listens to me. I know that you always hear and see me, but I want these Jews to believe that you are the one who sent me to save the lost.)

Pointing out to the audience that the lack of faith as the cause of the separation of man and the Creator,[65] Jesus is the bearer of the good news that God, moved by his sovereign love, welcomes those who confidently respond to the promise of the new alliance.

The plays illustrate the two possible options in the face of this salvific call: on the one hand, there are the characters who acknowledge with simplicity and gratitude that Jesus is the Redeemer, and on the other, there are those who do not believe in his word and reject him instead of welcoming him. In the first group, there is the blind man whom Jesus heals in the Play of the Samaritan woman, saying:

> Obre tu los ulls y veuràs;
> per la gran fe que tu fet às
> saràs absolt de ton peccat
> e de quest afany desliurat' (no. 15, ll. 193–96).

> > (Open your eyes and you will see; by the great faith that you have shown you will be acquitted of your sin, and freed of this eagerness).

---

we have just evoked so that they do not block us from a lived and creative understanding of this fundamental point'), Just, 'Glosses', p. 184.

65 'Pare, Senyor, en mi unit, | gràsias fas, com as oït. | Tostemps so cert que ous a mi; | mes, are us dich cridant axí: | per tot lo poble qui asi es / que puga dir tu m'as tremes, | lo qual vuy viu en gran peccat | per la lur incredulitat' ('Father, Lord, united in me, I thank you, as you have heard. I am always certain that you feel me; but I say to you, crying out like this: for all the people who are here who can say that you sent me, to those who today live in great sin because of their unbelief', no. 18, ll. 409–12).

In the same group there is the father of the possessed who says of his son:

> Io tinch fiansa que gorrà [...]
> Lo natzareu li pot aiudar! [...]
> Per cert io crech lo pot guarir.
> En exa fe io vull morir! (no. 27, ll. 42, 44, 49–50).

> (I am confident that he can cure him. [...] The Nazarene can help him. [...] In this faith I want to die!).

Another example is Martha, Lazarus's sister, who replies, 'verament confessa jo | que sou Cristo, fill de Déu viu' ('I truly confess that you are Christ, the Son of the living God', no. 17, ll. 121–22), when Jesus says to her:

> Jo só la resus[rre]chtió,
> vida, y qui en mi [creurà]
> de eterna mort no morrà.
> Jo li daré salvaci[ó] (no. 17, ll. 115–18).

> (I am the resurrection, the life, and who believes in me will not die of eternal death. I will give him salvation).

In the *Plays of the Passion*, Peter stands out, declaring himself ready to die for Jesus (no. 19, ll. 73–74, no. 27, l. 240, no. 38, ll. 231–34, and no. 42, ll. 565–67; Matthew 26. 35 and Mark 14. 31), then denies him three times (no. 19, ll. 245–48, no. 38, ll. 553–54, no. 42, ll. 846–50; see Matthew 26. 74, Mark 14. 71, and Luke 22. 60), but repentant still trusts in the merciful Father (no. 20, ll. 21–28, no. 21, ll. 41–44, and no. 41, ll. 83–86; Matthew 26. 75, Mark 14. 72, and Luke 22. 61–62), unlike Judas who, desperate for his guilt, takes his own life (no. 20, ll. 47–54 and no. 39, ll. 45–46; see Matthew 26. 6, Acts 1. 18–19). Both characters express the remorse for their guilt in the initial monologues of four of the twelve plays of the Passion cycle: Peter at the beginning of the *First Play of Good Friday* (no. 20, ll. 1–28) and of the *First Play of the Descent from the Cross* (no. 21, ll. 1–56), and Judas at the beginning of the *Second* and the *Third Play of Good Friday* (no. 28, ll. 1–28 and no. 39, ll. 1–8).

Among the Jews who appear in the Majorcan plays, there are those who, recognizing in Jesus the Messiah proclaimed in the Old Testament, are baptized (no. 10, ll. 13–58) and defend him, such as the members of the Sanhedrin or Great Jewish Council, Joseph of Arimathea, and Nicodemus (no. 17, ll. 169–70 and 183–86, no. 19, ll. 127–38, no. 27, l. 116–46; John 3. 2 and John 19. 39), and those who are outraged, accusing him of being a false prophet (no. 19, l. 255), son of the devil (no. 27, l. 79), lawbreaker (no. 19, l. 211), seducer (no. 19, l. 215), traitor (no. 19, l. 194 and 221b, and no. 27, l. 394), blasphemous (no. 19, l. 231), evil (no. 27,

THE SPIRITUAL DIMENSION OF THE MAJORCAN PLAY TEXTS   33

l. 110, no. 38, l. 15, no. 42, l. 71, no. 43, ll. 113, 173, and 262), and malefactor (no. 43, l. 114).

In the Majorcan plays, one of the most important accusations of the Sanhedrin, presided over by the high priest, is the alleged misappropriation of the name of God by Jesus. So, in the *First Play of Maundy Thursday*, Caiaphas interrogates him, asking:

> Digas, samarità malvat,
> lo sant disapte as trencat,
> lo poble vols tot pervertir
> y Déu te fas per aquell dir? (no. 19, ll. 249–52).

> > (Tell me, you wicked Samaritan, is it true that you have profaned the holy Sabbath, that you want to pervert the people, and that you make them call you God?).

In the *Second Play of Maundy Thursday*, Annas is appalled, saying:

> És vingut lo nazareu
> y à'l curat com si fos Déu.
> An-lo adorat davant de mi (no. 27, ll. 95–97).[66]

> > (The Nazarene has come and healed him as if he were God. They worshipped him before me).

In the *Third Play of Maundy Thursday*, Benjamin accuses Jesus: 'Entenent dona que Déu és | els simples qui no saben res!' ('He makes the simple, who know nothing, believe that he is God!', no. 38, ll. 19–20). In the Gospel sources, however, the accusation against Jesus is that of blasphemy for claiming to be the 'Messiah' and the 'Son of God' (Matthew 26. 63–65; Mark 14. 61–63).

The character of Jesus in the Majorcan plays reveals God's will for the resurrection and glorification of his only begotten Son, saying:

> Sapiau cert, en veritat
> que prés de ser resucitat
> lo Fill de l'hom se'n puiarà;
> el dret costat de Déu seurà,
> del seu Pare celestial
> y iudicant lo bé y mal (no. 28, ll. 104–09)

---

66 The divine nature of Jesus is the subject of the dialogue between Annas and the Father of the demon-possessed mute: 'Pare: Lo natzareu li pot aiudar. | Annàs: Com? Es ell Deu? | Pare: Així u e·ntès.' ('Father: The Nazarene can help him. Annas: How? Is he God? Father: That's how I understood it.' no. 27, ll. 44–45.

(Know for sure that after the resurrection of the dead, the Son of Man will be raised up. He will sit on the right side of God, his heavenly Father, judging good and evil)

and

> Si io u dich, sert, no me'n creureu,
> però io us dich a tots arreu
> que veureu, sert, en veritat,
> el Fill de la Verge asentat
> en los núvols del més alt çel,
> a la mà dreta de aquell
> qui as Pare celestial,
> de la virtut Déu eternal (no. 38, ll. 518–25).

(If I tell you the truth, you will not believe me, but I will tell you everywhere that truth: you will see the Son of the Virgin seated in the clouds of the highest heaven, to the right of Him who is the heavenly Father, and the eternal God of virtue).

The Majorcan Play Texts as a Source of Hope

In this final part, we look at the wording of the Majorcan play texts to show how the choice of words was likely to turn the plays into a source of hope for the community that created and witnessed the scenic representation of the main subjects of the history of the Salvation. The language employed in the plays reflects the solemn and festive way in which the medieval Majorcan dramaturgy stages the great themes of the Christian faith.

What prevails in this tradition is the commemorative and laudatory character of a drama that shows and celebrates the main events in the history of the Church and the foundations of the hope of the baptized community, completing and enriching the canonical motifs with the episodes transmitted by tradition and apocryphal texts. It is a theatre that, while avoiding the extremes of theological disquisition and popular entertainment, seeks to maintain a balance between exposing the truths of the faith and the emotional, reflective, and spiritual involvement of the participants.[67]

---

67 The Majorcan Passion drama of the late medieval period participates in the European current that Giulio Gasca Queirazza describes in the presentation of Anna Cornagliotti's edition of the Passione di Revello, when he says: 'La Passione e documento vivo di cultura impegnata nella testimonianza e nell'approfondimento di un valore, quello religioso, affermato come primario e proposto e coltivato come bene irrinunciabile del singolo individuo e dell'intera comunita: non intrattenimento o ricreazione, ma momento

Given the strong component of communitarian worship, it comes as no surprise that the by far most frequently used word in the plays is 'Déu' ('God', 836 occurrences). Negative words such as 'pecat', 'pecar', 'pecador', etc. ('sin', 'to sin', 'sinner', 354 occurrences), 'trist', 'tristor', 'entristit', etc. ('sadness', 'saddened', 'sad', 144 occurrences), 'malvat', 'maldat', 'malvestat', etc. ('evil', 'evilness', 81 occurrences) or the much less frequently used 'culpa', 'culpable', etc. ('guilt', 'guilty', 23 occurrences) and 'infern', 'infernal', etc. ('hell', 'hellish', 37 occurrences), lose much of their negative connotation as they appear in the light of Christ's redemptive death, expressed by words such as 'perdó', 'perdonar', etc. ('forgiveness', 'forgive', 71 occurrences), 'bondat' ('goodness', 70 occurrences), 'infinit', 'infinitament', etc. ('infinite', 'infinitely', 61 occurrences), 'Salvador', 'salvar', etc. ('Saviour', 'save', 59 occurrences), 'fe' ('faith', 58 occurrences), and 'Redemptor', 'redimir', 'redempció', etc. ('Redeemer', 'redeem', 'redemption', 53 occurrences).

The spiritually comforting tendency of the plays is reflected in the frequent use of positive words such as 'amor', 'amorós', 'amar', etc. ('love', 'loving', 'to love', 171 occurrences), 'alegria', 'alegre', 'alegrar', etc. ('joy', 'joyful', 'feel/cause joy', 160 occurrences), 'lloar', 'llaor', 'lloable', etc. ('to praise', 'praise', 'praiseworthy', 82 occurrences), 'cel', 'celestial', etc. ('heaven', 'heavenly/celestial', 91 occurrences), 'pietat', 'pies', etc. ('piety', 'pious', 51 occurrences), 'mercè', 'misericòrdia', etc. ('mercy', 33+18 occurrences), 'caritat', 'caritatiu', etc. ('charity', 'charitable', 44 occurrences) and 'pau' ('peace', 32 occurrences).

The word 'dolor' ('pain', 137 occurrences), when it is not related to the Saviour's suffering or to the affliction ('compassion') of those who witness the Passion, is inscribed in the hopeful context of the announcement of the cessation of human tribulations through divine intervention.

Another noteworthy aspect is that in the Majorcan plays there is a tendency to avoid the overflow of emotions: there are many exhortations not to be exalted,[68] to remain firm in the faith,[69] to comfort each other[70] and to measure the signs of pain so as not to confuse one another.[71] In this way, spectators are offered a model of moderation and sensitivity in

---

importante di vita.' ('The Passion is a living document of culture committed to the testimony and deepening of a value, the religious one, affirmed as primary and proposed and cultivated as an indispensable asset of the individual and of the entire community: not entertainment or recreation, but an important moment of life.') Gasca Queirazza, 'Prezentazione', v and x.

68 See no. 15, ll. 60–61; no. 18, l. 17; no. 21, ll. 57–58; no. 27, ll. 53 and 267–69; no. 38, l. 147; no. 42, ll. 337–39, and no. 43, l. 228.

69 See no. 20, ll. 182–89; no. 38, ll. 109–16 and 129–31; no. 39, ll. 376–83; no. 42, ll. 141–43, and no. 42, ll. 235–39.

70 See no. 42, ll. 370–79.

71 See no. 20, ll. 174–77, and no. 42, ll. 150–59. For an assessment of the Christian view of 'plant' (mourning), see De Martino, *Morte*, pp. 322–44.

human treatment, worthy of imitation and contrasting with the rudeness and cruelty of Jesus's antagonists.[72]

Finally, it is interesting to point out that the promptness of acting or of carrying out an order is a recurrent motif in the plays. Expressions such as 'prest', 'prestament', 'sens tardar', 'sens detenir', etc. ('quick', 'quickly', 'without delay') sum up to 437 occurrences, and expresses the attitude of prompt readiness that is expected from the faithful in response to God's call, reminiscent of the Pauline image of the runner in the race for the imperishable wreath in 1 Corinthians 9. 24–27.

Conclusion

Summing up our analysis, it can be stated that the anonymous playwrights of the Majorcan play texts consciously address the audience as members of the religious community in numerous ways: through the performance in a place of worship temporarily used as a stage, through the almost exclusively sung presentation of the play texts using the technique of the *contrafactum* of liturgical songs, through the role model function of those stage characters who respond to God's call with an attitude of reverence and receptiveness expressed in their words and gestures, through the

---

72 The harshness characterizes the members of the Sanhedrin and their executioners (no. 19, ll. 133–34, 206, 211–28, 230–34, 249–56, 261–62, and 269–76; no. 20, ll. 41–46, 61–68, 70–82, 85–88, 93–94, 109–10, 137–38, 145–49, and 154–55; no. 27, ll. 110, 128, 406–22, and 424–32; no. 28, ll. 29–32, 63–90, 220–21, and 234–39; no. 38, ll. 57–58, 450–51, 472–85, 494–95, 498–99, 504–13, 529–40, 589–94, 630–41, and 650–53; no. 39, ll. 17–20, 111–28, 253–56, 278–79, 290–91, 294–97, and 314–23; no. 42, ll. 308–9, 729–33, 744–47, 758–61, 767–71, 796–800, and 811–29; no. 43, ll. 1–5, 11–15, 111–15, 169–73, 196–98, and 262–65) and the character of Judas (no. 19, ll. 80–96a; no. 20, ll. 29–40 and 47–54; no. 28, ll. 1–20 and 33–46; no. 38, ll. 258–69 and 442–45; no. 39, ll. 1–8 and 21–48), while meekness and humility (Matthew 11. 29) are the attributes of Jesus (no. 19, ll. 41–43, 45–48, 157–60, 165–68, 257–60, and 263–64; no. 27, ll. 209–11, 213–16, and 345–54; no. 28, ll. 100–09 and 186–89; no. 38, ll. 330–31, 356–77, 422–25, 486–93, and 496–97; no. 39, ll. 183–86 and 324–27; no. 42, ll. 105–14, 380–84, 518–27, 603–57, 748–57, and 762–66; no. 43, ll. 31–35), of the apostles (no. 28, ll. 128–31; no. 42, 593–97; no. 43, ll. 199–213), and of the Virgin Mary (no. 20, ll. 162–73; no. 28, ll. 132–35; no. 38, ll. 169–78; no. 39, ll. 49–56, 61–68, and 372–75). Following the Gospel source, the character of Peter rages against Malchus in the Garden of Gethsemane (no. 19, ll. 195–200; no. 27, ll. 395–98; no. 38, ll. 452–57; no. 42, ll. 734–38), until he is admonished by Jesus for his belligerent attitude (no. 19, ll. 201–02; no. 27, ll. 399–402; no. 38, ll. 458–65; no. 42, ll. 739–43). In the *Second Play of Maundy Thursday*, there is a scene similar to the one of Malchus: during the last supper, Peter wants to know the name of the traitor so that he can split his head in half with the knife (no. 27, ll. 256–57).

portrayal of Jesus based both on the Gospel accounts and on the ecclesial tradition, and finally through a choice of words likely to inspire both joy over the good tidings and hope of redemption among the spectators and the actors who took part in the performance of these plays.

Bibliography

Manuscripts

Barcelona, Biblioteca de Catalunya, MS 1139

Edited Source Texts

Actes del martiri de sant Fructuós, bisbe de Tarragona, i els seus diaques sant Auguri i sant Eulogi, ed. by Rafael Serra Abellà (Tarragona: Arquebisbat de Tarragona, 2008)

Jacobus de Voragine, *Legenda aurea. Goldene Legende*, ed. and trans. by Bruno W. Häuptli, Fontes Christiani, 2 vols (Freiburg and others: Herder, 2014)

Teatre bíblic. Antic Testament, ed. by Ferran Huerta (Barcelona: Barcino, 1976)

Teatre hagiogràfic, ed. by Josep Romeu i Figueras, 3 vols (Barcelona: Barcino, 1957)

Teatre sobre la vida adulta de Jesús (segle XVI), ed. by Pere Santandreu Brunet, Bibliotheca Marian Aguiló, 35 (Barcelona: Universitat de les Illes Balears / Publicacions de l'Abadia de Montserrat, 2003)

Teatro medieval, vol. I: *El drama litúrgico*, ed. by Eva Castro (Barcelona: Crítica, 1997)

Secondary Material

Borgnet, Guy, 'Structure et sens de la Petite Passion des *Carmina Burana*: la figure de Jesus', *Fifteenth-Century Studies*, 13 (1988), 67–77

Cenoz, Guillermina, 'Teatro navideño catalán de técnica medieval' (unpublished doctoral thesis, Universitat Autònoma de Barcelona, Bellaterra, 1977)

De Martino, Ernesto, *Morte e pianto rituale: dal lamento funebre antico al pianto di Maria* (Turin: Editore Boringhieri, 1975)

Dominguez, Veronique, *La scène et la Croix. Le jeu de l'acteur dans les Passions dramatiques françaises (XIVe–XVIe siècles)* (Turnhout: Brepols, 2007)

Ehrstine, Glenn, 'Passion Spectatorship between Private and Public Devotion', in *Thresholds of Medieval Visual Culture: Liminal Spaces*, ed. by Elina Gertsman and Jill Stevenson (Woodbridge: Boydell and Brewer, 2012), pp. 302–20

——, 'Raymond Peraudi in Zerbst: Corpus Christi Theater, Material Devotion, and the Indulgence Microeconomy on the Eve of the Reformation', *Speculum*, 93/2 (2018), 319–56,

——, '*Ubi multitudo, ibi confusio*. Wie andächtig war das Spielpublikum des Mittelalters?', in *Das geistliche Spiel des europäischen Spätmittelalters*, ed. by Sieglinde Hartmann (Wiesbaden: Reichert, 2015), pp. 113–31

Gasca Queirazza, Giuliano, 'Presentazione', in *La Passione di Revello. Sacra rappresentazione quattrocentesca di ignoto Piemontesa*, ed. by Anna Cornagliotti (Turin: Centro Studi Piemontesi, 1976), pp. v–x

Just, Cassià M., 'Glosses per a una relectura de la Regla de Sant Benet', in *Regla de Sant Benet*, ed. by Cassià M. Just (Barcelona: Publicacions de l'Abadia de Montserrat, 2007), pp. 151–338

Kovács, Lenke, 'The Special Effects in the Majorcan Llabrés Manuscript (ms. 1139 Biblioteca de Catalunya) and in Late Medieval Catalan Drama', in *Mirabilia. Gli effetti speciali nelle letterature del medioevo*, ed. by Francesco Mosetti and Roberta Ciocca (Alessandria: Edizioni dell'Orso, 2014), pp. 321–36

Longtin, Mario, 'Prompting the Action: the Prologue, the Messenger and the Fool', in *The Narrator, the Expositor, and the Prompter in European Medieval Theatre*, ed. by Philip Butterworth (Turnhout: Brepols, 2007), pp. 191–209

Llompart, Gabriel, 'La devoció mariana de Mallorca a la història de la pietat i a la iconografia', in *Nostra Dona Santa Maria dins l'art mallorquí* (Palma de Mallorca: Caixa de Balears, «Sa Nostra», 1988), pp. 21–41

Mas, Joan, 'El teatre religiós del segle XVI', in *El teatre català dels orígens al segle XVIII*, ed. by Albert Rossich, Antoni Serra, and Pep Valsalobre (Kassel: Edition Reichenberger / Universitat de Girona, 2001), pp. 17–33

——, 'Tipologies de les passions catalanes del segle XVI', in *La Mort com a personatge, l'Assumpció com a tema, Actes del Seminari celebrat del 29 al 31 d'octubre de 2000, amb motiu del VI Festival de Teatre i Musica Medieval d'Elx*, ed. by Josep Lluís Sirera (Elx: Ajuntament d'Elx, 2002), pp. 253–75

Massip, Francesc, *La Festa d'Elx i els misteris medievals europeus* (Alacant: Institut de Cultura Juan Gil Albert, Diputació d'Alacant, Ajuntament d'Elx, 1991)

——, *La ilusión de Ícaro. Un desafío a los dioses. Máquinas de vuelo en el espectáculo de tradición medieval y sus pervivencias en España* (Madrid: Centro de Estudios y Actividades Culturales, Madrid, 1997)

——, 'Le vol scénique dans le drame médiéval et les survivances actuelles dans le théâtre traditionnel', *Oihenart. Cuadernos Lengua y Literatura*, 16 (1999), 7–15

Romeu i Figueras, Josep, *Teatre català antic. Volums d'homenatge a l'autor*, ed. by Francesc Massip and Pep Vila, 3 vols (Barcelona: Institut del Teatre de la Diputació de Barcelona, Curial, 1994–1995)

Shoemaker, William H., 'The Llabrés Manuscript and its Castilian Plays', *Hispanic Review*, 6 (1936), 239–55

Surtz, Ronald E., *The Birth of a Theater: Dramatic convention in the Spanish Theater from Juan del Encina to Lope de Vega* (Madrid: Princeton, 1979)

——, *Teatro medieval castellano* (Madrid: Taurus, 1983)

Symes, Carol, 'Liturgical Texts and Performance Practices', *Understanding Medieval Liturgy. Essays in Interpretation*, ed. by in Helen Gittos and Sarah Hamilton (Farnham: Ashgate, 2016), pp. 339–67

Young, Karl, *The Drama of the Medieval Church*, 2 vols (Oxford: Clarendon Press, 1933)

Online Resources

Bible Gateway, https://www.biblegateway.com/ (accessed: 4 February 2024)

Cantus Index: Catalogue of Chant Texts and Melodies, https://cantusindex.org (accessed: 4 February 2024)

ELIŠKA KUBARTOVÁ

'Reality Effect' in Religious Performances of the Passion

Depositio Crucis, Planctus Mariae, St Vitus Passion Play *from Bohemia**

▼ **ABSTRACT** This paper addresses the late medieval Passion devotion through the prism of phenomenology and cognitive theory. The concepts of visceral seeing, kinaesthetic empathy, and embodied schema are employed to explain the specific type of mimetic and emotional realism exhibited by various Passion media (texts, images, and performances). The argument is demonstrated on the examples of Marian lament, animated sculptures of Christus Patiens, a Bohemian fragment of the *St Vitus Passion Play*, and textual and visual representations of the *arma Christi*.

▼ **KEYWORDS:** kinaesthetic empathy, visceral seeing, embodiment, animated crucifixes, *planctus Mariae*, Marian lament, *St Vitus Passion Play*, Passion, *arma Christi*

---

* I would like to thank the late Bob Clark and the second, anonymous reviewer for all their insightful and inspiring comments and suggestions. Many thanks also to Glenn Ehrstine for correcting my English, as well as for his most helpful comments. The research presented in this paper has been funded by the Czech Science Foundation via project No. 21-18870S 'Medieval Bohemian Marian and Magdalenian Plancts as Textual and Cultural Performance'.

Eliška Kubartová (née Poláčková; kubartova@ics.cas.cz) is postdoctoral researcher at the Centre of Classical Studies, Institute of Philosophy (Czech Academy of Sciences, Prague) and Assistant Professor at the Department of Theatre and Film Studies, Palacký University Olomouc. Her professional interests comprise Classical (especially Roman) Theatre and Drama, Medieval Theatre and Drama, and Theatre Translation. Presently, she is secretary and treasurer of SITM.

European Medieval Drama, 27 (2023), 41–70
BREPOLS ❧ PUBLISHERS   10.1484/J.EMD.5.137677

My point of departure for this paper is my previous research on Marian Laments, a devotional genre that formed, from the thirteenth century onwards, part of the medieval worship that focused on the Passion of Christ and his salvific death on the Cross.[1] Depicting the Virgin Mary as a witness of her son's suffering, these Latin and vernacular compositions have been described as having a distinctly 'realistic' feel, representing the characters of Christ, Mary, and others as both deeply grounded in the historical realm of Scripture and partaking in the lived presence of the pious readers, listeners, or spectators. Rachel Fulton, for instance, aptly contends that the textual and performative discursive formations labelled as Passion devotion were carefully designed to prompt the devotee 'to apprehend *the reality* of Christ's sacrifice'.[2] To a similar effect, the visual representations of Christ's Passion have been acknowledged to maintain a certain mimetic realism of the everyday, employing familiar details such as soldiers playing dice at the foot of the cross, the contemporary garb of onlookers of the crucifixion, and existing species of plants and birds swarming the slopes of the Biblical Golgotha.

It has been demonstrated how these forms of visual realism, representative of medieval art, contributed to the theological meaning of these works, accentuating the human aspect of Christ as the Word 'bodied forth' and, in doing so, promoting the Eucharistic piety that flourished since the mid-thirteenth century as one of the outcomes of the Fourth Lateran Council's efforts to consolidate the faith and combat heresy, especially among the laity. In my forthcoming study on the mediality and reception of Marian Lament,[3] I link the purported 'reality effect'[4] to yet another distinctive feature of the genre, i.e. the noticeable 'dramatic effect' of Mary's lament over the dead, or nearly-dead, body of her son, which is sometimes termed in scholarship as the 'sense of action' or 'inner drama'.[5] I also focus on the narrative strategies adopted in Marian Lament to achieve the desired level of mimetic realism, including first-person narration, use of the dramatic present, references to the everyday in the depiction of the Biblical stories, etc. I have additionally identified the various religious,

---

1 Poláčková, *Verbum*, pp. 341–416; Poláčková, 'Planctus Mariae'; Poláčková, 'Marian Laments'; Kubartová, 'Negotiating'.

2 Fulton, *From Judgement to Passion*, p. 239; italics are the author's.

3 A prospective monograph, including editions of the Bohemian corpus of Marian laments, is forthcoming: Kubartová and others, *Worshipping*.

4 I borrow the term from Roland Barthes, though with slightly different connotations than are his original. See the original term in Barthes, 'The Reality Effect', and its appropriation for art and literary criticism in Borowski and Sugiera, 'Introduction', p. 137 (p. 141 for the relation of the term to the complementary notion of the *estrangement effect* of Bertolt Brecht).

5 E.g. McNamer, *Affective Meditation*; King, *Medieval Literature*, p. 119; Izydorczyk, 'The *Evangelium Nicodemi*', p. 90.

social, and psychological functions that the realistic quality of Marian laments conceivably aroused in the pious audience.

Presently, I would like to tackle the issue from a different angle to consider how far we can get in pursuing the notion of the alleged 'realism' of these compositions, beyond the sheer enumeration of the aesthetic strategies they employed and the functions they fulfilled for the original audiences. To discuss the purported realistic effect of Marian laments and other forms of Passion devotion, I employ several theoretical concepts based on the phenomenological and cognitive approaches to the study of human culture, drawing on similar research conducted recently in the area.[6] Before presenting the argument itself, a quick note on genetic taxonomy cannot be dispensed with. In this research, I deliberately broaden the source basis of my inquiry to include, besides the standard items of medieval theatrical performance, additional forms of medieval worship, such as sculptures, manuscripts, and other forms of performance than theatre proper. Indeed, as Glenn Ehrstine observes in his work on indulgenced religious spectatorship, 'a strictly bipartite approach to Christian rite and Christian theater [has] ultimately [proven to be] a false dichotomy', an anachronism owing more to the modern notion of secularization than to the actual catalogue of medieval performance genres.[7] The objective of this paper is, ultimately, to argue that the reality effect produced by discursive formations of the Passion is based on the same cognitive grounds, whether it concerns visual, textual, or performative representations of the scenes of Christ's suffering.

Arguably, the distinct form of realistic representation found in medieval textual and visual artefacts, as well as in the theatrical and cultural performances of the time,[8] can be conceptualized as embodied encounters with the divine,[9] in which meanings were communicated through both *representational* and *non-representational modes of signification*. It is the latter, phenomenal elements of religious performances with which the present work is concerned in particular, discussing the ways in which they contributed to the 'realistic effect' of various devotional practices related to the worship of Christ's Passion. The argument hinges on several key concepts of the recent cognitive-phenomenological treatment of late-Antique and medieval devotional praxes, namely the phenomena of *animateness, visceral seeing, kinesthetic sympathy/empathy*, and *embodied schemata*.

---

6 For the similar research methodology and material, see e.g. Stevenson, *Performance*; Dresvina and Blud, *Cognitive Sciences*; Karnes, *Imagination*; etc.

7 Ehrstine, 'Das geistliche Spiel'. See also Flanigan, *Liturgical Drama*; and Norton, *Liturgical Drama*.

8 Singer, *Traditional India*. See Shepherd, *The Cambridge Introduction*, pp. 42–43.

9 For the notion of embodiment, see Varela and others, *The Embodied Mind*; Lakoff and Johnson, *Philosophy*.

All of these conceptual clusters emerged from a rapidly developing research field, demarcated by a productive exchange between phenomenology and cognitive science, the integration of which has been of ample benefit for the historical study of performance, as the doyen of the cognitive research, Bruce McConachie, remarked already at the beginning of 1990s.[10] Theoretical and methodological fusion of the two fields of knowledge, as much as they are concerned with the corporeal and moment-to-moment quality of human life, brought deeper sensitivity to the inherently embodied nature of all human endeavour, in art as in 'real life'. In both, meaning does not prove to exist separately and independently of its agent, but is believed to be produced discursively, in the course of interaction between the world and self. What is of the utmost importance in this regard is the fact that neither the world nor the self engage in the process as abstract entities, but enter the encounter as inevitably material(ized) and historically, socially, and culturally situated.

Within the notion of human existence as inescapably *embodied* in nature, the above-mentioned concepts of the kinesthetic sympathy, etc., emphasize particularly the *processual* and *interactive* (*reciprocal, mimetic*) aspects of meaning formation in the artistic and real-life encounters, characterized as moments of dialogic interchange between two embodied agents, animate or non-animate (books, sculptures, props, etc.). Cognitive research concludes that we know, perceive, and understand the world primarily in and through the structure, capacities, and experiential history of our bodily apparatus. This ultimately corporeal experience of and with the world inevitably affects also the mental activities through which we process that experience, as George Lakoff and Mark Johnson described in their visionary study of bodied metaphors, and more extensively in their later work, *Philosophy in the Flesh* (1999).[11] Our perception and cognition can thus be conceptualized as an embodied activity, engaging our bodies in a constant physical and mental interaction with the surrounding environment. The interaction manifests itself even on the pre-intellectual level as a certain form of sensorimotor reflection or imitation, triggered by the activity of a particular group of brain cells, so-called *mirror neurons*. Discovered in the 1990s, these neurons are now believed to be responsible for a sensorimotor mimetic response observed in the brain of a person watching another person performing a certain target-based activity. The mirror neurons fire when we observe someone else executing an action, but they do much more than just that: they also activate corresponding neural centres in our brain responsible for performing the very same action we are observing in the other person. The mirror neurons thus 'relate

---

10 McConachie, 'Metaphors'.
11 Lakoff and Johnson, *Metaphors*; Lakoff and Johnson, *Philosophy*.

observed action to the observer's motor repertoire, activating neurons that are also responsible for performing that action'.[12]

Even though the exact working mechanism of mirror neurons is still debated, the same cannot be said about the importance of their discovery. Investigation of neural mirroring proved beyond any doubt that humans respond to others' movements, gestures, and expressions — once these are performed as goal-directed actions — by an unconscious process of motor simulation, reconstructing these same actions 'in their bodies' as if they performed them themselves. The implications of this finding are profound. First of all, the mechanism of neural mirroring foregrounded the importance of corporeality in communication and perception, acknowledged in medieval scholarship especially in the researches informed by the recent 'corporeal' and 'material turn' in humanities that equally pinpointed the relevance of the phenomenal aspects of medieval social and cultural forms for their comprehensive assessment.[13] More specifically, neurological research of human cognition emphasizes the significance of action for perception, conceiving of perception as a form of action insofar that when we watch other bodies move, we respond to their movement by enacting it vicariously in our own bodily apparatus.[14]

What does all this have to do with devotional performances of the Passion? Much, since acknowledging perception and cognition as processes inextricably embedded in human bodily apparatus allows us to confirm and expand further some of the observances previously made about the working mechanisms and effects of the Passion devotion. In what follows, I will suggest one possible application of the cognitive-phenomenological theories concerning embodied vision, animation, and imitation in devotional praxes related to the veneration of Christ's Passion and death, particularly texts and objects that formed part of the Good Friday ceremonies and a representative Passion Play from Bohemia. I argue that what has been identified in various Passion media as a representational mode conveying a kind of 'reality' or 'everyday effect' to their target audiences, engages even the entirely pre-intellectual level of human consciousness, the actual neural mechanisms of the cognitive apparatus. Having said all this, it cannot be overemphasized that, while being universal insofar that it comprises cerebral processes of all human beings regardless of their

---

12 Garner, *Kinesthetic Spectatorship*, p. 153. For Garner's extremely elucidating summary of the scholarship behind the mirror neurons, see pp. 153–61.

13 For the corporeal and material turn in medieval studies, a field too extensive to be summarized in full, see Lund and Semple, *A Cultural History*. Seminal are works by Catherine Walker Bynum, most famously her *Holy Feast*.

14 Noë, *Action*.

Theological Meaning of Devotional Gestures in the *Planctus of Cividale* Through the Lens of Embodied Cognition

The first example comes from the (para-)liturgical ceremonies of Good Friday, during which a cross, or crucifix, was first adored by the whole congregation and then taken down by the clergy and deposited in a place representing the Holy Sepulchre. An optional element of these rites was the chanting of a Marian Lament, presenting the Virgin as a witness to the mortal torments of her son, sometimes accompanied by other biblical characters. One such composition, the fourteenth-century *Cividale Planctus Mariae*, is perhaps best known for its abundant stage directions, which provide an unprecedently detailed repertoire of gestures that the clerics embodying the individual characters — Virgin Mary, John, Mary Magdalene, and Mary Jakobi — were supposed to perform, as seen in the following excerpt:

> IOHANNES:
> *Hic vertat se ad Mariam, suas lacrimas ostendendo.*
> Fleant materna viscera
> Marie matris vulnera.
> *Hic se percuciat.*
> Materne doleo
> que dici soleo
> *Hic salutet Mariam.*
> felix puerpera.
>
> MARIA MAIOR:
> *Hic amplectet unam Mariam ad collum.*
> Flete, fideles anime
> *Hic aliam.*
> flete, sorores optime,
> ut sint multiplices
> *Hic se percutiat.*
> doloris indices,
> planctus et lacrime.

---

15 Garner, *Kinesthetic Spectatorship*, p. 161.

AMBE MARIE:

Hic ambe Marie erigant se cum manibus extensis ad Mariam et ad Christum.
Cur merore deficis,
mater crucifixi?
Cur dolore consumeris,
dulcis soror nostra?
Sic oportet fieri
Hic se inclinant cum salute.
ut predixit psalmista.

MARIA MAIOR:

Hic se percuciat.
Triste spectaculum
Hic ostendat Christum.
crucis et lancee!
Hic ostendat latus Christi.
Clausum signaculum
mentis virginee
Hic se percuciat.
profunde me vulnerat.[16]

> (JOHN: *Let him turn to Mary, showing his tears.* 'The maternal heart
> of Mary weeps for the wounds.' *Let him beat himself.* 'I mourn the
> motherhood, which I said was', *let him hail Mary*, 'happy childbear-
> ing'. MARY MAJOR: *Let her throw her hands around the neck of one
> of the Marys.* 'Weep, most faithful of souls', *and around the neck of
> the other*, 'weep, best of sisters, so that all signs of sorrow', *let her
> beat herself*, 'may be multiplied with lamentation and tears'. BOTH
> MARIES: *Let both Maries raise their extended hands to Mary and
> Christ.* 'Why do you become faint, mother of the crucified one?
> Why are you consumed with sorrow, our sweet sister? Thus it was
> to be', *let them bow with respect*, 'as predicted by the psalmist'. MARY
> MAJOR: *Let her beat herself.* 'Sad spectacle', *let her point at Christ*, 'of
> cross and spear!' *Let her point at Christ's side.* 'The secret sign of a
> Virgin mind', *let her beat herself*, 'wounds me deeply'.)

Besides their deictic, foregrounding, and gaze-orienting function in the
performance of the lament, the individual gestures of this elaborated gestural script have been acknowledged to bear a central role in the physical

---

16 'Cividale Planctus', ed. by Young, p. 508. Translation is the author's, with the use of
translation by Davidson, 'Planctus Mariae', p. 282.

modes and gestural language of medieval piety.[17] Several scholars have argued persuasively that gestural representations, such as those enacted in the performance of the *Cividale Planctus*, as well as their static counterparts depicted in religious paintings and sculpture, served as visual cues, or prompts, instructing the devotee in the proper execution of devotional gestures. The movements displayed in these official religious representations, such as bowing, kneeling, raising one's hands, kissing, and prostrating, were thus sanctioned as the 'orthodox' patterns of movement, while the non-represented gestures were implicitly ruled out of the repertoire of the proper ritual behaviour.

Besides serving as patterns for the authorized modes of bodily veneration, realistic bodily gestures in religious representations have been also claimed to bridge the gap between the human and the divine world by the strong sense of verisimilitude between the represented actions, and the actual behaviour of human beings as experienced outside the religious encounter, in the everyday reality. In effect, such religious representations served as a graphic shorthand of the central Christian notion of God becoming man, in conveying Christ's humanity through the human actor representing him in the Passion Play, and through the anthropomorphic Christ puppet and the 'humanity' of other characters in the narration of his death during the ceremonies of the Good Friday.

Beyond the long-discussed concept of verisimilitude,[18] *visceral seeing*, a term coined by Patricia Cox Miller in her book *The Corporeal Imagination* (2009), can be instructive with regard to the purported effect of reality in the viewers' response to religious representations. According to Miller, who develops the term in relation to hagiographic imagery of late antiquity,

> visceral seeing is a way of naming one of the results of the (re)physicalizing of the senses in light of the view that the Incarnation had legitimized the material realm. [...] Hagiographical images of saintly bodies taught the reader how to bring together the 'real' and the transcendent, the material and the spiritual, in a single image. [...] Visceral seeing denotes a pictorial idiom in which the senses have cognitive status and the mind is materially engaged.[19]

Elsewhere, she adds that, '[t]his kind of embodied thoughtfulness was crucial to the experiential engagement of the beholder or reader with im-

---

17 See e.g. Stevenson, *Performance*, chapter 1; Flora, *The Devout Belief*; Davidson, *Gesture*, here specifically for the discussion of the devotional function of gestures in the *Cividale Planctus*; Ogden, 'Gesture', pp. 28–29.

18 Barthes, 'The Reality Effect'. See also Borowski and Sugiera, 'Preface', p. XXIV.

19 Miller, *The Corporeal Imagination*, pp. 12–14.

ages of the saintly body'.[20] Miller's definition suggests that the emphasized materiality of a devotional image, e.g. its focus on gesture as in the *Cividale Planctus*, facilitates the understanding of the theological meanings communicated by the image in rendering its abstract message more concrete, hence graspable — by materializing the immaterial, in Miller's words. Validating their own body as a site of meaning formation, the devout of late antiquity, like their medieval counterparts, could thus perceive the abstract notion of Christ's redemptive sacrifice as, literally, tangible and, as a result, accessible via one's own direct physical experience. In the Passion idiom, the gaping side wound of the crucified Christ can be cited as a particularly poignant example of the materialization of theological discourse. Often emphasized by a deictic gesture in a theatrical performance, or its prominent placement in the manuscript mise-en-page, the 'wound of love' (Bernard of Clairvaux) epitomized, in a way, the theological discourse of Christ as a safe place, a refuge, and the site of the ultimate unification with the divine.[21] Devotional images and writings communicated this message unambiguously through the depictions of the side wound in a shape of vulva or vagina, as well as by evocative descriptions of the *vulnus* as a site of physical encounter with Christ that can be touched, kissed, or even entered, either by imagination or by actual physical action.

The visceral representational idiom, and the corresponding viewing stance of the beholder, thus sheds light on the way in which the 'reality effect', or the sense of experiencing the divine as present here and now, contributed substantially in various Passion enactments to the expression of their catechetical meanings. In actualizing the human body as a projection screen for the display of abstract theological notions, the bodied nature of the divine Word-made-Flesh emerged not as a mere rhetorical figure, but as a powerful cognitive metaphor associating religious truths with the immediate human embodied experience.

The above-stated function of devotional gestures as patterns for the proper execution of individual devotional acts can be explored further with the use of yet another term adopted from the cognitive theory, i.e. the *embodied schema*. Mark Johnson, philosopher and linguist, took up the term to describe non-conscious kinesthetic patterns that arise from our embodied existence in the world, i.e. the motor capacities of our bodies and their interactions with the environment, such as execution of movement, watching others move, reaching out to other people and objects, etc.[22] The embodied schemata that arise unconsciously from such encounters do not vanish once the situation that generated them is over.

---

20 Miller, 'Visceral Seeing', p. 398.
21 For the scholarship about Christ's side wound, see Hollywood, 'That Glorious Slit'; Easton, 'The Wound'.
22 Johnson, *Body*, pp. 19–23.

They rather linger in the body, inscribed in the person's motor memory, ready to be recalled in a later situation similar to the original one. As Jill Stevenson puts it succinctly in her work on lay piety in late-medieval York, 'an embodied schema is both a pattern of past action as well as a pattern for future action'.[23] Consequently, it can be argued that the devotional bodily script enacted during the Mass of the Presanctified on Good Friday, when the *Cividale Planctus* was most probably performed as a part of the ceremony of the *Adoratio Crucis*,[24] was not only observed by the congregation, but also adopted unconsciously in their bodily repertoire. It could be 'called out' next time when they would find themselves in a situation that required veneration of a sacred image, e.g. encountering the cross/crucifix or the Eucharist exhibited in an *ostensorium* placed on the altar or carried in procession. As a result of the preceding internalization of the suitable repertoire of embodied schemata, a proper devotional gesture, such as clasping ones hands or bowing deeply, would emerge automatically in the believer's body. It would allow her or him to worship in an orthodox way and, at the same time, rendering her a member of a larger kinetic/kinesthetic community (e.g. those who worshipped properly, in contrast to those who committed heresy).

Tactility and Animation in the *Imago Christi*

Patricia Cox Miller's acknowledgement of the cognitive status of senses seems to be instructive also with respect to the second example of the reality effect in Passion representations, the mimetic sculptures of the crucified Christ employed in the ritual of Adoration, Deposition, and Entombment of the Cross during the ceremonies of Good Friday. The existence of these religious puppets, as they are sometimes called, and their employment in church rituals has been discussed extensively.[25] Elina Gertsman, Daniele Di Lodovico, and other scholars have shown how these objects contributed to the feeling of the 'real presence' of Christ in the ceremonies by their striking *naturalism* and unprecedented degree of *animateness*.[26] As regards the former, it has been demonstrated that the sculptures-puppets were often executed with careful attention to the naturalistic depiction of every single detail of Christ's tormented body. Bodily gestures expressing the excruciating pain experienced by the Saviour, such

---

23 Stevenson, *Performance*, p. 27.

24 Smoldon, *The Music*, p. 377.

25 A large scholarship exists regarding the animated liturgical puppets. Of general introductory nature is Kopania, *Animated Sculptures*. See also Kopania, 'Animated Sculptures'; and *Animating Medieval Art*, ed. by Gertsman.

26 Gertsman, 'Bewilderment'; Di Lodovico, 'Revising Devotion', pp. 121–74.

as inclined head, limp extremities, and half-closed eyes evocative of his near-unconscious state, were executed in minute carving; mimetic polychromy illustrated vividly the numerous marks of torture, such as blood profusely streaming down the suspended body, the pallid complexion of Christ's body and face, and his gaping wounds. These realistic/naturalistic artistic techniques, and many other, triggered the visceral mode of seeing in these 'crucifixi dolorosi', as they are sometimes called, investing the Saviour's suffering with substantial theological meanings (**Fig. 2.1**).

One of the theological meanings actualized in the distinctive materiality of such religious images was the ontological correspondence between the Eucharistic species and the flesh and blood of the Eschatological, resurrected Christ. This parallel was accentuated in some of these crucifixes through the verisimilitude between the drops of blood pouring copiously out of Christ's wounds and the wine grapes as a source of Eucharistic wine, creating a visual link between Christ's tormented body and the Eucharist.[27] To the same extent, the life-bringing power of the Saviour's sacrifice was 'embodied' in his vulva-shaped side-wound reminiscent of a birth canal, from which new life is known to be born in the actual world of the devotees as well as in the religious teaching that venerated the side-wound as a gateway through which the Church was born to the world at Calvary.[28]

Religious representations making use of such visceral imagery in communicating the complex theological meanings necessarily validated the role of senses for perception and cognition, as Miller rightly points out. Accessible primarily through the bodily senses (of sight, but also touch and smell, as the sculptures were kissed during the ritual of Deposition),[29] the emphasized corporeality of the image of crucified Christ conveyed, through the realistic depiction of his wounded flesh, the crucial message about the redemptive power of God's carnality, or 'in-fleshedness'. Arguably, the catechetical efficacy of such images was grounded in the above-mentioned process of motor simulation, or sensorimotor resonance, insofar that the neural system of the beholder responded to the representation of Christ's (and Mary's) torments by experiencing the effects of the torture vicariously in her/his own body. The embodied nature of the devotee's perceptual stance proves decisive for the proper understanding of the theological meanings inscribed in the *crucifixi dolorosi* of Christ's piteously human, yet ultimately redemptive death on the cross.

Yet another 'realistic' aspect of these sculptures was the deliberate employment of materials that triggered visceral response in the pious beholders through their tactile and olfactory qualities. As was already recounted, these and similar sculptures were supposed to be experienced

---

27 Bynum, *Wonderful Blood*, pp. 176–78.
28 See above, note 19 for reference.
29 Kopania, *Animated Sculptures*, pp. 168, 267, 271, and 316.

Figure 2.1. Crucifixus Dolorosus from Jihlava ('Přemyslid Crucifix'); first third of the fourteenth century. The Royal Canonry of Premonstratensians at Strahov. Photo: NoJin, Wikimedia Commons.

not only by sight, but also by touching and smelling them especially during the ritual of the Adoration of the Cross, in which first the clergy, and then the whole congregation, approached the cross one by one and kissed the wounds of the Saviour in an act of utmost veneration. The significance of the sensual qualities of such physical pious encounters, such as kissing and touching devotional books and relics, cannot be overestimated, as

Caroline Walker Bynum, Jill Stevenson, Hans Belting, Eric Palazzo, and others have demonstrated in their respective works on the subject of medieval sensual piety.[30]

Made up of linden wood and other species renowned for their softness as well as distinct smell and warmth, reminiscent of the qualities of human skin, the sculptures were supposed to simulate the human body not only through their visual execution (e.g. the naturalistic depiction of swollen veins and lacerated flesh), but also through their texture and scent — as did the manuscripts, for that matter, made of parchment, distinguished by analogous sensual qualities like these soft kinds of wood. The 'fleshiness', or verisimilitude, of the sculptural representations of Christ in his carnal state could be further emphasized by application of 'real' materials, such as animal hair and textiles, representing respectively Christ's scalp and loincloth.[31]

As Jill Stevenson argues, such material characteristics of these works of art were by no means incidental, but played a decisive part in communicating the devotional message of Christ's carnal, fleshy, embodied nature that rose in importance over the fourteenth and fifteenth century in relation to Eucharistic piety. Referring to her own research and other studies of English mystery plays, Stevenson claims that the physical actuality of the actors' onstage presence highlighted the human nature of the incarnated Christ, which was part and parcel of the high and late medieval devotional idiom.[32] In theatrical (Passion Play) as well as in textual (*Cividale Planctus*) and visual (*crucifixi dolorosi*) religious representations, Christ's human substance was thus pinpointed to emphasize the religious dogma of the divine word made flesh through the medium of visual and textual performance. Such interpretation of these representations, according to cognitive science, was engendered by the embodied nature of the devotee's perceptual position from which (s)he beheld Christ as an embodied entity, too, in his image made of parchment, wood, or human flesh. The bodily situated perception of the believers seemed to prepare the grounds, so to speak, for the message of God's incarnation. As Stevenson succinctly puts it, 'the bodily state shared by viewer and image helps to ensure a clear devotional interpretation'.[33]

Last but not least, it has been argued that the devotional significance of the religious puppets of the crucified Christ presided in their ability to 'enliven' the moments from salvation history, rendering them familiar

---

30 Stevenson, *Performance*; from Caroline Walter Bynum see esp. Bynum, *Dissimilar Similitudes*; Belting, *An Anthropology*; Palazzo, *L'invention chrétienne*; Palazzo, *Le souffle de Dieu*.

31 Karmon, 'The Sacro Monte'; Kopania, *Animated Sculptures*, p. 146.

32 Stevenson, *Performance*, p. 135.

33 Stevenson, *Performance*, p. 34.

Figure 2.2. Crucifixus Dolorosus from Drasty (previously Hradčany); around 1350. Carmel of St Joseph in Prague. Photo: Petr Uličný.

and, thus, more relevant to the pious viewer. Ingenious technological mechanisms of joints and pulleys were used to make it possible for the image to be suspended on the cross for veneration, deposited, carried in a procession, and laid in the tomb in the manner of an actual human body. In order to enhance the realistic effect of a tortured man, some of the sculptures, especially those made in northern Italy, were supplemented with a movable tongue. It could be protruded and pulled back to imitate even the slightest traits of Christ's mortal suffering, referring perhaps also to his last words ('It is finished', John 19. 30), articulated, one can imagine, with the greatest efforts of his quickly escaping vital forces[34] (**Fig. 2.2**).

---

34 Kopania, *Animated Sculptures*, p. 31.

While considered by some to have been superficial theatrical effects, at best, or a crude trick of the medieval Church for manipulating the laity, at worst, the kinetic qualities of these sculptures served, in fact, similar devotional purpose as the earlier examples of mimetic realism cited in this study. Cognitive theory holds that motility, or the ability to move, is distinguished as a crucial characteristic of human existence as embodied in nature, underscoring the 'phenomenological inseparability of aliveness and movement'.[35] According to this view, human experience with and in the world is inherently dynamic: we recognize ourselves and the others as living entities largely because of the ability of our/their bodies to execute a goal-oriented as well as unintentional movement, such as expansion and shrinking of the chest when we are breathing, instinctive swallowing of saliva, or the contractions of the heart muscle pumping the blood around the body. Experiencing the sculpture of Christ in movement thus enables the pious onlooker to see it as being 'truly alive', rather than as a static devotional image. This animate quality of such sculptures largely contributed to their signification as enactments of the 'live' Christ in his Eucharistic and eschatological form.

Beyond the purpose of representing Christ as resurrected, hence, alive, the religious sculptures such as these have been recognized to elicit a certain affective response in the viewer, a trait which gave name to the whole strand of high and late medieval piety, that of affective devotion.[36] Originating in the thirteenth century in the devotional culture of the Cistercians and the reformed orders, mostly of Franciscan provenance, the affective forms of devotion, according to Sarah McNamer, 'portray Christ not as King or Lord but as "Jesu": a pitiable human victim who stoops under the weight of the cross',[37] triggering an affective response to his sacrifice by creating a strong sense of participation of the devotees in the scenes of Passion. This sense of active participation in the sacred events was achieved in Passion texts, images, and performances by the use of poetic devices such as the first-person singular, present tense, deixis, use of everyday materials and motifs, but perhaps most importantly by placing the devotee in the viewing position of an immediate witness to Christ's suffering. In the affective devotional encounters, the devotee was encouraged to step into the shoes, so to speak, of the sacred characters — Virgin Mary, Mary Magdalene, Saint John, and others — in order to experience the moments of Christ's torture with unprecedented immediateness through the power of 'imaginative performance as a primary means of

---

35 Garner, *Kinesthetic Spectatorship*, p. 6.

36 For introduction to this devotional mode, see Clark, 'Spiritual Exercises', pp. 276–81; McNamer, *Affective Meditation*.

37 McNamer, *Affective Meditation*, p. 29.

producing emotion', and 'driving rhythm that has profound somatic effects' and 'stir[s] up passionate compassion for Jesus', as McNamer puts it.[38]

Cognitive scholars take pains to show how movement, or rather kinesthesia, 'the experience one has of one's movements as a result of the sensations generated by one's muscles, joints, tendons, and the vestibular and other systems involved in balance and orientation',[39] contributes not only to our self-awareness as living bodies, but also to the generation of affect and emotions. Essentially, cognitive research has proven that 'movement and affect are inseparably involved with each other'.[40] This is to say that each and every movement we produce and watch others produce, in reality as in artistic representations, is affectively charged, prompted by, accompanied, and/or followed by emotion. Labelled as sensorimotor resonance, this bodily mechanism has been recognized as particularly important insofar as the generation of *empathy* is concerned.

This social ability, which has grown extremely popular in human sciences over the past few decades as an analytical tool, tends to be described as the ability to walk in someone else's shoes or 'the act of recognizing and sharing another person's feelings, sensorimotor experiences, and/or perspectives'.[41] Apparently, this definition conforms very well to the medieval conception of affective piety. Both the theological notion of *compassio* and modern empathy, thus seem to involve a certain form of 'inner imitation' (*Nachahmung*, Theodor Lipps) or 'inner mimicry' (John Martin), grounded in the rudimentary, kinesthetic level of experience.[42]

The *compassio*, or compassion with the suffering Christ, was considered a cornerstone of various affective devotional practices that encouraged devotees to ruminate over the Passion narratives recounting Christ's suffering often with the help of visual aids, such as the crucifixes mentioned earlier in this study or other similar images, e.g. Pieta, Deposition, *Imago Pietatis*, and *arma Christi*. The mental images induced by the concurrent mental work of reading and viewing (or, indeed, merely picturing the respective *Andachtsbilder*) were 'enlivened' by the imagination of the pious meditant and, in effect, triggered in her/him a bodily response of sympathy, pity, commitment and, in some cases, even an urge to suffer the same torments as the Saviour did in the Passion narrative.[43]

Cognitive science calls this visceral simulatory mechanism 'kinesthetic empathy', describing it as a mode of motor resonance in which the

---

38 McNamer, *Affective Meditation*, pp. 29, 30, 179.

39 Garner, *Kinesthetic Spectatorship*, p. 2.

40 Garner, *Kinesthetic Spectatorship*, p. 21.

41 Garner, *Kinesthetic Spectatorship*, p. 224; see also e.g. Cameron, *Metaphor*, pp. 9–10.

42 Lipps, 'Empathy'; Martin, *America Dancing*, pp. 47–52.

43 For the notion of devotional *compassio*, see McNamer, *Affective Meditation*, pp. 25–57; Delaurenti, *La contagion des émotions*.

movement production and perception are aligned in an epistemic formation, in which the act of producing a movement is always accompanied by neural simulation of the same movement in the body of the percipient. This interpersonal sensorimotor resonance, cognitive theory holds, enables us to approach within the reach of the embodied experience of others. By recreating the kinesthetic experience of another person unconsciously in our own bodies, we make the first step towards the more intellectual modes of empathy, such as the 'emotional empathy' and 'cognitive empathy'. The vicarious experience of motor capacities, abilities, and habits of the others, nevertheless, seems to be a necessary precondition for these higher modes of interpersonal resonance.[44]

The mechanism of kinesthetic empathy seems to be all too clear when regarding the interaction of two or more people. However, I aim to proceed still further in the current line of thought, asking whether the kinesthetic empathy could be induced as a result of the rumination over a lifeless object, too, e.g. the visual and textual representations of crucified Christ, animated like certain *crucifixi dolorosi*. The following case study to this point comprises three elements of medieval Bohemian Passion idiom, namely the *St Vitus Passion Play*, the *Planctus Mariae* from the *Passional of Abbess Kunigunde*, and an example of the *arma Christi* image-text[45] extant in the same manuscript, that was in use in the Benedictine Convent of St George in Prague.

Verbal Staging in *St Vitus Passion Play* from Bohemia

Cognitive research has shown that the mirroring activity of human neural system is not restricted exclusively to the actions performed by other living body(ies) here and now; a similar simulatory process actually occurs in our brain even when we simply imagine the (targeted) actions, hear sounds referring to the execution of such actions, or see inanimate objects perform the given actions. As Staton Garner, Jr. puts it, 'mirror neurons activate when one imagines an action by thinking or reading about it or when one hears an action being recounted (in storytelling, for instance)'.[46]

In the light of these findings, the notions of *verbal staging* and *theatre of the mind*, known from the previous research on literary perception,

---

44 Reynolds and Reason, *Kinesthetic Empathy*; Garner, *Kinesthetic Spectatorship*, pp. 2–25.
45 A term coined by visual and media scholar W. J. T. Mitchell to describe hybrid media that combine visual and textual layer as an equal basis in the process of meaning creation: Mitchell, *Picture Theory*, esp. pp. 70, 89nn. For the vast employment of Mitchells term to the analysis of medieval Passion culture, see my upcoming work on Bohemian lament, Kubartová and others, *Worshipping*.
46 Garner, *Kinesthetic Spectatorship*, p. 154.

seem to retain greater poignancy as their intuitive workings are placed on more stable grounds by the neurological study of human brain. Both terms claim, each from a slightly different angle, that a textual performance can be conceived as corollary to a theatrical performance insofar as both represent a kind of 'staging' or 'enactment' of a narration that renders the represented actions, regardless of their intent, 'vivid' and 'dramatic'. Both the notion of verbal staging and theatre of mind shed light on the significance of the reader's/listener's imagination in the process of meaning formation, identifying the mind of the recipient as an ultimate site of the 'mental performance' incited by certain kinds of literature. Developing the argument further with the use of the findings of cognitive phenomenology, it can be argued that a similar process of motor resonance (or kinesthetic empathy) is in operation in both performative and textual representations, since each of them elicits a certain mimetic response in the reader's/viewer's body triggered either by watching something happen or by imagining it happening, respectively. Consequently, the textual and performative encounters can be equally successful in producing an empathic bodily response, even if the former do not represent any actual movement that the recipient's body could empathically imitate straight away. For example, the compassionate response to Christ's suffering could be elicited not only by watching a performance of a Passion play, but also by taking part in a Good Friday ceremony featuring the chanting of a Marian lament, meditating over a textual version thereof, or observing an image of *arma Christi*,[47] referring to Christ's suffering in a metonymic way. Let us consider all these three examples into more detail.

In Passion plays and mystery cycles, Christ's suffering was notoriously represented not as an abstract idea but as a 'real thing', entrenched in the actuality of the lived world of the spectators who, in Jill Stevenson's words, 'understood the cycle [or similar religious representations] as a living story that began in the past and continued through their own lives and into their futures'.[48] A heterogenous blend of the sacred narrative of the Biblical past and the actual present of the spectators, the unique phenomenality of the Pasion performance inevitably informed how the spectators understood its religious meanings. At the same time, the 'vivid', enlivened materiality of the theatrical enactment also conditioned particular sensorimotor responses that got inscribed, in the process of watching the performance and even after its end, in the audience's minds in the form of an embodied schema, imprinted in their bodies to be retrieved later in a situation similar

---

47 The term denotes visual and/or textual representations of the instruments of Christ's Passion in medieval literature and art, reaching as far back as the ninth century and gaining prominence in the fourteenth and fifteenth centuries especially in relation to Passion idiom; see *The Arma Christi*, ed. by Cooper and Denny-Brown.

48 Stevenson, *Performance*, p. 99.

to that which originally incited the schema,[49] as discussed earlier with regard to the devotional gestures in the *Cividale Planctus*. For instance, a vivid description of Christ's tormented body in the fragment of the *St Vitus Passion Play* from Bohemia, seen from the perspective of Joseph of Arimathea, made the audience to re-enact vicariously the sensorimotor experience of a person in pain (Christ), as well as a person in mourning (Joseph). Both these bodily patterns effectually imprinted in the motor memory of the audience in the course of the encounter, leaving a distinct somatic and cognitive trace.

Kinesthetic empathy triggered by various Passion media had two impacts. First, it laid grounds for a more complex and intellectual modes of empathic response to Christ's suffering, such as the *compassio*, a religious virtue praised highly by medieval theologians. Second, it created embodied schemata, or patterns of movement, that the spectators could apply in their future encounters with image of suffering Christ — or anyone else suffering, for that matter. Such response could be triggered by a theatrical representation, as in the performance of a Passion play, but also through more orthodox religious genres, e.g. textual composition enacted during (para-) liturgical ceremonies and other devotional performances (such as the *Cividale Planctus* and *Planctus Mariae* from the *Passional of Abbess Kunigunde*, discussed below), or stationary images, e.g. crucifixes and images of the tools of Christ's passion, yet to be considered.

In his monologue from a fourteenth-century Bohemian *St Vitus Passion Play*, Joseph of Arimathea is depicted as approaching the cross and observing desperately, yet dedicatedly the suspended body of Christ. Curiously, the audience could perhaps compare Joseph's pious description of the corporeal marks of Saviour's suffering with their immediate visual analogy captured by the religious puppet that might have been used to stage the scene.[50]

> *Tunc vadant ad crucem. Tunc Iozeph, stans ante crucem, dicit.*
> Auvech, tvórče milostivý,
> tvój svatý život nelstivý
> tak jest *náramně proražen*
> i všem na divy *obnažen*.
> Spasiteli všeho světa
> me vesele, ma roznieta,
> tak sta *zbite ruče i nožie*,

---

49 See Stevenson, *Performance*, pp. 89–92, 99–104.

50 While a human actor undoubtedly represented Christ in the scenes where the character was supposed to speak (ll. 314–44, 375–82), it is possible, even more likely, that a liturgical puppet replaced the actor in the Deposition scene. Kamil Kopania and Daniele Di Lodovico argue to this point: Kopania, *Animated Sculptures*, p. 200; Di Lodovico, 'Revising Devotion', pp. 135–45.

> v té *hlavici ostré hložie,*
> *v tvém bočie rána veliká:*
> *kakož kříže neproniká?*
> Proši tvé milosti bože,
> vezmi mi duši v nebeské ložie.
> *Tunc deponant corpus et Jozeph dicit.*[51]

> (Let them then go to the cross. Then, let Joseph, standing before the cross, say: 'Oh, merciful creator, your truthful body was so utterly pierced and uncovered for everyone to watch. Saviour of the whole world, my joy, my elation, how beaten are your hands and *legs*, the sharp thorns in your head, and such a big wound in your side! How is it that it does not go all through? I ask for your mercy, my God, take my soul to the heavenly bed.' Let them then take the body of Christ down from the cross and Joseph say [...].)

The passage from the *St Vitus Passion play* can be compared, in its focus on the material outcomes of Christ's suffering and the form of their rendering, with another Bohemian Passion text, the *Planctus Mariae* from the *Passional of Abbess Kunigunde*. Here, a similar verbal depiction of Christ's suffering occurs in a graphic enumeration of the numberless ways in which Christ's body was tormented, emphasis being put on the particular objects serving as a means of the mutilation process, and the bodily traces of the torture. All this is exemplified poignantly in the following extract from the lament, which was most probably intended for recitation by and to the nuns of the Benedictine convent of St George at the Prague Castle that occurred, according to the local breviary, on Good Friday after Vespers.[52]

> Illud corpusculum, quod spiritus sanctus in meis visceribus illi conpegerat, quod per teneritudine nec super terram sine dolore incedere poterat, tot flagellorum ictibus dilaceratum est, tot malleorum percussionibus, clavorum quid confossionibus perforatum est, quod a planta pedis usque ad verticem, non est in eo sanitas.[53]

> (This body, that the Holy Spirit composed inside my loins, that was so tender that it could not tread the ground without pain, this body has been lacerated by so many strokes of the scourge and by so many blows of hammers, and pierced by so many nails that there is not a single healthy spot to be found on his body from head to toe.)

---

51 'Svatovítský zlomek', ed. by Máchal, p. 131; emphases and translation are the author's.

52 Prague, National Library, MS XIII E 14d, fol. 74ʳ.

53 *Planctus Mariae*, Passional of Abbess Kunigunde, Prague, National Library, MS XIV A 17, fol. 16ʳ; translation is the author's.

Both renderings of Christ's torments, one performed and one recited, must have elicited a visceral empathic response in the pious recipients, engaging the capacity of their bodily apparatus to vicariously imitate the sensorimotor experience of another person while watching that person perform an action — or merely hear the action being recounted, to reiterate Garner's explanation of the workings of neural mirroring mechanism. Disrobing, battering, piercing, and nailing the body of Christ was, thus, automatically and unconsciously simulated by the viewers/listeners, producing substantial devotional effects (e.g. feeling compassion with the suffering Christ, learning the proper devotional gestures to venerate his sacrifice, etc.).

As has been already suggested, we may argue that even a static image that does nothing more than insinuate the individual actions of Christ's torment could be enough, if cognitive theory is not mistaken, to elicit in the viewers' bodies similar kind of response as did the performative and textual representations thereof. As recounted earlier, cognitive research seems to have proven by now that emotional simulation occurs not only when we watch an action being performed, or hear it recounted, but also when we hear the mere sounds related to the execution of such action or see inanimate objects perform it.[54]

The latter situation can be evidenced by the devotional use of the depictions of *arma Christi*, tools of Christ's suffering that started appearing from the thirteenth century onwards in textual representations, desk painting, murals, and manuscript illumination.[55] The individual items, such as splinters from the wood of the cross, spikes from the crown of thorns, etc., were also gathered in the collections of relics, that were kept in churches and exhibited publicly at various festive occasions. In Prague, one of such prominent occasions was the Feast of the Holy Lance and Nails, established by the Pope in 1354 on the direct appeal from Emperor Charles IV (1316–1378). Relics kept in the imperial, royal, and St Vitus treasury were exhibited on a wooden scaffold at the Cattle Market, today's Charles Square in the Prague New Town, for the locals and pilgrims to venerate, including a number of Passion items, e.g. 'clavus de sinistra manu, pars tunice purpuree in qua Christus fuit coronatus, pars spongie cum qua Christus fuit potatus', etc.[56] If the findings of cognitive scientists are correct, 'dynamic' and 'enlivened' exhibition of the tools of Christ's torments, such as the one at Prague Cattle Market, or at its successor in Nuremberg, instituted in 1424,[57] provoked a bodily response in the audi-

---

54 Garner, *Kinesthetic Spectatorship*, p. 154.
55 See Cooper and Denny-Brown, 'Introduction'.
56 Kubínová, *Imitatio Romae*, pp. 238–56, 291–98.
57 Ehrstine, 'Indulgenced Affect'.

ences comparable to that of seeing a live person inflicting and receiving torments by the same devices as the ones displayed at the Feast.

A similar effect must have been produced also by the pictorial counterpart of these public exhibitions, the depiction of *arma* in manuscript illumination and painting. One such illumination can be found in the already mentioned *Passional of Abbess Kunigunde* from Bohemia, where images of the tools accompany a set of mystical and affective tracts written by a Dominican priest Kolda of Koldice. Elaborating on the salvific ramifications of God's excruciating sacrifice, the Latin prose meditations encouraged the users of the manuscript to contemplate the position of the human soul as the testamental Bride of Christ, a devotional trope promoted by the works of Bernard of Clairvaux and other theologians of the time. Applying the findings of cognitive theory on the reading practices of the manuscript, it follows that its users did not need the actions related to the individual *arma* to be actually performed, nor even recounted, in order to experience pious compassion with the tormented Saviour. In fact, it was enough for them to stage the respective acts of mutilation in their own 'mind theatres' with the aid of visual cues provided by the images of the arms and textual cues from the accompanying treatises, such as the description of Christ's wounds quoted above. As for the depiction of the *arma*, two of them can be found in the manuscript: one representing the *arma* conspicuously in the manner of theatrical props ready to be used in a stage performance (**Fig. 2.3**), and another in which their effects can be already seen on the mutilated body of Christ pending on the cross (**Fig. 2.4**). The sensorimotor system of the viewers was quick to respond to these visual and textual 'prompts', not only conjuring vivid mental images of the scenes of Christ's suffering, but also eliciting an empathic response to his suffering and inscribing sensorimotor patterns derived from this input, such as weeping and wringing one's hands, in their somatic apparatus.

Conclusion

In this essay, I drew upon several conclusions of previous scholarship regarding the 'reality effect' of late medieval devotional media, observed in texts, objects, and performances depicting the Passion. Presuming that this aesthetic strategy 'was really there' in the corresponding events and works of art, I argued that their alleged 'realism' should not be considered an aesthetic quality alone, but also a perceptual one insofar as it was grounded in a specific modality of medieval devotional spectatorship — and any spectatorship, for that matter —, the inevitably embodied nature of human perception and cognition. As the surrounding world inevitably comes to us through the gateway of corporeal senses located in our bodily organs,

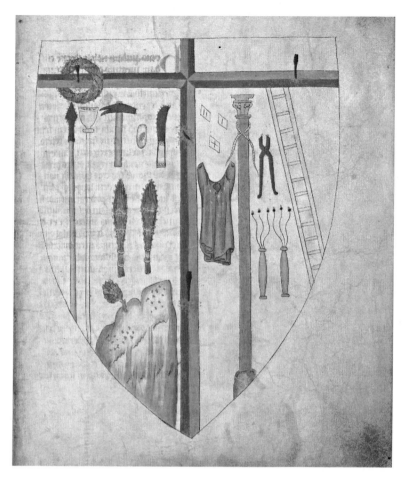

Figure 2.3. *Arma Christi, Passional of Abbess Kunigunde*, Prague, National Library of the Czech Republic, MS XIV A 17, fol. 3^r. Photo: National Library of the Czech Republic.

all our cognitive processes, even the most intellectual ones, germinate on a much more primordial level, in our corporeal experience of life. I explored here, in particular, the mechanism of a neurosomatic simulatory response, in which cells known as mirror neurons, activated by the perception of a targeted action, trigger a somatoneural activity in parts of the cerebral cortex responsible for the execution of the same action. Thus, watching an action, or imagining it with the aid of visual or acoustic cues, we vicariously experience the same action, unconsciously and automatically, in our own bodies.

64   ELIŠKA KUBARTOVÁ

Figure 2.4. *Arma Christi, Passional of Abbess Kunigunde*, Prague, National Library of the Czech Republic, MS XIV A 17, fol. 10ʳ. Photo: National Library of the Czech Republic.

This mechanism, I believe, can be instructive in explaining various observations previously made about the function of the objects and performances designed to enhance devotion to Christ's Passion, such as the animated crucifixes, scripts for the Good Friday ceremonies, and affective Passion meditations. Each in its unique way, all these religious media provoked a distinctive form of affective resonance in the bodies of their recipients, presenting mimetically concrete ('realistic'), visceral images of embodied actions related to Christ's suffering. The primary considerations seem to validate at least three religious functions associated in scholarship with this kind of Passion representations. They contributed to the communication of theological meanings related to the notion of Christ's human nature and its Eucharistic consequences; imprinted proper devotional gestures in the somatic patterns of the pious viewers/readers/listeners in the form of an embodied schema; and incited a pre-intellectual kinesthetic sympathy towards the suffering God that could be developed toward a more complex religious affect, such as the compassion with Christ's humanity, which enabled the devotee to recognize also her/his own pitifulness and sinfulness through accepting one's own share in God's suffering.

The synergy of cognitive and phenomenological approaches to medieval devotional performance practices does not bring any substantially new observations on its own. It nonetheless validates previous findings from the viewpoint of the operations of human mind in a distinct spectatorial position (of the viewer, reader, or listener) that was then — and still is — inescapably and intrinsically embodied in nature.

Bibliography

Manuscripts

Prague, National Library, MS XIII E 14d (Breviary)
——, MS XIV A 17 (*Passional of Abbess Kunigunde*)

Edited Source Texts

'Cividale Planctus', in Karl Young, *The Drama of the Medieval Church*, vol. I
(Oxford: Clarendon Press, 1933), pp. 507–12
——, Davidson, Audrey Ekdahl, 'Planctus Mariae From Cividale', *Comparative Drama*, 42/3 (2008), 271–85
'Svatovítský zlomek', in Jan Máchal, *Staročeské skladby dramatické původu liturgického* (Prague: Česká akademie císaře Františka Josefa pro vědy, slovesnost a umění, 1908), pp. 126–40

Secondary Material

Animating Medieval Art, ed. by Elina Gertsman = *Preternature: Critical and Historical Studies on the Preternatural*, 4/1 (2015)
Barthes, Roland, 'The Reality Effect', in Roland Barthes, *The Rustle of Language* (Berkeley: University of California Press, 1989), pp. 141–48
Belting, Hans, *An Anthropology of Images: Picture, Medium, Body* (Princeton: Princeton University Press, 2011), reprint 2014
Borowski, Mateusz and Malgorzata Sugiera, 'Introduction to Chapter Three', in *Fictional Realities/Real Fictions: Contemporary Theatre in Search of a New Mimetic Paradigm*, ed. by Mateusz Borowski and Malgorzata Sugiera (Newcastle: Cambridge Scholars Publishing, 2007), pp. 136–48
——, 'Preface: From the Realism of the Representation to Realism of Experience', in *Fictional Realities/Real Fictions: Contemporary Theatre in Search of a New Mimetic Paradigm*, ed. by Mateusz Borowski and Malgorzata Sugiera (Newcastle: Cambridge Scholars Publishing, 2007), pp. VII–XXVIII
Bynum, Caroline Walker, *Christian Materiality: An Essay on Religion in Late Medieval Europe* (New York: Zone Books, 2011)
——, *Dissimilar Similitudes: Devotional Objects in Late Medieval Europe* (New York: Zone Books, 2020)
——, *Holy Feast and Holy Fast: The Religious Significance of Food to Medieval Women* (Berkeley: University of California Press, 1987)
——, *Wonderful Blood: Theology and Practice in Late Medieval Northern Germany and Beyond* (Philadelphia, Pa.: University of Pennsylvania Press, 2007)

Cameron, Lynne, *Metaphor and Reconciliation: The Discourse Dynamics of Empathy in Post-conflict Conversations* (New York: Routledge, 2011)

Clark, Robert L. A., 'Spiritual Exercises: The Making of Interior Faith', in *The Oxford Handbook of Medieval Christianity*, ed. by John Arnold (Oxford: Oxford University Press, 2017), pp. 271–88

Cooper, Lisa H., and Andrea Denny-Brown (eds), *The Arma Christi in Medieval and Early Modern Material Culture. With a Critical Edition of 'O Vernicle'* (London: Routledge, 2014)

A Cultural History of Objects, ed. by Julie Lund and Sarah Semple, vol. II (London: Bloomsbury Academic, 2021)

Delaurenti, Béatrice, *La Contagion des émotions: Compassio, une énigme médiévale* (Paris: Classiques Garnier, 2016)

Di Lodovico, Daniele, 'Revising Devotion: The Role of Wooden Sculptures in Affecting Painting and Devotion in the Late Medieval Period in Italy (XIIth–XVth Century)' (unpublished doctoral thesis, University of Washington, 2016)

Dresvina, Juliana, and Victoria Blud, *Cognitive Sciences and Medieval Studies: An Introduction* (Cardiff: University of Wales Press, 2020)

Easton, Martha, 'The Wound of Christ, the Mouth of Hell: Appropriations and Inversions of Female Anatomy in the Later Middle Ages', in *Tributes to Jonathan J. G. Alexander: The Making and Meaning of Illuminated Medieval and Renaissance Manuscripts, Art and Architecture*, ed. by Susan L'Engle and Gerald Guest (London: Harvey Miller, 2005), pp. 395–414

Ehrstine, Glenn, 'Das geistliche Spiel als Ablassmedium. Überlegungen am Beispiel des Alsfelder Passionsspiels', in *Religiöses Wissen im mittelalterlichen und frühneuzeitlichen Schauspiel*, ed. by Klaus Ridder and others (Berlin: Schwabe, 2021), pp. 259–97

Flanigan, Charles Clifford, *Liturgical Drama and Dramatic Liturgy: A Study of the Quem Queritis Easter Dialogue and Its Cultic Context* (Ann Arbor: University Microfilms International, 1981)

Flora, Holly, *The Devout Belief of the Imagination: The Paris 'Meditationes Vitae Christi' and Female Franciscan Spirituality in Trecento Italy* (Turnhout: Brepols, 2009)

Fulton, Rachel, *From Judgement to Passion: Devotion to Christ and Virgin Mary, 800–1200* (New York and Chichester: Columbia University Press, 2002)

Gertsman, Elina, 'Bewilderment Overwhelms Me', *Preternature: Critical and Historical Studies on the Preternatural*, 4/1 (2015), 1–12

Gesture in Medieval Drama and Art, ed. by Clifford Davidson (Kalamazoo: Medieval Institute Publications, 2001)

Hollywood, Amy, 'That Glorious Slit: Irigaray and the Medieval Devotion to Christ's Side Wound', in *Luce Irigaray and Premodern Culture: Thresholds of History*, ed. by Teresa Krier and Elizabeth H. Harvey (London: Routledge, 2004), pp. 105–25

Izydorczyk, Zbigniew, 'The *Evangelium Nicodemi* in the Latin Middle Ages', in *The Medieval Gospel of Nicodemus: Texts, Intertexts, and Contexts in Western Europe*, ed. by Zbigniew Izydorczyk (Tempe: Medieval and Renaissance Texts and Studies, 1997), pp. 43–101

Johnson, Mark, *The Body in the Mind: The Bodily Basis of Meaning, Imagination, and Reason* (Chicago: The University of Chicago Press, 1987)

Karmon, David, 'The Sacro Monte at Varallo and the Choreography of an Olfactory Landscape', *Future Anterior: Journal of Historic Preservation, History, Theory, and Criticism*, 13/2 (2016), 57–75

Karnes, Michelle, *Imagination, Meditation and Cognition in the Middle Ages* (Chicago: University of Chicago Press, 2011), reprint 2017

Kinesthetic Empathy in Creative and Cultural Practices, ed. by Dee Reynolds and Matthew Reason (Bristol: Intellect, 2012)

King, Pamela M., *Medieval Literature, 1300–1500* (Edinburgh: Edinburgh University Press, 2011)

Kopania, Kamil, *Animated Sculptures of the Crucified Christ in the Religious Culture of the Latin Middle Ages* (Warsaw: Neriton, 2010)

——, 'Animated Sculptures of the Crucified Christ: Origins, Development and Impact', *Material Religion. The Journal of Objects, Art and Belief*, 14/4 (2018), 545–58

Kubartová, Eliška, 'Negotiating Gender Roles in High-Medieval Bohemian Literature and Performance: Marian and Magdalenian Laments', in *Communicating the Passion: Socio-Religious Function of an Emotional Narrative*, ed. by Pietro Delcorno and Holly Johnson [forthcoming]

Kubartová, Eliška, and others, *Worshipping Like a Woman. Marian and Magdalenian Laments From Medieval Bohemia* (Turnhout: Brepols [planned 2025]).

Kubínová, Kateřina, *Imitatio Romae — Karel IV. a Řím* (Praha: Artefactum, 2006)

Lakoff, George, and Mark Johnson, *Metaphors We Live By* (Chicago: The University of Chicago Press, 1980)

——, *Philosophy in the Flesh: The Embodied Mind and Its Challenge to Western Thought* (New York: Basic Books, 1999)

Mazzon, Gabriela, *Pathos in Late-Medieval Religious Drama and Art: A Communicative Strategy* (Leiden and Boston: Brill and Rodopi, 2018)

McConachie, Bruce, 'Metaphors We Act By: Kinesthetics, Cognitive Psychology, and Historical Structures', *Journal of Dramatic Theory and Criticism*, 8/2 (1993), 23–45

McNamer, Sarah, *Affective Meditation and the Invention of Medieval Compassion* (Philadelphia: University of Pennsylvania Press, 2010)

Miller, Patricia Cox, *The Corporeal Imagination: Signifying the Holy in Late Ancient Christianity* (Philadelphia: University of Pennsylvania Press, 2009)

——, 'Visceral Seeing: The Holy Body in Late Ancient Christianity', *Journal of Early Christian Studies*, 12/4 (2004), 391–411

Mitchell, W. J. Thomas, *Picture Theory: Essays on Verbal and Visual Representation* (Chicago: University of Chicago Press, 1994), reprint 2014

The Music of the Medieval Church Dramas, ed. by William Lawrence Smoldon and Cynthia Bourgeault (London: Oxford University Press, 1980)

Noë, Alva, *Action in Perception* (Cambridge, MA: MIT Press, 2004)

Norton, Michael Lee, *Liturgical Drama and the Reimagining of Medieval Theatre* (Kalamazoo: Medieval Institute Publications, 2017)

Ogden, Dunbar H., 'Gesture and Characterization in Liturgical Drama', in *Gesture in Medieval Drama and Art*, ed. by Clifford Davidson (Kalamazoo: Medieval Institute Publications, 2001), pp. 26–47

Palazzo, Éric, *L'invention chrétienne des cinq sens dans la liturgie et l'art au Moyen Âge* (Paris: Les Éditions du Cerf, 2014)

———, *Le souffle de Dieu: l'énergie de la liturgie et l'art au Moyen Âge* (Paris: Les éditions du Cerf, 2020)

Poláčková [Kubartová], Eliška, 'Marian Laments from Medieval Bohemia: Performing Suffering and Redemption Through Compassion', *European Medieval Drama*, 25 (2021), 65–90

———, 'Planctus Mariae: Performing Compassion as a Means of Social Promotion', *Theatralia*, 23/2 (2020), 74–91

———, *Verbum caro factum est: Performativita bohemikální literatury 14. století pohledem divadelní vědy* (Prague: Filosofia, 2019)

Stevenson, Jill, *Performance, Cognitive Theory, and Devotional Culture: Sensual Piety in Late Medieval York* (Basingstoke: Palgrave MacMillan, 2010)

Traditional India: Structure and change, ed. by Milton Singer (Philadelphia: American Folklore Society, 1959)

Varela, Francisco J. and others, *The Embodied Mind: Cognitive Sciences and Human Experience* (Cambridge, MA: MIT Press, 1991)

CLARA STRIJBOSCH _____

Singen und Wiegen

Das Weihnachtslied 'Ecce mundi gaudia' im Wienhäuser Liederbuch

▼ **ABSTRACT** This article discusses the song 'Ecce mundi gaudia' in the *Wienhäuser Song Book* (c. 1500) in its literary and cultural context. The song derives from a group of Christmas carols found in manuscripts belonging to women connected with the Devotio Moderna movement in the triangle Zwolle (The Netherlands)–Cologne–Wienhausen (Germany). In all instances well-known material about Jesus's infancy or youth is embedded within an existing Latin frame. Unlike similar songs, the Wienhäuser song 'Ecce mundi gaudia' has a second refrain containing words typically found in lullabies, which might indicate a Christmas cradling tradition. Several sources witness that cradling could end up in a dance around the Christmas cradle, even in church. Probably the Wienhäuser song 'Ecce mundi gaudia' accompanied a tradition of cradling at Christmas in Wienhausen.

▼ **KEYWORDS:** women, *Devotio Moderna*, Christmas song, cradle song, medieval Christmas dance, *Wienhäuser Song Book*, Macaronic song, Joseph, convent drama, Wienhausen.

Clara Strijbosch (c.b.m.strijbosch@uu.nl) studied piano at the Utrecht Conservatory, and Dutch language and Literature at Utrecht University, where she earned her doctorate in 1995 with a thesis on the Irish Saint Brendan (published in 2000 in Dublin as *The Seafaring Saint*). She has been a researcher in the Departments of Musicology and Dutch Literature at several European and South-African Universities. Since 2000 she has been working as an independent researcher and journalist, publishing on medieval travel stories and on songbooks of the later Middle Ages.

Das *Wienhäuser Liederbuch*, das in der zweiten Hälfte des fünfzehnten Jahrhunderts oder in Teilen kurz nach 1500 im niedersächsischen Nonnenkloster Wienhausen zusammengestellt worden ist, enthält auf vierzig vollständig beschriebenen Papierblättern vierundfünfzig Lieder, von denen siebzehn auf Latein und sechs in einer lateinisch-deutschen Mischsprache abgefasst sind; die übrigen sind auf Niederdeutsch. Zwei dieser niederdeutschen Lieder weisen einen lateinischen Kehrreim auf.[1] Eines der beiden ist ein kurzes Weihnachtslied mit dem lateinischen Kehrreim 'Ecce mundi gaudia' (fol. 29^r).[2] In diesem Beitrag wird durch einen Vergleich mit verwandten Weihnachtsliedern versucht, das Lied 'Ecce mundi gaudia' in sein kulturelles und religiöses Umfeld einzubetten. In einem zweiten Schritt wird überprüft, ob das Lied bestimmte Hinweise zu einer Eigenart sonstiger 'Kindelwiegenlieder' enthält. Kam es bei diesem Lied zu einem Wiegen des Kindes? Ging das Wiegen mit einem Tanz aus Freude über die Geburt Christi einher?

Durch die so gewonnenen Erkenntnisse wäre ein weiterer Schritt dazu getan, der Charakterisierung des Wienhäuser Liedguts und des religiösen Festalltags in Wienhausen näherzukommen und den Brauch des 'Weihnachtstanzes' genauer zu umreißen.

Singen und Dichten

Das Lied 'Ecce mundi gaudia' im *Wienhäuser Liederbuch* passt zu einer Gruppe von Weihnachtsliedern aus Handschriften von Frauen aus dem Bereich zwischen Zwolle und Köln, die der Devotio moderna zuzuordnen sind. Die Devotio moderna, die sich ausgehend vom Fluss IJssel von etwa 1400 an rasch über das Rheingebiet und Nord-West-Deutschland verbreitete, war eine sehr erfolgreiche Reformbewegung, die auf die innere spirituelle Entwicklung ihrer Angehörigen abzielte. Angestrebt wurde ein Leben in einer frommen Gemeinschaft, wobei sich vor allem Frauen zu solchen Gemeinschaften hingezogen fühlten.[3] Aus einem solchen Umfeld stammt auch ein Lied aus der Liederhandschrift Berlin, SBB-PK, mgo 190, das ebenfalls den Kehrreim 'Ecce mundi gaudia' aufweist. Die Handschrift ist um 1480 im Bistum Utrecht entstanden, wahrscheinlich in einer

---

1 Wienhausen Klosterarchiv, Ms. 9, vgl. 'Wienhäuser Liederbuch', hg. von Alpers; zur Musik siehe Sievers, 'Die Melodien'; zur Datierung siehe Roolfs, 'Das *Wienhäuser Liederbuch*', S. 264. Von der in der Edition Alpers, S. 2, genannten Anzahl von 59 Liedern sind die Nummern 45 bis 49 abzuziehen, weil es sich hier um Gebete handelt.

2 Vgl. *leticia* abgekürzt *le* (Str. 3–6), *plena gratia* abgekürzt *pl gr* Str. 2 und 6. 'Wienhäuser Liederbuch', hg. von Alpers, S. 25. Das Lied wird nach der Kehrreimzeile 'Ecce mundi gaudia' bezeichnet.

3 Für eine rasche Einblick in das Funktionieren von Liedern in der Devotio moderna siehe De Morrée, *Voor de tijd*, S. 18–24.

SINGEN UND WIEGEN 73

Frauengemeinschaft der Devotio moderna. Beide Lieder werden hier zum Vergleich zitiert:[4]

Wienhäuser Liederbuch, fol. 29ʳ

1. Do de tyd wart vullenbracht,
ecce mundi gaudia
do bewisede god syne krafft,
sine fine leticia.
O virgo Maria, tu es plena gratia,
pie pie so se nunne so
mater Jhesu, make uns vro.

2. Dor stunt eyn ezel und eyn rinth [*Refr.*],
dar wart gheboren dat leve kynt [*Refr.*].

3. Do dat kynt gheboren wart [*Refr.*],
do en haddet neynen wyndeldock [*Refr.*].

4. Josep toch syne hoseken uth [*Refr.*]
unde makede dem kynde eyn wyndeldock [*Refr.*].

5. Se operden dem kynde eyn grote solt [*Refr.*],
wirok, myrren unde golt [*Refr.*].

6. Se nam dat kynt by ore hant [*Refr.*]
unde vorede dat in Egiptenlant [*Refr.*].

(**1.** Als die Zeit gekommen war, seht die Freuden der Welt, bewies Gott seine Macht. Immerwährende Freude, o Jungfrau Maria, du bist voll der Gnaden. Liebes, liebes süßes Kind, Mutter Jesu, mach uns froh. **2.** Da standen ein Esel und ein Ochse [*Refr.*]. Dort wurde das liebe Kind geboren [*Refr.*]. **3.** Als das Kind geboren wurde [*Refr.*], hatte es keine Windel [*Refr.*]. **4.** Josef zog seine Hosen aus [*Refr.*] und machte dem Kind daraus eine Windel [*Refr.*]. **5.** Sie opferten dem Kind einen großen Schatz [*Refr.*], Weihrauch, Myrrhe und Gold [*Refr.*]. **6.** Sie nahm das Kind an ihre Hand [*Refr.*] und führte es nach Ägypten [*Refr.*].)

---

4 Berlin, SBB-PK, Ms. Berlin 190; *Liederenhandschrift*, hg. von Mertens, S. 306–07; für Fragen der Datierung und Lokalisierung siehe Mertens, S. 43–45. Die Übersetzungen verlassen zwangsläufig die Kategorie der wörtlichen Übertragung, sobald sie die mittelalterlichen Texte in einem gängigen Gegenwartsdeutsch wiedergegeben. So erscheinen die zahlreichen Diminutive in den Texten in der deutschen Übersetzung nicht; es handelt sich um einen typisch niederländischen Sprachgebrauch.

Berlin, SBB-PK, mgo 190, fol. 38ᵛ

1. Kinder, swijcht, so moecht di horen
ecce mundi gaudia
hoe heer Jhesus is gheboren.
in te sunt solempnia,
o virgo Maria,
dei plena gracia.

2. Denghel die die bootscap brachte [*Refr.*],
quam ter maghet inder nachte [*Refr.*].

3. Hi gruesete also vriendelike [*Refr.*]
mitten heer van hemelrike [*Refr.*].

4. Hi seide datse soude ontfaen [*Refr.*]
Jhesum Cristum, sonder waen [*Refr.*].

5. Dat was een wonderlic dinc [*Refr.*],
die maghet mit een woert ontfinc [*Refr.*].

6. Si droech hem maenden neghen [*Refr.*],
als vrouwen bi naturen pleghen [*Refr.*].

7. Gheboren wert di edel dracht [*Refr.*]
tsnachts in couder midder nacht [*Refr.*].

8. Men leiden in een cribbeken [*Refr.*],
Jhesum dat suete kindekijn [*Refr.*].

9. Dat kint moet sijn ghebenedijt [*Refr.*]
ende sijn moeder in alder tijt [*Refr.*].

(**1.** Kinder, schweigt, so könnt ihr hören, seht die Freuden der Welt, wie Jesus der Herr geboren wurde. In dir ist die Heiligkeit, o Jungfrau Maria, voll der Gnaden Gottes. **2.** Der Engel, der die Botschaft brachte [*Refr.*], kam zur Magd in der Nacht [*Refr.*]. **3.** Er grüßte sie sehr freundlich [*Refr.*] im Namen des Herrn vom Himmelreich [*Refr.*]. **4.** Er sagte, dass sie empfangen werde [*Refr.*] den Herrn Jesus Christus fürwahr [*Refr.*]. **5.** Das war ein Wunder [*Refr.*], die Magd empfing durch ein Wort [*Refr.*]. **6.** Sie trug ihn neun Monate [*Refr.*], so wie Frauen das natürlicherweise tun [*Refr.*]. **7.** Geboren wurde die edle Frucht [*Refr.*] in der Kälte, mitten in der Nacht [*Refr.*]. **8.** Man legte ihn in die Krippe [*Refr.*], Jesus, das süße Kind [*Refr.*]. **9.** Das Kind soll gebenedeit sein [*Refr.*] und seine Mutter in Ewigkeit [*Refr.*].)

Man zögert, diese beiden Texte Variationen eines einzigen Lieds zu nennen: Bis auf das Weihnachtsmotiv haben sie bloß einen Teil des Kehrreims 'Ecce mundi gaudia' gemeinsam. Vom Format her stimmen sie überein: zwei volkssprachige Zeilen, unterbrochen von einem ebenfalls zweigeteilten lateinischen Kehrreim. Inhaltlich erzählt Wienhausen die ganze Weihnachtsgeschichte von der Geburt Jesu bis zur Flucht nach Ägypten, Berlin mgo 190 dagegen vor allem die Verkündigung durch Gabriel und das Wunder, dass Maria durch das Wort empfing.

Es gibt um 1500 mehrere Lieder, die eine Mittelstellung zwischen den beiden inhaltlich weit auseinanderliegenden Liedtexten Wienhausen und Berlin mgo 190 einnehmen, wie zum Beispiel ein Lied aus dem Liederbuch der Catharina van Rade sowie ein Lied der Anna von Köln:

Catharina van Rade, Köln, HA, 7010 W 25, fol. 157ᵛ–58ʳ
1. Die coutste nacht die oit gewaert
O virgo Maria
Dat was doen jhesus geboren was
Domine fulgencia ave plena gracia.

2. Hij waert geleit in einre cribben [*Refr.*].
Ein luttel hoys dat was sijn bedde [*Refr.*].

3. Jhesus is een suete kernne [*Refr.*].
Daer omme craken wi dese noetkens geern [*Refr.*].

[…]

5. Maria sette Jhesus op haeren scoet [*Refr.*].
Sij gaff hem einen appel roet [*Refr.*].

6. Maria soude jhesus ein papke maken [*Refr.*].
Her joseph ginck die stexkens rapen [*Refr.*].[5]

   (**1.** Die kälteste Nacht, die es je gab, o Jungfrau Maria, war, als Jesus geboren wurde. Glanz der Heiligkeit. Gegrüßet seist du voll der Gnaden. **2.** Er wurde in eine Krippe gelegt [*Refr.*], etwas Heu war sein Bett [*Refr.*]. **3.** Jesus ist ein süßer Kern [*Refr.*], deswegen knacken wir diese Nüsse gerne [*Refr.*]. […] **5.** Maria setzte Jesus auf ihren Schoß [*Refr.*], sie gab ihm einen Apfel rot [*Refr.*]. **6.** Maria sollte Jesus einen Brei kochen [*Refr.*], Josef sammelte das Kleinholz [*Refr.*].)

---

5 Es folgen noch drei Strophen mit verschiedenen Tätigkeiten aus dem Bereich des Haushalts und schließlich eine Darstellung der Himmelfahrt.

Anna von Köln, Berlin, SBB-PK, mgo 280, fol. 22ʳ–24ᵛ

1. It wart geboren in eynre nacht,
o virgo Maria,
eyn cleynes kynt van groisser macht,
o benivolencia, o o o virgo Maria.

2. So kalde necht men nye en vant [*Refr.*],
als do dat kynt geboren wart [*Refr.*].

3. Si lachten in yn eyn kribbelyn [*Refr.*],
hou dat was syn beddekyn [*Refr.*].

4. Dair en was alles guetz neit me [*Refr.*],
her Joseph reis syn hoesen enzwei [*Refr.*].

5. Si wanten it in eyn doechelyn [*Refr.*],
doe bleckden eme syn voeselyn [*Refr.*].

6. De moder solde eyn pepgen machen [*Refr.*],
her Joseph moist dat hoiltzgen raiffen [*Refr.*].⁶

> (**1.** Es wurde geboren in einer Nacht, o Jungfrau Maria, ein kleines
> Kind von großer Macht. O Gnade, o o o Jungfrau Maria. **2.** Eine
> so kalte Nacht gab es noch nie [*Refr.*], wie als Jesus geboren wurde
> [*Refr.*]. **3.** Sie legten ihn in eine Krippe [*Refr.*], Heu war sein Bett
> [*Refr.*]. **4.** Da gab es überhaupt nichts [*Refr.*], Josef riss seine Hosen
> entzwei [*Refr.*]. **5.** Sie wickelten ihn in ein Tuch [*Refr.*], da blieben
> seine Füße nackt [*Refr.*]. **6.** Die Mutter sollte einen Brei bereiten
> [*Refr.*], Josef musste das Kleinholz sammeln [*Refr.*].)

Das erste Lied stammt aus einem Devotionale aus dem Jahr 1487, das
der Catharina von Rade gehörte und das im oder für das Maastrichter Ter-
tiarissenkloster Maagdendries geschrieben worden war.⁷ Das zweite Lied
ist im Liederbuch der Anna von Köln enthalten, das größtenteils im zweiten Viertel des sechzehnten Jahrhunderts im Rheinland zusammengestellt
worden ist. Beide entstanden wahrscheinlich in eine Frauengemeinschaft,

---

6 Es folgen noch vierzehn Strophen mit der ganzen Weihnachtsgeschichte bis zur Flucht nach
Ägypten.

7 Köln, Historisches Archiv, 7010 (W) 25, fol. 157ᵛ–58ʳ; über Herkunft und Schreiberin
siehe Van Luijtelaar, 'Colofonconventies', S. 65–66; Edition in der *Nederlandse Liederenbank*,
https://www.liederenbank.nl/text.php?recordid=25315&lan=nl (Zugriff: 21. Dezember 2022).

beeinflüsst durch die Devotio moderna.[8] Sie enthalten beide den zweiten Teil des Kehrreims, wie er auch in Wienhausen und Berlin mgo 190 vorkommt, mit Variationen: 'o virgo Maria, Domine fulgencia, etc.' oder 'o virgo Maria, o benivolencia, etc.' Die Zeile 'Ecce mundi gaudia' haben beide nicht. Catharina van Rade erwähnt am Anfang die extreme Kälte in der Weihnachtsnacht. Zudem kennt Anna von Köln Strophen, die davon handeln, dass Josef seine Beinkleider auszieht, um daraus Windeln für das Kind zu machen. Beide haben eine weder in Wienhausen noch in Berlin mgo 190 vorkommende Strophe über Maria, die für das Kind Brei kochen soll, und Josef, der dafür Kleinholz sammelt.

Ob Wienhausen oder Berlin mgo 190 möglicherweise am Anfang der Tradition steht, lässt sich nicht feststellen. Vielmehr handelte es sich offenbar auch damals schon um ein weitgefasstes, thematisches Feld, auf das nach Bedarf zurückgegriffen werden konnte. So befindet sich in Annas von Köln Liederbuch ein zweites Lied mit dem Kehrreim 'Ecce mundi gaudia' — aber hier lautet der zweite Teil des Kehrreims 'sio fiolenlcia [*sic*], o virgo Maria, o plena gratia' (fol. 27ᵛ–28ʳ).[9] Dieses Lied setzt mitten in den weihnachtlichen Geschehnissen ein und beginnt mit Aussagen darüber, wie Jesus Holz sammelt, mit einem Blasebalg das Feuer anfacht und seiner Mutter beim Breikochen hilft — was in den vorhin zitierten Liedern Josefs Aufgaben sind. Dann folgen bei Anna von Köln drei in diesem Zusammenhang merkwürdige Strophen (Str. 4–6):

1. Jhesus nam dat korffgen in syn hant,
ecce mundi gaudia,
he las de spaengen, da he sy vant,
sio fiolenlcia
o virgo Maria, o plena gratia

2. He nam dat puystergen in syn hant [*Refr.*],
he bleyss dat vuyrgen, dat it brant [*Refr.*].

3. He nam dat leffelgen in syn hant [*Refr.*],
he halp synre moder dat moisgen koichen [*Refr.*].

4. O Maria, verwar dyn kynt [*Refr.*],
he geit des aventz also spaede [*Refr.*].

---

8 Berlin, SBB-PK, mgo 280; Anna von Köln, *Liederbuch*, hg. von Salmen, S. 14–15; für Datierung, Lokalisierung und kodikologische Beschreibung siehe De Morrée, *Voor de tijd*, S. 122, 220–26, und 324–37.

9 Vgl. Anna von Köln, *Liederbuch*, hg. von Salmen, S. 16.

5. Ick en kans verwaren neit [*Refr.*],
he hait de reyne hertgens lieff [*Refr.*].

6. Jhesus had eynen kruysen cop [*Refr.*],
vyl kruyser dan eyn wynranck top [*Refr.*].

> (**1.** Jesus nahm den Korb in die Hand, siehe die Freuden der
> Welt, er sammelte Kleinholz, wo immer er es fand. Unbefleckte, o
> Jungfrau Maria, o du voll der Gnaden. **2.** Er nahm den Blasebalg
> in die Hand [*Refr.*], er fachte das Feuer an, bis es brannte [*Refr.*].
> **3.** Er nahm den Löffel in die Hand [*Refr.*], er half seiner Mutter
> den Brei zu kochen [*Refr.*]. **4.** O Maria, behüte dein Kind [*Refr.*], es
> geht abends spät aus [*Refr.*]. **5.** Ich kann ihn nicht davon abhalten
> [*Refr.*], er liebt die reinen Herzen [*Refr.*]. **6.** Jesus hat einen Locken-
> kopf [*Refr.*], lockiger als eine Weinranke [*Refr.*].)

Hier wird Maria ermahnt, ihren Sohn zu behüten, der abends ausgeht,
woraufhin sie erwidert, dass sie das nicht könne, denn ihr Sohn liebe die
reinen Herzen. Ähnliche Strophen gibt es in Berlin, SBB-PK, mgo 185.
Die Handschrift ist Ende des fünfzehnten Jahrhunderts entstanden, und
zwar in der Gegend von Zwolle, dem Kerngebiet der Devotio moderna.[10]
Auch dieses Lied enthält einen 'Ecce mundi gaudia'-Kehrreim. Die Fassung
Berlin mgo 185 beginnt mit dem Motiv, dass Jesus als Liebhaber abends
die Jungfrauen besuchte und dass Maria ihn nicht davon abhalten konnte,
gefolgt von Hausarbeiten wie dem Sammeln von Holz und dem Kochen
von Brei. In diesem Lied ist das Motiv von Jesus als Liebhaber breiter
und umfassender ausgearbeitet als später in Annas von Köln lückenhafter
Fassung. Ebenso trifft man gleich in der ersten Strophe auf die Metapher
der Weinranke, wie in der letzten Strophe von Annas von Köln Lied.

1. HEre Jhesus uwen brunen cop
exe mondy gaudio
Hi bloeyt als enen wyngaerts cnop
cia fya lencia
O virgo Maria / O plena gracia

2. Heer Jhesus rockelkijn dat was groen [*Refr.*]
ende al syn lyfken als ene bloem [*Refr.*].

---

10 Berlin, SBB-PK, mgo 185, *ca.* 1475–1505; für die Datierung, Lokalisierung und
kodikologische Beschreibung siehe De Morrée, *Voor de tijd*, S. 64 und 314–23; über
Weihnachtslieder in dieser Handschrift S. 71–81). Das Lied auf S. 254–57 ist hier nach
der diplomatischen Edition, *Liederhandschrift*, hg. von van der Poel u. a. (Lied 74)
wiedergegeben.

3. Heer Jhesus is een auentganger [*Refr.*],
tot eenre Jonferen was alle syn ganc [*Refr.*].

4. Sy hebbe my lief sy mynnen my seer [*Refr.*],
daer om byn ic byden Joncferen geerne [*Refr.*].

5. Maria huedet uwen soen [*Refr.*],
datten v die jonferen niet en nemen [*Refr.*].

6. Ick en kans ghehueden nicht [*Refr.*],
hi heeft di reyne herten lief [*Refr.*].

7. Ic heb sy oec also duer gecost [*Refr.*],
daerom en mach ic er niet wesen af [*Refr.*].

8. Hi nam en corf in syn hant [*Refr.*],
hi las die sprockelkyn daer hise vant [*Refr.*].

9. Hi nam die cruke hi haelden water [*Refr.*],
hy halp sinre moeder dat moesken caken [*Refr.*].
Amen.

1. Herr Jesus, dein strahlender Kopf, siehe die Freuden der Welt, blüht wie eine Weinranke. Unbefleckte, o Jungfrau Maria, o du voll der Gnaden. **2.** Der Rock des Herrn Jesus war grün [*Refr.*] und sein ganzer Körper wie eine Blume [*Refr.*]. **3.** Jesus geht abends immer aus [*Refr.*], jedes Mal zu einer der Jungfrauen [*Refr.*]. **4.** Sie lieben mich, sie lieben mich sehr [*Refr.*], deswegen bin ich gerne bei den Jungfrauen [*Refr.*]. **5.** Maria, behüte deinen Sohn [*Refr.*], auf dass die Jungfrauen ihn dir nicht nehmen [*Refr.*]. **6.** Ich kann ihn nicht davor behüten [*Refr.*], er liebt die reinen Herzen [*Refr.*]. **7.** Ich habe auch so teuer dafür bezahlt [*Refr.*], deswegen kann ich nicht davon lassen [*Refr.*]. **8.** Er nahm einen Korb in seine Hand [*Refr.*], er sammelte Kleinholz, wo immer er es fand [*Refr.*]. **9.** Er nahm den Krug, er holte Wasser [*Refr.*], er half seiner Mutter den Brei zu kochen [*Refr.*]. Amen.)

Dieses Lied entfernt sich weit vom traditionellen Weihnachtslied. Das einzige, was beide noch verbindet, ist der Kehrreim. Nicht Jesu Geburt, sondern seine Jugend wird beschrieben. Seine 'Liebesabenteuer' sind derart plastisch dargestellt, dass frühere Herausgeber diese nicht anders als Profanisierung einer geistlichen Liebe betrachten konnten. Es ist jedoch eher denkbar, dass in diesem gesprächartigen Liedtext der Erlösungsgedanke in das Weihnachtslied eingegangen ist. Jesus selbst erläutert, warum Maria ihn nicht am Besuch der reinen Jungfrauen hindern kann, denn für deren Herzensreinheit habe er teuer bezahlt. Somit ist weniger von einer profanisierten als von einer frauenmystischen Liebe die Rede.[11] Offenbar waren innerhalb des Musters eines gespaltenen Kehrreims wie 'Ecce mundi gaudia [...], O virgo Maria, etc.' diverse Variationen der ergänzenden Sätze und der Motive um Jesu Geburt, Jugend und Liebe möglich — wie ein Vers- oder Strophenmosaik.

Nicht nur die jeweiligen beiden volkssprachigen Verse kannten Varianten, auch der Kehrreim selbst war offensichtlich variabel. Das lateinische Weihnachtslied, dem der Kehrreim dieser Lieder entlehnt ist, lautet:

> Ecce mundi gaudium
> Ecce salus gentium
> Virgo parit filium
> Sine violentia
> Ave virgo regia
> Dei plena gratia[12]

>> (Siehe die Freude der Welt, siehe das Heil der Völker: Die Jungfrau gebiert einen Sohn ohne Schmerzen. Ave Jungfrau, Königin, voll der Gnaden Gottes.)

Die Formulierung 'sine violentia' bezieht sich auf das Dogma, dass Maria sündenlos empfangen und geboren wurde, sündenlos empfangen hat und ohne Schmerzen ihr Kind geboren hat — damit ist alles Körperliche von ihrer Mutterschaft ferngehalten.[13] Diese für Nonnen so wichtigen Begriffe der 'unberührten' Empfängnis und der schmerzlosen Geburt des Kindes Jesus präsentieren sich in den hier besprochenen Liedern äußerst unterschiedlich. Wienhausen hat 'sine fine leticia', Berlin mgo 190 'in te sunt solempnia', Catharina van Rade 'domine fulgencia', Anna von Köln hat einmal 'o benivolencia', und einmal das merkwürdige 'sio fiolenlcia' und in Berlin mgo 185 steht 'cia fya lencia'. Diese letzten beiden Formulierungen sind zweifellos Verschreibungen für 'sine violentia'.

Es braucht wenig Kunstfertigkeit, ein Lied mit gespaltenem Kehrreim zu dichten: Notwendig sind lediglich zwei Verse zu einem Thema aus der Weihnachtsgeschichte, die sich reimen. Eine Reihe von Motiven, die ebenfalls in anderen Themenkreisen zu dem Zusammenstellen von Liedern

---

11 Knuttel, *Geestelijk lied*, S. 217–18. Mehr Verständnis hat De Morrée, *Voor de tijd*, S. 79, die das Lied deutet als eine Feier der Liebe zwischen Christus und der Schwester der Devotio moderna, die mit Christus 'verheiratet' ist.

12 *Analecta hymnica*, hg. Blume u. a., Bd. xx, S. 95, Nr. 8076.

13 Über die Unbefleckte Empfängnis Mariens und Jungfrauengeburt im späteren Mittelalter siehe Söll, *Mariologie*, S. 164–93. Beide Dogmen gewährleisteten, dass Maria vom ersten Augenblick an vom Fehl der Erbsünde bewahrt blieb und auch bei Mariä Verkündigung durch den Engel oder bei der Geburt nicht gesündigt habe oder geschädigt wurde.

geführt hat, bezeugt folgendes kleine Lied aus der Handschrift Annas von Köln:[14]

1. Edel mynsch, vernemet snel,
Ecce mundi gaudium,
wie der engel Gabriel,
Virgo Maria, du bis plena gratia.

2. Van Gode her neder wair gesant [*Refr.*]
tzo Nazaret in Galaleen lant [*Refr.*].

3. Tzo eynre maget dair he sy vant [*Refr.*],
Maria was sy genant [*Refr.*] (fol. 172ᵛ).

> (**1.** Edler Mensch, vernehme rasch, siehe die Freuden der Welt, wie der Engel Gabriel, Jungfrau Maria, du bist voll der Gnaden, **2.** Von Gott hinabgesandt wurde [*Refr.*] nach Nazareth in Galilea [*Refr.*], **3.** zu einer Jungfrau, wo er sie fand [*Refr.*], Maria war sie genannt [*Refr.*].)

Hier wird statt der Weihnachtsgeschichte das Verkündigungsmotiv vom 'Ecce mundi'-Kehrreim durchkreuzt. Stereotype Verse und Motive standen offensichtlich zur Verfügung, und der Kehrreim hält das Ganze zusammen. Die Variationsbreite der neugedichteten Lieder ist dabei so groß, dass man nicht mehr sagen kann, was jeweils die Vorlage war und wer was entlehnt hat.

Im Vergleich zu den oben vorgestellten Liedern ist das Wienhäuser Lied inhaltlich konsistent und ohne allzu viele individuelle Details versehen, es weist ein gewisses Bildungsniveau auf. Die Formulierung 'sine violentia' ist durch die farblose, aber korrekte lateinische Phrase 'sine fine leticia' ('Freuden ohne Ende') ersetzt. Der Reim 'vullenbracht–krafft' in der ersten Strophe ist auf Deutsch nicht rein. Im Niederländischen würde er lauten 'vullenbracht–kracht', was einen reinen Reim ergibt. Vielleicht schimmert hier eine niederländische Quelle durch. Die Reime auf 'wyndeldock' in den Strophen 3 und 4 funktionieren gar nicht; man könnte die Verse nur mit Hilfe einer Wortumstellung reimend gestalten ('Kindel–Windel'). Diese Reimproblematik legt den Schluss nahe, dass das Wienhäuser Lied, genau wie fast alle 'Ecce mundi gaudia'-Lieder, vermutlich auf einer mündlichen und (teilweise?) niederländischen Vorlage beruht.

Alle Äquivalente des Wienhäuser Liedes sind in Liederbüchern aus Frauenkonventen aufzufinden oder stammen von mit der Devotio

---

14 Anna von Köln, *Liederhandschrift*, hg. von Salmen, S. 57.

moderna verbundenen Frauen. Einer der wichtigsten Vertreter dieser Bewegung in Nordwestdeutschland war der in Zwolle geborene Windesheimer Chorherr Johannes Busch.[15] Ab 1465 hat er die norddeutschen Heideklöster und auch Wienhausen reformiert. Dabei fand 1469 in Wienhausen die gewalttätige Vertreibung der Äbtissin Katharina von Hoya statt — sie kehrte ein Jahr später als Nonne zurück.[16] Zwischen den Häusern der Devotio moderna und Frauen aus dem Wienhäuser Umfeld hat es offensichtlich einen gemeinsamen Liederschatz gegeben und die geteilte Tradition, nach dem Muster lateinischer Kehrreime selber Lieder zusammenzustellen.

Ein Motiv aus dem Wienhäuser Lied bestätigt die Verbindung zum Liederschatz der Devotio moderna und zum Rheingebiet: das Motiv der Hosen Josefs,[17] die als Windel des frischgeborenen Kindes dienen. Es erscheint auch in einem der Lieder Annas von Köln, im *Hessischen Weihnachtsspiel* und im Lied in Berlin mgo 185.[18]

Josefs Hosen bzw. die Windeln Jesu und das Kleid Mariens sind berühmte Reliquien im Aachener Domschatz, die seit der ersten Hälfte des vierzehnten Jahrhunderts und bis heute während der Aachener Heiltumsfahrt öffentlich präsentiert werden. In zahlreichen Liedern, Bildern und Pilgerberichten wird bezeugt, dass es bei der Geburt Christi nichts gab; Josef habe sofort die Hosen von seinen Beinen genommen und daraus Windeln geschnitten. Es gibt auch die Variante, dass das Kind in das Kleid Mariens gewickelt worden sei, das diese bei der Verkündigung durch den Engel getragen habe.[19] Beide Notlösungen illustrieren die dürftigen Umstände bei der Geburt Christi: kein Haus, kein Bett und extreme Kälte.

Eine winzige Scherbe (**Fig. 3.1**), die in Wienhausen aufgefunden worden ist, zeigt eine thronende Maria mit Krone und Hemd. Wahrscheinlich standen auf der gegenüberliegenden Hälfte, wie es üblich war, Josefs Hosen.[20] Die Scherbe ist wahrscheinlich der Überrest eines Andachtsbilds, das mit der Aachener Heiltumsfahrt zusammenhängt. Es bestätigt die Verbindungen zwischen Wienhausen und dem nordwestlichen Rheingebiet.

---

15 Windesheim, in der Nähe von Zwolle war das 'Urväterhaus' der Devotio moderna.

16 Riggert-Mindermann, *Klosterreform*, S. 120, 123.

17 Mit den Hosen Josefs ist wohl die Beinbekleidung gemeint; vgl. dazu De Coo, 'Addenda', S. 249. Über die Verbreitung des Motivs siehe De Coo 'In Josephs Hosen', passim und De Coo, 'Addenda', passim.

18 *Liederhandschrift*, hg. von van der Poel u. a., S. 216–20, hier S. 217, Incipit 'Uan vrouden ons die kynder syngen'; [...] 'Josep die toech alte hant | Die hasen vanden benen syn | diemen ons noch taken latet sien | ende daertoe dat wal hilige cleet daer god syne menscheit in ontfenck'.

19 Siehe De Coo, 'In Josephs Hosen', vor allem Abbildungen 14 und 18–22, S. 158 und S. 161–63; auch De Coo 'Addenda'; Williams, *Josephs Hosen*, S. 37–54).

20 Appuhn, 'Der Fund', S. 203; auch in De Coo, 'Addenda', S. 251, wo argumentiert wird, dass wahrscheinlich daneben Josefs Hosen sichtbar waren.

Figure 3.1. Fragment eines Andachtsbilds aus Kloster Wienhausen. Photo: Kloster Wienhausen.

Wiegen und Tanzen

Nur in der Wienhäuser Fassung hat das Lied 'Ecce mundi gaudia' zwei Verse im Kehrreim, die in anderen Fassungen des Liedes nicht vorkommen und die alle Strophen beschließen: 'pie pie so se nunne so | mater Jhesu, make uns vro' ('liebes, liebes Kindlein süß, Mutter Jesu, mach uns froh'). Kehrreime mit 'sus, sus, susa ninna' und ähnlichen Besänftigungsformeln gelten als Indizien für ein Wiegenlied.[21] Ob allerdings ein Kehrreim mit 'sus, sus', etc. ausreicht, um ein Lied als 'Wiegenlied' zu kennzeichnen, ist die eine Frage, ob man sich dazu tatsächlich wiegend bewegte, ist eine zweite. Beide Fragen werden im Folgenden nach einleitenden Überlegungen zur grundsätzlichen Möglichkeit, in Kirchen und Klöstern zur Weihnachtszeit zu tanzen, näher beleuchtet. Notgedrungen werden Belegstellen aus einem weiteren Bereich als nur dem oben erwähnten Dreieck Zwolle–Köln–Wienhausen angeführt, gibt es doch in diesem Dreieck kaum Hinweise auf einen Brauch des Wiegens oder Tanzens am Weihnachtsfeiertag.

Dass ein Wiegen oder Tanzen zum Wienhäuser Lied passen würde, geht an erster Stelle aus seiner Form hervor: Das Lied ist in allen oben genannten Handschriften ein Rondeau, ein einstimmiges lateinisches Lied mit Kehrreim, wobei die zweizeilige Strophe durch den ersten Vers des Kehrreims unterbrochen wird. Die einfache Struktur von Rondeaus und Rondelli ist: AB aA ab AB (Großbuchstabe = Kehrreim); kennzeichnend ist der halbierte Kehrreim (A) mitten in der Strophe.[22] Religiöse lateinische Rondeaus waren meistens Kontrafakte von weltlichen Rondeaus, wobei sowohl die weltlichen als auch die religiösen Varianten als Tanzlieder dienten. So sind in einer Handschrift des dreizehnten Jahrhunderts mit französischem Organum zwei Abbildungen von Klerikern erhalten, die sich wie bei einem Reigen an der Hand halten.[23] Die eine (**Fig. 3.2**) befindet auf einem Blatt neben der Aufschrift 'Musica Mundana' ('Musik von Körper und Seele'), die zweite, in den Gebärden sehr ähnliche, befindet sich am Anfang einer Reihe von Rondeaus.[24] Rondeaus sind durch eine klare melodische und metrische Struktur gekennzeichnet, die zum Tanzen einlädt, und sie enthalten einen ansprechenden, leicht singbaren

---

21 Van Duyse, *Het oude Nederlandsche Lied*, Bd. 3, S. 1886 erwähnt als weitere Besänftigungsworte in niederländischen und deutschen Weihnachtsliedern 'susa ninna susa noe' oder 'sujo, sujo', oder auch 'suze nanje'. Er gibt die folgende Erklärung: susa ist Besänftigungswort, ninne heißt 'Liebchen'; Mak, *Middeleeuwse kerstliederen*, S. 74, Anm., erwähnt 'verla zu-zu-zu', 'verla-zu-ze nynno', oder 'valasus' und Varianten. Kohler, *Martin Luther*, S. 77, Anm. 34 nennt *susaninne* als Ausdruck für ein Wiegenlied eine Tautologie, zusammengesetzt aus *susen* (sausen): 'mit summendem Laut ein Kind einwiegen', und *ninne* aus der Kindersprache für 'Kindchen'; so auch Mak, *Middeleeuwse kerstliederen*, S. 79, Anm. 2.

22 Wilkins, *Rondeau*. Über ihre Funktion als Tanzlieder siehe Stevens, *Words*, S. 178–96.

23 Florenz, Biblioteca Medicea-Laurenziana, Plut. 29. 1, fol. 428^r, Knäble, *Tanzende Kirche*, Abb. 9, eine der wichtigen Quellen für Polyphonie in Notre Dame. Vgl. Stevens, *Words*, S. 515. Über die Form des Tanzes als Kreis oder Reigen siehe Knäble, *Tanzende Kirche*, S. 310.

24 Zur mittelalterlichen Dreiteilung von Musik in *Musica mundana, musica humana* und *musica instrumentalis* vgl. Haar, *Music*. Die *musica humana* steht zwischen der *Musica mundana* (u. a. Sphärenmusik) und der hörbaren *musica instrumentalis* (Vokal- und Instrumentalmusik).

Figure 3.2. Florenz, Biblioteca Medicea-Laurenziana. Ms Plut. 29.1, fol. 428ʳ. Photo: Biblioteca Medicea-Laurenziana.

Kehrreim. Dem entspricht die einzige überlieferte Melodie eines 'Ecce Mundi'-Liedes.[25]

Es gibt außer der Rondeau-Form noch einige weitere Aspekte, die 'Ecce mundi gaudia' mit Tanzliedern verbinden. Erstens ist es schlichtweg die Jahreszeit, für die dieses Lied vorgesehen ist: Die Tage um Weihnachten waren auch in Kirchen und Klöstern eine Zeit der Ausgelassenheit und der tanzartigen Spiele. In seiner *Summa de ecclesiasticis officiis* (1162) erwähnt der französischer Theologe Jean Belethus vier Tänze, die zwischen Weihnachten und dem Dreikönigsfest von vier unterschiedlichen Gruppen von Klerikern aufgeführt wurden.[26] Die französischen Kathedralen und Kirchen des zwölften oder dreizehnten Jahrhunderts, auf die er sich bezieht, sind zwar keine Frauenklöster in der Lüneburger

---

25 Stevens, *Words*, S. 188–89; nur eines der oben erwähnten Lieder wurde mit Musik überliefert (Berlin SBB-PK, mgo 190, fol. 38ᵛ; *Liederenhandschrift*, hg. von Mertens, S. 306–07; Transkription in Van Duyse *Het oude Nederlandsche Lied*, Bd. III, S. 1858); Form und Akzente sind gleich wie die des Wienhäuser Liedes (abgesehen von der Erweiterung des Kehrreims in Wienhausen).

26 'Fiunt autem quatuor tripudia post natiuitatem Domini in ecclesia, leuitarum, sacerdotum, puererum, id est minorum etate et ordine, et subdiaconorum, qui ordo incertus est.' Johannes Beleth, *Summa*, hg. von Douteil, S. 134.

Heide, andere Nachrichten erlauben jedoch eine Verallgemeinerung seines Berichts und eine Annäherung an den Wienhäuser Konvent.

Zu hohen Feiertagen wurden an verschiedenen Bischofshöfen und in Klöstern Tanzveranstaltungen abgehalten.[27] In Breslau bezahlte ein Abt im Jahr 1468 einen Musiker für das Spielen von Tänzen, bei welcher Gelegenheit auch Frauen in das Kloster eingeladen waren.[28] Es muss bei solchen Veranstaltungen dermaßen lustig zugegangen sein, dass das Magdeburger Konzil von 1403 ausdrücklich verbot, Spiele zum Gedenken eines Heiligen oder unter dem Vorwand des Brauchtums in eigener oder fremder Tracht zu veranstalten. Das Verbot galt für alle Nonnen der Provinz in ihren Klöstern oder Kirchen, ganz gleich welchen Ordens. Auch war es künftig nicht gestattet, dass durch Auswärtige irgendwelche Spiele oder Theateraufführungen an irgendeinem Ort stattfanden, ob mit oder ohne Masken.[29] Derartige Vorschriften vermochten jedoch in den zwei nachfolgenden Jahrhunderten nicht den Brauch, in Klöstern Maskenspiele zu veranstalten, zu stoppen. Zu diesen Spielen wurde offenbar auch getanzt: Der schlesische Ritter Hans von Scheinichen berichtet 1576, an einem Mummenschanz der adligen Nonnen des St. Marienklosters in Köln teilgenommen zu haben: 'Wir waren also lustig mit den Nonnen, tanzten und tranken sehr viel'.[30]

Das Leben in Wienhausen vor der großen Reform im Jahr 1469 wurde als 'relativ frei' und 'sinnenfroh' gekennzeichnet.[31] Ausgelassenes Tanzen und reichliches Trinken sind zwar nicht belegt, aber ein Wiegen oder Tanzen ist durchaus denkbar, vor allem in einem schlichteren Sich-Wiegend-Bewegen.[32] Nach der Reform wird sich Wienhausen notgedrungen den strengeren Normen der Devotio moderna angeglichen haben und dürfte wohl in der Folge weniger tanzfreudig gewesen sein.

Anders als in den sonstigen Handschriften enthält die Wienhäuser Fassung von 'Ecce mundi gaudia' im Kehrreim Besänftigungsworte wie 'pie pie so se nunne so'. Diese Ergänzung unterstreicht die Vermutung, dass

---

27 Siehe Salmen, *Tanz*, S. 23–32 und Knäble, *Tanzende Kirche*, S. 158–61.

28 Salmen 'Tanzen', S. 70–71.

29 'Prohibemus etiam, ne de cetero moniales nostre provincie in monasteriis vel ecclesiis suis sub quocumque colore in memoriam alicuius sancti vel presumptu consuetudinis, in suo proprio habitu vel alieno, ludos facere presumant, sine larvis, cum larvis, nec etiam per extraneos ludos aliquos seu spectacula quecumque fieri permittant.' Salmen, 'Tanzen', S. 72.

30 Salmen, 'Tanzen' gibt aus dem fünfzehnten und sechzehnten Jahrhundert mehrere Beispiele von Spielen in Klöstern, sogar von gemischten Tänzen, an denen angeblich Kleriker und Laien, Männer und Frauen teilgenommen haben.

31 Koldau, *Frauen*, S. 72; zu den Folgen der Reform vgl. Riggert-Mindermann, 'Klosterreform', S. 123–26.

32 Die neueste Datierung des Liederbuchs als zum größten Teil um oder nach 1500 (Roolfs, 'Wienhäuser Liederbuch', S. 264) würde das ganze Liederbuch nach dieser Reform platzieren, aber es ist sehr wohl möglich, dass vorreformierte Lieder dann doch noch eingeschrieben wurden.

es sich hier um ein Lied handeln dürfte, das weihnachtliche Wiegenfeiern begleitete und zu dem man sich möglicherweise wiegend bewegte oder tanzte.

Aus vor allem deutschen, österreichischen und niederländischen Zeugnissen ist bekannt, wie weihnachtliche Wiegenfeiern vorsichgingen und teilweise auch, welche Lieder dazu gesungen wurden. Es gehörte wohl schon Mitte des zwölften Jahrhunderts zu den Gepflogenheiten, eine Kindelwiegenfeier zu veranstalten, in der in einer (Schaukel-)wiege eine das Jesuskind darstellende Holzpuppe lag, anstatt in der biblisch bezeugten Krippe. Das wird aus der Ablehnung des Brauchs durch Gerhoh von Reichersberch klar, der in *De investigatione Antichristi* (1160–1163) schreibt, dass man bildlich die Wiege des kindlichen Erlösers vorführe, das Wimmern des Kleinen, die mütterliche Gestalt der Wöchnerin [...]. Er spricht hierbei offensichtlich von einer Wiegenfeier in einer Kloster- oder Stiftskirche aus der Salzburger Gegend.[33] Von den für derartige Feiern hergestellten Wiegen, zur individuellen oder gemeinsamen Benutzung, sind etliche erhalten. Sie bezeugen einen weit verbreiteten Wiegenbrauch, vor allem in Deutschland, Österreich und den südlichen Niederlanden.[34] Obwohl es für den nordniederländischen Bereich eine Überlieferungslücke gibt, stammt eines der wenigen Zeugnisse dafür, wie eine Schaukelwiege benutzt wurde, aus dem Klarissenkloster in Amsterdam. Das Kloster bekam vom Beichtvater Bartholomeus eine Wiege geschenkt, nachdem er gesehen hatte, wie Kinder in der Weihnachtszeit beim Liedersingen das Kindlein Jesus wiegten. Bartholomeus' Absicht war es, dass die Nonnen damit wie kleine demütige Kinder Jesus wiegen und in ihren Herzen bewahren sollten,[35] ein Brauch, der von Weihnachten bis Maria Lichtmess (2. Februar) währte. Bartholomeus deutet dabei das Wiegen zu einer geistlichen Übung um: Die Wiege steht bei ihm für das demütige Herz, sie ist ausstaffiert mit dem Kissen der Liebe, den Perlen der Tugenden usw. An beiden Seiten der von ihm beschriebenen Wiege gab es drei Seile, mit deren Hilfe sie geschaukelt werden konnte, und während des Schaukelns,

---

33 Gerhoh, *De inuestigatione*, hg. von Stülz, S. 130–31: 'Exhibent preterea imaginaliter et saluatoris infantie cunabula, paruuli uagitum, puerpere uirginis matronalem habitum [...]'.

34 Keller, *Wiege*, S. 195–204. Von den zweiunddreißig erhaltenen Schaukelwiegen bis 1600 sind elf südniederländischer Herkunft, zwei südniederländischer oder deutscher, eine niederrheinischer oder niederländischer, sechs deutscher Herkunft und nur eine vielleicht aus den nördlichen Niederlanden (Listen in Keller, *Wiege*, S. 205–09). Toepfer, 'Kindel', S. 131 erwähnt fünfzehn Wiegen, die bei einem Brand im Brigittenkloster Marienwohlde gerettet wurden, 'die von einer individuellen Verehrung des Jesuskindes zeugen.'

35 'op-dat wy al-te-samen als cleyne oetmoedighe kinderen Jesum alsoe moechten wieghen ende bewaeren in onser herten [...]. [...] ghemeynlyck [...] van kersmis tot lichtmisse'. Ampe, 'Uit de kerstvroomheid', S. 171 und 180). Es betrifft hier Aufzeichnungen von Schwester Weyncken von 1565.

das für das demütige Gebet stehe, begannen kleine Glocken zu klingeln, so dass Gottes Aufmerksamkeit darauf gelenkt werde.[36]

Die Handlung des Wiegens konnte mittels einer spirituellen Deutung legitimiert werden. So ging sie auch in Visionen ein, z. B. in eine Vision der Mystikerin Margarethe Ebner, die das ihr geschenkte Jesuskind aus seiner Wiege auf ihren Schoß nimmt und es küsst — ob leibhaftig oder nur im geistigen Sinne, bleibt in der Schwebe.[37] Im Kloster Ebstorf, unweit von Wienhausen, waren das Kind und die Krippe wichtige Objekte der Andacht.[38] Obwohl sich aus Wienhausen selbst keine Wiege oder Krippe erhalten hat, ist es sehr wohl möglich, dass auch hier eine Jesus-Figur umsorgt oder gewiegt wurde, wie das sonst offenbar in Frauenklöstern geschah.[39]

Der klösterliche oder auch häusliche Kindelwiegenbrauch ist ein Kern der Spiele, die sich von dem frühen fünfzehnten Jahrhundert an entwickelten; neben einer Wiege mit einem Christkind wurden auch Maria, Josef und andere Figuren dargestellt und es entfaltete sich eine kleine dramatische Handlung.[40] Wie ein derartiges Spiel vor sich ging, lässt sich aus einer Tegernseer Handschrift aus der Mitte des fünfzehnten Jarhnunderts ableiten: Zu Weihnachten erklinge der fröhliche Hymnus 'a solus ortus cardine', heißt es dort, und während man beim 'resonet in laudibus' das Kindlein wiege, fange Unsere Frau [Maria], dargestellt von einer Person, an zu singen: 'Joseph lieber *neve* [Verwandter/Vertrauter] mein'. Dann antworte ihr die andere Person, Josef: 'Gerne, meine liebe *muome* [Verwandte/Vertraute]', woraufhin der Chor den anderen Vers in einer dieser Weisen singe. Danach setze der Chor ein.[41] Hier ist beim Kindelwiegen ein dialogischer Wechselgesang zwischen den dramatisierten Personen Josef, Maria und dem Chor bezeugt. Sie singen drei Gesänge: den Hymnus 'a solus ortus cardine', das 'resonet in laudibus' und das 'Wiegenlied par

---

36 Vgl. Janota, *Studien*, S. 143–47; Keller, *Wiege*, S. 121–25.

37 Ebner, *Werke*, hg. von Strauch, S. 90.22–91.12. Die Vision von Margaretha Ebner datiert vom 26. Dezember 1344.

38 Schlotheuber, *Klostereintritt*, S. 292–94.

39 Für weitere Beispiele siehe Keller, *Wiege*, S. 133–34; Toepfer, 'Kindel', S. 131–36. Janota, *Studien*, S. 143–48 nimmt an, dass der Kindelwiegenbrauch seinen Ursprung in Frauenklöstern fand. Aus Wienhausen fehlen 'beweiskräftige Requisiten' für einen Wiegenbrauch. Sievers, *'Die Melodien'*, S. 43–44.

40 Zur Gattungsbezeichnung vgl. Berthold, *Kindelwiegenspiele*, S. 208–09.

41 'Zw den weynachten der fröleich ympnus A solis ortu cardine vnd so man daz kindel wiegt über das Resonet in laudibus hebt vnnser vraw an ze singen in ainer person Yoseph lieber neve mein. So antwort in der andern person Yoseph geren liebe mueme mein Darnach singet der kor dy andern vers in ainer dyenner weis Darnach der Chor'. München, BSB, cgm 715, fol. 4ʳ, hier zitiert nach: Janota, *Studien*, S. 127. Zu den Bezeichnungen 'Neffe' und 'Tante' in Analogie zur Andeutung eines Verwandtschaftsverhältnisses siehe Toepfer, *'Vom marginalisierten Heiligen'*, S. 48.

excellence', 'Joseph lieber neve myn'.[42] Zwei Handschriften aus Prag und Krakau, beide um 1400, geben unter dem Titel 'Ordo personarum ad cunabulum' eine ausführliche Beschreibung einer Wiegenfeier.[43] In einem Leipziger Kantionale von *ca.* 1420 findet man den ganzen Gesang beim Kindelwiegen, mit Hinweisen zum Vorgang.

> *Maria singt*
> Joseph liber neve myn
> hilf mir wygen myn kindelin
> daz got musse deyn loner syn
> yn hymmilreich (fol. 115^{r-v})[44]
>
> > (Joseph, mein lieber Vertrauter, hilf mir mein Kindlein zu wiegen, so dass Gott es dir im Himmelreich lohnen möge.)

Diese Szene ist in einigen Kindelwiegenspielen des fünfzehnten und sechzehnten Jahrhunderts breit ausgemalt. Das farbigste und detaillierteste Bild bietet das *Hessische Weihnachtsspiel* (1450–1460).[45] Josef antwortet hier auf Marias Bitte:

> Ia, Maria, das wel ich thun gerne
> got unßerm herre
> und wel meilichen singen
> und gar frolich umb die wiegen springen! […]
> Sellenfro, knecht myn,
> singe mit mir und loss uns frolich syn! (V. 167–72; fol. 4^{r})
>
> > (Ja, Maria, dass tue ich gerne für Gott unseren Herrn, und ich will gerne voller Freude und ganz fröhlich um die Wiege springen […]. Sellenfro, mein Knecht, singe mit mir und lass uns fröhlich sein!)

Die entsprechende Spielanweisung lautet: 'Und hier tanzen Josef und der Knecht um die Wiege, und sie singen: "In dulce iubilo".[46] Die Engel singen daraufhin: 'sunt impleta' (einen Teil des 'resonet in laudibus'). In

---

42 Zur Kennzeichnung von 'Joseph lieber neve mein' als Christkindwiegenlied par excellence vgl. Keller, *Wiege*, S. 129. Die Literatur über 'resonet in laudibus' und 'Josef lieber neve' ist sehr umfangreich. Für eine erste Orientierung hilft Wachinger, 'Resonet'.

43 Prag, UB, Ms. IV.G.8; Krakau, UB, Ms. 2251. Angaben nach Ameln, 'Resonet', S. 69–72). Das Grundgerüst bildet hier das *Canticum Simeonis*, d. h. der Lobgesang Simeons auf den Messias.

44 Leipzig, UB, Ms. 1305, hier zitiert nach Ameln, 'Resonet', S. 68. Es handelt sich um eine Kantionale, die vor und nach 'Josef lieber neve' zwei sehr beliebte Weihnachtsgesänge aufzeigt: 'dies est leticie' und 'in dulci iubilo'. Janota, *Studien*, S. 135–36.

45 'Hessisches Weihnachtsspiel', hg. von Froning, S. 902–37. Versangaben im Folgenden nach dieser Ausgabe.

46 'Et sic servus et Ioseph corisant per cunabulum cantando: "In dulce iubilo".'

einer späteren Szene umtanzen auch noch Mägde und Wirte die Wiege. Wie man diese Tänze beurteilen soll, lässt sich allerdings fragen. Die Mägde und Wirte im Spiel sind freche, zänkische Leute und Josef ist eine ambivalente Figur, die zwar rührend, zugleich aber auch tollpatschig Mutter und Kind umsorgt und sich das Bier gerne schmecken lässt. Am Ende des Spiels, als Luzifer mit seinen Teufeln überlegt, wie sie nach Jesu Geburt überhaupt noch Seelen für die Hölle gewinnen können, meint der Teufel Beelzebub, dass es ausreiche, Mägde zum Tanzen zu verführen, das werde alle Beteiligten auf den Pfad der Sünde führen (V. 760–75). Luzifer beschließt das Ganze mit den Worten: 'Wenn wir uns nächstes Jahr gesund wieder treffen, werden wir (nur er und die seinen oder auch das ganze Publikum?) fröhlich singen und tanzen'. Der Verfasser des Spiels bewertet offensichtlich den Tanz nicht (oder nicht nur) positiv. Vielleicht hat er sogar Josefs Tanz nur hinzugefügt, um ihn noch lächerlicher vorzuführen, als er schon ist.[47]

Ausgesprochen hausbacken wirkt Josef, wenn er in einer vorangehenden Szene das Kind mit improvisierten Windeln versieht, um es nachher zu wiegen:

> Eya, libe Maria,
> vol gnaden bistu unnd gude pia
> hie sint zwo alt hoszen,
> der kund ich nij geloszen!
> dy sint nicht gar glantz
> unnd sint by den lucheren gantz:
> andersz habe ich nicht mer!
> reich mir das kint her:
> ich wel es legin in die wiege und wel im singen:
> susze, liebe ninne! (V. 598–607)

> > (Eia, liebe Maria, voller Gnaden bist du und eine gute Sühnerin. Hier sind zwei alte Hosen, von ihnen konnte ich mich nie trennen. Sie sind nicht mehr ohne Makel und sind nur neben den Löchern ganz. Anderes habe ich nicht mehr! Reich mir das Kind, ich will es in die Wiege legen und will für es singen: 'Schlaf, Kindchen, schlaf'.)

Josef benutzt hier die Worte 'susze, liebe ninne', die traditionsgemäß als *pars pro toto* eines Wiegenlieds gesehen werden können.

Ob das *Hessische Weihnachtsspiel* auf einen aus der Realität bekannten Weihnachtstanz um die Wiege zurückgreift, lässt sich nicht festlegen.

---

47 Siehe Toepfer, '*Vom Marginalisierten Heiligen*', S. 46 über die unterschiedliche Bewertung der Lächerlichkeit Josefs. Dass auch Luzifer um die Wiege tanzt (Toepfer, 'Kindel', S. 130), lässt sich aus dem Text nicht herleiten.

Derartige Tänze hat es jedoch gegeben. Salmen erwähnt eine tänzerische Ausführung zu Weihnachten beim Kindelwiegen im Frauenkloster Preetz (Schleswig-Holstein).[48] In einer Chronik bezeugt ist der Weihnachtstanz in der fränkischen Stadt Hof. Dort tanzten zu Weihnachten beim Vespergottesdienst in der Kirche, 'wo man nach alter Gewohnheit das Kindchen Jesus wiegte', offenbar möglichst alle Kirchgänger. Der Organist spielte 'resonet in laudibus', 'in dulci jubilo' und 'Joseph lieber Joseph mein', der Chor sang die Antwort. Diese Gesänge luden wegen ihrer Proportion (Wohlklang und Takt) 'etliche Massen' zum Tanz ein, die Knaben forderten die kleinen Mädchen auf und tanzten um den Hochaltar, das machten auch die Alten, die den Jüngeren vortanzten und so der frohen, freudenreichen Geburt Jesu Christi auf allzu ausgelassene Weise gedachten.[49] Dieses Beispiel bestätigt, dass sich auch Laien, Alt und Jung, am Kindelwiegen in der Kirche beteiligten, und dass dies sogar in einen Tanz um den Altar münden konnte.[50]

Aus Münster wird berichtet, dass die Knaben bei der Weihnachtsfeier um eine Krippe alle 'auff vnd nidder springen vnd mit den henden zusamen schlagen', während das 'resonet in laudibus' gesungen wurde.[51] Das *Brixener Dommesnerbuch* erwähnt um 1560, dass Domschüler und ihre Lehrer an einem derartigen Brauch teilhatten. Nach der Komplet, anschließend an das 'nunc dimittis', stellte der Mesner die Wiege auf den Altar. Zwei Schüler wiegten das Kind, während die anderen sangen. Beim 'puer natus est' wurde das Kind zum Kuss herumgereicht. Die Zeremonie wurde jeden Sonntag vom Neujahrstag bis Lichtmess wiederholt.[52] Die Empfehlung an den Mesner, er möge 'eyn gaysl' (eine Peitsche) mitnehmen, 'dan die puebm seint vast vnzogen' ('weil die Buben sehr ungezogen sind'),

---

48 Leider gibt es weder in Salmen, *Tanz*, S. 29 noch in Salmen, 'Tanzen', S. 70 einen Nachweis für diese Mitteilung.

49 'Am Heiligen Christag zur vesper, da man nach alter gewonheit das kindtlein Jesus wiegete, wie mans nennet, und der organist das "Resonet in laudibus in dulci jubilo", item "Joseph, lieber Joseph mein", schluge, auch der chor darauff sunge und sich solche gesenge wegen ihrer proportion [sic!] etlichermassen zum tantz schicketen, da pflegeten die knaben kleine mägdlein in der kirchen auffzuzihen und umb den Hohen Altar zu tantzen, welches auch wol alte betagte lappen theten, den jungen vortanzeten, sich der frolichen freudenreichen geburt Jesu Christi nach euserlicher groberweis dadurch zu erinnern'. Widman, *Chronik*, hg. von Rösler, S. 321. Gemäß einer Aufzeichnung auf der nächsten Seite (S. 322, April 1528) bezieht sich dieses Zitat auf Weihnachten 1527. Ich danke Carla Dauven, Manuel Hoder und Regina Toepfer für ihre Bemühungen, dieses Zitat zu finden und zu interpretieren. Siehe auch Nürnberg, *Der Jahreswechsel*, S. 51–53.

50 Siehe Keller, *Wiege*, S. 116 für Beispiele aus Pappenheim (1511), Brixen (um 1559) und Sterzing (1548).

51 Witzel, *Psaltes*, fol. 163[r].

52 Feichter, *Brixener Dommesnerbuch*, hg. von Hofmeister-Winter, fol. 19[v], 29[r]–30[v], 32[r] und 43[r] (S. 131, 152–56 und 179). Ich danke Andrea Hofmeister herzlich für ihre Hilfe, diese Zitate zu finden.

zeigt, dass die Schüler beim Ritual wohl nicht mucksmäuschenstill sitzen-
blieben.

Weniger ausgelassen scheint das Wiegen im Familien- und Bekannten-
kreis des Kölner Kaufmanns und Ratsherrn Hermann Weinsberg vor sich
gegangen zu sein. Da wurde zwischen 1559 und 1591 beim Singen der
lateinischen Lieder 'puer nobis nascitur', 'puer natus est nobis' und 'dies est
laetitiae' das Kindlein gewiegt ('das Kintgin gew(i)eget'). Im Jahr 1584
hat ein anwesender Wachtrupp mitgesungen; es fehlt hier die Angabe zu
einem möglichen Wiegen zu diesem Lied.[53] Ob Weinsberg mit 'Wiegen'
ein gemeinsames Singen und sich Bewegen meinte oder das Schaukeln
einer Wiege, lässt sich nicht feststellen.[54]

Ende des sechzehnten Jahrhunderts wurde in der Amsterdamer Oude
Kerk eine Wiege mit der Holzfigur eines kleinen Kindes in Windeln auf
den Hochaltar gestellt. Eltern begleiteten ihre Kinder, die eine Wiege mit
Holzpuppe und Glöckchen bei sich trugen, in die Kirche. Als der Priester
während der Messe anfing, das Kind auf dem Altar zu wiegen und 'Eia,
Eia, Eia' sang, fingen auch alle Kinder an, ihre 'Kinder' zu wiegen und 'Eia'
zu singen.[55] Sie füllten mit ihrem Glockenklang den ganzen Kirchenraum
aus und die Orgel unterstützte 'auf eine ganz besondere Weise' das Ganze.
Offensichtlich ging es laut und fröhlich zu. Der Gewährsmann, der reformierte Presbyter Walich Syvaertsz, charakterisiert den Brauch als kindisch
und lächerlich. Er zeigt sich empört, dass die Katholiken ihren Kindern zu
Hause in der Weihnachtszeit dieses 'Puppenwerk' beibrachten.[56]

---

53 Weinsberg, *Liber Iuventutis*, fol. 407^v-8^r (1560), fol. 421^{r-v} (1562) und fol. 462^v (Anno
   1564); 'den 25 december uff einen montag war der hillige christag [...]. Und haben
   mit allem unsem gesinde daß hoichzit s. Jacob gehalten und zu Weinsberch daß kindtlin
   gewiget, und gesongen, puer nobis nascitur'. *Liber Senectutis*, fol. 322^r (1581 [= 1580]); 'uff
   Christabent ist min 23. fanenwacht uff die Eigelsteinsportz gefallen, und wiewol uff das
   hoichzit ein ungelegener tag ware, darzu unseletich witter, noch dannest zouch ich in
   groissen regen uff die Eigelsteinsportz, Dr. Acht heubtmann mit sinem fanen van s.
   Maximinenstrass uff s. Severinsportz. Da beslossen wir zu 12 uren das alte jar, fingen
   do an zu singen: "Puer natus est nobis" und "Dies est laetitiae" und machten uns mit dem
   neuwen geborn kintlin Jesu frolich'. *Liber Senectutis*, fol. 481^v, '1584 den 24. dez.'; auch noch
   Liber Decrepitudinis, fol. 246^v (1592 [= 1591]).
54 Keller, *Wiege*, S. 135.
55 Zu welchem Gesang dieses 'Eia Eia' gehörte, lässt sich nicht feststellen: entweder
   zur Sequenz 'eya recolamus laudibus piis', zu 'magnum nomen domini Emanuel'
   (Acquoy, 'Kerstliederen', S. 245, Anm. 2) oder zu 'resonet in laudibus'.
56 Walich Syvaertsz schreibt in der Vorrede seiner *Roomsche mysterien* (Amsterdam, 1604),
   fol. 2^v-3^r: 'Sy weten hoemen op Kersdach een wieghsken met een Beeldeken daer inne,
   nae een cleyn kindeken ligghende in de luyers gefatsoneert, opt hooch Autaer plachten
   te setten: ende dat d'Ouders hare kinderen met een wieghsken ende schelle in de kercke
   leyden: ende als de Priester onder de Misse het kindeken opt Autaer staende begoste te
   wieghen ende te singhen Eia, Eia, Eia, etc. zoo vinghen de kinderen voort mede aen elck
   zijne kindeken te wieghen ende Eia te singhen, maeckende daer benevens een groot gheluyt
   ende gheclanck met haere schellen, dat de gheheele kercke daer van vervult was: waer

Er war nicht der einzige protestantische Verfasser, der im sechzehnten Jahrhundert gegen das Kindelwiegen agierte. Sebastian Franck schreibt in seinem *Weltbuch* (1534):

> Zů Weinnacht begeen sy die kindtheit Christi also/ sy setzen ein wiegen auff den altar/ darein ein geschnitzt kind geleget/ diß wiegen die statt kind ein grosse menge/ springen vnnd tantzen umb das kind in einem ring/ darzů die alten zůsehen/ vnd mitt singen mit vil seltzamen liedlin/ von dem neüwgebornen kindlin (fol. 50ᵛ).[57]

> (Zu Weihnachten feiern sie wie folgt die Kindheit Christi: Sie setzen eine Wiege auf den Altar, in die eine geschnitzte Holzpuppe gelegt ist. Diese wiegen sie statt eines Kindes. Eine große Menge springt und tanzt im Kreis um das Kind. Die Alten schauen zu und singen viele eigenartige Lieder von dem neugeborenen Kind.)

Derartige Nachrichten vermelden auch einige andere anti-katholische Autoren.[58] Luther selbst äußert sich nicht gerade wohlwollend und schreibt: 'da man zu weynachten das kindlin gewigt und mit reymen affenspiel getrieben hat.'[59] Anderswo macht er in einer seiner Aussagen klar, wie fest zu Beginn des sechzehnten Jahrhunderts der Brauch in der Weihnachtszeit verankert war: Der Festkalender fängt an, sagt er in einer Predigt aus dem Jahr 1533, mit 'den Wygenachten, da wir das kindlin wiegen und spielen mit unserem lieben HERRN jnn der mutter schyoss'.[60] Es lässt sich schwer sagen, ob Luther gegen den Brauch an sich war, oder nur gegen dessen allzu ausgelassenen Ausprägungen.[61] Ein Jahrhundert später waren jedenfalls Syvaertsz' Amsterdamer Glaubensgenossen nicht mit dem Vorgang — oder nur mit der Musik? — bei der weihnachtlichen Wiegenfeier einverstanden. Der reformierte Kirchenvorstand der Oude Kerk agierte gegen das Orgelspiel beim Kindelwiegen, eine Gelegenheit, zu der der Organist, Dirck Sweelinck, 'viele Papisten' eingeladen hatte. In Januar 1645 wurden zwei Abgeordnete zu Dirck geschickt, um ihn zur Ordnung zu rufen.[62]

---

onder de Orghel op eene sonderlinghe wyse was spelende, die het spel hielp vercieren.' Zitiert nach: Acquoy, 'Kerstliederen', S. 245. Syvaerts stützt sich auf Erinnerungen seiner ehemaligen Glaubensgenossen; siehe Roodenburg, *Onder censuur*, S. 56; S. 60 über Walich Syvaertsz und sein vernichtendes Urteil über den Wiegenbrauch.

57 Franck, *Weltbuch*. Es ist die Rede von einer Weihnachtsfeier in Franken.

58 Zusammenfassend Keller, *Wiege*, S. 138–42.

59 Luther, 'Fastenpostille (1525)', WA 17/II, S. 208.35–209.1.

60 Luther, 'Predigt (1533)', WA 37, S. 48.41–49.1.

61 Kohler, *Martin Luther*, S. 77–80.

62 'Dewyl de Organist van de Oude Kerk zich voorgenomen heeft het kindeken te wiegen en daartoe vele papisten genoodigd' hat, wurde am 12. Januar 1645 entschieden, dass die Kirchenmeister versuchen werden derartige Abergläubigkeiten ('zulke superstitiën') abzuwehren. *Repertorium der Protocollen van de gereformeerde Kerkeraad te Amsterdam*,

Kohler vermutet, dass Weihnachtstänze (d. h. der Brauch des Kindelwiegens mit Tanz um die Wiege) im sechzehnten Jahrhundert so sehr in Verruf geraten waren, dass sie untersagt wurden und nur in Restformen oder als Kinderspiel überdauerten.[63] Die Zeugnisse aus Amsterdam und Hof zeigen jedoch, dass der Brauch Mitte des sechzehnten oder sogar siebzehnten Jahrhunderts in katholischen Kreisen nicht nur von Kindern an abseitigen Orten oder außerhalb der Kirche gepflegt wurde. Vielmehr wurde damals das Kindelwiegen anscheinend von strenggläubigen Protestanten als verwerfliche, papistische Gewohnheit betrachtet, doch es sind gerade diese protestantischen Gegner des Brauchs, denen wir viele Nachrichten über die Tradition und die Weihnachtstänze verdanken.

In mittelniederländischer Sprache gibt es von geistlichen Spielen mit Kindelwiegenszenen keine Spur. Auch die beiden im deutschsprachigen Gebiet überaus beliebten Wiegenlieder 'resonet in laudibus' oder 'Joseph lieber neve' sind in niederländische Liederbücher nur spärlich oder gar nicht eingegangen.[64] Wenn man ausschließlich Lieder, die bei Wiegenspielen oder — bräuchen vorkommen, als 'Wiegenlieder' deuten will, sind aus niederländischen Gegenden kaum Weihnachts — bzw. Wiegenlieder überliefert, außer die bei Weinsberg genannten und auch die in niederländischen Liederbüchern breit überlieferten Lieder 'dies est laetitiae' und 'puer nobis nascitur'. Eine derart strenge Eingrenzung würde allerdings vieles ausschließen, was, näher betrachtet, sehr wahrscheinlich beim Wiegenbrauch gesungen wurde.[65]

Ein niederländisches Lied, das möglicherweise ein Bindeglied zwischen Wiegenkehrreim und Kindelwiegenbrauch darstellt, befindet sich in einer privaten Devotionshandschrift von *ca.* 1470, wahrscheinlich aus der Gegend von Sint-Truiden (südliche Niederlande, heute Belgien). 'Dit is eyn devoet lietgen van den heilighen kerste' ('Dies ist ein frommes Lied vom heiligen Christ') enthält etliche Strophen, in denen jeweils ein Körperteil des Jesuskindes genannt wird, woraufhin man diesen Körperteil berührt, gefolgt von einer Bitte um Jesu Schutz. Die zwei Verse der Strophe werden immer durch den Kehrreim 'sussoe nynnoe' getrennt.[66] Der

---

UB Uva Collectie W. Moll, Afd. Hss, no. 85 (Protokoll VIII, fol. 14), zitiert nach Klönne, 'Amstelodamensia', S. 265. Dirck Sweelinck war Sohn und Nachfolger des Komponisten-Organisten Jan Pieterszoon Sweelinck.

63 Kohler, *Martin Luther*, S. 79.

64 Das Lied 'magnum nomen', das in deutschen Quellen oft vorkommt, zusammen mit oder als Refrain von 'resonet in laudibus', ist dagegen häufig in niederländischen Liederbüchern zwischen 1500 und 1550 vertreten, vgl. *Nederlandse Liederenbank* ('magnum nomen') und Wachinger, 'Resonet in laudibus', K. 1227–28).

65 Keller, *Wiege*, S. 129, hält sich an das strenge Kriterium, nur das als 'Kindelwiegenlied' zu bezeichnen, was als Lied in Wiegenfeiern oder Wiegenspielen Verwendung fand.

66 Gent, UB, Ms. 1330, fol. 46ᵛ–47ᵛ. Das Lied folgt hier auf einen 'liber generationis', der in der ersten Weihnachtsmesse gelesen wird. Datierung und Lokalisierung nach Reynaert,

erste Vers lautet: 'Sy namen dat kindekijn metten teenen' (sie fassten das Kindlein an den Zehen). Das Berühren des Christuskindes kann nur in übertragenem Sinn an einer Figur in einer (Schaukel)wiege stattgefunden haben, aber eine haptische Berührung ist sehr wohl denkbar: plastisch wird vorgeführt, wie man an den Zehen das Berühren begann und an Füßen und Fersen fortsetzte.

Auch Benennungen der Handlung des Wiegens ('Nu wieghen wy') und der wiederholte Kehrreim mit Besänftigungsworten ('sus sus'), wie sie in verschiedenen niederländischen und deutschen Weihnachtsliedern vorkommen, suggerieren ein Mitsingen und wiegendes Mitbewegen der Beteiligten bei einen Wiegenbrauch. Ein Gewährsmann dafür, 'susa ninna' als Begleitung zum Kindelwiegen zu betrachten, ist niemand geringerer als Luther, der in seiner *Christtag-Nachtmittagspredigt* aus dem Jahr 1531 das pervertierte 'susa ninna' das 'Wiegenlied des Teufels' nannte: 'sein Sause liebe Nunne'.[67] Der Kehrreim steht bei ihm offensichtlich als *pars pro toto* für den gesamten Brauch.[68]

Einige deutsche und niederländische Lieder enthalten neben einem Kehrreim mit Worten zum Wiegen Hinweise, die sie in die Nähe der Wiegenlieder rücken. Das ist z. B. der Fall in einer Übersetzung von 'en trinitatis speculum', in der jedes Mal die dritte Zeile ein 'Eya' enthält, und als Kehrreim ein wiederholtes 'zuy wel, lieve nynne'.[69] Das Lied wurde wahrscheinlich im Wechselgesang mit dem Wiegenlied 'puer nobis nascitur' gesungen.[70] Das Lied 'Een alre lieffelicken een' ('Eine allerliebste Person') hat als Kehrreim:

Catalogus, Bd. II, S. 167. Ein Besitzernachweis auf fol. 29ʳ aus dem sechzehnten oder siebzehnten Jahrhundert sagt: 'desen boeck hooert [*sic*] toe' ('dieses Buch gehört') 'enken van houen'.

67 Luther, 'Predigt am Sonntach nach Weihnachten, nachmittags (1534)', *WA* 34/II, S. 551.17.

68 z. B. in dem Lied 'Ioseph ginck van nazareth to bethleem' (Utrecht, UB, 16 H 34, fol. 63ᵛ–64ʳ, um 1500, vielleicht Zwolle), mit Kehrreim 'Susanyn susanyn nu weigen wi, nu weigen wi, dat also suete lieue kindelyn' ('jetzt wiegen wir, jetzt wiegen wir, dass allerliebste Kindchen'). Die Berliner Handschrift mgo 185 enthält inmitten von einundzwanzig Weihnachtsliedern nur eines mit einem Wiegenkehrreim: 'Ons genaket die auent sterne' ('uns nähert sich der Abendstern', hier S. 220–22), in dem dargestellt wird, wie Maria das Kind auf den Schoß nimmt, es küsst und ihm ein Bad bereitet. Der Kehrreim lautet: '"susa nynna susa noe" | sagte Maria zum lieben Jesus'. 'Abendstern' passt gut zu Hinweisen, dass das Kindelwiegen meistens am Ende des Tages stattgefunden hat, vgl. Janota, *Studien*, S. 142 und 145. Die Handschrift Catherina Tirs (Münster, um 1588) enthält ein Lied, in dem Joseph ein *weygen leyt* mit der Zeile singt: 'zusen innyne suze'. *Niederdeutsche geistliche Lieder*, hg. von Hölscher, S. 124, Lied 64, Str. 3.

69 Berlin, SBB-PK, mgo 190, fol. 6ᵛ; Trier, StB, Ms. 322/1994 4°-II, fol. 213ᵛ; Utrecht, UB, 16 H 34, fol. 55ʳ. In der Trierer Handschrift werden Latein und die Volkssprache verwendet; die beiden anderen Handschriften verwenden Latein mit niederländischer Schlusszeile.

70 Berlin, SBB-PK, mgo 190, fol. 6ᵛ, *Liederenhandschrift*, hg. von Mertens, S. 173, Überschrift 'Repeticio super Puer nobis nascitur'; auch in Utrecht, UB, 16 H 34

suyo suyo suyo su
suyo suyo suyo su
suyo suyo suyo su
lieve susters is dat niet nu.[71]

(Suyo suyo suyo su [3×], liebe Schwestern ist das nicht Neues?).

Die Themen sind sowohl Geburt und Krippenandacht als auch Erlösung. Der Kehrreim scheint zum Wiegen einzuladen und die erhebliche Strophenzahl von neunundfünfzig würde es zulassen, dass jede Beteiligte in einem Wiegenkreis eine Strophe singen konnte.

Wiegenlieder in Wienhausen

Alles in allem scheint es angemessen, jene Lieder, in denen direkt zum Wiegen aufgerufen wird, als Wiegenlieder zu bezeichnen, und Lieder mit einem *suja*-Kehrreim als mögliche Wiegenlieder, d. h. Lieder, bei denen gewiegt werden konnte, entweder durch die wiegende Bewegung des eigenen Körpers oder durch das Schaukeln einer Wiege. Auch das 'Ecce mundi gaudia' im *Wienhäuser Liederbuch* kann mit seinem Kehrreim 'pie pie suse nunne so' auf einen möglichen Brauch des Kindelwiegens hindeuten.

Die Grenze zwischen einer heftigen inneren Emotion und deren äußeren Verkörperung durch Bewegung oder Tanz war nicht fest umrissen und es hat Momente gegeben, in der diese Grenze überschritten wurde, auch (oder gerade) in Klöstern. In den Schwesterbüchern des Klosters Adelhausen (südlich von Freiburg, auf 1318 datiert) wird erwähnt, die Schwester Adelheid Geishörnlin sei offensichtlich nach einer überwältigenden spirituellen Erfahrung dermaßen freudvoll erfüllt gewesen, dass sie so wild um den Altar wirbelte, dass ihr das Blut aus Mund und Nase geschossen sei.[72] Ähnlich verhielt sich die Kirchberger Schwester Mechthild von Waldeck, als göttliche Liebe und Gotteserfahrung in ihre Seele gefahren sei. Die Seele sei aufgesprungen, was ihr wie eine leibhaftige Erfahrung vorgekommen sei; ihre Seele habe im Inneren alle Bewegungen gemacht, die unsere Schwestern mit ihren Körpern zum Ausdruck brachten, wenn sie jubilierten, und unzählige Male konnte sie es nicht an sich

---

Andeutungen von Wechselzeilen. In anderen Handschriften lautet der Kehrreim 'o susze libe min' (Trier), 'zuza lieue nynno' (Utrecht).

71 Wien, ÖNB, 12875, fol. 25ᵛ (Ende des fünfzehnten Jahrhunderts, wahrscheinlich aus einem Frauenkloster), *Het geestelijk lied*, hg. von Bruning u. a., S. 50.

72 Anna von Munzingen, 'Chronik', hg. von König, S. 166, 'Vnd vnser Herre der erfulte ir begirde [...] vnd die süssigkeit vnd das wunder, d[a]z von ir wart, das was also gross, das si vff fuor vnd zwirbelet vmb den altar, vnd schoss ir das bluot ze munde vnd zuo nasen vs'; sehe auch Lewis, 'Music', S. 168.

halten, ohne dass wir es bemerkten.[73] Was genau vor sich ging, wenn man derart heftige Emotionen nicht an sich halten konnte, bleibt leider ungewiss: Wurde gesprungen, gestikuliert, sogar getanzt? Im Hinblick auf Kindelwiegenbräuche erwägt Regina Toepfer:

> Hörten sie andächtig zu oder summten sie leise mit, beteten sie inbrünstig oder bewegten sie ihren Körper im Takt der Melodie? Hielten manche vielleicht gar eine eigene Jesuskindfigur im Arm um sie gleichfalls in Schlaf zu wiegen?[74]

Diesen Ansatz verfolgend kann man sich fragen, ob die Sängerinnen von Wiegenliedern ihre innere Freude in eine körperliche Wiegebewegung umsetzten oder sogar in einen Tanz um das 'Jesuskind'? Ein Kehrreim wie 'nu wiegen, nu wiegen wi', ist ohne Schaukelbewegung der Wiege, des eigenen Körpers oder beider kaum vorzustellen. Das Zeugnis des Kölners Hermann Weinsberg suggeriert, dass sich die Singenden beim Wiegen des Kindeleins tatsächlich im Rhythmus mitbewegt hätten. Die oben erwähnten Wiegenlieder nennen teilweise das Wiegen oder Schaukeln explizit und offenbar ging dies bei Laien manchmal in ein ausgelassenes, frohes Springen und Tanzen über, sogar um den Altar. Die erwähnten Zeugnisse aus Hof, Brixen, Köln und Amsterdam beziehen sich auf improvisierte Laientänze in der Kirche oder zu Hause. Ob das in Klöstern ebenso vor sich ging, lässt sich nicht sagen. Institutionalisiert war der Tanz um die Wiege oder Krippe wahrscheinlich nicht, und fest choreografiert war er schon gar nicht.

Ob in Wienhausen gewiegt wurde? Die Ausbreitung mit den zum Wiegen nahezu auffordernden Besänftigungsworten 'pie pie suse nunne so' im Kehrreim von 'Ecce Mundi gaudia' lässt es vermuten. Dass nur das Wienhäuser Lied diese Wiegewörter eingefügt hat, bedeutet vielleicht, dass in Wienhausen das Wiegen zur Weihnachtsfeier gehörte. Dieser Gedanke wird darüber hinaus dadurch gestützt, dass es im *Wienhäuser Liederbuch* auch ein eindeutiges Wiegenlied gibt: das deutsch-lateinische Lied 'Dat was eyn eddel juncfrowe fyn'.[75] Die letzte Strophen dieses Lieds lauten:

---

73 'und gotlicher mynn und bevindung gotes in ir sel in ir fur, als sie auf sprung, und daucht sie nach warer bevindung, das ir sel inwendig alle die geperd het, die unser swester ausswendig heten, so sie jubilirten, und an zal dick mocht sie sich nicht enthalten, das wir sein innen wurden'. 'Aufzeichnungen', hg. von Roth, S. 119, *Kirchberger Schwesterbuch*, erste Hälfte vierzehntes Jahrhundert. Diejenige, die am Wort ist, ist die Verfasserin der *Kirchberger Schwesterbücher*; siehe auch Lewis, 'Music', S. 169.

74 Toepfer, 'Kindel', S. 131.

75 'Wienhäuser Liederbuch', hg. von. Alpers, Nr. 16, S. 11, fol. 14[v].

De krubbeke was syn wegelyn,
quam mater sibi dedit,
dat houweken was syn beddekyn,
quam bos et asinus comedit.

Nu wege wege dat kindelyn;
et plane iubilemus –
dat plassede jo myt den hendeken –
et fortiter cantemus.

> (Die Krippe war seine Wiege, die ihm die Mutter gab, das Heu
> war sein Bett, das Ochse und Esel fraßen. | Jetzt wiege, wiege das
> Kindelein; und wir singen laut sein Lob, dass es in die Händchen
> klatscht, und wir singen noch lauter.)

Dieses schlichte, refrainlose Lied enthält eine klare Aufforderung dazu,
das Kind beim Singen zu wiegen, worüber es sich freut. Es bestätigt die
Annahme, dass für die Wienhäuser Nonnen das Kindelwiegen sehr wohl
zur Weihnachtsfeier gehört habe.

Mit dem Lied 'Ecce mundi gaudia' lassen sich das Kloster Wienhausen
und seine Bewohnerinnen in die kulturell-mystischen Traditionen der Devotio moderna eingliedern; der häufige Gebrauch von Diminutiven sowie
die Tatsache, dass dem oftmals unreinen Reim in der niederdeutschen
Volkssprache ein reiner Reim im Niederländischen entspricht, schafft zudem auf sprachlicher Ebene eine Nähe zum Sprachbereich der Devotio
moderna. Der Refrain mit Wiegenwörtern ('pie pie su se nunne so') und
die für das Tanzlied kennzeichnende Rondeaustruktur sprechen dafür,
dass man sich in Wienhausen beim Singen dieses Liedes tatsächlich wiegend bewegte.

Bibliographie

Unedierte Quellen

Handschriften und Archivalien

Berlin, Staatsbibliothek zu Berlin Preußischer Kulturbesitz, mgo 280: Anna von
    Köln

————, mgo 185: Liederhandschrift

————, mgo 190: Liederhandschrift

Florenz, Biblioteca Medicea-Laurenziana, Plut. 29. 1

Gent, Universitätsbibliothek, Ms. 1300

Kassel, Universitätsbibliothek, 2° Ms. poet. et roman. 19: *Hessisches*
    Weihnachtsspiel

Köln, Historisches Archiv, 7010 (W) 25: Catharina van Rade

Trier, Stadtbibliothek, Ms. 322/1994 4°-II

Utrecht, Universitätsbibliothek, 16 H 34

Wien, Österreichische Nationalbibliothek, 12875

Wienhausen, Archiv des Zisterzienserinnen-Klosters, Hs. Nr. 9

Frühdrucke

Franck, Sebastian, *Weltbuch: Spiegel unn bildniss des gantzen erdboden* [. . .]
    (Tübingen: Morhart, 1534) (VD16 F 2168)

Witzel, Georg, *Psaltes Ecclesiasticus* (Mainz: Behem, 1550) (VD16 W 4006)

Edierte Quellen

Analecta hymnica medii aevi, hg. von Clemens Blume u. a., 55 Bde (Leipzig:
    Reisland, 1886–1922)

Anna von Köln, *Liederbuch (um 1500)*, hg. von Walter Salmen und Johannes
    Koepp (Düsseldorf: Schwann, 1954)

Anna von Munzingen, 'Chronik', hg. von Johann König, *Freiburger Diözesan Archiv*,
    13 (1880), 129–236

'Aufzeichnungen über das mystische Leben der Nonnen von Kirchberg bei Sulz
    Predigerordens während des XIV. und XV. Jahrhunderts', hg. von Ferdinand
    Roth, *Alemannia*, 21 (1893), 103–48

Ebner, Margaretha und Heinrich von Nördlingen, *Werke. Ein Beitrag zur Geschichte*
    der deutschen Mystik, hg. von Philipp Strauch (Freiburg: Mohr, 1882)

'En trinitate speculum', https://www.liederenbank.nl/text.php?
    recordid=29474&lan=nlG (Zugriff: 21. Dezember 2023)

Feichter, Veit, *Die Schriften des Brixner Dommesners Veit Feichter (ca. 1510–1560)*, hg. von Andrea Hofmeister-Winter, Bd. I: *Das Brixner Dommesnerbuch. Mit elektronischer Rohtextversion und digitalem Vollfaksimile auf CD-ROM*, Innsbrucker Beiträge zur Kulturwissenschaft. Germanistische Reihe, 63 (Innsbruck: Institut für Deutsche Sprache, Literatur und Literaturkritik, 2001)

Het geestelijk lied van Noord-Nederland in de vijftiende eeuw: De Nederlandse liederen van de handschriften Amsterdam (Wenen ÖNB 12875) en Utrecht (Berlijn MGO 190), hg. von Eliseus Bruning u. a. (Amsterdam: Vereniging voor Nederlandse muziekgeschiedenis, 1963)

Gerhoh von Reichersberg, 'Des Propstes Gerhoh von Reichersberg Abhandlung *De inuestigatione Antichristi*', hg. von Jodok Stülz, *Archiv für Kunde österreichischer Geschichts-Quellen*, 20 (1858), 127–88

Gesungene Innigkeit: Studien zu einer Musikhandschrift der Devotio Moderna (Utrecht, Universiteitsbibliotheek, Ms. 16 H 34, olim B. 113). Mit einer Edition der Gesänge, hg. von Ulrike Hascher-Burger (Leiden: Brill, 2002)

'Hessisches Weihnachtsspiel', in *Das Drama des Mittelalters*, hg. von Richard Froning, Teil III (Stuttgart: Union, 1892), S. 902–37 (Nachdr. Darmstadt: Wissenschaftliche Buchgesellschaft, 1964)

Johannes Beleth, *Summa de ecclesiasticis officiis*, hg. von Herbert Douteil (Turnhout: Brepols 1976)

Liederenhandschrift Berlijn 190. Hs. Staatsbibliothek zu Berlin – Preussischer Kulturbesitz germ. oct. 190, hg. von Thom Mertens u. a., Middeleeuwse Verzamelhandschriften uit de Nederlanden, 12 (Hilversum: Verloren, 2013)

Liederhandschrift Ms. Berlin 185, hg. von Dieuwke van der Poel u. a., https://www.dbnl.org/tekst/_han028hand01_01/ (Zugriff: 21. Dezember 2023)

Luther, Martin, *Werke. Weimarer Ausgabe* (*WA*), hg. von J. K. F. Knaake u. a., 120 Bde (Weimar: Böhlau, 1883–2009)

'Middelnederlandsch Kerstliedje', hg. von J. G. R. Acquoy, *Archief voor Nederlandsche Kerkgeschiedenis*, 4/3 (1893), 334–36

Niederdeutsche geistliche Lieder und Sprüche aus dem Münsterlande, hg. von Bernhard Hölscher (Berlin: Hertz, 1854)

Weinsberg, Hermann, *Autobiographische Aufzeichnungen*. Digitale Gesamtausgabe. Hg. von der Abteilung für Geschichte der Frühen Neuzeit und Rheinische Landesgeschichte des Instituts für Geschichtswissenschaft der Universität Bonn, https://www.weinsberg.uni-bonn.de/ (Zugriff: 21. Dezember 2023)

Widman, Enoch, *Chronik der Stadt Hof*, hg. von Maria Rösler (Neustadt: Schmidt, 2015)

'Wienhäuser Liederbuch', hg. von Paul Alpers, *Niederdeutsches Jahrbuch*, 69–70 (1943–1947), 1–41

Forschungsliteratur

Acquoy, J. G. R., 'Kerstliederen en Leisen', Reprint der Ausgabe Amsterdam 1887, *Archief voor Nederlandsche Kerkgeschiedenis*, 6 (1897), 217–72

Ameln, Konrad, 'Resonet in Laudibus' – 'Joseph lieber Joseph mein', *Jahrbuch für Liturgik und Hymnologie*, 15 (1970), 52–112

Ampe, Albert, 'Uit de kerstvroomheid der zestiende eeuw: Onbekend werk van Bartholomeus van Middelburg', *Ons geestelijk erf*, 41 (1967), 123–90

Appuhn, Horst und Christian von Heusinger, 'Der Fund kleiner Andachtsbilder des 13. bis 17. Jahrhunderts in Kloster Wienhausen', *Niederdeutsche Beiträge zur Kunstgeschichte*, 4 (1965), 157–238

Berthold, Luise, 'Die Kindelwiegenspiele', *Beiträge zur Geschichte der deutschen Sprache und Literatur*, 56 (1932), 208–24

De Coo, Joseph, 'Addenda zum Weihnachtsmotiv des Josefshosen', *Aachener Kunstblätter*, 43 (1972), 249–61

——, 'In Josephs Hosen Jhesus gehwonden wert', *Aachener Kunstblätter*, 30 (1965), 144–84

De Morrée, Cécile, *Voor de tijd van het Jaar: Vervaardiging, organisatie en gebruikerscontext van Middelnederlandse devote liedverzamelingen (ca. 1470–1588)* (Hilversum: Verloren, 2017)

Haar, James, 'Music of the Spheres', in *Grove Music (online)* (Oxford: Oxford University Press, 2001), https://doi-org.proxy.library.uu.nl/10.1093/gmo/9781561592630.article.19447 (Zugriff: 21. Dezember 2023)

Janota, Johannes, *Studien zu Funktion und Typus des deutschen geistlichen Liedes im Mittelalter*, MTU, 23 (München: Beck, 1968).

Keller, Peter, *Die Wiege des Christuskindes: Ein Haushaltsgerät in Kunst und Kult* (Worms: Wernersche Verlagsgesellschaft, 1998)

Klönne, Bernardus, 'Amstelodamensia. Het Kindekewiegen in de Oude Kerk', *De Katholiek*, 104 (1893), 262–74

Kohler, Erika, *Martin Luther und der Festbrauch*, Mitteldeutsche Forschungen, 17 (Köln: Böhlau, 1959)

Koldau, Linda Maria, *Frauen – Musik – Kultur. Ein Handbuch zum deutschen Sprachgebiet der Frühen Neuzeit* (Wien: Böhlau, 2005)

Knäble, Philip, *Eine tanzende Kirche. Initiation, Ritual und Liturgie im spätmittelalterlichen Frankreich* (Köln: Böhlau, 2016)

Knuttel, J. A. N., *Het geestelijk lied in de Nederlanden voor de kerkhervorming* (Rotterdam: Brusse, 1906, Reprint Groningen und Amsterdam: Bouma/Hagen, 1974)

Lewis, Gertrud Jaron, 'Music and Dancing in the Fourteenth-Century Sister-Books', in *Vox mystica: Essays on Medieval Mysticism: In Honor of Valerie Lagorio*, hg. von Anne Clark Bartlett u. a. (Cambridge: Brewer, 1995), S. 159–69

Mak, J. J. und Eliseus Bruning, *Middeleeuwse kerstliederen* (Utrecht: Het Spectrum, 1948)

Nürnberg, Ute, *Der Jahreswechsel im Kirchenlied: Zur Geschichte, Motivik und Theologie deutscher und schweizerischer Lieder* (Göttingen: Vandenhoeck & Ruprecht, 2016)

Reynaert, Joris, *Catalogus van de Middelnederlandse Handschriften in de Bibliotheek van de Rijksuniversiteit te Gent*, 2 Bde (Gent: Universität Gent, 1984–1996)

Riggert-Mindermann, Ida-Christine, 'Die Klosterreform und ihre Auswirkungen auf die Lüneburger Kloster', in *Weltbild und Lebenswirklichkeit in den Lüneburger Klöstern. IX Ebstorfer Kolloquium vom 23. bis 26. März 2011,* hg. von Wolfgang Brandis and Hans-Walter Stork (Berlin: Lukas, 2015), S. 119–28

Roodenburg, Herman, *Onder censuur: De kerkelijke tucht in de gereformeerde gemeente van Amsterdam, 1578–1700* (Hilversum: Verloren, 1990)

Roolfs, Friedel Helga, 'Das *Wienhäuser Liederbuch* – eine kodikologische Annäherung', in *Passion und Ostern in den Lüneburger Klöstern. Bericht des VIII. Ebstorfer Kolloquiums Kloster Ebstorf, 25. bis 29. März 2009,* hg. von Linda Maria Koldau (Ebstorf: Kloster Ebstorf, 2010), S. 245–64

Salmen, Walter, *Tanz und Tanzen vom Mittelalter bis zur Renaissance,* Terpsichore, 3 (Hildesheim: Olms, 1999)

——, 'Tanzen in Klöstern während des Mittelalters', *Michaelsteiner Konferenzberichte,* 55 (1999), 67–74

Schlotheuber, Eva, *Klostereintritt und Bildung: Die Lebenswelt der Nonnen im späten Mittelalter. Mit einer Edition des 'Konventstagebuchs' einer Zisterzienserin von Heilig-Kreuz bei Braunschweig (1484–1507),* Spätmittelalter und Reformation, 24 (Tübingen: Mohr Siebeck 2004)

Sievers, Heinrich, 'Die Melodien des *Wienhäuser Liederbuchs*', *Niederdeutsches Jahrbuch,* 69–70 (1943–1947), 41–46

Söll, Georg, *Mariologie,* hg. von Michael Schmaus u. a., Handbuch der Dogmengeschichte, 3/4 (Freiburg: Herder, 1978)

Stevens, John, *Words and Music in the Middle Ages: Song, Narrative, Dance and Drama, 1050–1350* (Cambridge: Cambridge University Press, 1986)

Toepfer, Regina, 'Kindel, Wiege, Windel: Zur Interaktion mit sakralen Objekten in Weihnachtsritualen und Spielen', *European Medieval Drama,* 25 (2021), 119–41

——, 'Vom marginalisierten Heiligen zum hegemonialen Hausvater: Josephs Männlichkeit im *Hessischen* und in Heinrich Knausts *Weihnachtsspiel*', *European Medieval Drama,* 17 (2013), 43–68

Van Duyse, Florimond, *Het oude Nederlandsche lied: Wereldlijke en geestelijke Liederen uit vroegeren tijd. Teksten en melodieën,* 4 Bde (Den Haag und Antwerpen: Nijhoff und De Nederlandsche Boekhandel, 1903–1908)

Van Luijtelaar, Inge, 'Colofonconventies in middeleeuwse handschriften uit vrouwenkloosters in de Nederlanden' (Masterthesis, RU Nijmegen, 2015)

Wachinger, Burghart, 'Resonet in laudibus', in *Die deutsche Literatur des Mittelalters. Verfasserlexikon,* 2. Aufl., hg. v. Kurt Ruh u. a., 11 Bde (Berlin u. a.: de Gruyter, 1978–2008), Bd. VII (1989), Sp. 1226–31

Wilkins, Nigel, 'Rondeau', in Grove Music (online) (Oxford: Oxford University Press, 2001), https://doi-org.proxy.library.uu.nl/10.1093/gmo/ 9781561592630.article.23782 (Zugriff: 21. Dezember 2023)

Williams, Anne, 'Josephs Hosen: Devotion and Humor', in Anne Williams, *Satire, Veneration and St. Joseph in Art, c. 1300–1550* (Amsterdam: Amsterdam University Press, 2019), S. 37–89

Internetressourcen

De Digitale Bibliotheek voor de Nederlandse Letteren (DBNL), https://www.dbnl.org/ (Zugriff: 21. Dezember 2023)
Nederlandse Liederenbank (KNAW und Meertens Instituut), http://www.liederenbank.nl (Zugriff: 21. Dezember 2023)

ANGELIKA KEMPER

Gesang auf dem Sinai

Dynamische Räume und Signale der Transgression im
Mühlhäuser (thüringischen) Katharinenspiel

▼ **ABSTRACT** The Thuringian *Play of St Catherine*,
dating from the middle of the fourteenth century,
deals with the martyrdom of the saint herself and the
martyrdom of several other figures. Their appearances
are not only accompanied by heavenly figures, but are
also acoustically emphasized by chants. The play thus
shows an intense tonal design, its numerous liturgical
chants have a commentary effect and mark the
figures' passage into transcendence. The play also
reveals a complex use of space and adds dynamic
spaces, which are created performatively, to its fixed
stage locations. Based on the play's spatial and sound
direction, the contribution examines how spatial and
acoustic means are used, how 'this world' and 'the
next world' are marked and what effects can be
achieved with this, especially in a hagiographic
context.

▼ **KEYWORDS:** space, sound, saints plays, legends,
play direction, simultaneous stage, liturgical songs,
media, St Catherine, *Mühlhäuser (thüringisches)
Katharinenspiel*

Angelika Kemper (Angelika.Kemper@aau.at) has studied German, Latin,
Middle- and Neo-Latin philology. She was promoted Dr.phil. at the University of
Mannheim, and Dr.habil. at the University of Klagenfurt. Since 2019 she is
Associate Professor for Medieval German Language at Literature at the
University of Klagenfurt.

European Medieval Drama, 27 (2023), 105–130
BREPOLS ❦ PUBLISHERS

10.1484/J.EMD.5.137680

Für ein Legendenspiel sollten die Gestaltung von Raum und Klang eigentlich, so könnte man annehmen, nebensächlich sein — es steht schließlich eine Person, der oder die Heilige, in der Mitte des Spielgeschehens und im Zentrum der Heilsdidaxe. Doch für eine inszenatorische Realisierung sind die Fragen nach dem bespielten Raum, dem evozierten Raum und der weiteren — etwa klanglichen — Ausgestaltung solcher Räume elementar, da sie Seh- und Hörgewohnheiten aufrufen und eine Signalwirkung entfalten. Es geht in Legendenspielen um Übergänge in transzendente Bereiche und um wunderhaftes Geschehen, so dass die mit Heiligenlegenden befassten Stücke Vermittlungen zwischen irdischer Welt und Jenseits aufzeigen.[1] Die Stücke unterstützen damit die Laienkatechese und den Heiligenkult, aber sie interpretieren auch den Weltzustand: Sie präsentieren eine von Gegensätzen geprägte, gewaltsame Welt und dienen entsprechend der Verlautbarung von Appellen, die auf die Lebensführung zielen und den himmlischen Lohn in Aussicht stellen. Die dramatisierte Heiligenfigur wird insofern als Vermittlungsinstanz aufgebaut, die an Diesseits und Jenseits teilhat. Die Stücke nutzen zur Darstellung dieser Konstellation, wenn transzendente Übergänge erfolgen, auch Räume und klangliche Signale als theatrale Mittel. Diese stellen dann nicht nur ästhetische Momente dar, sondern können je nach Ausgestaltung zugleich auf die Heilsbedeutung des Gesehenen und Gehörten weisen; sie müssen anhand des überlieferten Spieltexts rekonstruiert werden, was der folgende Beitrag unternimmt.

Als Beispiel für ein Legendenspiel wurde das *Mühlhäuser (thüringische) Katharinenspiel* ausgewählt. Das Stück geht auf eine Vorlage zurück, die um 1340/1350 im nördlichen Thüringen entstanden war; die Handschrift lässt eine zur Aufführung bestimmte Texteinrichtung erkennen, sie erfasst die Textanfänge lateinischer Gesänge und enthält lateinische Bühnenanweisungen.[2] Das Stück ist als einziges der deutschsprachigen Märtyrerspiele dieser Zeit vollständig überliefert und kann wegen seiner komplexen Raumverwendung und seiner intensiven klanglichen Ausgestaltung als geeignetes Beispielmaterial für das vorliegende Thema dienen.

Im Ganzen enthält das Spiel zwanzig lateinische Gesänge, die durch die Darsteller vorzutragen waren, weshalb wohl Kleriker zu den Aufführenden zählten.[3] Das Stück ist in einer Handschrift des Stadtarchivs Mühlhausen

---

1 Hierzu Schulze, *Geistliche Spiele*, S. 183. Schulze weist auf die Tendenz zur geschlossenen Form in Legendenspielen hin und hält fest, dass diese in 'Kontakt mit den biblischen Spielzyklen' entstanden seien.

2 Die lateinischen Gesänge wurden durch die Schreiberhand hervorgehoben. Nach Beckers Angabe sind in der Mühlhäuser Handschrift — mit einer Ausnahme — alle Gesänge nur mit dem Textanfang verzeichnet; *Das Spiel*, hg. von Beckers, S. 3.

3 Aufgrund des musikalischen Befundes äußerte schon Wilhelm Creizenach die Vermutung, dass Kleriker und Schüler als Aufführende vorgesehen waren; siehe Creizenach, *Geschichte*, S. 127.

überliefert, wobei im Folgenden die Edition Otto Beckers' (Breslau 1905) als Textgrundlage verwendet wird.[4]

Das Legendenspiel behandelt das Martyrium der Katharina von Alexandria, einer historisch nicht belegbaren Gestalt, die unter Maxentius (Kaiser, 306–312 n. Chr.) gestorben sein soll. Die frühesten schriftlichen Zeugnisse zu ihrer Gestalt sind im östlichen Kulturraum zu verorten, während sie offenbar erst seit dem achten/neunten Jahrhundert im lateinischen Westen Bekanntheit erlangte.[5] Die im Hoch- und Spätmittelalter populär gewordene Heilige zählte seit dem vierzehnten Jahrhundert zur Gruppe der Nothelfer, worauf der Spieltext ausdrücklich hinweist. Das prolog- und epilogfreie Spiel setzt ohne Bericht über die Vorgeschichte ein, indem sich zu Beginn eine Spielerprozession, von lateinischem Gesang begleitet, auf den Bühnenplatz bewegt. Die Handlung des Stücks konzentriert sich auf die Auseinandersetzung mit dem paganen Herrscher Maxentius und zeigt ein mehrstufiges Martyrium der Hauptfigur, wobei wiederholt Wunder auftreten und die göttliche Lenkung des Geschehens verdeutlichen. Nicht nur die Wunderereignisse, auch die Martyrien werden akkumuliert. Katharinas Peinigung wird von einer Reihe anderer Martyrien begleitet, da sich durch das Auftreten der Protagonistin weitere Figuren bekehren und dafür Strafe leiden: Die herbeigeholten Gelehrten nehmen eine Disputation mit ihr auf, lassen sich zum Christentum bekehren und erdulden das Martyrium im Feuer. Die Folterknechte bereiten ein mit Messern besetztes Rad für Katharina vor, welches jedoch durch ein göttliches Wunder zerstört wird. In der Folge bekehren sich die Königin und der Vertraute des Maxentius und erleiden auf Geheiß des Herrschers ebenfalls das Martyrium. Zum Schluss lehnt Katharina ein letztes Mal den Götzenglauben ab, worauf ihre Hinrichtung folgt; sie wird zur Ent-

---

4 Das Spiel ist überliefert in der Handschrift Mühlhausen, Stadtarchiv, cod. 20, fol. 45rb–47vb. Der Umfang beträgt — Biermanns Zählung folgend — ca. 750 Verse, der Text ist in nordthüringischer Mundart verfasst. Biermann, 'Mühlhäuser Katharinenspiel', Sp. 721–23. Zitate aus dem Spieltext folgen der Edition: *Das Spiel*, hg. von Beckers, S. 128–57 (Angaben aus dieser Edition sind versehen mit der Sigle *KSp* für *Katharinenspiel*).

5 Hierzu Frutaz, 'Katharina', Sp. 60–61; Assion, 'Katharina', Sp. 1055–73; siehe auch die Informationen bei Schill, 'Ikonographie', S. 14–16. — Die Katharinenlegende fand in deutschen und lateinischen Versionen, in Prosa und Versen weite Verbreitung. Ihr Ursprung wird in einer *Passio* angesetzt, wobei eine griechische Urfassung der Legende offenbar bereits im sechsten oder siebten Jahrhundert vorhanden war; sie wurde bearbeitet und in eine lateinische Fassung umgeformt. Die Legende war im Westen wohl seit dem achten/neunten Jahrhundert bekannt, im zwölften Jahrhundert lag eine kompilierte lateinische 'Standardfassung' vor (*Vulgata*, für die drei Fassungen unterschieden werden können), während deutschsprachige Legenden erst seit dem dreizehnten Jahrhundert (Versform) und vierzehnten Jahrhundert (Prosa) belegt sind. Vgl. Assion, 'Katharina', Sp. 1055–58.

hauptung vor die Stadt geführt, spricht zu der versammelten Menge[6] und richtet ein Gebet an Gott, das ihre Nothelferfunktion unterstreicht. Schließlich kommt die *Dominica persona* mitsamt Maria und Engeln auf die Bühne, um sie in Empfang zu nehmen. Das Spiel zeigt im Übrigen bei allen Martyrien die direkt anschließende Aufnahme in den himmlischen Bereich, da göttliches Personal die neuen Glaubenszeugen unter Gesang begrüßt und in das Himmelreich einlädt. In der Schlusspartie des Spiels wird der Körper Katharinas zum Berg Sinai geleitet, auf dem die Bestattung stattfindet, wonach die Heilige auf einem Himmelsthron Platz nimmt. Über die bühnenpraktische Realisierung dieser komplexen Szene, die eine Aufteilung in Körper und erlöste Seele vornimmt, kann an dieser Stelle nur spekuliert werden.[7] Der gemeinsame Gesang des 'Te deum' beschließt die Handlung, bevor noch eine kurze, zehn Verse umfassende Teufelsszene folgt, die Maxentius' Ankunft in der Hölle zeigt und mit dem Ausschwärmen der Teufel endet.

Die folgende Untersuchung soll auf der textlichen Basis des Mühlhäuser Legendenspiels die räumliche und klangliche Gestaltung überprüfen und darlegen, wie sie im Rahmen der Regie eingesetzt und koordiniert werden; Szenen transgressiven Charakters haben dabei Priorität. Daran anknüpfend kann erschlossen werden, welche Aufgaben räumliche und klangliche Mittel in der Inszenierung erfüllen und welches Wirkungskalkül mit ihnen verbunden ist, da sie im Spiel zur Sinnerzeugung beitragen können. Auch ist zu beachten, dass manche Spielräume in einer Freilichtaufführung nicht an festen Bühnenorten zu lokalisieren sind, sondern offenbar primär durch Aktion belegt sowie durch weitere theatrale Mittel charakterisiert wurden; will man sie aus heutiger Sicht identifizieren und analysieren, dann wirkt der fluide Charakter dieser Räume hinderlich.[8] Den Bedingungen einer Simultanbühne scheint es daher angemessen, den in der theaterwissenschaftlichen Forschung gebräuchlichen Begriff des 'performativen Raumes' aufzugreifen, der die gewissermaßen erspielten[9] Schauplätze des geistlichen Spiels kennzeichnet. Er kann — nach Erika Fischer-Lichte — durch Bewegung wie durch das 'Erklingen von Lauten' verändert werden, also auch gestisch, sprachlich oder gesanglich

---

6 Sie äußert in der Ansprache ihre Erlösungsgewissheit, da ihr ein Platz im Himmel bereitet sei; *KSp*, V. 637.

7 Vgl. Koch, 'Formen', S. 30, die diesen Aspekt für die narrative Legendenversion (*Passional*) hervorhebt.

8 Zur Problematik der Szeneneinteilung ähnlich Biermann, *Die deutschsprachigen Legendenspiele*, S. 16–17, der darauf hinweist, dass Legendenspiele in der Regel eine weniger gut einsehbare Szeneneinteilung zeigten als Oster- und Passionsspiele.

9 So Kirchner, *Raumerfahrung*, S. 9.

evoziert sein.[10] Die Gestaltung solcher dynamischen Räume wird also aufmerksam zu beachten sein. Ihr ephemerer Charakter gewinnt, so ist anzunehmen, durch Klanglichkeit an Einprägsamkeit und Bedeutung. So wird den Märtyrerfiguren des *Katharinenspiels* in ihrem Übergangsstatus zwischen Diesseits und Jenseits jeweils Gesang, gewissermaßen eine akustische *beatificatio*, zugestanden.[11] Dieser Übergangsschritt wird im Folgenden besondere Beachtung finden, da er über das Spielgeschehen hinausweist: Die Auswertung der räumlichen und klanglichen Mittel soll die Darstellung von 'Diesseits' und 'Jenseits' in der Inszenierung erhellen und deutlich machen, wie diese Bereiche — speziell der jenseitige Bereich — durch Regiemaßnahmen markiert und für das Spielgeschehen geöffnet werden. Daraus lassen sich einige hagiographische Folgerungen ableiten, die den Untersuchungsgang abschließen. Vergleichend sollen bei der Untersuchung einige zeitnah entstandene Legenden- und Endzeitspiele herangezogen werden, um die gewonnenen Beobachtungen in knapper Form einzuordnen. Dies sind das *Moselfränkische Katharinenspiel*, das *Mittelschlesische Dorotheenspiel* und das *Thüringische Zehnjungfrauenspiel*, das nicht nur etwa zeitgleich in derselben Region entstanden ist, sondern auch in einer Überlieferungsgemeinschaft mit dem Mühlhäuser Spiel vorliegt.[12]

Die Dimension des Raumes

Das *Mühlhäuser Katharinenspiel* umfasst einige konkrete Bühnenorte,[13] die in den Bühnenanweisungen und im Sprechtext benannt werden. Zu ihnen zählen Himmel und Hölle, Katharinas Haus, Maxentius' Palast, ein Kerker, eine Marter- und Hinrichtungsstelle, dazu ein neutraler Aktionsraum oder Platz für Massenszenen und Botengänge, wo sich wohl auch das Publikum befand. Weitere Bühnenorte sind anzunehmen, auch wenn sie im Text nur angedeutet werden oder punktuell zum Einsatz kommen. Dies sind das Haus des Cursates, der Katharina nach dem Befehl des Herrschers unter seine Aufsicht nimmt, und der Berg Sinai, der am Ende der Handlung den Ort der feierlichen Bestattung darstellt. Diese Episode ermöglicht damit

---

10 Hierzu vgl. Fischer-Lichte, *Ästhetik*, S. 187; Kirchner, *Raumerfahrung*, S. 9. Siehe auch die einschlägige Studie von Barton, 'Inszenierung', S. 440–41 und 448; Barton legt in einer differenzierten Schichtung das Raumkonzept mittelalterlicher Theaterbühnen dar.

11 Zugleich handelt es sich bei den Gesangsvorträgen um Akte liturgischer Verehrung, die in das Spiel Eingang finden.

12 Vgl. *Das Spiel*, hg. von Beckers, S. 4. Zitate aus dem *Moselfränkischen Katharinenspiel* (*MKSp*) erfolgen nach der Edition von Bierhals Jefferis, *Ein spätmittelalterliches Katharinenspiel*; Zitate aus dem *Mittelschlesischen Dorotheenspiel* (*MSDSp*) richten sich nach dem von Ukena edierten Text, *Die deutschen Mirakelspiele*, Bd. II.

13 Vgl. die Auflistung bei Biermann, *Die deutschsprachigen Legendenspiele*, S. 19–20.

den Vorgang einer *translatio* (Überführung)[14] auf der Bühne und erstellt eine Verbindung zum Kult der populären Heiligen, deren Gebeine der Legende nach im Katharinenkloster am Berg Sinai ruhen, wo sie heilsames Öl hervorbringen und Wunder wirken. Die wunderhaften Umstände des Todes der Märtyrerin werden auch in der *Legenda aurea*[15] festgehalten, welche für die Handlungsgestaltung des *Mühlhäuser Katharinenspiels* — wohl neben anderen hagiographischen Quellen — als Vorbild diente.[16]

Zur Erfassung des Raumes ist zu ergänzen, dass zwei Verweise auf reale städtische Örtlichkeiten am Ende des Spieltexts erfolgen, da die Teufelsfiguren u. a. zur 'kapellichen vor den greten' (*KSp*, V. 699)[17] eilen und damit eine Erfurter Lokalität in das Spiel einbeziehen. Die Hinweise legen nahe, dass die thüringische Stadt als Aufführungsort vorgesehen war, wenngleich keine Spielnachricht überliefert ist. Ein geeigneter Platz zur Aufführung wäre in der Tat der Erfurter Domhügel, wo die um 1330 errichteten 'Cavaten' (Stützkonstruktionen) am Fuß des Hügels als Prozessionshalt bzw. Bühnenort denkbar sind; eine Verwendung des Domhügels selbst als 'Berg Sinai' wäre somit naheliegend.[18] Im Ganzen ist es angebracht, in Übereinstimmung mit Heinrich Biermanns Zählung, für das *Mühlhäuser Katharinenspiel* eine weitläufige Simultanbühne mit etwa zehn Bühnenständen anzusetzen.[19]

---

14 Es sind hiermit die Übertragungen der Körper von Heiligen bzw. der Reliquien bezeichnet, auch die zugehörigen rituell-liturgischen Vorgänge; das Spiel greift offenbar die Folge von Erhebung (*elevatio*), Überführung (*translatio*) und Empfang (*adventus*) auf sowie die Niederlegung (*depositio*). Überführungen fanden seit 350 statt; seit dem 11. Jahrhundert wurden Ostensionsfeste durchgeführt sowie Reliquienprozessionen abseits der Heiligenfeste. Vgl. Heinzelmann, 'Translation', Sp. 947–49.

15 Jacobus de Voragine, *Legenda aurea*, hg. von Maggioni, Kap. CLXVIII (S. 1211–12). Das Milchwunder, die Translatio des Körpers durch Engel zum Berg Sinai sowie das heilsame Öl werden in der *Legenda aurea* benannt.

16 Beckers nahm die *Legenda aurea* als einzige Quelle an, vgl. *Das Spiel*, hg. von Beckers, S. 125. Weitere Einflüsse und Vorlagen wurden in der Forschung diskutiert, wobei Bierhals Jefferis, *Ein spätmittelalterliches Katharinenspiel*, S. 1 und 237, das *Passional* und das *Märterbuch* (um 1300) als Quellen anführt. Dagegen war die *Legenda aurea* oder ein ihr nahestehender Text von Biermann und Ukena als Hauptquelle benannt worden, vgl. Biermann, *Die deutschsprachigen Legendenspiele*, S. 31, und Ukena, *Die deutschen Mirakelspiele*, Bd. I, S. 50.

17 Laut Königshof, *Zur Geschichte*, S. 199, handelt es sich um 'das Drillhäuschen auf dem Domplatz', wo Gefangene ausgestellt wurden.

18 Vgl. Fasbender, 'Erfurt', S. 127; vgl. auch Königshof, *Zur Geschichte*, S. 113–15, der sich eingehend mit den Bühnenverhältnissen befasst und annimmt, dass ein freier Platz genutzt wurde (vor dem Dom oder der Barfüßerkirche) und dass Bühnenpodeste zur Anwendung kamen.

19 Mehrere prozessionsartige bzw. spektakelhafte Aufzüge — insbesondere die Eintritte in Himmel und Hölle — waren vorgesehen, daher ist von einem eher großen Bühnenplatz auszugehen. Siehe zur Anzahl der Bühnenorte Biermann, 'Mühlhäuser (thüringisches) Katharinenspiel', Sp. 722.

Die Abfolge der verwendeten Spielorte[20] erweist, dass am Beginn des Stücks neutrale Bühnenorte bevorzugt werden, die der irdischen Welt und dem Alltagsbereich angehören. So kann das Publikum an das graduelle Einsetzen der überirdischen Handlung angenähert werden, die sich durch Auftritte von Teufel und Erzengel entspinnt. Das Publikum erhält durch diese Figuren vorab Erklärungen des Geschehens und wird nicht unvermittelt mit Gewaltszenen und Höllenfahrten konfrontiert. Überhaupt sind auch die Martern Katharinas nach dem Prinzip der Steigerung angelegt (es folgen Inhaftierung, Auspeitschen, Hungerfolter, Rad, Enthauptung), das für die Dramaturgie des gesamten Spiels leitend ist. Sobald allerdings die Konflikthandlung zwischen heidnischem Herrscher und Märtyrerin einsetzt, verlagert sich das Geschehen an den Hof und in den Machtbereich der Heiden. Der ausgedehnte Mittelteil der Handlung (*KSp*, V. 96–605), welcher die Martyrienfolge umfasst, verändert die Bühnenorte dann in auffälliger Weise. Hier werden Orte der Peinigung und jenseitige Orte im Wechsel ins Spiel gebracht, so dass sich wiederholt scharfe Kontraste bei den verwendeten Bühnenräumen ergeben, ihrer Zugehörigkeit zum himmlischen und höllischen Bereich entsprechend. Es ergibt sich folgender Ablauf: Nach den Hofszenen werden — für die Gelehrten — Marterplatz und Himmel als Spielorte herangezogen, dann erweist sich als neuer Schauplatzschwerpunkt der Kerker Katharinas; er wird im Spieltext zweimal benannt — einmal in der Figurenrede, einmal in der Bühnenanweisung — und erscheint als ambivalenter Bühnenort, da er als Ort der unentrinnbaren Erniedrigung und der Gotteserscheinung zugleich fungiert. Da sonst im Sprechtext nur eine knappe Kommunikation der Figuren erfolgen kann, insofern sie zumeist in kurzen Dialogen ihre Appelle, Bekenntnisse und Forderungen äußern, ist die Gesprächsszene im Kerker, die Katharina und ihre Besucher zeigt, für das laienkatechetische Ziel der Glaubensstärkung bemerkenswert. Hier wird das Publikum zum ersten Mal mit einem Hinweis auf die *imitatio Christi* versehen, die der Königin als künftiger Märtyrerin bevorsteht:

KATHERINA:
du salt an deme dreten tage,
[vorwar ich di daz sage],
zu deme hemelriche vare. (*KSp*, V. 365–67)

> (KATHARINA: Du wirst am dritten Tage, das sage ich dir fürwahr, ins Himmelreich eingehen.)

Die für Katharina vorgesehene Radmarter ist auf dem Marterplatz lokalisiert: 'Milites portant rotam. | Tunc Katherina flexis genibus orans ad

---

20 Die Bestimmungen von Raum und Ort in der kulturwissenschaftlichen Diskussion erläutert Günzel, *Raum*, S. 50–68.

dominum [...]. Tonitrus frangit rotam' (*KSp*, V. 445a–b, V. 459a: 'Die Soldaten tragen das Rad, dann betet Katharina kniend zum Herrn [...] Ein Donnerschlag [d. h. Blitz] zerbricht das Rad'). Als der Marterversuch fehlschlägt, kommt sogleich die Hölle als Bühnenort ins Spiel: 'Tunc diaboli ducunt eos [tortores] ad infernum | clamando: "Ho, ho"' (*KSp*, V. 459b–c: 'Dann führen die Teufel die Folterknechte zur Hölle, während sie rufen: "Ho, ho"'). Ein Teufel kommentiert die Höllenfahrt der Folterknechte:

> Lucifer, vil liber here,
> wi komen mit grozen eren.
> wi haben wol gevaren,
> wi brengen eine groze schare. (*KSp*, V. 460–63)

> (Luzifer, liebster Herr, wir kommen mit großen Ehren. Wir waren erfolgreich, wir bringen eine große Schar.)

Danach wird der Marterplatz[21] für die Peinigung und Hinrichtung der Königin eingesetzt sowie für das Martyrium des Porphirius und seiner Soldaten, denen jeweils Auftritte der himmlischen Figuren folgen, die sie in das Himmelreich einladen; eine entsprechende Bühnenaktion, bei der die Darsteller begleitet vom göttlichen Personal den himmlischen Bereich betreten, ist denkbar. Der Schlussteil, der das finale Martyrium Katharinas enthält, ist dann wieder durch einen Wechsel des Schauplatzes ausgezeichnet. Hier ist ein 'Platz vor der Stadt' (der Anweisung 'vor di stat' entsprechend) als Bühnenplatz vorgesehen (*KSp*, V. 627). Der Ortswechsel wird von der komplexen darstellungstechnischen Aufgabe begleitet, die legendengemäßen Handlungsräume zu evozieren, dies sind der Berg Sinai und der Himmel, der selbst Ort der Handlung wird. Die Bühnenanweisungen zur wundersamen Übertragung des Körpers zum Sinai lauten:

> Tunc statim decollat [Cursates] eam [Katharina], quo facto Angeli veniunt cum thuribulis, Dominica persona cum Maria et corpus sepeliunt in monte Sinai cantando: 'Gratulemur in honore'. (*KSp*, V. 661a–d)

> (Dann enthauptet Cursates sie sogleich; nachdem das geschehen ist, kommen Engel mit Weihrauchfässern, die göttliche Person und Maria. Sie begraben den Körper auf dem Berg Sinai, wobei sie singen: 'Gratulemur in honore'.)

Die Aufnahme in den Himmel wird mit der folgenden Bühnenanweisung bezeichnet: 'Dominica persona elevat Katherinam et ducit eam ad |

---

21 Hierbei ist nicht klar, ob derselbe Platz für alle Martern genutzt wurde oder ob der Platz 'außerhalb der Stadt' für die Königin und Katharina reserviert war.

thronum cantando: "Veni, sponsa christi"' (*KSp*, V. 669a–c: 'Die göttliche Person erhebt Katharina und führt sie zum Thron mit dem Gesang: "Veni, sponsa christi"'). Die Erhebung der Märtyrerin beinhaltet ihre Platzierung auf dem Himmelsthron, so dass es wohl naheliegend ist, dass die Inszenierung die Heilige mit ihren bekannten Attributen[22] wie einer Krone oder einem Rad dem Publikum präsentierte. Im Kontrast erfolgt nun die Öffnung der Hölle, in die der heidnische Herrscher verbracht wird.

Die kontrastiv gestaltete Dimension des Raumes nutzt damit offenbar eine symbolische Grundlage, sie weist auf zeitgenössisch gängige semantische Anspielungshorizonte. Gerade jedoch die prozessionsartigen bzw. spektakelhaften Himmel- und Höllenfahrten deuten darauf, dass das Raumkonzept des Spiels auch den performativen, erspielten Raum umfasst, der sich durch Aktion, Gestik, Sprache usw. etabliert. Dieser dynamische Raum, der mit den statischen Schauplätzen während der Handlung im Wechsel zum Einsatz kommt, ist trotz seiner mangelnden Definierbarkeit für die Wirkung eines Legendenspiels grundlegend. Er umschließt das jenseitige Eingreifen, präsentiert damit die Besitzergreifung des irdischen Raumes, so dass er einen hermeneutischen Schlüssel für das Verständnis von Lohn und Strafe bereithält und ein beunruhigendes Potential für die Affektlage und Heilssorge der Rezipientenseite besitzt.[23]

In einem Vergleich mit anderen zeitnah entstandenen Legendenspielen, dem *Mittelschlesischen Dorotheenspiel* (ca. 1350) und dem *Moselfränkischen Katharinenspiel*,[24] ist zunächst auffallend, dass diese Spiele eine deutlich reduzierte Verwendung überirdischen Personals aufweisen und auf die eindrücklichen Himmel- und Höllenfahrten verzichten; nur das Mühlhäuser Spiel führt die *Dominica persona* auf die Bühne. Die Ansetzung der Bühnenorte weist ansonsten in allen drei Legendenstücken auf eine analoge Bühnenaufteilung, da der Hof oder das Praetorium, das Haus der Märtyrerin usw. in allen Beispielen vergleichbar vorliegen. Die performative, dynamische Raumgestaltung ist in beiden Stücken minimiert, was sich mit der Beobachtung deckt, dass das Moselfränkische Spiel ohnehin eine eher narrative Wiedergabe der Legende bezweckte. Ebenso fehlen in beiden Vergleichsbeispielen lateinische liturgische Gesangspartien.[25] Daraus lässt sich mit Blick auf die Gattungszuordnung der Stücke folgern,

---

22 Hierzu zählen Rad, Krone, Buch, Schwert und Palme; siehe Frutaz, 'Katharina', Sp. 60–61.

23 Zur Frage der Kollusion und der Präsentation von Heiligkeit vgl. auch Kemper, 'Bewegte Grenzen', S. 143–74.

24 Das Spiel folgt zeitlich wohl dem Mühlhäuser Text nach; vgl. Bierhals Jefferis, *Ein spätmittelalterliches Katharinenspiel*, S. 57, die (auf Basis der Handschrift) den Zeitraum der Entstehung zwischen 1430 und 1450 annimmt.

25 Das *Mittelschlesische Dorotheenspiel* enthält einen volkssprachlichen Gesang, das *Moselfränkische Katharinenspiel* erwähnt zum Schluss einmal Gesang bei der Aufzählung der Wunder, der aber nicht Teil der Handlung ist, sondern nur berichtet wird (*MKSp*, V. 941: 'Man horte daß gesenge groiß').

114 ANGELIKA KEMPER

dass eine routinierte Spieltätigkeit des Oster- und Passionsspieltyps im Hintergrund des *Katharinenspiels* gestanden haben könnte, da hier die lateinischen Gesangspartien, das Agieren der Figur Christi auf der Bühne sowie einige einschlägige Szenenmuster (Höllenfahrt, Seelenfang, sadistische Folter, Auferstehung) bereits vorgeprägt waren.[26]

Die klangliche Gestaltung des Raumes

In einem nächsten Schritt soll die klangliche[27] Dimension erörtert und — anhand des Textmaterials — ihr Beitrag zur Generierung von Sinn umrissen werden. Dabei stehen die lateinischen Gesänge als auffälligstes Element im Vordergrund. Sie finden sich im Spieltext in dichter Folge v. a. zu Beginn und am Schluss der Spielhandlung, während im Mittelteil jeweils punktuell Gesangspartien vorliegen. Dies ist der Fall, wenn die Martyrien beendet sind und die Aufnahme in den Himmel präsentiert wird, wobei himmlische und menschliche Figuren im Wechsel ihren Part vortragen.[28]

Das Textmaterial der Gesänge entstammt, Heinrich Biermanns allgemeiner Zuordnung folgend, dem 'vortridentinischen Brevier'; eine genauere Zuweisung an mögliche Quellen ist bislang nicht erfolgt, da im

---

26 Es liegt wohl v. a. eine Angleichung der Protagonistenrolle zugrunde, die angesichts der Vorstellung einer *imitatio Christi* naheliegt.

27 Unter Klang wird im Folgenden ein akustisches Phänomen verstanden, das sich anders als das Geräusch mit einem 'klare[n] Höreindruck' verbindet und bei Klängen 'erkennbarer Höhe' als Ton wahrgenommen wird; vgl. Dietel, *Wörterbuch*, S. 154.

28 Die Reihe der Gesänge lautet nach ihrem Erscheinen im Text wie unten angegeben; angeführt werden nur die Textanfänge (Incipits), wobei sich die Angabe von Sammlungen bzw. Quellen an Beckers Edition orientiert (zur Identifizierung der Gesangstexte dienten die Edition *Analecta hymnica*, hg. von Blume u. a. [hier und im Folgenden abgekürzt als *AH*], und Hartkers *Antiphonarium* mit der zugehörigen Überlieferung St. Gallen, SB, Cod. Sang. 390 und Cod. Sang. 391): 'Testimonium domini' [vgl. Psalm 18. 8; *AH* Nr. 3, Bd. 28, S. 17]; 'Voce cordis' [Hymnus 'De sancta Katharina', *AH* Nr. 72, Bd. 26, S. 210]; 'Cum dominante manu' [*AH* Nr. 74, Bd. 26, S. 216]; 'Rex decies' [*AH* Nr. 74, Bd. 26, S. 216]; 'Probasti, domine, cor nostrum' [vgl. Psalm 16. 3]; 'Venite benedicti patris mei' [vgl. Matthäus 25. 34]; 'Isti sunt sancti' [vgl. Offenbarung 7. 14; I Makkabäer 2. 50]; 'Vidisti, domine, agonem meum' [*Hartker-Antiphonar*, Cod. Sang. 390, S. 123]; 'Veni, electa mea' [vgl. Psalm 44. 12; Hohes Lied 4. 8; *AH* Nr. 8, Bd. 28, S. 33]; 'O miranda[m] mulieris' [*Hartker-Antiphonar*, Cod. Sang. 388, S. 450]; 'Sanctus, sanctus' [*Trishagion*]; 'Bonum certamen certavi' [vgl. II Timotheus 4. 7–8; I Korinther 15. 10; *Hartker-Antiphonar*, Cod. Sang. 391, S. 94]; 'Sancti mei, qui in hoc saeculo' [vgl. II Timotheus 4. 7–8; *Hartker-Antiphonar*, Cod. Sang. 391, S. 137]; 'Isti sunt sancti [siehe oben]; 'Expecto pro te gladium' [*AH* Nr. 69, 71, 72 und 74, Bd. 26, S. 199, 209, 210 und 218]; 'Veni, electa mea' [siehe oben]; 'Gratulemur in honore' [*AH* Nr. 69 und 74, Bd. 26, S. 201 und 215]; 'Veni, sponsa christi' [vgl. Psalm 44. 12; Hohes Lied 4. 8; *Hartker-Antiphonar*, Cod. Sang. 391, S. 189]; 'Regnum mundi' [*Hartker-Antiphonar*, Cod. Sang. 391, S. 14].

Verlauf des Mittelalters die Zahl der verwendeten Texte und Melodien stark anwuchs und die Textgestalt des Breviers im vierzehnten Jahrhundert gerade bei Heiligenfesten regional schwankte.[29] Ein Vergleich mit dem Mainzer Brevier, das für die Stadt Erfurt wegen der Zugehörigkeit zum Bistum Mainz maßgeblich erscheint, bietet sich daher an, um die verwendeten gregorianischen Gesänge und den lateinischen Textbestand in Annäherung zu fassen; sie können zur präziseren Deutung des Spiels beitragen. Anhaltspunkte für die Herkunft des Liedgerüsts kann auch die partielle Überschneidung mit dem Gesangsmaterial des *Thüringischen Zehnjungfrauenspiels* bieten, denn beide Spiele verfügen über zahlreiche geistliche Gesänge und zeigen gemeinsame Züge der Einbindung von liturgischem Gesang. Offenbar wurden in der Region umfangreiche Liedgerüste v. a. aus Antiphonen und Responsorien zur Spielgestaltung herangezogen, die durch ihre teils dialogische Anlage die Entwicklung der entsprechenden Szenen erleichterten.[30] Die Studie von Renate Amstutz zum *Thüringischen Zehnjungfrauenspiel* (*Ludus de decem virginibus*) soll daher im Folgenden einbezogen werden, da sie den liturgischen Kern dieses Spiels — freilich ohne Berücksichtigung des deutschen Texts — rekonstruiert hat und einen Vergleich der beiden Spiele möglich macht.[31]

Die verwendeten Texte in den Gesängen des *Katharinenspiels* sind häufig dem Katharinenfest zuzuordnen, jedoch auch den Festen anderer Märtyrerinnen, Märtyrer und Heiligen.[32] Wie bei anderen geistlichen Spielen wurde das Liedgerüst vom Bearbeiter aus verschiedenen liturgischen Textteilen zusammengestellt, so dass auch andere Heiligenoffizien und das Commune Sanctorum berücksichtigt wurden, wenn es sich textlich anbot. So zählt das zahlreich überlieferte Responsorium 'Regnum mundi' etwa zum Fest verschiedener Heiliger bzw. zum Gemeingut mehrerer weiblicher Heiliger (u. a. Agatha, Dorothea, Lucia, Margarita, Ma-

---

29 Vgl. Simmler, 'VII. Text-, Teiltext- und Textteilallianz', S. 478, sowie Biermann, *Die deutschsprachigen Legendenspiele*, S. 28. Die von Biermann herangezogenen Breviere stammen alle aus späterer Zeit, dem fünfzehnten und sogar sechzehnten Jahrhundert (vgl. Biermanns Literaturverzeichnis, S. 308). Die von ihm identifizierte Hauptquelle, das *Breviarium Romanum*, wird mit einer Ausgabe des Jahres 1541 angeführt; insofern sollte die Annahme Biermanns erneut an Quellentexten überprüft werden.

30 Eine dialogische Struktur weisen 'Probasti, domine, cor meum' und 'Veni, electa mea' auf, eine erklärende Ich-Rede bieten 'Expecto pro te gladium' und 'Vidisti, domine, agonem meum'.

31 Speziell die gemeinsamen Gesänge der beiden Spiele können hierdurch erschlossen werden; vgl. Amstutz, *Ludus*. Die Autorin arbeitet mit liturgischen Handschriften der Diözese Mainz und greift u. a. das Temporale, Sanctorale und Commune Sanctorum auf. Vgl. Mertens, 'Klang', S. 34.

32 Biermann, *Die deutschsprachigen Legendenspiele*, S. 29–32, nennt ohne nähere Begründung das *Breviarium Romanum* als Hauptquelle und verweist auf die hierbei häufig anzutreffende Verwendung der *Legenda aurea*.

ria Magdalena, Katharina).[33] In der Tat wäre daher ein Brevier, das als Textsorte einen intertextuellen Zuschnitt hat und Texte und Gesangteile verschiedener Provenienz einbindet (sowie im Aufbau variieren kann, je nach Verwendungszweck), als Vorlage des *Katharinenspiels* denkbar; die breviertypische Kombination von Gesang, Lesung/Bericht (Bibel, Legende, Martyrologien) und Gebet wird auch im Märtyrerspiel bei der Wiedergabe der Katharinenlegende in Umrissen erkennbar.[34] Wenn man ein spätmittelalterliches Beispiel des Mainzer Breviers heranzieht, zeigt sich jedoch eine Abfolge von Antiphonen und Responsorien, die eindeutig vom Liedgerüst des *Mühlhäuser Katharinenspiels* abweicht, bereits ersichtlich an 'Virginis eximie katherine' zu Beginn des Brevierabschnitts zum Katharinenfest und dem etwas später folgenden Hymnus 'Pange lingua' (fol. 295$^{\text{r–v}}$).[35] Die im Mainzer Brevier eingefügten sechs Lectiones, die den Inhalt der Katharinenlegende berichten, teilen die Legendenhandlung in sinnvoll gewählte Abschnitte, indem sie einzelne Handlungsschritte und Martyrien benennen: 1. Die Konfrontation Katharinas mit Maxentius, 2. die Einladung der Gelehrten und Katharinas Stärkung durch den Engel, 3. die Disputation und den Tod der Gelehrten, 4. die Kerkerhaft Katharinas und die Martyrien der Königin und des Prophirius, 5. die Radmarter, 6. die Enthauptung und Bestattung Katharinas. Jedoch auch hier wird deutlich, dass das Brevier kaum als direkte Vorlage gedient haben kann, da beide Versionen — das Spiel und das Brevier — eine teils verschiedene Reihenfolge der Episoden wählen: Die Radmarter wird im Spiel früher vorgeführt, während das Brevier diese Marter als eigenen Punkt der Betrachtung ansetzt und erst nach dem Tod der Königin und des Porphirius einfügt. Das Spiel bietet dabei die bessere Verkettung der Ereignisse, da es das Martyrium der Königin als Folge der Wundererfahrung bei der Radmarter vorführt. Auch sind die Martyrien der Königin und des Porphirius im Spiel getrennt worden, um sie jeweils ausführlicher zu präsentieren, während die Lectio 4 des Breviers sie zusammenführt und in einem Satz recht knapp berichtet.

Die Spielvorlage bemüht sich auch sonst um eine Verständnissicherung der Liturgieteile. Die lateinischen Texte der Gesänge des Spiels werden bei

---

33 Vgl. die Übersicht https://cantus.uwaterloo.ca/id/007524 (Zugriff: 20. Dezember 2023).

34 Die Funktion des Gebets ist freilich im *Katharinenspiel* gegenüber der Legendendarbietung und den Gesängen zurückgenommen; vgl. zur Textsorte 'Brevier': Simmler, 'VII. Text-, Teiltext- und Textteilallianz', S. 478–79.

35 Zum Vergleich herangezogen wurde u. a. die Inkunabel *Breviarium Moguntinum* (Straßburg: Grüninger, 1487), fol. 295^{r}–97^{r}. Die systematische Prüfung der liturgischen Überlieferung, die auch Nachbarbistümer einschließt, ist im Rahmen dieses Beitrags nicht zu leisten. Da die Mainzer liturgische Tradition jedoch eine vergleichsweise konstante Anlage in melodischer und textlicher Hinsicht zeigt, wie Macardle herausstellt, scheint es zulässig, eine spätere Quelle heranzuziehen; siehe Macardle, 'Die Gesänge', S. 264 (zur Leistung liturgischer Studien in Lokalisierungsfragen siehe S. 269).

der Martyrienfolge des Mittelteils und in der finalen Erhebung Katharinas fast ausnahmslos durch die folgende Figurenrede in die Volkssprache übertragen,[36] während die Gesänge zu Beginn nicht durch Übersetzung oder Paraphrase zugänglich gemacht wurden. Da die inhaltlichen Züge der lateinischen Texte insgesamt die Handlungsschwerpunkte der Inszenierung aufgreifen und deren Darstellungstendenzen untermauern,[37] ist eine nur dekorative Funktion der liturgienahen Passagen ausgeschlossen. Die Gesänge erweisen sich dabei stets — mit einer Ausnahme, dem Eingangsgesang des Herrschers — als der himmlischen Sphäre zugehörig.

Wenn man die einzelnen Abschnitte des Spiels verfolgt, dann enthalten die Gesänge der Eingangsprozession bei Maxentius und den *Adoratores*, also den Gelehrten,[38] Responsorien zum Katharinenfest, wobei den Figuren jeweils die sie selbst betreffenden Textpassagen zugeteilt sind.[39] Sie tragen in diesen Gesängen das Legendengeschehen episch berichtend vor. Die anderen Prozessionsvorträge sind von der *Dominica persona* zu hören sowie von Katharina mit den Engeln, die hier eine Sängergruppe bilden; diese Gesänge konturieren deutend die Legendenhandlung, da sie die Eigenschaften der Heiligen zusammenfassen (Weisheit, Unschuld, Reinheit), wie es die Antiphon der *Dominica persona* leistet:

Testimonium Domini fidele,
Sapientiam praestitit parvulae,
Hostis ideo saevissimus
Non dominatus est eius.
Innocentiam retinens
Mundumque cor diligens
Per poenas temporales
Portas introivit aeternales.[40]

> (Als zuverlässiges Zeugnis gewährte der Herr der jungen Frau Weisheit, so bemächtigte sich der gewaltig tobende Feind ihrer nicht. Die Unschuld bewahrend, das reine Herz liebend, ging sie durch weltliches Leiden ein in die ewigen Pforten.)

Die zehn Gesänge des Mittelteils stehen jeweils im Kontext des Martyriums der Märtyrerinnen und Märtyrer und der Einladung ins Himmelreich.

---

36 Dies geschieht in paraphrasierender Weise, nicht in wörtlicher Übersetzung.

37 So wird die Königin nach ihrem Martyrium von der *Dominica persona* empfangen mit 'Veni, electa mea', ein bekehrter Soldat singt bei seinem Martyrium 'Bonum certamen certavi'; vgl. *KSp*, V. 529b und 578c.

38 Es handelt sich wohl um einen Übertragungsfehler auf der Basis der *Legenda aurea*, die diese Figuren als 'oratores' anführt, *KSp*, V. 176c.

39 So Ukena, *Die deutschen Mirakelspiele*, Bd. I, S. 59.

40 Der Text ist nicht vollständig in der Handschrift verzeichnet und wird angeführt nach *AH* Nr. 3, Bd. 28, S. 17; Hervorhebung ergänzt.

Sie begleiten in einem erkennbaren Schema dieses Geschehen — auf die menschlichen Figuren, die selbsterklärend ihre Ergebenheit benennen, antworten die himmlischen Figuren, die sie ins Himmelreich laden und nochmals deutend und affirmativ die Vortrefflichkeit der Märtyrerinnen und Märtyrer akzentuieren.

So singen z. B. die Gelehrten einen Psalmvers 'Probasti, domine, cor meum' (Ps 16. 3), der auf ihre Prüfung verweist, die Königin singt 'Vidisti, domine, agonem meum', ein auf die Marter der Heiligen Agatha verweisender Textabschnitt, der bereits in Hartkers *Antiphonarium* enthalten war und die Aspekte der Weigerung und des Kampfes betont. Auf die Anrufung an den Herrn antworten jeweils die Gesänge der *Dominica persona*, die ihnen das Himmelreich verheißt.[41] Den Abschluss der Gesangsfolge bilden Vorträge der *Angeli*, die den Heiligenstatus betonen wie z. B. nach dem Martyrium der Gelehrten, als sie 'Isti sunt sancti' singen (*KSp.*, V. 298a–b). Die gesangliche Abfolge ist also grundsätzlich dreischrittig angelegt.[42] Dabei ist ein Steigerungsprinzip zu beobachten, da im Fall der Königin der Engelsgesang ausgeweitet wird und das Trishagion angehängt ist, und in der Passage des Martyriums Katharinas sechs Gesangspartien zu hören sind.[43] Der klangliche Höhepunkt des Spielschlusses scheint auf dem Berg Sinai angesiedelt zu sein, auf dem alle himmlischen Figuren (*Angeli*, *Dominica persona*, Maria) gemeinsam agieren — sie bestatten den Körper Katharinas — und singen. Die letzten Gesangspartien des Spiels ('Gratulemur in honore', 'Veni, sponsa Christi', 'Regnum mundi'), die vor dem abschließenden 'Te deum' erfolgen, unterstützen dabei jeweils eine geistliche Lesart der vorgeführten Legendenhandlung. Sie akzentuieren den Aufstieg zum himmlischen Sitz und die Verachtung der Welt sowie die brautmystische Liebe nach Vorbild der Psalmen und des Hohelieds; wie andere Quellen zeigen, deutende Passagen des Mainzer Breviers aus dem fünfzehnten Jahrhundert, ist es für das Katharinenfest durchaus üblich, den *mons* Sinai des Legendenschlusses mit mehrfacher Bedeutung zu versehen und den geistlichen bzw. christologischen Sinn hervorzuheben: Der Berg ist der Ort der mosaischen Gebote und der Begräbnisort Katharinas; zugleich steht er für Christus ('qui christus est') und er wird damit zum Ziel der gläubigen Breviernutzer ('ad montem qui christus est pervenire

---

41 In ihnen lässt sich einmalig ein wörtlicher Anklang an die *Legenda aurea* nachweisen ('Veni, electa mea'). Die aus Psalmtext und Hohelied stammende Wendung erscheint, wiederholt variiert, zahlreich in *AH*.

42 Vgl. Ukena, *Die deutschen Mirakelspiele*, Bd. I, S. 87; Königshof, *Zur Geschichte*, S. 104.

43 Dies sind ein Gesang der Märtyrerin ('Expecto pro te gladium'), die Antwort der *Dominica persona* ('Veni, electa mea'), der Jubelgesang der himmlischen Figuren auf dem Berg Sinai ('Gratulemur in honore'), eine erneute Einladung der *Dominica persona*, die Weltabsage der Heiligen ('Regnum mundi [...] contempsi') und der gemeinsame Gesang des 'Te deum'.

valeamus').[44] Diese explizite Gleichsetzung des überirdisch konnotierten Berges mit Christus selbst vermeidet das *Katharinenspiel* in seinen lateinischen und volkssprachlichen Texten, doch die mystische Sinnschicht, die die Hauptfigur als Auserwählte kennzeichnet, ist auch hier fassbar.

Die Aufhebung der alltäglichen Wirklichkeit wird zudem in den Gesängen, welche die Martyrien begleiten, akustisch umgesetzt und hörbar gemacht. Diese Gesänge enthalten ausnahmslos die Vorträge der gerade in der Bühnenhandlung verstorbenen Märtyrerinnen und Märtyrer — so dass auch die gerade in der Spielhandlung Getöteten zu singen beginnen.[45] Die gesanglichen Vorträge führen damit gewissermaßen die augenblickliche Auferstehung der Person vor und sie gestalten im Medium liturgischen Gesangs — wie Elke Ukena konstatiert — den 'metaphysischen Schritt[] von der Zeitlichkeit in die Ewigkeit'.[46] Erkennbar ist der Gesang ein festes akustisches Signal der Heiligkeit oder Heiligwerdung,[47] denn sie wird immer musikalisch signalisiert und erscheint auf diese Weise als Verbindung des Diesseits mit dem Jenseits. Die Gesänge erfüllen dabei, betrachtet man die kommunikative Ebene, die Funktion der inhaltlichen Rekapitulation, des Lobs, des Lohnversprechens und des Kommentars.[48]

Vergleicht man nun die Gestaltung des *Mühlhäuser Katharinenspiels* mit anderen Legendenspielen, so lässt sich festhalten, dass weder das *Moselfränkische Katharinenspiel* noch das *Mittelschlesische Dorotheenspiel* eine auch nur annähernd vergleichbare gesangliche Ausgestaltung erfahren haben. Das *Dorotheenspiel* fügt lediglich an einer Stelle einen Gemeindegesang[49] ein — den Leis 'Nu bitte wir den heyligen geyst' —, während das *Moselfränkische Katharinenspiel* ganz auf Gesang verzichtet. Doch ist das etwa zeitgleich entstandene *Thüringische Zehnjungfrauenspiel*[50] dem *Mühlhäuser Katharinenspiel* in dieser Hinsicht vergleichbar, da es über eine umfangreiche gesangliche Ausgestaltung verfügt in Form von neunundzwanzig lateinischen Vorträgen — Responsorien, Invitatorien und Antiphonen —, die meist ins Deutsche übertragen wurden, wobei es eine

---

44 *Breviarium Moguntinum*, fol. 295ᵛ (*Collecta*). Auch die eingesehene Version des *Breviarium Romanum* enthielt diese Formulierung in der einleitenden *Oratio*, *Breviarium Romanum* (Venedig: Jenson, 1478), fol. 371ʳ.

45 Von der Königin heißt es etwa: 'Tunc Regina sepulta cantat', *KSp*, V. 521d.

46 Ukena, *Die deutschen Mirakelspiele*, Bd. I, S. 85.

47 Zur Entwicklung der Kanonisation siehe Brinker, *Formen*, S. 9–10; Rosenfeld, *Legende*, S. 26–27.

48 So die Deutung Ukenas, *Die deutschen Mirakelspiele*, Bd. I, S. 86–87.

49 Vgl. die Edition durch Ukena, *Die deutschen Mirakelspiele*, Bd. II, S. 338.

50 Die Datierung für die Mühlhäuser Fassung A (577 Verse) ist zwischen 1350 und 1370 anzusetzen; die Darmstädter Fassung B verzichtet auf lateinische Gesänge (687 Verse) und ist auf 1428 zu datieren. Siehe Schulze, *Geistliche Spiele*, S. 176; Linke, 'Thüringische Zehnjungfrauenspiele', Sp. 916. Für Fassung A könnte ein lateinisches liturgisches Spiel die Vorstufe gewesen sein, da nach Amstutz ein komplettes lateinisches liturgisches Spiel als Grundlage der Gesänge denkbar wäre (ebd.).

Gruppe von vier Gesängen mit dem *Katharinenspiel* teilt.[51] Das Responsorium 'Testimonium domini' ist beiden Spielen gemeinsam, das von der Gruppe der himmlischen Figuren (*Thüringisches Zehnjungfrauenspiel*) bzw. der *Dominica persona* (*Mühlhäuser Katharinenspiel*) an prominenter Stelle gesungen wird, während die anfängliche Spielerprozession stattfindet. Amstutz setzt hierfür einen ausgedehnten, festlichen und musikalisch reich gestalteten Vortrag an, dessen Text über den zugrundeliegenden Psalmvers (18. 8) hinausgegangen sein dürfte.[52] Sie nimmt für diesen Gesang eine regionale Sonderverwendung an, die nicht in liturgischen Handschriften nachgewiesen werden könne, doch ist der Text des Responsoriums auch andernorts überliefert und mit dem Fest der Hl. Margarita verbunden. Eine liturgische Quelle, die eine Verwendung in Thüringen nahelegt, ist zwar nicht greifbar, aber durch ein in Rasdorf (Hessen) entstandenes Antiphonale lässt sich zumindest ein nahe an der Region verwendetes liturgisches Gesangsbeispiel zu diesem Heiligenfest belegen.[53]

Das zweite gemeinsame Responsorium stellt 'Regnum mundi' dar, welches nicht zum älteren Bestand gregorianischer Gesänge zählt, sondern erst ab dem dreizehnten und vierzehnten Jahrhundert verbreitet ist.[54] Dieser Gesang wurde als Teil der 'consecratio virginum' eingesetzt, spielte damit eine Rolle bei der Zeremonie der Aufnahme angehender Nonnen in ihren neuen Stand; der Text des Responsoriums, der eine Absage an die Welt enthält und als Ich-Aussage formuliert ist, ist für diesen Zweck überaus passend.[55] Der Gesang ist im *Katharinenspiel* in das Finale der Handlung eingereiht, als Katharina von der *Dominica persona* zum Thron geführt wird, und auch im *Zehnjungfrauenspiel* erscheint der Gesang — durch zweimalige Darbietung — in seiner Bedeutung hervorgehoben. Beide Spiele ergänzen eine deutschsprachige Übersetzung des lateinischen Gesangstexts.

Der Gesang 'Veni electa mea' erscheint ebenfalls in beiden Spielen, er wird im *Katharinenspiel* an zwei Stellen aufgeführt und dem Martyrium der Königin sowie dem Martyrium Katharinas beigegeben (beide Gesänge

---

51 *Das Spiel*, hg. von Beckers, S. 4.

52 Amstutz, *Ludus*, S. 89.

53 Vgl. Amstutz, *Ludus*, S. 89. Zum genannten Antiphonale bzw. Responsorium siehe Fulda, Hochschul- und Landesbibliothek, 100 Aa 55, fol. 118ᵛ. Die Handschrift, die auch einen Osterspieltext enthält, ist in der ersten Hälfte des fünfzehnten Jahrhunderts entstanden und war für das Kollegiatstift Rasdorf (Kreis Fulda) geschrieben worden (https://fuldig.hs-fulda.de/viewer/fullscreen/PPN432340890/244/); von den zwanzig Gesängen des *Katharinenspiels* sind sechzehn in diesem Antiphonale verzeichnet, freilich über den gesamten Codex verstreut.

54 Amstutz nimmt eine Verbreitung v. a. durch den Dominikanerorden an, siehe *Ludus*, S. 93–95.

55 Amstutz, *Ludus*, S. 97. Der Gesang ist bereits in einem Mainzer Pontificale des zwölften Jahrhunderts enthalten und nimmt hier eine herausragende Stelle ein, siehe S. 210.

werden durch die *Dominica persona* vorgetragen). Texte, die diesem Incipit entsprechen, sind in Form von Antiphon und Responsorium gut belegt.[56] Im Fall des *Katharinenspiels* wird erst bei der zweiten Darbietung eine vereindeutigende deutsche Übersetzung ('trut', 'frundin', *KSp*, V. 648) unmittelbar angefügt — soweit es das verkürzte Incipit erkennen lässt —, während auf den ersten Gesang folgend zunächst der Grund für die Erwählung im deutschen Text benannt wird. Der aus den Psalmen (44. 12) und dem Hohelied (4. 8) abgeleitete lateinische Text markiert — nicht anders als im *Zehnjungfrauenspiel* — den Übertritt der weiblichen Figuren in die mystische Umgebung des himmlischen Bräutigams, wie es das im Spiel verwendete deutsche Vokabular nahelegt. Auch dieser Gesang ist für die Zeremonie der 'consecratio virginum' verwendet worden, da der Bischof als Vertreter Christi diese Worte singen soll, wenn die Übergabe von Schleier und Ring bevorsteht.[57]

Auch das 'Sanctus, sanctus' ist beiden Spielen gemeinsam, es folgt im *Katharinenspiel* der Krönung der zur Märtyrerin gewordenen Königin und wird von einem Engel vorgetragen; im *Zehnjungfrauenspiel* eröffnet das dreifache Sanctus einen Preisgesang der klugen Jungfrauen. Im Fall des *Zehnjungfrauenspiels* merkt Amstutz den quasi-eucharistischen Charakter der Szene an, insofern der Eintritt der Figuren in den Himmel vorgeführt wird und die Haltung der Adoration mit diesem Gesangseinschub betont scheint;[58] im *Katharinenspiel* ist eine ähnliche Funktion naheliegend, dann folgt ohne weitere Verzögerung die Rede des Maxentius, die die Handlung vorantreibt und Porphirius und sein Martyrium ins Zentrum rückt. Der Gesang hat hier erkennbar zugleich den Charakter eines Szenenabschlusses, so dass die Aufnahme und Krönung der Märtyrerin beendet ist.

Die Verteilung der Gesänge weist in beiden Spielen Ähnlichkeiten auf, denn die Eingangsprozession wird im *Zehnjungfrauenspiel* ebenso wie die himmlische Krönung der Klugen gesanglich unterlegt; im mittleren Handlungsteil vor der Aburteilung der Törichten ergibt sich ein steter Wechsel aus gesprochenen und gesungenen Passagen. So sind eine ähnliche Darstellungstechnik und Handlungsanlage gewählt, um das eschatologische Potential der Parabel zu betonen, denn die Aufnahme in die himmlische Gemeinschaft und die Verstoßung in die Hölle werden auch hier aufgegriffen.[59]

---

56 Amstutz, *Ludus*, S. 213. Die Autorin geht für das *Zehnjungfrauenspiel* von einer Aufführung als Responsorium aus, indem die *Dominica persona* und die *Angeli* abwechselnd singen (S. 221).

57 Amstutz, *Ludus*, S. 210–11 und 225, beruft sich auf das Pontificale des Wilhelm Durandus (Ende des dreizehnten Jahrhunderts).

58 Amstutz, *Ludus*, S. 236.

59 Im zweiten Fall ist dies effektvoll mit Klagen ausformuliert. Eine Verbindung zu den Marienklagen der Osterspiel-Tradition führt Beckers an, siehe *Das Spiel*, hg. von Beckers, S. 39.

Raumregie und Klangregie

Die Raumregie und Klangregie des *Katharinenspiels* scheinen in der Weise koordiniert zu sein, dass nur bestimmte Bühnenräume gezielt eine klangliche Hervorhebung erfahren. Dies betrifft v. a. den Marterplatz, der wiederholt Ort der himmlischen Erscheinungen ist und von dem die himmelfahrtsähnlichen Abläufe ihren Ausgang nehmen.[60] Bei der Erhebung Katharinas ist die Verbindung mit der himmlischen Sphäre in größtmöglicher Deutlichkeit gegeben, durch Figuren, vielfachen Gesang und prozessionsartige Proxemik. Die mediale Kombination unterstützt zugleich die dogmatisch erlaubte Vorstellung von der unmittelbaren Heiligkeit der Märtyrerinnen und Märtyrer.[61] Wie anhand dieses Befundes deutlich wird, sind es gerade die dynamischen, erspielten Räume, die intensiv gesanglich ausgestaltet sind und durch ihre fluide Räumlichkeit einen Übergangsbereich zur Transzendenz markieren. Obwohl sie keinen festen Bühnenort besitzen, sind sie handlungsimmanent und heilsdidaktisch mit hoher Bedeutung geladen. Die Gesänge des Übergangsbereichs dienen dazu, ähnlich wie in liturgischen Partien des Oster- und Passionsspieltyps, den Sinn erläuternd abzusichern; dies steht im Einklang mit der seit Augustinus vorliegenden theologischen Maßgabe, dass nicht die *poena*, sondern allein die *causa* das Martyrium ausmache.[62] Die *poena*, die Pein der Märtyrerfiguren, wird den Zuschauern nie unkommentiert überlassen, so dass die *causa* immer wieder zur Sprache kommt und mit Verdienst und Lohn erklärt wird. Die Klangregie hat insofern eine musikalisch-ästhetische und eine kommunikative Aufgabe, ebenso hat sie eine aufmerksamkeitslenkende und gewissermaßen gattungstypisch disziplinierende Funktion, da sie nach den Szenen körperlicher Gewalt darauf abzielt, die geistlichen Inhalte zu stützen und die Transzendenz zu inszenieren.

Raum und Klang sind Teil eines Wirkungskalküls und werden durch den Spielleiter überlegt eingesetzt. Durch ihre Betonung der transgressiven Vorgänge und des exzeptionellen Handlungsrahmens, der die entsprechenden Szenen auszeichnet, bilden sie die Grundlage für nachdrückliche Wirkungseffekte. Der Spielleiter bedient sich schließlich nicht nur eines fluiden Raumes, sondern mit dem Gesang auch einer per se

---

60 Der Marterplatz scheint zwar eine Konkretisierung der bedrohlichen 'Sündenwelt' zu sein, in Kontrast zum Himmel, doch ist gerade dieser Platz in der Raumkonzeption des Stücks mit der überirdischen Welt verknüpft.

61 Da Christus im Märtyrer gegenwärtig sei (Tertullian, *De pudicitia*, 22, PL II. Sp. 1027), ist diesem nach der kirchlichen Tradition der 'Charakter eines Heiligen' eigen; die Apokalypse des Johannes legt nahe, dass Märtyrer sofort nach dem Tod in die unmittelbare Nähe Gottes gelangen (Offenbarung 7. 15). Zu Tertullian vgl. Frutaz u. a., 'Martyrer', Sp. 129; Rahner, 'Martyrium', Sp. 136; Henze, 'Martyrer', Sp. 1440.

62 Siehe Frutaz u. a., 'Martyrer', Sp. 127–28 (mit Verweis auf Augustinus, *Ep.* 89. 2; *Enarrationes in Psalmos* 34, 2, 1, PL XXXIII, Sp. 310; PL XXXVI, Sp. 333).

transitorischen Kunst; speziell die göttlichen Begegnungen des Spiels sind mit ihnen ausgestattet und als Übergangsereignisse markiert, so dass die Grenzen zwischen irdischer und jenseitiger Handlung aufgelöst erscheinen. Die epiphanischen Szenen sind ferner mit einem überirdischen Figurenkreis versehen sowie mit einer exzeptionellen Körperlichkeit der Märtyrerinnen und Märtyrer in ihrem Zwischenzustand zwischen Diesseits und Jenseits; doch mehr noch sind sie geprägt durch das Geschehen einer Transformation, die den Kern des Szenentyps 'Himmelfahrt' darstellt: Gerade sie ist schwierig abzubilden, am sichtbarsten ist sie in Katharinas Erhebung nach Ablegen ihres Körpers — nach der Bestattung auf dem Berg Sinai ist Katharina weiter als Figur in Aktion —, wobei dies jedoch theologisch unkommentiert bleibt.[63] Die Verwendung des fluiden Raumes stellt unter diesen Umständen eine hagiographische Raumpraxis[64] dar, die Grenzen durchlässig erscheinen lässt und den spezifischen Zwischenzustand der Hauptfiguren dramaturgisch übersetzen und ausdrücken kann. Im *Katharinenspiel* bildet diese Raumpraxis den Rahmen der Heiligwerdung der Märtyrerinnen und Märtyrer. Ihre Heiligwerdung konstituiert sich so nicht nur durch hagiographische Topoi wie Bekenntnis, Tugendbeweis und Tod, sondern beruht auf einem Zwischenstatus und einem Zwischenort zwischen den sonst symbolischen Raumordnungen der physischen Bühne. Zugleich kommt es hier zu Präsenzeffekten: In ihm verschwimmen die zeitlichen Grenzen zwischen Vergangenheit und Gegenwart, da Legendenspiele in der Regel auf die Heilsereignisse der antiken Zeit nur im Modus des Vergangenen eingehen können und die Zeit nach Christi Erdenleben fokussieren, während das *Katharinenspiel* ein Bemühen zeigt, die Christusfigur intensiv und möglichst häufig als handelnde Figur einzusetzen. Die Hauptfigur Katharina ist nicht nur durch Erinnerung, Appell und imitatives Leiden an der Heilsgewinnung beteiligt, sondern die *Dominica persona* führt die Heilsgewinnung mehrfach an Beispielfiguren vor. Die Auferstehung wiederholt sich so in Form einer Aufnahme ins Himmelreich an verschiedenen Figuren als gegenwärtiges Geschehen. Der in das Märtyrerleben verlegte Konflikt zwischen christlicher Einstellung und sündenverfallener Mitwelt ist für das Publikum leicht zu aktualisieren und auf die Alltagswelt zu übertragen. Katharina

---

63 Vgl. *KSp*, V. 661a–c und später V. 681a. Ob hier ein 'Auferstehungsleib' sichtbar gemacht werden soll, bleibt unklar. Markante theologische Positionen in dieser Diskussion vertraten Origenes (er unterscheidet zwischen Materialität und Form/Eidos, wobei letztere für Identität sorge) und Thomas von Aquin (er nimmt an, dass dieselben Materieteile wiederbelebt würden, die der irdische Leib besaß). Vgl. Ratzinger, 'Auferstehungsleib', Sp. 1052–53. Das Beharren der kirchlichen Tradition, dass der Erdenleib eine Rolle spiele, wird als Teil antignostischer Argumentation erläutert von Greshake, 'Auferstehung', Sp. 1200.

64 Zur situativ sich konstituierenden 'Raumpraxis' gegenüber der 'Raumordnung' als Bezugsrahmen siehe Kramer und Dünne, 'Einleitung', S. 18–19.

spricht in ihrer letzten Figurenrede von der Ablehnung von Reichtum und Ehre sowie ihrer Verachtung der Welt; auch hier ist Aktualisierung und Vergegenwärtigung als Wirkungsintention des Spiels erkennbar, und die Heilige gewinnt Imitabilität.[65]

Hagiographische Beobachtungen

Zum Schluss sollen einige hagiographische Beobachtungen festgehalten werden. Die dramaturgische Konzeption gestaltet die Heiligwerdung Katharinas als einen Aufstiegsprozess, im räumlichen und geistlichen Sinn, aber auch als eine Folge von wunderhaften Ereignissen, die nach weltlichen Gesetzen nicht erklärbar sind. Heilsökonomische Vorstellungen treten hinzu, denn gegenüber der Leistung der Heiligen ist im *Katharinenspiel* auffallend die Gnade als bestimmendes Moment zurückgedrängt — sie wird nur zweimal[66] erwähnt. An ihre Stelle treten das heroische Verhalten und der verdiente Lohn, die zahlreich in den Figurenreden angeführt werden mit Begriffen aus dem Wortfeld des Streitens und der Stärke; ein Engel kommentiert den Tod der Königin etwa: 'Eia, nu moge wi alle wol merke | an deser juncvrowen groze sterke' (*KSp*, V. 538–39).

Dieses Wortfeld bestimmt die semantische Färbung der Redepassagen und verrät zugleich die hagiographische Deutung des Martyriums. Es manifestiert sich eine Heiligkeitsvorstellung, die deutlich das Virtus-Ideal in den Figurenreden herausstellt und den eschatologischen Horizont der Martyrien erweckt, der bereits in der jüdischen Tradition vorlag, dann in frühchristlicher Zeit und auch in der Apokalypse des Johannes belegt ist; die Ideen von der Krone des Lebens und dem Triumph im Jenseits, der die Glaubenszeugen erwartet, werden in der Apokalypse des Johannes vorgebracht (Offenbarung 2. 10; 6. 9–11; 20. 4).[67] Die Figur Katharinas spricht so etwa nach der göttlichen Erscheinung im Kerker zu Maxentius: 'diner pine inachte ich nicht, | wan Got der ladit mich' (*KSp*, V. 416–17). Die *Dominica persona* öffnet den Märtyrern und Märtyrerinnen unmittelbar nach ihrem Tod das göttliche Reich: '[Nu] komit, ie gebenediten, | in mines vater riche' (*KSp*, V. 591–92). Auch führt die *Dominica persona* im Handlungsfinale als Grund für Katharinas Leiden ausgerechnet die Gerechtigkeit an, die sie den Verlockungen der Heiden vorzog:

---

65 Hierzu speziell Weitbrecht, '*Imitatio* und Imitabilität', S. 204–19, die das performative Potential der *Imitatio* untersucht.

66 *KSp*, V. 664 und 689. Zur zentralen Bedeutung der Gnade im theologischen Verständnis des Martyriums siehe Scheuer, 'Martyrer', Sp. 1441.

67 Die theologische Tradition vermittelt außerdem die Vorstellung, die Märtyrer seien Beisitzer beim Jüngsten Gericht; siehe Frutaz u. a., 'Martyrer', Sp. 129 (ohne genauen Beleg).

wan du dorch mich hast gehat
mangir hande ungemach,
und dorch di gerechtikeit
woldis lide jamer und leit (*KSp*, V. 674–77)

> (Denn du hast für mich manches Leid erlitten und für die Gerechtigkeit wolltest du Jammer und Schmerz erdulden)

So wird mit dem Gerichtskontext eine Akzentsetzung aufgerufen, die das Stück zugleich inhaltlich mit dem *Thüringischen Zehnjungfrauenspiel* verbindet. Die dynamischen Räume und klanglichen *beatificationes* vermitteln eine leistungsorientierte, aber hoffnungsvolle Aussicht auf das Jenseits; die Aufnahme in den Himmel und die Heiligwerdung werden gezielt mit einem klanglichen Signum versehen, das in den Gesangsfolgen eine dialogische Form aufweist.

Der Gerichtskontext und die Teufelsszenen sowie die weitgehend fehlende Gnadenperspektive bilden jedoch das Gegengewicht und manifestieren zugleich bekannte theologische Diskussionsfelder der spätmittelalterlichen Frömmigkeitsgeschichte, die das Spiel erfassen. Die Wahrnehmung und Deutung dessen, was auf dem Bühnenplatz physisch vorlag und sich als dynamisches Geschehen entfaltete, war anspruchsvoll: Diese komplexe Aufgabe betrifft auch die Wahrnehmung von Diesseits und Jenseits, die mittels der Elemente Raum und Klang in das Bühnengeschehen integriert wurden.

Bibliographie

Unedierte Quellen

Handschriften

Fulda, Hochschul- und Landesbibliothek, 100 Aa 55
St. Gallen, Stiftsbibliothek, Cod. Sang. 390
————, Cod. Sang. 391

Inkunabeln

Breviarium Moguntinum (Straßburg: Johann Grüninger, 1487) (GW 05398)
Breviarium Romanum (Venedig: Nicolas Jenson, 1478) (GW 05101)

Edierte Quellen

Analecta hymnica medii aevi, hg. von Guido Maria Dreves u. a., 55 Bde (Leipzig: Reisland, 1886–1926), Bd. XXVI (1897) und XXVIII (1898): *Historiae rhythmicae* 6 und 7
Augustinus, Aurelius, 'Opera Omnia', in *Patrologiae Cursus Completus* (*PL*), *Series Prima*, hg. von Jacques-Paul Migne, Bd. XXXIII und XXXVI (Paris: Migne, 1865)
Iacopo da Varazze [Jacobus de Voragine], *Legenda aurea*, hg. von Giovanni Paolo Maggioni, Millennio Medievale, 6/2, 2. Aufl. (Florenz: SISMEL, 1998)
Das Spiel von den zehn Jungfrauen und das Katharinenspiel, hg. von Otto Beckers, Germanistische Abhandlungen 24 (Breslau: Marcus, 1905)
Tertullian, Quintus Septimius Florentius, 'Opera Omnia', in *Patrologiae Cursus Completus* (*PL*), *Series Prima*, hg. von Jacques-Paul Migne, Bd. II (Paris: Migne, 1844)

Forschungsliteratur

Amstutz, Renate, *Ludus de decem virginibus. Recovery of the Sung Liturgical Core of the Thuringian Zehnjungfrauenspiel*, Studies and Texts, 140 (Toronto: Pontifical Institute of Mediaeval Studies, 2002)
Assion, Peter, 'Katharina von Alexandrien', in *Die deutsche Literatur des Mittelalters. Verfasserlexikon*, 2. Aufl., hg. von Kurt Ruh u. a., 11 Bde (Berlin u. a.: De Gruyter, 1978–2008), Bd. IV (1983), Sp. 1055–73
Barton, Ulrich, 'Inszenierung und Transzendierung von Räumlichkeit im Passionsspiel', in *Orte der Imagination – Räume des Affekts. Die mediale Formierung des Sakralen*, hg. von Elke Koch u. a. (Paderborn: Fink, 2016), S. 439–60

Bierhals Jefferis, Sibylle Anna, *Ein spätmittelalterliches Katharinenspiel aus dem Cod. Ger. 4 der University of Pennsylvania: Text und Studien zu seiner legendengeschichtlichen Einordnung*, Göppinger Arbeiten zur Germanistik, 430 (Göppingen: Kümmerle, 2007)

Biermann, Heinrich, 'Die deutschsprachigen Legendenspiele des späten Mittelalters und der frühen Neuzeit' (Diss., Universität Köln, 1977)

——, 'Mühlhäuser (thüringisches) Katharinenspiel', in *Die deutsche Literatur des Mittelalters. Verfasserlexikon*, 2. Aufl., hg. von Kurt Ruh u. a., 11 Bde (Berlin u. a.: De Gruyter, 1978–2008), Bd. VI (1987), Sp. 721–23

Brinker, Klaus, 'Formen der Heiligkeit. Studien zur Gestalt des Heiligen in mittelhochdeutschen Legendenepen des 12. und 13. Jahrhunderts' (Diss., Universität Bonn, 1966)

Creizenach, Wilhelm, *Geschichte des neueren Dramas*, 3 Bde (New York: Blom, 1965), Bd. 1: Mittelalter und Frührenaissance

Dietel, Gerhard, *Wörterbuch Musik* (München: DTV; Kassel u. a.: Bärenreiter, 2000)

Fasbender, Christoph, 'Erfurt', in *Schreiborte des deutschen Mittelalters. Skriptorien – Werke – Mäzene*, hg. von Martin Schubert (Berlin u. a.: De Gruyter, 2013), S. 119–49

Fischer-Lichte, Erika, *Ästhetik des Performativen*, 10. Aufl., edition suhrkamp, 2373 (Frankfurt a. M.: Suhrkamp, 2017)

Frutaz, Amato Pietro, 'Katharina', in *Lexikon für Theologie und Kirche*, 2. Aufl., hg. von Josef Höfer u. a., 14 Bde (Freiburg: Herder, 1986), Bd. VI (1986), Sp. 60–61

——, 'Martyrer', in *Lexikon für Theologie und Kirche*, 2. Aufl., hg. von Josef Höfer u. a., 14 Bde (Freiburg: Herder, 1986), Bd. VII (1986), Sp. 127–33

Greshake, Gisbert, 'Auferstehung der Toten. V. Theologie- und dogmengeschichtlich, VI. Systematisch-theologisch', in *Lexikon für Theologie und Kirche*, 3. Aufl., hg. von Walter Kasper u. a., 11 Bde (Freiburg u. a.: Herder, 1993–2001), Bd. 1 (1993), Sp. 1198–206

Günzel, Stephan, *Raum. Eine kulturwissenschaftliche Einführung*, 3. Aufl., utb, 5360 (Bielefeld: transcript, 2020)

Heinzelmann, Martin, 'Translation', in *Lexikon des Mittelalters*, 9 Bde (München: DTV, 2002), Bd. VIII (2002), Sp. 947–49

Henze, Barbara, 'Martyrer, Martyrium. III. Historisch-theologisch', in *Lexikon für Theologie und Kirche*, 3. Aufl., hg. von Walter Kasper u. a., 11 Bde (Freiburg u. a.: Herder, 1993–2001), Bd. VI (1997), Sp. 1439–41

Kemper, Angelika, 'Bewegte Grenzen. Beobachtungen zum kollusiven Potential "heiliger" Figuren und Gegenstände im *Mühlhäuser (thüringischen) Katharinenspiel*', *European Medieval Drama*, 25 (2021), 143–74

Kirchner, Thomas, *Raumerfahrung im geistlichen Spiel des Mittelalters*, Europäische Hochschulschriften, XXX/20 (Frankfurt a. M. u. a.: Lang, 1985)

Koch, Elke, 'Formen und Bedingungen von Sprachgewalt in Katharinenlegende und -spiel', in *Blutige Worte. Internationales und interdisziplinäres Kolloquium zum Verhältnis von Sprache und Gewalt*, hg. von Jutta Eming u. a., Berliner Mittelalter- und Frühneuzeitforschung, 4 (Göttingen: V&R unipress, 2008), S. 15–30

Königshof, Kaspar, *Zur Geschichte des geistlichen Theaters in der Stadt Erfurt und ihrer Umgebung. Geschrieben anläßlich der 1250-Jahrfeier der Stadt Erfurt im Jahre 1992* (Leipzig: St. Benno, 1992)

Kramer, Kirsten und Jörg Dünne, 'Einleitung. Theatralität und Räumlichkeit', in *Theatralität und Räumlichkeit. Raumordnungen und Raumpraktiken im theatralen Mediendispositiv*, hg. von Jörg Dünne u. a. (Würzburg: Königshausen & Neumann, 2009), S. 15–32

Linke, Hansjürgen, 'Thüringische Zehnjungfrauenspiele', in *Die deutsche Literatur des Mittelalters. Verfasserlexikon*, 2. Aufl., hg. von Kurt Ruh u. a., 11 Bde (Berlin u. a.: De Gruyter, 1978–2008), vol. IX (1995), Sp. 915–18

Macardle, Peter, 'Die Gesänge des *St. Galler Mittelrheinischen Passionspiels*. Ein Beitrag zu Rekonstruktion und Lokalisierung', in *Die Vermittlung geistlicher Inhalte im deutschen Mittelalter. Internationales Symposium, Roscrea 1994*, hg. von Timothy R. Jackson u. a. (Tübingen: Niemeyer, 1996), S. 255–70

Mertens, Volker, 'Klang und Sinn. Beobachtungen und Überlegungen zur Musik in geistlichen Spielen', in *'Wat nyeus verfraeyt dat herte ende verlicht den sin'. Studien zum Schauspiel des Mittelalters und der Frühen Neuzeit*. Festschrift für Carla Dauven-van Knippenberg zum 65. Geburtstag, hg. von Elke Huwiler u. a. (Leiden und Boston: Brill Rodopi, 2015), S. 32–52

Rahner, Karl, 'Martyrium', in *Lexikon für Theologie und Kirche*, 2. Aufl., hg. von Josef Höfer u. a., 14 Bde (Freiburg: Herder, 1986), Bd. VII (1986), Sp. 134–38

Ratzinger, Joseph, 'Auferstehungsleib', in *Lexikon für Theologie und Kirche*, 2. Aufl., hg. von Josef Höfer u. a., 14 Bde (Freiburg: Herder, 1986), Bd. I (1986), Sp. 1052–53

Rosenfeld, Hellmut, *Legende*, 4. Aufl., Sammlung Metzler, 9 (Stuttgart: Metzler, 1982)

Scheuer, Manfred, 'Martyrer, Martyrium. IV. Systematisch-theologisch', in *Lexikon für Theologie und Kirche*, 3. Aufl., hg. von Walter Kasper u. a., 11 Bde (Freiburg u. a.: Herder, 1993–2001), Bd. VI (1997), Sp. 1441–43

Schill, Peter, 'Ikonographie und Kult der Hl. Katharina von Alexandrien im Mittelalter. Studien zu den szenischen Darstellungen aus der Katharinenlegende' (Diss., LMU München, 2005)

Schulze, Ursula, *Geistliche Spiele im Mittelalter und in der Frühen Neuzeit. Von der liturgischen Feier zum Schauspiel. Eine Einführung* (Berlin: Schmidt, 2012)

Simmler, Franz, 'VII. Text-, Teiltext- und Textteilallianz "Brevier"', in *Textsorten und Textallianzen um 1500*, hg. von Mechthild Habermann u. a., Literarische und religiöse Textsorten und Textallianzen um 1500, 1 (Berlin: Weidler, 2009), S. 478–501

Ukena, Elke, *Die deutschen Mirakelspiele des Spätmittelalters. Studien und Texte*, 2 Bde, Arbeiten zur Mittleren Deutschen Literatur und Sprache, 1 (Bern u. a.: Lang, 1975)

Weitbrecht, Julia, '*Imitatio* und Imitabilität. Zur Medialität von Legende und Legendenspiel', *Beiträge zur Geschichte der deutschen Sprache und Literatur*, 134 (2012), 204–19

Internetressourcen

Cantus: A Database for Latin Ecclesiastical Chant. Inventories of Chant Sources, https://cantus.uwaterloo.ca/id/007524 (Zugriff: 20. Dezember 2023)

SUSANNA SCAVELLO

Du Moyen Âge à aujourd'hui

Sainte Barbe en scène

▼ **ABSTRACT** We will consider two levels of the character of the martyred saint — her body and her word — while questioning the contradiction between these two dimensions from a performative point of view, if we imagine the saint Barbe mysteries coming to life on stage. Furthermore, we will try to make distinctions between image, narrative, and dramatization of late medieval female martyrdom in terms of reception. We will first question the presumed passivity and sexualization of the heroine's body that has been proposed by contemporary readings that see the martyr primarily as an object of male desire and gaze. We will discuss the reaction of the character's body to the violence suffered in the theatre. Then we will examine the manifestation of the speech of Barbe, between joy, provocation and 'implacable decision', thus showing the paradoxical presence of the saint on the scene. We will conclude by wondering why we should revive these medieval plays on today's stages.

▼ **KEYWORDS:** mystery, St Barbara, St Agata, gender, violence, catharsis, special effects, body, speech, independence, actualization.

Susanna Scavello (susanna.scavello@hotmail.it) is postdoc researcher for Theatre Studies at the Université Paris Nanterre. Her PhD dissertation (cotutelle: University of Bologna and Université de Picardie Jules Verne) dealt with heroines in fourteenth- to sixteenth-century French theatre.

European Medieval Drama, 27 (2023), 131–160
BREPOLS ❧ PUBLISHERS   10.1484/J.EMD.5.137681

Nous allons considérer dans cet article deux aspects du personnage de la sainte martyre au théâtre, son corps et sa parole, en questionnant la contradiction qui existe entre ces deux dimensions, si on imagine les mystères de sainte Barbe prenant vie sur scène.[1] Nous tenterons en outre de distinguer de quelle façon la représentation iconographique, la narration et la dramatisation du martyre féminin au Moyen Âge tardif supposent une réception différente, car le medium influence la réflexion qu'on peut mobiliser sur de telles représentations. Notre propos se concentrera en premier lieu sur le corps de l'héroïne, sur la réaction de son corps à la violence subie. Nous nous interrogerons sur ses prétendues passivité et impassibilité et sur les lectures contemporaines qui en ont été faites, lesquelles la présentent avant tout comme objet du désir et du regard masculins (*male gaze*). Après quoi nous aborderons la manifestation de sa parole, entre joie, provocation et, pour le dire avec Artaud, 'décision implacable'. Le propos s'achèvera en se demandant quel pourrait être le sens de faire renaître les pièces médiévales de sainte Barbe sur les scènes d'aujourd'hui. Tout en considérant le contexte large, européen, des drames hagiographiques au féminin, le texte sur lequel s'appuiera davantage notre réflexion est le *Mystère de sainte Barbe en cinq journées* (BnF fr. 976, xve siècle) :[2] sainte Barbe s'avère la sainte la plus représentée au Moyen Âge et celle dont nous possédons le plus grand nombre de textes dramatiques conservés en France.[3] Des références intertextuelles avec le *Mystère de sainte Barbe en deux journées* et la *Sacra Rappresentazione* toscane de sainte Agathe[4] enrichiront notre analyse.

1. Passivité du corps, entre sexualisation et impassibilité

Le corps de la martyre tel que représenté sur la scène serait-il vraiment, d'un côté, sexualisé, et de l'autre, passif et imperturbable ?

La plupart des réflexions critiques qui ont été proposées sur les représentations du martyre féminin au Moyen Âge envisagent la figure de la sainte qui se sacrifie pour le Christ et qui subit avec une résistance étonnante des violences atroces en termes de corps passif sexualisé, en raison même du caractère genré de ces supplices (mastectomie, prostitution

---

1 La présente réflexion s'inspire des questions dont nous avons discuté dans notre thèse et qui méritent d'être analysées davantage, voir Scavello, *Les femmes*.

2 *Le Mystère*, dir. Longtin *et al.*

3 Nous connaissons une vingtaine d'attestations de représentations de son mystère entre la France et les Flandres, et trois textes : le mystère manuscrit en cinq journées, un rôle de Barbe (édition : Chocheyras, *Le théâtre*, pp. 93–108) et un mystère en deux journées, imprimé, du début du xvie siècle ('*Mystère*', dir. Longtin)..

4 'Rappresentazione', dir. Toschi.

forcée, etc.).[5] Certains critiques se sont intéressés à la réception possible de tels spectacles, tant par le spectateur médiéval que par un possible spectateur d'aujourd'hui, en s'appuyant pour justifier leur propos sur l'enluminure de Jean Fouquet représentant sainte Apolline (xve siècle). Cette image, bien connue de tous les historiens du théâtre médiéval, a nourri la vision qu'ils se faisaient de la sainte martyre suppliciée, dans et en dehors de la fiction théâtrale. Autrement dit, une représentation iconographique, visuelle, a été superposée à celle de la martyre telle que jouée sur la scène du théâtre. Or de nombreuses études ont souligné la dimension illusionniste de cette peinture, et sa profonde différence avec la mimésis théâtrale[6]. Une autre référence, la théorie féministe de Laura Mulvey sur le male gaze, des années 1970, a suscité l'adhésion de certains chercheurs.[7] Ainsi Marla Carlson[8] ou Robert Potter (ce dernier dans le cadre du ixe colloque de la SITM, en 1998) se sont interrogés sur les réactions du public médiéval au spectacle de violence extrême offert par l'acharnement sur le corps d'une jeune vierge pendant le martyre, un spectacle qu'ils considèrent comme pornographique, tout en s'interrogeant sur la possible réponse du lecteur-spectateur d'aujourd'hui :

> Nevertheless, it seems to me that what has transpired in the theatrical assault on the body of Saint Barbara is deeply pornographic. The audience has been invited to participate, voyeuristically, in the defilement of a virgin ; simultaneously, they have been provided with the edifying illusion that they are witnessing not something degrading, but something inspiring — the triumph of a holy martyr-in-the-making. This seems to my eye to be a highly compromised aesthetic and moral transaction, but certainly one with built-in popular appeal.[9]

Ce trait voyeuriste a été repris par Francesc Massip dans une récente étude sur la fiction de la torture dans les drames religieux, et dans un précèdent ouvrage, écrit en collaboration avec L. Kovács, consacré à la *Consueta de Santa Agata*, où on cite précisément Robert Potter.[10] L'historienne de l'art Martha Easton avait également convoqué voyeurisme et caractère

---

5 Voir les pièces consacrées à sainte Agathe et à sainte Barbe, qui subissent l'amputation des seins et à sainte Agnès, condamnée à s'exhiber nue dans un lupanar et victime d'une tentative de viol.

6 Dominguez, 'La scène et l'enluminure'.

7 Laura Mulvey, cinéaste et critique cinématographique britannique pose la première la question du *male gaze* comme facteur déterminant dans la culture dans Mulvey, 'Visual Pleasure'. Nous signalons la traduction française dans Mulvey, *Au-delà du plaisir*, pp. 36–66.

8 Carlson, 'Spectator Responses'.

9 Potter, 'Pornography'.

10 Massip, 'Cuerpo', p. 113 ; Massip et Kovács, 'The Late Medieval Catalan Play', p. 270. *La consueta de santa Agata* est la seule pièce catalane conservée avec une protagoniste féminine.

pornographique, pour interroger la réception des représentations visuelles du martyre de sainte Agathe :

> For some medieval male viewers respect and esteem for St Agatha and her suffering probably vied with an interest in her body and the sadistic, voyeuristic potential of her torture scene. Agatha becomes a conflation of sacrificial victim and sexual woman. Centuries after martyrdom essentially ended in the orthodox Christian West, texts and images such as those of the *Golden Legend* fulfilled the popular interest in women's bodies with their graphic depictions of the semi-nude or fully nude bodies of female martyrs and the myriad ways in which they were tortured. Margaret Miles terms this obsessive interest in female anatomy 'religious pornography'.[11]

Il est intéressant de remarquer que ce paradoxe, qui dit tout le caractère perturbant et ambigu de la célébration chrétienne de la sainteté féminine, a été décrit en termes de 'compromis', non seulement par Potter, mais aussi, plus récemment, par Massimo Bonafin à propos de la scène de l'exposition d'Agnès dans le lupanar, dans le jeu provençal qui lui est consacré, où le regard masculin complaisant de l'auteur et des spectateurs internes et externes à la représentation théâtrale se mêlerait à l'intention édifiante du texte.[12] Jonathan Beck également, dans une étude pionnière sur le sujet, avait comme Potter fait référence à la notion de pornographie, en rapprochant les *fatistes* médiévaux 'de leurs successeurs d'aujourd'hui (*fatistes modernes*) chez qui on voit les fantasmes de la frustration masculine se donner libre cours dans une littérature et un cinéma porno-vengeurs'.[13]

Dans les sources dramatiques, le corps de la sainte est en effet de plus en plus amplement donné en spectacle au fil du texte : de la mire du persécuteur et des tyrans, le corps de Barbe passe au spectacle public. C'est la même procédure que l'on observe dans le *Jeu de Sainte Agnès*,[14] où la jeune fille, d'abord objet du regard et du désir du fils du préfet, Apodixeis, le devient ensuite des ribauds à l'intérieur du bordel, puis de la foule des Romains qui réclament son exécution sur le bûcher. Or, à la différence des hagiographies en vers des XIIᵉ–XIIIᵉ siècles analysées par Brigitte Cazelles,[15] dans les textes *par personnages*, l'héroïne martyre ne devient jamais à proprement parler une victime muette et passive, puisqu'elle déploie au contraire face au supplice une parole éloquente. Si on considère les transpositions dramatiques, il faut se poser cette question : le corps de la martyre est-il, comme celui de l'Apolline de Fouquet, un corps insensible

---

11 Easton, 'Saint Agatha', p. 98.
12 Bonafin, 'Alcune considerazioni', p. 278.
13 Beck, 'Sexe', pp. 27–28.
14 *Il mistero*, dir. de Santis.
15 Cazelles, *The Lady*, p. 51.

DU MOYEN ÂGE À AUJOURD'HUI   135

cohérent avec le motif du saint indemne de la tradition hagiographique, et se trouve-t-il aux antipodes de celui de la mystique, expressif à l'excès dans ses manifestations de souffrance corporelle en imitation du Christ ?[16] Et, autre question essentielle, le personnage de la sainte était-il joué par un acteur ou par une actrice ?

Les lectures qui ont été proposées nous semblent plus pertinentes pour les domaines iconographique et hagiographique que pour celui des représentations théâtrales. Il en ressort l'image d'une héroïne-victime, objet passif de violence, d'agression sexuelle, du regard masculin, le corps se confondant avec l'esprit, la passivité relevant du corps tout autant que de l'esprit. Nous aimerions mettre à jour ces analyses partielles, quoique fines et suggestives, en considérant dans sa globalité l'action de l'héroïne martyre dramatisée, action qui ne se borne pas au martyre du corps. En effet, à bien écouter les répliques de Barbe, pétries de volonté et de conscience, elle ne se manifeste pas comme victime passive, même dans l'acmé de son martyre. Que se passe-t-il donc de singulier dans les textes théâtraux ? En quoi réside l'écart entre l'Apolline de Fouquet et l'héroïne sainte des mystères ? La martyre est-elle passive sur scène ? Le scénario s'avère complexe, riche en contradictions, surtout dues au fait que le théâtre, mimésis par excellence de la réalité, nécessite un certain réalisme et présente un personnage incarné, paradoxalement caractérisé par un divorce entre le corps et les mots, à mi-chemin entre douleur et joie. Face à des tortures inhumaines, le corps de la sainte serait-il représenté comme impassible dans la performance du martyre ? Et encore, est-il possible que la force rhétorique des héroïnes ne soit pas soutenue par un corps vibrant, que leur voix vigoureuse émane d'un corps insensible ?

1.1. Un corps sexualisé ?

Les supplices infligés au corps de Barbe par des bourreaux qui en sont à la fois agents et spectateurs concernent aussi des zones corporelles marquées d'un sens sexuel, caractéristiques de la féminité de la jeune fille, créant ainsi un contraste plus aigu entre l'aspiration de la vierge à une intégrité pure et le morcèlement physique exhibé de son corps. Dans le *Mystère de Barbe en deux journées*, voici le commentaire d'un tyran quand la sainte est battue, pendue au gibet : 'Je luy donray sus la mamelle | Tant que mon courget en fauldra' (vv. 1984–85). À quoi l'on peut associer la scène du supplice des torches ardentes dans une fresque de Lorenzo Lotto (1524), où les torches brûlent le corps de Barbe au niveau des seins et

---

16 Carlson, 'Spectator Responses'.

du ventre.[17] La mutilation des seins, en frappant un organe au Moyen Âge comme aujourd'hui érotisé, et en outre emblématique de la prérogative maternelle de la femme,[18] est particulièrement brutale. C'est ce qui arrive à Agathe — dont les seins coupés sont l'attribut iconographique — comme à Barbe, qui subit également le supplice de la mastectomie, quoique son attribut soit plutôt la tour où elle a été enfermée par son père. Ce type de supplice remonte pour les deux saintes à la tradition hagiographique mais reçoit une amplification particulière dans les pièces, surtout dans le cas de sainte Barbe. Toujours dans le mystère en deux journées, après la quatrième guérison du corps de Barbe par les anges et face à la témérité de la jeune fille, Marcien franchit un degré de brutalité supplémentaire en décidant de mutiler les seins de Barbe. Il ajoute de l'horreur à la scène en ordonnant aux tortionnaires de : 'jetter és chiens ses mamelles !' (v. 2281). Les bourreaux, rivalisant de zèle pour mieux achever leur tâche, s'efforcent de satisfaire le tyran. C'est le second bourreau qui l'emporte, en jetant aux chiens 'la mammelle bien jolie', et en touchant mieux la cible, dans une jubilation macabre. À un tel supplice, Barbe répond avec la violence des invectives qui caractérisent sa parole tranchante, comme nous le verrons plus tard.

Dans la version en cinq journées, Marcien explicite verbalement sa volonté d'offenser Barbe dans sa féminité :

> Tranché ses memelles du corps
> Comme chose trés diffamable
> Et en femme vituperable ! (vv. 16621–23).

> (Tranchez les seins de son corps : c'est une action blâmable et honteuse pour une femme !)

Et nous retrouvons le détail sadique d'utiliser des 'cousteaulx esbrecher',

> Affin que la longue trencheure
> Et la tardive desrompeure
> Plus de mal luy face et douleur (vv. 16626–28).

> (Afin que la profonde entaille et la déchirure prolongée lui procurent plus de mal et de douleur.)

Le bourreau Talifart souligne en outre que la beauté physique de Barbe sera ainsi ruinée en sa 'plus belle forme':

---

17 Lotto décore la chapelle Suardi, dans la *Villa* des Comtes Suardi à Trescore Balneario (Bergame), avec des fresques inspirées des vies de sainte Barbe et de sainte Brigitte.

18 Wirth, *L'image*, pp. 73–94.

TALIFART

Voustre corps de beaulté paré
Tantoust sera lait et difforme !
Vous perdéz la plus belle forme
Qui soit en beaulté feminine. (vv. 16647–51)

> (Votre corps paré de beauté sera bientôt laid et déformé ! Vous
> perdrez la plus belle forme de la beauté féminine.)

Un autre, Marpault, parle du sein de Barbe comme 'Gentille Ymaigerie
formelle | En beauté parfaicte et formee' (vv. 1660–61). Le corps de la
martyre dont on remarque la beauté s'avère toujours objet du regard des
personnages masculins, suggérant ainsi une analyse genrée des représentations du martyre. M. Easton, en s'appuyant sur les représentations icono-
graphiques du martyre de sainte Agathe, insiste sur la violence sexuelle
qu'un tel supplice signifie et 'sanctifie', si l'on prête attention moins à la
signification théologique, qu'à la 'visual response' du spectateur face à ces
images, à leur 'visual effect'. Tout en admettant la polysémie symbolique
du sein féminin, la chercheuse soutient que les représentations médiévales
de l'amputation de la sainte sont bien des 'images of sexual violence
justified in the name of religion'. Or, dans le *Mystère de sainte Barbe en cinq
journées*, les répliques de l'héroïne manifestent clairement qu'en mutilant
ses seins, c'est le côté maternel et nourricier que l'on viole : la sainte le
reproche ainsi à Marcien, alors qu'il incite les bourreaux à scier davantage :

MARCÏAN

Saiéz ! Sayéz ! El[le] ne dit
Mot ne demy. El ne sent rien !

BARBARA

Que dirai ge, trés felon Chien,
Tirant crüel trés depiteulx ?
N'es tu point confus ne honteux
De faire a pucelle transcher
Ce que tu as voulu succéz
En ta mere ou temps d'enfance ?
Tu as prins jadis ta substance
Et pasture maternelle
De ta memelle naturelle
De quoy véz cy les deux pareilles.
Tu es criminel a merveilles ! (vv. 1667–79)

> (MARCIAN : Sciez ! Sciez ! Elle ne dit pas un traître mot. Elle ne
> sent rien ! BARBARA : Que devrais-je dire, chien scélérat, cruel et
> pitoyable tyran ? N'éprouves-tu pas de trouble ni de honte à faire
> trancher à une jeune fille ce que tu as voulu sucer à ta mère au

temps de ta petite enfance ? Tu as pris alors ta subsistance et ta nourriture du sein qui t'étais naturel, et dont tu vois ici les deux pareils. Tu es un monstrueux criminel !)

L'image ne peut manquer d'évoquer la substance humaine que le Christ a reçue de la Vierge Marie, à laquelle Notre Dame même, en tant que personnage du mystère, fait précisément référence quand elle demande à son fils d'aller couvrir Barbe, honteusement exposée après avoir été mutilée. La référence à l'allaitement maternel se retrouve dans les répliques d'Agathe, dans la représentation florentine, lorsqu'elle subit le même supplice :

O perfido crudel tristo tyranno
che non ti se ribaldo vergognato
d'aver tagliato quel che più d'un hanno
alla tua madre havesti già poppato[19].

(Oh perfide, cruel, misérable tyran, toi, vaurien, qui n'as pas eu honte d'avoir coupé ce que pendant plus d'une année tu avais jadis tété à ta mère.)

Clément Saliou, quant à lui, sans aucune mention d'une implication sexuelle, voit

dans cette torture spécifique un outrage indirect dirigé contre la Vierge Marie puisqu'une des caractéristiques de ces personnages est d'être vierge et de vouloir le rester, à l'image de Marie. En les mutilant de la sorte, il s'agit d'empêcher toute possibilité symbolique d'une nouvelle Incarnation et de manière générale d'éliminer toute possibilité de vie.[20]

Il nous semble que la dimension de violation de la féminité sexuelle et maternelle de la femme — sans toutefois exclure l'interprétation théologique, en parfaite cohérence avec le cadre culturel et idéologique où ces pièces médiévales s'inscrivent — doive également être envisagée, à la lumière des commentaires concernant sa beauté physique, en particulier, celle de la partie du corps mutilé. Nous voici précisément face à la situation de 'compromis' précédemment évoquée, ou, disons plutôt, de paradoxe : celui de ces personnages, dont la beauté sainte est en même temps une beauté séduisante. Barbe, quant à elle, ne parle qu'à travers le langage de l'esprit et transpose le discours des bourreaux sur un plan spirituel, en déclarant avoir les seins de l'âme, par elle consacrés à Dieu dès son enfance, bien entiers et nourrissant sa vertu spirituelle et intellectuelle :

---

19 Toschi, 'Rappresentazione', p. 60.
20 Saliou, 'Disloquer', p. 180.

Mais j'ay mes memelles entieres
Dedans mon ame qui nourissent
Trestouz les sens qui d'icelle yssent,
Lesquelz j'ay a Dieu consacré
Dés enfance ! (vv. 1685–89)

> (Mais je garde au dedans de mon âme mes seins entiers, qui nourrissent toutes les facultés qui en émanent et que j'ai consacrées à Dieu dès mon enfance !)

Cette constatation revient dans les mots qu'Agathe adresse à Quintien, avec le même procédé syntaxique de l'adversative, qui marque la conscience réconfortante d'une nourriture intérieure :

ma sappi ch'io non ho di questo affanno
ch'io n'ho mille nell'anima appicato
con le qual mi nutrisco e nutrirai
quando sposa a Giesu mi consacrerai.[21]

> (Mais sache que moi, je n'ai pas de telles inquiétudes, car j'en ai mille attachés à mon âme, avec lesquels je me nourris et je me nourrirai quand je me consacrerai épouse de Jésus.)

Tant la référence à l'allaitement maternel que celle aux seins de l'âme dérivent de l'hagiographie de sainte Agathe, comme en témoigne la *Légende Dorée* : 'Ego habeo mamillas integras intus in anima mea ex quibus nutrio omnes sensus meos quas ab infantia domino consecraui'.[22] En revanche, un tel motif n'est pas présent dans l'hagiographie de Barbe — alors qu'on le retrouve dans des dramatisations plus tardives de sa légende

Autre question : la nudité de l'héroïne était-elle véritablement montrée dans les scènes de supplice ? Il nous semble difficile de l'imaginer si le rôle était interprété par un homme, comme dans le cas du mystère de sainte Barbe représenté à Metz en 1485, où la protagoniste était jouée par un jeune garçon.[23] Dans ce cas nous sommes en présence d'un travestissement. Même si le déguisement était une pratique courante dans le théâtre médiéval, il est légitime de s'interroger, dans le sillage de Robert Clark,

---

21 Toschi, 'Rappresentazione', p. 60.

22 Iacopo da Varazze, *Legenda Aurea*, dir. Maggioni, XXXIX : 'De sancta Agatha', p. 298.

23 Petit de Julleville, *Les Mystères*, t. II, p. 48, qui s'appuie sur la *Chronique* de Metz de Philippe de Vigneulles. De même, dans le *Mystère de saint Martin* de Seurre d'Andrieu de la Vigne, il n'y a aucune femme sur scène, seulement des hommes. On en trouve la preuve dans la liste des acteurs que l'on fait suivre du nom de leurs personnages, voir Andrieu de la Vigne, *Le Mystère*, dir. Duplat, pp. 105–15.

sur l'aspect potentiellement transgressif d'une telle performance *queer*.[24] Certes les saintes, à l'instar d'autres rôles féminins importants (la Vierge ou Marie-Madeleine), pouvaient également être jouées par des femmes, comme en témoignent les listes des acteurs de certaines pièces et l'attestation d'actrices professionnelles — le mythe des premières comédiennes remontant à la *commedia dell'arte* ayant été désormais abandonné.[25] Dans l'iconographie de l'époque, les martyres torturées sont en général nues jusqu'à la ceinture,[26] quoique sainte Barbe, dans la légende peinte par Lotto évoquée plus haut, soit représentée entièrement nue pendant la scène du supplice des torches et après la mutilation. Quant à la nudité des personnages martyrisés en scène, une didascalie du *Mystère de saint Étienne Pape* (1548), indique par exemple que le choix est laissé au bon vouloir du maître de jeu.[27]

Plutôt alors que la présence d'un acteur masculin ou non, montré nu ou non, un autre aspect typique et essentiel du théâtre médiéval pourrait aider à (re)considérer l'idée courante d'une martyre 'victime sexuelle' : la pratique des trucages et des effets spéciaux pour les scènes de martyres. Elle a fait l'objet d'intéressantes éditions et études, plus ou moins récentes, basées sur les livres de conduite des meneurs du jeu, véritables manuels de mise en scène,[28] sur les comptes de dépenses d'un spectacle ou sur les didascalies mêmes des textes dramatiques.[29] Lors des événements merveilleux, y compris les supplices ou les décollations, les corps des personnages étaient souvent des 'corps feints', des mannequins et, même dans le cas où les rôles étaient tenus par des acteurs ou des actrices, les parties mutilées, puis rattachées, étaient réalisées par des *feintes* ; toute blessure ou effet sanglant était représenté grâce à des trucages (couleurs, postiche de chair, armes feintes, etc.). L'artifice des agressions était donc patent, malgré la mise en œuvre d'une certaine illusion.

Rappelons ainsi que, lors du miracle de la guérison des seins d'Agathe dans la *sacra rappresentazione*, saint Pierre attache les seins feints au corps de la sainte en prison. Une didascalie externe ('Sancta Agata essendo guarita rende gratie a Dio') et une interne, dans les paroles que, ranimée dans

---

24 L'approfondissement de la question du travestissement et du drag dépasse le propos de cet article. Pour une discussion sur le thème, voir Clark and Sponsler, 'Queer Play'.

25 Voir Muir, 'Woman', la mise à jour de Parussa, 'Le théâtre' et Prevenier, 'Quand un honorable bourgeois'.

26 Voir, par exemple, les miniatures de l'Histoire de Sainte Catherine du *Livre de Belles Heures du Duc de Berry*, chef-d'œuvre de codex enluminé du début du XVe siècle, analysées par Easton, 'Feminism'.

27 Le maître de jeu M. Bousselot, voir Petit de Julleville, *Les Mystères*, t. II, op. 626–27 ; Le Hir, 'Les indications'.

28 *Le livre*, dir. Chohen ; *Il quaderno*, dir. Brovarone.

29 Bordier, 'La violence' ; Dominguez, 'Entre la feinte et le rire' ; Bouhaïk-Gironès, 'Trois documents' ; Massip, 'Cuerpo'.

sa ferveur, elle adresse à Dieu pour son corps guéri ('e or sanato m'hai el corpo necto | e le mammelle rappicchate al pecto',), nous laissent envisager la réalisation d'un trucage : Saint Pierre colle, de toute évidence, des seins feints à sa poitrine, sans que le public s'en aperçoive (par exemple derrière un voile) et Agathe retrouve ainsi son intégrité physique. Nerida Newbigin met à juste titre l'accent sur le caractère fictionnel de ces martyres féminins sur scène, au-delà du sexe de l'acteur-interprète :

> Whether she (the virgin saint) is played by a boy (the dolci canti or 'sweet songs' of the Santa Barbara play may suggest child actors), or by a young man, or by a woman in an all-female context, the audience will not see lust-inspiring female flesh; they will see body-suits ; they will not see real breasts, they will see stage breast that can be hacked off and miraculously restored. The incitement to lust is accompanied by a repudiation of all sexuality.[30]

Le spectacle d'un corps feint, ou contrefait avec des *feintes*, qui subit une prétendue violence 'sexuelle', qu'il soit féminin ou travesti, peut-il susciter sur le public, au Moyen Âge comme aujourd'hui, une forme de jouissance érotique et sadique ? La représentation des parties du corps morcelé dans les mystères hagiographiques était un trait typique des scènes de torture, quel que soit au demeurant le sexe du protagoniste. Ces spectacles violents offraient en effet aux *maîtres es secrets* l'occasion de mettre en œuvre l'étendue de leur savoir-faire pour 'montrer des martyres de plus en plus détaillés', car 'l'homme de théâtre est un technicien et le théâtre montre ce que peut réaliser le théâtre'.[31] Il ne faut pas oublier non plus que le traitement dramatique du corps torturé et réifié de la sainte, dégradé jusqu'à l'état d'animal cuit, de plat prêt à être consommé, comme il arrive souvent dans le *Mystère de sainte Barbe en cinq journées*, dégage un effet comique paradoxal.[32] Ce rire macabre relève lui aussi de l'esthétique dissonante des mystères, notamment des mystères de la Passion :[33] c'est à la lumière de la Passion du Christ, sans dimension genrée, qu'il faut aussi lire la réification et l'humiliation corporelle des martyres, caractérisant tout autant les saints que les saintes, dans l'actualisation performative du martyre archétypique.

On peut en conclure que l'usage des trucages, de même que les conventions (acteurs pour interpréter les rôles féminins) et l'esthétique propres au jeu médiéval peinent à produire une vision érotisée d'un corps féminin nu objet de violence. Le dispositif théâtral gigantesque de la fin

---

30 Newbigin, 'Agata', p. 88.

31 Koopmans, 'L'équarrissage', p. 119.

32 Le corps du saint est offert comme nourriture aux bourreaux, qui le 'mangent', tout comme les saints 'mangent' leurs coups — exprimés souvent par des métaphores alimentaires, voir Faivre, 'Martyrs', pp. 124–25.

33 Dominguez, *La scène*, p. 96.

du Moyen Âge ne peut pas être, en termes de spectacle, si facilement comparable à la vision cinématographique — le cinéma étant réaliste et illusionniste par essence — vision cinématographique à laquelle il a pourtant été fait référence, en s'appuyant sur la théorie de Laura Mulvey, pour justifier le *male gaze* également à l'œuvre dans la représentation médiévale du martyre féminin. Est-il alors judicieux de parler d'un contenu pornographique ? Dans notre perspective, à propos de scènes de violence extrême, et si l'on tient pour acquis que le harcèlement exercé sur le corps de la sainte martyre relève d'une forme d'assaut sexuel, il serait plus approprié et constructif de convoquer la notion aristotélicienne de catharsis[34] et celle contemporaine d''empathie négative' :[35] nous pourrions ainsi concevoir une libération des émotions négatives et des pulsions agressives chez les spectateurs qui sympathisent avec les bourreaux ou le personnage souffrant. Cela rejoint aussi la perspective de Bernard Faivre sur la fonction de la violence dans les mystères, comme moyen nécessaire pour susciter l'émotion du public et donc garantir l'efficacité esthétique des pièces.[36] Sans comparer aussi facilement que le fait Potter un film de Lars von Trier avec un drame hagiographique du Moyen Âge, nous sommes convaincue du pouvoir cathartique que ce théâtre pouvait exercer sur le public, parce que celui-ci était 'subliminally rassured'[37] sur le fait que les corps meurtris sur scène ne subissaient pas une violence réelle, que le sang répandu était feint ou qu'il s'agissait aussi de corps feints ! De plus, cette 'immersion dans le bas corporel' avait pour fonction d'exacerber la distance entre l'homme-spectateur et la puissance divine témoignée par l'âme du saint en gloire : l''innocence théâtrale' médiévale montre ce qui est montrable,[38] alors que cet aspect donnerait aujourd'hui matière fertile à une opération de *cancel culture*.

La possible dimension cathartique de la violence sur scène n'a suscité aucune attention, alors qu'elle permettrait de nuancer, ou au moins de

---

34 Nous nous y référons en tant que concept esthétique universellement utilisé par les études d'histoire et d'esthétique théâtrales, en précisant que le Moyen Âge ne connaît pas la *Poétique* d'Aristote, publiée à Venise en traduction latine par Lorenzo Valla en 1498 et redécouverte en France seulement au milieu du XVIe siècle. L'anachronisme est donc conscient et voulu.

35 Fusillo, 'Guardare' ; pour un aperçu complet de l'esthétique de l'empathie négative, en perspective intermédiale, nous renvoyons à Fusillo et Ercolino, *Empatia*.

36 Faivre, 'Martyrs', p. 129.

37 Potter, 'Pornography'. Le film cité est *Breaking the waves* qui raconte le sacrifice pour amour d'une jeune-fille qui a des traits de « sainteté », où la dimension sacrée du martyre se mêle à la motivation toute terrestre d'une passion charnelle.

38 'Les mystères baignent dans une innocence théâtrale, où tout est montrable, de l'action la plus haute à la torture la plus basse, parce que nous sommes au théâtre et qu'en tant que spectateur, j'ai le droit de m'esclaffer aux saillies ordurières de ces bouffons sanglants que sont les bourreaux, avant d'entonner à pleine voix le *Te Deum* qui accompagne la montée du saint au Paradis'. Faivre, 'Martyrs', p. 131.

problématiser, l'interprétation parfois univoque, négative et machiste, qui a été proposée pour les représentations médiévales des martyres féminins. La notion d'empathie négative, qui caractérise une identification avec les héros négatifs et qui appelle la fonction de purification, permettrait même de mettre en évidence une possible utilité de la mise en scène des passages les plus terrifiants par leur violence et leur misogynie. Il s'agirait d'entrevoir dans les pièces la possibilité de la sublimation esthétique d'une *libido* violente, précisément avec la finalité (positive) d'éviter la pratique réelle d'une telle violence, en assurant donc une fonction de contrôle social des instincts les plus bas. Au metteur en scène potentiel d'aujourd'hui le choix d'un traitement esthétique qui puisse communiquer au public avec la pudeur nécessaire.

1.2. Un corps impassible ?

Le théâtre médiéval offre aux regards du spectateur un corps souffrant à l'instar de celui de la mystique, un corps 'transgressif' et qui n'est pas 'silencieux', comme le suggère M. Carlson, en se référant justement à l'Apolline peinte : l'appareil des effets spéciaux que nous venons d'évoquer vise précisément à simuler la souffrance de la sainte martyrisée. Dans les représentations de la fin du Moyen Âge, où la mimésis demande des corps et des voix réels, une question s'impose donc avec force : la souffrance du personnage calque-t-elle les *impossibilia* hyperboliques de la *passio* et du motif du saint indemne ? Comment le plaisir et l'impassibilité du corps pendant les tortures se traduisent-ils sur scène ? Est-ce grâce à l'invulnérabilité du corps face aux tortures que la joie de l'âme est rendue possible ?

Au théâtre, l'héroïne prend la parole pendant la mise en œuvre des tortures et son corps est présent, face aux spectateurs, l'acteur/actrice n'étant pas toujours remplacé.e par un mannequin ou une poupée, comme cela se produit de façon systématique pour la représentation de l'exécution capitale, où le personnage, n'ayant pas de répliques, est silencieux. L'usage de masques qui pourraient reproduire l'expression sereine du saint à l'approche de la couronne du martyre est documentée dans un texte catalan hagiographique, la *Consueta de saint Crispí y santa Crespinià* ;[39] en revanche, nous n'avons pas ce genre d'attestation (masques ou expression que l'on donnerait au visage du mannequin) dans le domaine français.[40] On pourrait certes envisager que lorsqu'un mannequin subit des supplices, un vrai acteur, caché, prononce les répliques,[41] mais nous savons que des

---

39 Massip, 'Cuerpo', p. 109.

40 Je remercie Marie Bouhaïk-Gironès pour ses suggestions à ce sujet.

41 Comme il arrive dans la scène de la torture de l'âme de Judas, réalisée par une feinte, dans la *Passion* de Jean Michel, voir Dominguez, *La scène*, pp. 195–96.

membres feints de corps font aussi partie des accessoires des spectacles, comme nous l'avons vu pour la *sacra rappresentazione* de sainte Agathe et cela implique la présence de l'acteur et la mise en place d'artifices particuliers : si l'acteur demeure indemne, le personnage saint qui exprime de la joie l'est-il lui aussi, comme c'est le cas dans les narrations hagiographiques ?

On sait que sur la scène du Moyen Âge, les signes de violence sur le corps des saints ou du Christ étaient recherchés et réalisés à travers des techniques parfois complexes, en pleine cohérence avec la signification théologique et la visée édifiante de tels spectacles : une violence nécessaire.[42] Ainsi, au début de la quatrième journée, Barbe est livrée au prévôt Marcien, qui face à la fermeté de ses positions religieuses et à son attitude audacieuse et méprisante à son égard, manifeste contre elle une fureur croissante. Sous ses ordres, en une seule première séance d'horreur, les tyrans déchirent sa chair au nerf de bœuf, la fouettent au cilice, parsèment de sel ses plaies. Même la trêve de l'enfermement en prison n'en est pas une, car Marcien la fait équiper de cailloux pointus afin que, même endormie, Barbe ne trouve pas la paix ! C'est alors que le ciel intervient et descend dans la prison obscure en l'éclairant après la prière de Barbe, où elle verbalise pour la première et unique fois la souffrance corporelle qu'elle éprouve. L'expression de sa peine s'effectue face à Dieu, alors que la sainte n'avait montré aucune vulnérabilité lors de l'exécution des tortures par les tyrans. Dans une tirade au rythme rapide, en vers pentasyllabiques, une parole fragmentée semble refléter le morcellement de son corps par les cailloux :

> De deul je lermie,
> La char me fremie,
> Le tourment m'est grief !
> Helas, quel meschief !
> Ses esclatz pour brief
> Entrent en mon corps. (vv. 15598–603)

> (Je pleure de douleur, ma chair tremble, le supplice m'est pénible ! Hélas, quelle méchanceté ! Ces éclats entrent vivement dans mon corps.)

Ce corps souffrant entre en contradiction avec le corps imperturbable et impassible du récit hagiographique et de l'iconographie du martyre féminin. Dans la théorie de Carlson basée sur l'enluminure d'Apolline, la chercheuse attribue l'impassibilité du corps martyrisé à l'idéal de l'église

---

42 Dominguez, *La scène*, pp. 77–106, pour l'analyse de la 'poétique du corps souffrant'.

et de la société autour d'un corps féminin religieux fermé, silencieux, qui s'oppose à celui, transgressif, de la mystique :

> Apollonia, eyes shut, presents an emblem of the closed, sealed body recommended by the church ; the silent martyr thus models the silent women, epitomized by the anachoress but also desirable with the society at large,[43]

sans préciser qu'il s'agit pourtant de l'héritage d'un topos hagiographique et martyriel traditionnel très ancien. Selon la chercheuse, en n'exprimant pas les excès d'une participation affective totale, la représentation de saintes martyres — exemptes de toute souffrance — semblerait cohérente avec l'idéologie dominante du Moyen Âge tardif, méfiant à l'égard de certaines manifestations mystiques extrêmes. Le corps de la mystique se révèle, de ce point de vue, un corps subversif par rapport à la norme, en s'auto-déterminant dans l'infliction de peines et dans la traversée de l'abjection, pour atteindre l'humiliation extrême et la mortification de la chair. Par contraste, le corps 'silencieux' de la martyre serait dépourvu de toute qualité subversive, surtout si on le considère comme objet passif de violence : la figure blanche, rigide, séraphique, aux yeux fermés de l'enluminure de Fouquet est l'emblème parfait d'une telle conception. Mais, comme le conclut Carlson elle-même dans sa réflexion, c'est bien dans la distance qui sépare le corps réprimé de la martyre de celui, expressif à l'excès, de la mystique en extase, que le spectateur, surtout féminin, peut trouver son rôle actif et dialogique. L'engagement dans ce dialogue se situerait précisément dans la coparticipation à la douleur de la martyre torturée, dont le corps silencieux se révèlerait, ainsi, 'double-voiced' :

> The spectacle of torture, silently welcomed, thus presents both a warning against ecstasy and an opportunity to experience it. In Bakhtinian terms, the silent martyr's body is double-voiced, and neither voice is given the final word ; nor do these voices resolve into a dialectical synthesis.[44]

Cette perspective est très intéressante, car elle dépasse celle du 'male gaze' et accueille, enfin, tant la possibilité d'une empathie avec la martyre en proie au supplice, que le rôle actif d'un public féminin. Reste cependant le fait qu'au théâtre le corps de la martyre, loin d'être 'réprimé', imperturbable et potentiellement souffrant, porte les signes concrets d'une souffrance vraisemblable, manifestée à travers les trucages et que, malgré cela, l'empathie avec le personnage est entravée à cause du discours même de la sainte, comme nous le verrons plus tard.

---

43 Carlson, 'Spectator Responses', p. 14.
44 Carlson, 'Spectator Responses', p. 15.

1.3. *Le paradoxe en scène*

Comme nous l'avons remarqué, en cohérence avec les mystères de la Passion, la souffrance du corps saint est simulée et le corps donne à voir une douleur 'réelle'. Dans nos pièces hagiographiques cela produit une contradiction par rapport au statut du personnage, la sainte indemne : la représentation des traces sanglantes des tourments, dans leur évidence matérielle, suffit-elle à nous faire penser que le personnage réponde aux lois naturelles, en étant joué en tant que corps souffrant, alors qu'il déclare se réjouir dans l'âme et ne pas éprouver de douleur pendant les tortures ? L'ambiguïté est forte : l'acteur/actrice qui joue Barbe fait-il/elle semblant d'éprouver souffrance ou joie ? Y a-t-il cohérence entre l'esprit et les mots qui disent la joie à chaque tourment et le corps agressé qui les subit ? Il/elle joue-t-il/elle davantage l'être humain vulnérable ou la sainte déjà participant de la dimension éternelle du ciel et donc invulnérable, comme le veut l'hagiographie ? Dans la version scénique du martyre, le corps et l'âme ne peuvent qu'être ensemble, du moins tant que la sainte est en vie. On s'attend à trouver une synthèse des deux aspects, celui de la souffrance et celui de la joie.

Le motif traditionnel de la métamorphose de la douleur en plaisir pourrait, en outre, avoir comme effet d'atténuer la violence que ces histoires contiennent. Dans cette dynamique paradoxale, en effet, la punition même de la rébellion de la sainte est amortie, puisque, dans un sens, elle est désirée par la martyre, qui s'approche ainsi de plus en plus de la joie céleste de son âme. La façon de rendre sur scène cette contradiction influence naturellement la réception que les spectateurs en ont et sa signification : si l'acteur/actrice ne joue pas la souffrance, l'acharnement sur le corps de sainte Barbe devient un procédé maniériste et une distance plus marquée s'établit entre le personnage et le spectateur, le *pathos* se trouvant amorti par l'état de jouissance du personnage. L'âme de la sainte se réjouit et son corps avec elle, dans une sereine impassibilité qui pourrait nous rappeler l'Apolline peinte aux yeux fermés.

Même si on constate le manque de documents sur l'*actio* théâtrale à cette époque en France — les premiers traités datant du xviiᵉ siècle — en s'appuyant sur des témoignages indirects liés aux réactions du public ou au contexte social de la pratique théâtrale, la critique a supposé un jeu plutôt codifié dans la gestuelle et dans l'usage de la voix, influencé, d'un côté, par la culture rhétorique et, de l'autre, par les formes fixes du discours poétique, comme le rondeau. Le 'message' à communiquer étant proclamé par le comédien dans l'espace public, l'on imagine plutôt une forme de déclamation très musicale et rythmée. Reste le fait, qu'en termes de jugement du jeu, il s'agit d'une vision partielle, comme le remarque à juste titre Clément Saliou.[45] Toutefois, même si à l'époque un tel type de performance pouvait produire une distance marquée entre spectateurs et acteurs, le jeu n'étant pas naturaliste, dans la perspective d'une mise en scène du mystère aujourd'hui, la question du jeu et de l'émotion qu'il produit sur le public nous semble essentielle. Néanmoins, la représentation d'un personnage totalement en extase paraît, même en termes d'esthétique théâtrale médiévale, difficile à imaginer au regard de l'appareil des secrets qui recherche la manifestation d'une chair violentée. En outre, nous avons des témoignages de spectateurs, amateurs d'un jeu de l'acteur suscitant la compassion.[46] C'est pourquoi la vision d'un personnage impassible, modelé sur l'image de Fouquet, nécessite d'être repensée : le corps de la martyre au théâtre n'est pas un corps vraiment silencieux, ni si différent de celui de la mystique, car l'on pourrait imaginer la sainte manifestant de la douleur avec les gestes d'un corps souffrant, tels les cris et les larmes,[47] en cohérence avec l'exhibition des effets sanglants. C'est là précisément que se situe l'écart de la scène par rapport au texte dramatique, tout comme l'écart du théâtre par rapport à la narration et à l'iconographie hagiographiques.

Et pourtant, d'un point de vue dramaturgique, les personnages ne se plaignent pas dans les pièces (la réplique de Barbe souffrante citée *supra* représente, comme nous l'avons dit, une exception dans le mystère). Le seul moment de faiblesse des saintes se manifeste dans la demande de secours à Dieu, qui arrive avant qu'elles ne puissent ressentir la douleur des supplices puis, pour guérir leur chair blessée — qui doit quand même apparaître blessée sur scène pour être guérie. La mise en spectacle des légendes saintes, avec ses illusions techniques, montre bien autre chose que les hypotextes narratifs, et au théâtre le corps a droit de parole autant que la voix qui récite le texte. L'on peut alors envisager que la sainte-personnage apparaisse en tant qu'être dont les gestes du corps — humain — expriment la souffrance, mais dont l'esprit s'élève en même temps à un statut surnaturel manifesté, quant à lui, par l'action d'une parole constamment en communication avec Dieu (un beau défi pour le jeu d'acteur d'aujourd'hui). Et si Barbe se montre en scène avec un corps

---

45 Voir l'utile aperçu de Saliou, 'Vie théâtrale', pp. 85–92. Le lien entre pratique judiciaire et théâtre comique, autour d'une culture de la rhétorique, quant à lui, a été démontré par Bouhaïk-Gironès, *Les clercs*. Voir aussi de la même historienne le récent 'Le mystère', surtout pp. 130–40, pour un aperçu à jour sur le jeu et la voix des acteurs dans le mystère.

46 Un témoignage concerne précisément le spectacle de Metz que nous avons cité *supra*, où Barbe est joué par Lionard, un jeune garçon, qui fait pleurer le public et fascine les spectateurs, voir Petit de Julleville, *Histoire*, t. II, p. 48. Voir aussi Lalou, 'Les tortures', p. 46.

47 Voir Schmitt, *La raison*, pp. 316–20. Voir aussi la gestuelle suggérée par la puissance dramatique du *Planctus* de Marie en deuil dans la Passion du *Palatinus* et dans les autres *Mystères de la Passion*, où la mère du Christ apparaît comme personnage théâtral à part entière, Dominguez, *La scène*, pp. 252–87.

vulnérable et sensible, l'effet de *pathos* en sera renforcé, l'identification des spectateurs avec elle se produira davantage, que si elle se montre totalement insensible aux agressions. Mais nous allons vérifier cette hypothèse, en nous appuyant sur le discours de l'héroïne.

2. Une parole qui proclame la joie et l'affermissement de l'esprit

Barbe souffre-t-elle 'pour de vrai' ? Ses répliques, ses mots manifestent aussi au théâtre une parole qui exprime la joie, voire l'extase, pendant les supplices, comme le veut la tradition hagiographique du miraculeux. Dans la plus ancienne représentation dramatique médiévale de martyre que l'on connaisse, chez Hrotsvita (Xe siècle), en particulier dans le *Sapientia*, une scène très émouvante présente Sagesse, la mère des trois sœurs martyrisées (Foi, Espérance et Charité), en proie à une réaction troublante , cohérente avec cette dynamique oxymorique : quand Foi doit être finalement décollée, Sagesse n'éprouve pas elle non plus de douleur, mais de l'allégresse, et ses larmes sont des larmes de joie : 'O filia, filia, non confundor, non contristor, sed valedico tibi exultando et osculor os osculosque prae gaudio lacrimando'.[48] En outre, alors que dans les dialogues dramatiques de Hrotsvita, comme dans les *passiones*, le corps des personnages, par son statut de corps transfiguré, déjà au-delà des lois terrestres, est clairement invulnérable, les effets du 'réalisme' de la scène du Moyen Âge tardif, quant à eux, montrent des souffrances corporelles en provoquant une représentation fort ambiguë, comme nous l'avons montré. Mais si le corps souffre, l'âme se renforce et jouit : la dynamique oxymorique prend précisément origine dans le fait que la souffrance du corps est la condition nécessaire à la véritable joie de l'esprit. Plus le corps souffre, plus l'âme se rapproche de la conquête de son salut éternel, comme le souligne Barbe, lors d'un rare moment où les bourreaux manifestent de la pitié pour elle : 'ces tourments me sont profitables / pour mon salut finalement' (vv. 15105–6). Et lorsqu'elle est brutalement fouettée, la jeune fille révèle à Marcien, sur le mode du sarcasme, qu'elle ressent un plaisir plus grand que celui qu'il prend au lit, probablement en compagnie de quelqu'un. La comparaison avec le plaisir sexuel, qui pourrait sembler inconvenante dans un tel contexte, s'avère toutefois cohérente avec le vocabulaire érotique à travers lequel le langage mystique exprime l'amour divin au Moyen Âge, comme le montre la double acception de l'usage des mots 'délices'/'délit' : pour Barbe, il est question d'un plaisir de l'âme, comme elle l'explique, alors que pour Marcien, on reste dans le domaine éphémère des sens :

---

48 Hrotsvita, *Théâtre*, dir. Goullet, pp. 234–79.

Barbara

Je prens, véz tu, plus de delices
Que tu ne faiz en ung beau lit
Quand y couches a ton delit !
Le travail, fatigacïon,
L'angoesseuse vexacïon
Que donnes a mon pouvre corps
Vituperablement de hors,
Mon ame, dedans, esclarcist
Et la parfaict et l'enforsist,
Car mon gré la reczoit. (vv. 1535–44)

>(Je prends, vois-tu, plus de plaisir, que quand tu couches dans
>un beau lit pour ta jouissance ! Le tourment, la fatigue et le harcè-
>lement violent que tu infliges éhontément à mon pauvre corps, à
>l'extérieur, éclaircit mon âme à l'intérieur et la perfectionne et la
>fortifie, c'est pourquoi je le reçois de bon gré.)

Voici l'explicitation de la signification du martyre : les tourments 'de hors',
sur le corps, qu'elle endure patiemment font naître la clarté au 'dedans'
de son âme. L'effet de ce contraste est troublant, notamment quand le
personnage exprime sa jouissance tout en décrivant les signes matériels
que son corps porte, comme dans ce passage du mystère en deux journées,
où Barbe est battue violemment par de 'gros nerfs' :

Ma chair est toute pourfendue
Et de coups et de playes fendue.
Las, tant je suis en grant esmoy !
Mais je suis toute resjouÿe.
Mon createur, je te rens grâces. (vv. 2020–24)

>(Ma chair est toute déchirée, et fendue par les coups et les bles-
>sures. Ah, je suis tellement bouleversée ! Mais je m'emplis de joie.
>Mon créateur, je te rends grâce.)

Les assauts subits deviennent pour la sainte, non seulement des motifs de
plaisir, mais encore de force et de courage. Le côté actif du personnage
et son héroïsme face aux supplices ressortent particulièrement dans le
mystère en cinq journées, où Barbe explique sa résistance à travers des
images très efficaces, qui disent sa constance et son désir de surpasser ces
épreuves. Après qu'elle a été brûlée avec des torches, elle se compare à
une tour stable, à l'abri du vent. La chaleur des lampes ardentes, au lieu de
l'anéantir comme une boule de glace, la renforce et la rend paradoxalement
vivante, en lui donnant couleur ('Je m'endurcis et pren couleur'), tout en
lui apportant la liesse que le salut imminent lui garantira pour l'éternité
('Car c'est pour ma salvacïon'). C'est pourquoi le spectacle de son sang qui

coule, lorsque son corps a été déchiré par des peignes de fer, au lieu de l'affaiblir comme le croit Alimodes :

> Tu voiz respandu a oultrance
> Ton sang et ne te peuz mater :
> Cela te deust espoventer (vv. 16283–85).

> (Tu vois répandu à l'excès ton sang et tu n'arrives pas à t'épuiser : cela devrait t'effrayer.)

lui donne au contraire un plus grand courage dans la bataille, s'agissant d'un 'parfaict regard', qui lui rappelle la 'merveille' du drap 'taincte en sang' du Christ, avec qui elle partage la passion.

3. Éloquence, indépendance, volonté irréductible

La parole de la martyre ne se borne pas à proclamer la joie de l'âme, mais manifeste le caractère inébranlable et indépendant du personnage, qui sape la hiérarchie traditionnelle et les rapports de pouvoir entre les genres. Avant et pendant les supplices, Barbe agit à travers un discours ferme et conscient, qui exprime sa résistance et sa supériorité intellectuelle face à la brutalité des bourreaux ou à la cuistrerie des antagonistes. Déjà affranchie de son père et de ses maîtres, dont elle refuse la proposition de mariage et la doctrine païenne, Barbe se montre cohérente, du début à la fin de la représentation, à sa propre pensée : elle défend son choix de vivre aux côtés du Christ et l'acceptation souffrante de son propre destin, qui doit passer par le sacrifice extrême du martyre. L'héroïne médiévale du mystère se montre ainsi capable d'une volonté et d'une décision 'implacable', en représentant à nos yeux non seulement un modèle de sainteté chrétienne, mais aussi un personnage digne du théâtre de la cruauté artaudien, au sens 'philosophique' et existentiel plus que physique :

> Et philosophiquement parlant d'ailleurs qu'est-ce que la cruauté ? Du point de vue de l'esprit cruauté signifie rigueur, application et décision implacable, détermination irréversible, absolue.[49]

---

49 Artaud, *Le théâtre*, pp. 153–55 : 'Première lettre sur la cruauté', ici p. 156. Le théâtre ('dans le sens de création continue') qui ne possède pas la conscience qu'au centre du 'tourbillon de vie qui dévore les ténèbres', du 'tourbillon volontaire du bien', il y a 'un noyau de mal de plus en plus réduit, de plus en plus mangé', n'est pas considéré comme utile : 'Une pièce où il n'y aurait pas cette volonté, cet appétit de vie aveugle, et capable de passer sur tout, visible dans chaque geste et dans chaque acte, et dans le côté transcendant de l'action, serait une pièce inutile et manquée', Artaud, *Le théâtre*, pp. 155–56 : 'Deuxième lettre'.

La singularité radicale de la sainte réside surtout dans son éloquence savante et audacieuse et dans sa prise de parole publique (un tabou pour les femmes depuis Saint Paul) : pour défendre leur virginité et gagner le salut céleste, les vierges martyres assument des comportements qui étaient, en général, considérés comme masculins au Moyen Âge. C'est surtout l'action, en tant qu'acte verbal, le discours éloquent de l'héroïne, qui produit des effets concrets dans la réalité et a le pouvoir de la métamorphoser : outre qu'elle cause la rage furieuse du persécuteur dans le conflit verbal dramatisé dans les pièces, sa parole puissante suscite des réactions (de gêne ou d'admiration) et des conversions, qui sont le fruit de ses facultés intellectuelles et d'une rhétorique agissante — et pas seulement le résultat de forces surnaturelles extérieures. L'on pense aux prédications d'Apolline et aux spéculations philosophiques de Catherine avec les sages païens qu'elle arrive à convertir dans les *sacre rappresentazioni* ou à la dispute de Barbe avec les deux docteurs Alphons et Amphoras, où la relation maître/élève se renverse au point que les deux maîtres renoncent, désespérés, à leur projet pédagogique et ramènent la jeune fille, rhétoriquement invincible, à son père. Barbe est elle-même l'allégorie d'une conception du savoir chrétien par opposition au savoir païen qui n'est pas guidé par Dieu : elle est une sainte du savoir, comme en témoignent les collèges portant son nom.[50] De ce point de vue, un personnage interprété à l'époque par un homme devait être moins troublant qu'une interprétation féminine.

À la témérité du corps, manifestée par l'inébranlable endurance de Barbe aux supplices, conséquence de sa ferme foi, s'associe ainsi une témérité de la voix qui, indomptée, affronte les personnages masculins et se traduit dans un discours ferme et tranchant, entre fierté, dévotion et sarcasme. Son agressivité verbale provoque une croissante agressivité corporelle chez les bourreaux : gonflés de colère et d'orgueil à cause de sa résistance étonnante et de sa parole rebelle, ils s'acharnent contre son corps dans le crescendo de violence que nous connaissons. Les bourreaux ordonnent à plusieurs reprises à la 'victime' de faire taire sa voix dérangeante. Lors du supplice des torches, Barbe offre son corps comme un plat prêt à être consommé et invite son persécuteur à s'en servir, avec le sarcasme provocateur qui la caractérise. Le rondeau triolet met bien en exergue le duel entre les deux parties. Loin de rester muette pendant les tourments, forte de sa grâce ('Maintenant ma vertu reluist'), Barbe tourne en dérision ses adversaires, qui sont assommés par son 'bruyt' :

---

50 Barbe n'est pas seulement la protectrice des travailleurs exposés aux périls (pompiers, mineurs), mais aussi l'une des saintes patronnes des écoliers et des étudiants (de même que Catherine d'Alexandrie) : on songe, par exemple, au Collège de Sainte Barbe fondé à Paris au xvie siècle sur la montagne Sainte-Geneviève.

MARCÏAN
Tais toy, Garce, cesse ton bruyt,
Tu m'estonne[s] tout le cerveau !

BARBARA
Maintenant ma vertu reluist.

ALIMODES
Taist toy, Garce, cesse ton bruyt !

BARBARA
Mon corps est present asséz cuyt,
Menguë ma char, trés ort Boureau. (vv. 16177–82)

> (MARCIAN : Tais-toi, chienne, ferme ta gueule ! Tu me casses
> la tête ! BARBARA : maintenant ma vertu rayonne. ALIMODES :
> Tais-toi, chienne, ferme ta gueule ! BARBARA : mon corps est à
> présent assez cuit, mange ma chair, sale bourreau.)

Mais l'éloquence remarquable du personnage, l'esprit d'entreprise dont le
chrétien Origène fait l'éloge chez la jeune fille, son courage et sa liberté
à défier les lois parentales et sociales ne conviennent pas aux femmes
'normales' : c'est précisément dans les répliques des trois femmes de
Nicomédie que le traditionnel point de vue misogyne est mis en scène,
à l'occasion des requêtes aux dieux pendant le sacrifice que Dioscorus
organise pour sa fille : 'Femme se taise ou parle bassement' souhaite
Cassandra, et voici le vœu d'Athalanta :

> Dieux infiniz, par la voustre puissance,
> Besséz ung pou des femmes le langaige :
> A leurs mariz maintesfois font nuyssance
> Pa[r] trop parler par fierté de couraige.
> C'elles parloint pou, ce seroit avantaige.
> Bon leur seroit avoir humilité.
> Les mariz ont deshonneur et dommaige
> Quant femmes ont par foiz auctorité. (vv. 3541–48)

> (Dieux éternels, par votre pouvoir, modérez un peu le langage des
> femmes : elles font souvent tort à leurs maris quand elles leur
> parlent avec un cœur trop audacieux. Si elles parlaient peu, ce serait
> une bonne chose. Ce serait bien qu'elles soient modestes. Les maris
> sont déshonorés et blessés quand les femmes montrent parfois de
> l'autorité.)

Et pourtant le *fatiste* — consciemment ? — donne voix à une protagoniste
qui incarne l'exact contraire de ce modèle féminin silencieux : le texte

nous semble ambigu, et cette ambiguïté cohérente avec le double visage de la martyre que l'on trouve dans les représentations théâtrales, celui de la femme sainte et selon le point de vue ennemi, celui de la sorcière dangereuse.[51] Barbe s'avère précisément une 'maulvaise teste', et ne parle certainement pas à voix basse, comme le voudrait Cassandra, car elle fait valoir ses arguments, tout en exprimant sa voix authentique. Le 'vice' dont les femmes de Nicomédie demandent le remède aux dieux correspond exactement à la puissance de la voix féminine (la tant redoutée 'auctorité' qui menace les 'mariz'), un remède mis en œuvre dans nos pièces à l'encontre de femmes dissidentes, par des hommes (im)puissants qui se croient des dieux.

De plus, en refusant les avances de riches et puissantes prétendantes, la martyre manifeste une maîtrise complète de son corps. Elle en assume le contrôle de façon rigoureusement indépendante, jusqu'à la mort, quand elle affirme sa volonté d'être tourmentée pendant le martyre, qui, loin d'être subi, s'avère librement recherché comme condition pour accomplir le mariage céleste. Cela est encore plus vrai si l'on considère que Barbe refuse même d'être plainte par les spectatrices indignées du spectacle obscène qui la voit contrainte à se promener nue dans les rues de Nicomédie après avoir été mutilée à la poitrine. Tout en se montrant située sur un autre plan que ces femmes 'trop humaines', les trois femmes de Nicomédie, Barbe récuse leur pitié :

> BARBARA
> O ! nobles Dames et Matrones
> Et Cueurs feminins bieneuréz,
> Je vous pry que vous ne plouréz
> Ma passïon : mon cueur la veult !
> Et si Nature vous esmeult
> A pitié et compassïon
> Et d'avoir recordacïon
> De moy qui suys une innocente,
> Par une lÿesse rescente
> Ejouÿsséz vous, je vous pry,
> Avec moy sans faire nul cry. (vv. 17894–904)

> > (Ô nobles dames et épouses, et cœurs féminins bien heureux, je vous prie de ne pas pleurer mon martyre : mon cœur le désire ! Et si Nature vous pousse à éprouver pitié et compassion et à porter témoignage pour moi qui suis innocente, avec moi réjouissez-vous d'une fraîche joie, je vous prie, sans proférer aucun cri.)

---

51 Je renvoie à Scavello, 'Une "pureté".

Mario Longtin rapproche cette réaction de Barbe de celle du Christ à la huitième station de la croix, quand il invite les femmes de Jérusalem 'à ne pas pleurer sur lui, mais bien sur elles-mêmes et sur leurs enfants' (Luc, 23. 27–31),[52] en voyant dans ce refus de pitié une autre preuve de la proximité de l'héroïne avec son modèle christique : Barbe s'était en effet comparée au Christ qui subit la passion précisément au début de la quatrième journée, quand démarre la séquence des supplices qui la conduira à sa propre passion. Barbe, femme sainte, sait que la beauté de son corps est éphémère ('Ne vous chaille de ma beaulté | Corporelle qui est instable !', vv. 17840–41)

Nous sommes donc en face d'une parole résolue et déstabilisante, miroir d'une pensée illuminée qui place Barbe sur un plan supérieur, du point de vue chrétien, celui de l'esprit et du cœur, alors que les femmes et les hommes qui la pleurent raisonnent sur un niveau totalement terrestre et se préoccupent de son beau corps meurtri. De telles répliques nous confirment que le martyre, bien que subi, se transforme en geste de volonté activement recherché par l'héroïne, montrant en cela combien ces personnages médiévaux ne peuvent en rien coïncider avec des figures de victimes féminines vulnérables, simples objets du regard masculin. Il nous semble que le refus de compassion, conjugué avec la proclamation de la joie dans la souffrance et la témérité d'une parole insoumise et éloquente, ont pour effet d'affaiblir la participation émotive ('empathie positive') du public envers un personnage qui serait souffrant et victime par essence, parce qu'ils lui permettent de se pencher davantage sur son esprit, que sur son corps agressé, objet privilégié de l'attention des chercheurs. Cet aspect accroît la complexité du personnage et l'effet de son action sur le public. Malgré la représentation sur scène de son corps vulnérable, Barbe s'avère une héroïne forte et incarne moins un modèle féminin d'intégrité morale qu'un sujet indépendant et libre, dans la maîtrise de sa pensée et de son corps.

4. Conclusion : incarnation et jeu

Il y a d'abord un intérêt et scientifique et artistique à envisager la mise en scène des mystères de sainte Barbe, afin de mieux en comprendre la dramaturgie, en éprouvant par exemple sur scène la contradiction entre corps souffrant et esprit joyeux, à savoir l'écart entre la tradition hagiographique narrative et son transcodage dans le nouveau langage théâtral, par définition intermédial : faire renaître ces objets dans leur dimension originale, face à un public, permettrait sans doute d'éclairer certaines des

---

52 Longtin, 'Chœur', p. 318.

questions que nous avons posées. L'exploration pratique d'une mise en scène pourrait laisser entrevoir la réponse que la seule lecture des textes, aussi visionnaire soit-elle, ne peut pas atteindre.

La renaissance de ces pièces sur les scènes d'aujourd'hui prend également à nos yeux une signification éthique et sociale, surtout si on assume une perspective consciemment médiévaliste sur l'action de la martyre au théâtre, perspective que nous avons déjà suggérée dans notre analyse. Le statut double et paradoxal du personnage, modèle de perfection chrétienne et femme dissidente, pourrait être lu de la manière suivante : sainte, Barbe est martyrisée car elle doit partager la souffrance avec le Christ Rédempteur et le rejoindre, ainsi, pour une union mystique ; femme indépendante et rebelle, l'héroïne médiévale est torturée car elle affirme et revendique jusqu'au bout un choix de vie transgressif et une gestion autonome de son propre corps, comme sujet féminin libre, en somme. Sous cette lumière, l'exhibition du corps supplicié, objet du 'male gaze' de ses bourreaux, n'est alors que la conséquence de la manifestation de l'esprit du personnage, qui se joue au niveau verbal, éthique et intellectuel. Loin de représenter une victime passive, le théâtre médiéval offre au spectateur d'aujourd'hui un modèle de femme forte et indépendante : c'est précisément à cause de sa force et de sa résistance que la martyre fait l'objet d'un traitement punitif ou, selon les points de vue, devient le sujet de son martyre.

Dans notre perspective contemporaine, la répression violente de cette figure rebelle, n'est pas uniquement la punition de la chrétienne dans un monde païen, mais apparaît comme la censure d'une femme libre tout court. Plutôt que de se limiter à voir la martyre comme corps réifié ou sexualisé, il faudrait alors considérer, en déplaçant le regard, que, c'est parce qu'elle n'est pas un simple corps qu'elle est censurée et réprimée. La proclamation de sa joie dans la douleur physique, sa parole mordante et provocatrice, son refus de la compassion, pourraient favoriser une réflexion critique plus complexe, dans une 'dimension brechtienne' du théâtre médiéval,[53] et inviter à une méditation, non seulement sur la signification chrétienne de l'incarnation,[54] mais aussi sur le courage, sur la liberté de choix et d'expression de l'héroïne. Une telle réflexion conduit nécessairement le lecteur — et spectateur — à se focaliser sur le sujet dans sa totalité, sans se limiter à la simple visualisation d'un corps passif objet de violence ou de désir.

Sujet féminin qui donne sens à sa vie, à la lumière d'un idéal qu'elle choisit de façon autonome par rapport au microcosme familial et au

---

53 Potter, 'The Brechtian dimension' : il s'agit d'une formulation anachronique et d'un renversement de périodisation voulu, l'approche brechtienne est précisément une approche inspirée par les mystères.

54 Dominguez, 'Entre la feinte et le rire'.

macrocosme social, Barbe trouve son impulsion dans l'amour inconditionnel du Christ et son action est guidée et ne prend sens que dans l'horizon chrétien. Pour un public contemporain, le Christ pourrait fonctionner comme métaphore d'un sens, d'un idéal, que la protagoniste recherche et auquel elle est fidèle, qui guide son combat de vie de façon radicale, en cohérence avec elle-même et avec ses désirs. Ce théâtre nous offre ainsi un personnage qui 'a prise sur le monde', pour le dire avec Simone de Beauvoir. L'on pourrait ainsi sortir de la dynamique conjugale — quoique sublimée — d'époux et d'épouse célestes, en libérant le Christ et la martyre du joug du genre, sur lequel l'imaginaire occidental de matrice chrétienne s'est fondé. La redécouverte contemporaine de ces pièces pourrait permettre une telle sortie et une telle libération, en transposant la dialectique sainte/idéal christique vers un sens universalisant, en sortant de l'idéologie religieuse chrétienne, qui naturellement connote l'époque médiévale. En outre, la répression violente de la liberté du corps et de l'esprit de Barbe entre en forte résonnance avec notre actualité, en suscitant une réflexion sur le prix que, dans certains contextes, même occidentaux, les femmes doivent encore payer pour affirmer de façon autonome leur pensée et leur action, et maîtriser leur corps à leur gré.

Enfin, nous considérons que seule l'expérimentation sur scène pourrait permettre de dépasser ou simplement de mieux comprendre les impasses et les paradoxes que les textes médiévaux nous présentent, et de résoudre les dichotomies que nous avons discutées (douleur/joie, corps passif/parole active, objet sexuel/sujet libre) dans la dimension performative, où la parole s'incarne dans le corps des acteurs, où l'écriture laisse la place à l'oralité, et où l'action et les effets scéniques prennent vie face à des spectateurs en chair et en os. C'est dans cette 'co-présence corporelle'[55] de tous les acteurs de l'action théâtrale que nous voyons le nouvel avenir de ces pièces médiévales.

---

55 Fischer-Lichte, *Estetica*, p. 67 et s.

Bibliographie

Sources éditées

Andrieu de la Vigne, *Le Mystère de Saint Martin 1496*, dir. André Duplat (Genève: Droz, 1979)

Hrotsvita, *Théâtre*, dir. Monique Goullet (Paris: Les Belles Lettres, 1999), pp. 234–79

Iacopo da Varazze, *Legenda Aurea*, dir. Paolo Maggioni (Florence: Edizioni del Galluzzo, 2007)

Le livre de conduite du régisseur et le compte des dépenses pour le mystère de la Passion joué à Mons en 1501, dir. Gustave Cohen (Paris: Champion, 1925)

Il mistero provenzale di Sant'Agnese, dir. Silvia de Santis (Rome: Viella, 2016)

Le Mystère de sainte Barbe en cinq journées, BnF fr. 976, dir. Mario Longtin *et al.* (à paraître)

Le*Mystère de sainte Barbe en deux journées*, BN Yf 1652', dir. Mario Longtin (thèse inédit, Université McGill, Montréal, 1996)

'Rappresentazione di Santa Agata', dans *Sacre rappresentazioni toscane dei secoli XV e XVI*, dir. Paolo Toschi (Florence: Olschki, 1969), n. 2

Textes secondaires

Artaud, Antonin, *Le théâtre et son double* (Paris: Gallimard, 1964).

Beck, Jonathan, 'Sexe et genre dans l'hagiographie médiévale: les mystères à saintes', *Le Moyen Âge français*, 19 (1986), 18–33

Bonafin, Massimo, 'Alcune considerazioni sul Miracolo di Sant'Agnese', dans *La scena assente. Realtà e leggenda sul teatro nel Medioevo*, dir. Francesco Mosetti Casaretto (Alessandria: Edizioni dell'Orso, 2006), pp. 269–79

Bordier, Jean-Pierre, 'La violence du mystère', *Littératures Classiques*, 73/3 (2010), 95–108

Bouhaïk-Gironès, Marie, *Les clercs de la Basoche et le théâtre comique* (Paris: Champion, 2007)

——, ' *Le mystère de Romans* (Paris: éditions EHESS, 2023)

——, 'Trois documents sur les feintes, les secrets et leurs maîtres (XVe–XVIe s.)', *Revue d'Histoire du Théâtre*, 278/2 (2018), 15–21

Carlson, Marla, 'Spectator Responses to an Image of Violence: Seeing Apollonia', *Fifteenth-Century Studies*, 27 (2002), 7–20

Cazelles, Brigitte, *The Lady as Saint: A Collection of French Hagiographic Romances of the Thirteenth Century* (Philadelphia: University of Pennsylvania Press, 1991)

Chocheyras, Jacques, *Le théâtre religieux en Savoie au XVIe siècle*, Publications romanes et françaises, 115 (Genève: Droz, 1971)

Clark, Robert et Claire Sponsler, 'Queer Play: The Cultural Work of Crossdressing in Medieval Drama', *Medieval Studies*, 28/2 (1997), 319–44

Dominguez, Véronique, 'Entre la feinte et le rire: les supplices sur la scène des mystères (xvᵉ–xviᵉ siècles)', dans *Du Diable au Corps*, dir. J.-P. Dupouy et E. Gaucher-Rémond, *Camaren*, 3 (2010), 111–27

——, *La scène et la croix: le jeu de l'acteur dans les passions dramatiques françaises (xivᵉ–xviᵉ siècles)* (Turnhout: Brepols, 2007)

——, 'La scène et l'enluminure. *L'Apolline* de Jean Fouquet dans le livre d'Heures d'Étienne Chevalier', *Romania*, 122 (2004), 468–505

Easton, Martha, 'Feminism', *Studies in Iconography*, 33 (2012), 99–112

——, 'Saint Agatha and the Sanctification of Sexual Violence', *Studies in Iconography*, 16 (1994), 119–38

Faivre, Bernard, 'Martyrs, bourreaux et spectateurs', *Littératures classiques*, 73/3 (2010), 121–32

Fischer-Lichte, Erika, *Estetica del performativo. Una teoria del teatro e dell'arte*, trad. S. Paparelli (Rome: Carocci, 2014)

Fusillo, Massimo, 'Guardare il male a distanza: empatia negativa, paura catarsi', *Psiche*, 1 (2020), 283–96

Fusillo, Massimo et Stefano Ercolino, *Empatia Negativa. Il punto di vista del male* (Milan: Bompiani, 2022)

Koopmans, Jelle, 'L'équarrissage pour tous ou la scène des mystères dits religieux', *Littératures Classiques*, 73/3 (2010), 109–20

Lalou, Élisabeth, 'Les tortures dans les mystères: théâtre et réalité, xivᵉ–xvᵉ siècle', *Medieval English Theatre*, 16 (1994), 37–50

Le Hir, Yves, 'Les indications scéniques dans le mystère de saint Etienne Pape de Nicolas Loupvent', *Bibliothèque d'Humanisme et Renaissance*, 42/3 (1980), 661–76

Longtin, Mario, 'Chœur à chœur: le *Mystère de sainte Barbe en cinq journées* et le roman médiéval', dans *De l'Oral à l'écrit, le dialogue à travers les genres romanesque et théâtral*, dir. Corinne Denoyelle (Orléans: Paradigme, 2015), pp. 301–26

Massip, Francesc, 'Cuerpo afligido, cuerpo mutilado: la puesta en escena de la tortura en el teatro medieval', dans *Lo scandalo del corpo. Studi di un altro teatro*, dir. Carla Bino *et al.* (Milano: Vita e Pensiero, 2019), pp. 105–14

Massip, Francesc et Lenke Kovács, 'The Late Medieval Catalan Play of St Agatha: Introduction, Text and Translation', in *Performance, Drama and Spectacle in the Medieval City. Essays in Honour of Alan Hindley*, dir. Catherine Emerson *et al.* (Leuven: Peeters, 2010), pp. 267–94

Muir, Lynette, 'Woman on the Medieval Stage: The Evidence from France', *Medieval English Theatre*, 7 (1985), 107–19

Mulvey, Laura, *Au-delà du plaisir visuel. Féminisme, énigmes, cinéphilie* (Sesto San Giovanni: Éditions Mimesis, 2017)

——, 'Visual pleasure and narrative cinema', *Oxford Journals*, 16/3 (1975), 802–16

Newbigin, Nerida, 'Agata, Apollonia and Other Martyred Virgins: Did Florentines Really See these Plays Performed?', *European Medieval Drama*, 1 (1997), 77–100

Parussa, Gabriella, 'Le théâtre des femmes au Moyen Âge: écriture, performance et mécénat', dans *Théâtre et révélation. Donner à voir et à entendre au Moyen Âge*, dir. Catherine Croizy-Naquet *et al.* (Paris: Champion, 2017), pp. 303–21

Petit de Julleville, Louis, *Histoire du théâtre en France, Les Mystères*, 2 vols (Paris: Hachette, 1880)

Potter, Robert, 'The Brechtian dimension of Medieval Drama', *Renaissance du théâtre médiéval*, XIIe colloque de la Société internationale du théâtre médiéval, Lille, 2–7 juillet 2007, dir. Véronique Dominguez (Louvain: Presses universitaires de Louvain, 2009), pp. 203–18

——, 'Pornography and the Saints' Play', Presented at the Ninth Colloquium of the Société Internationale pour l'Étude du Théâtre Médiéval, Odense, Denmark, 1998, en ligne http://www.sitm.info/history/1998–2001/ SITM_files/papers/Robert_Potter.html (accès: 25 Decembre 2023)

Prevenier, Walter, 'Quand un honorable bourgeois de Malines, 'marié avec une bonne et honeste femme', s'encanaille dans une compagnie de théâtre en marge de la bonne société (1475)', dans *La Permission et la Sanction. Théories légales et pratiques du théâtre (XIVe–XVIIe siècle)*, dir. M. Bouhaïk-Gironès, J. Koopmans, K. Lavéant (Paris: Classiques Garnier, 2017), pp. 141–63

Saliou, Clément, 'Disloquer pour renaître: la torture et ses effets dans les vies de saints dramatisées des XVe et XVIe siècles', dans *Corps béants, corps morcelés: altération et constellation du corps dans les arts scéniques et visuels*, dir. Julie Postel et Marie Garré Nicoară (Louvain-la-Neuve: EME éditions, 2018), pp. 175–86

——, 'Vie théâtrale dans le Nord-Ouest de la France (Bretagne, Pays de la Loire, Poitou, Aunis) du XIIIe au XVIe siècle' (thèse inédite, Université de Rennes 2, 2019)

Scavello, Susanna, 'Les femmes fortes de la scène médiévale : martyres entre ciel et terre. Étude comparative des héroïnes du théâtre français des XIVe–XVIe siècles' (thèse inédite, Université de Bologne et Université de Picardie Jules Verne, 2021)

——, 'Une "pureté contagieuse": le pouvoir de la sainte dans le théâtre médiéval (XIVe–XVIe siècles)', *Quaderni di Filologia Romanza*, 28/29 (2021–2022), 123–48

Schmitt, Jean-Claude, *La raison des gestes dans l'Occident médiéval* (Paris: Gallimard, 1990)

Wirth, Jean, *L'image du corps au Moyen Âge* (Florence: Edizioni del Galluzzo, 2013)

CORA DIETL

Catechism and Miracles as Arguments in Religious Debate

Hanns Wagner's Play of St Ursus

▼ **ABSTRACT** The paper suggests a confessional reading of Hanns Wagner's play about St Maurice and St Ursus, staged for the 100th anniversary of Solothurn's admission to the Swiss Confederation in 1581. Wagner uses diverse verbal and theatrical methods of religious persuasion, addressing an audience of mixed confession, who are given the role of 'the people'. By contrast with the ruler, who is the most negatively portrayed, the 'people' are shown to be convinced by words that visibly come true and by miracles, accepting the major Catholic prayers, and the Catholic understanding of baptism and of sainthood.

▼ **KEYWORDS:** Hanns Wagner, Solothurn, St Ursus, saints plays, school plays, Reformation, Swiss Confederation, persuasion, baptism, miracles.

Cora Dietl (cora.dietl@germanistik.uni-giessen.de) is professor of medieval and Early Modern German literature at the University of Giessen. Since her post-doc thesis about Neo-Latin drama in Southern Germany (Tübingen, 2004), one of her major fields of research has been fifteenth- and sixteenth-century theatre.

European Medieval Drama, 27 (2023), 161–188
BREPOLS ❧ PUBLISHERS

10.1484/J.EMD.5.137682

Figure 6.1. Franz Graff, Reconstruction of the old minster of St Ursus before 1763 (copper engraving, 1855). Photo: City Archive of Solothurn.

When in 1581 Solothurn celebrated the 100th anniversary of its admission to the Swiss Confederation, Hanns Wagner, schoolmaster at the Latin school of St Ursus and organist at the minster of St Ursus,[1] wrote a play about Solothurn's major patron saint in two parts.[2] It was staged on 27 and 28 August on Solothurn's minster square, the *Kronenplatz*[3] (**Fig. 6.1**).[4]

The Swiss Confederation had been under enormous pressure since the Reformation, which had caused strong tensions between the Reformed and the Roman Catholic members.[5] For Solothurn as a Roman Catholic city, celebrating the centennial of the admission to the Confederation

---

1 For the biography see: R. Kully, 'Wagner'.
2 For the whole paper see the chapter 'Solothurn' in Dietl and others, *Inszenierungen von Heiligkeit*.
3 For a discussion of the placement of the stage see: R. Kully, 'Nachwort', pp. 397–99; Biermann, 'Nachwort', pp. 242–43.
4 The dimensions of this image are not correct; the street to the right of the minster is narrow, and there is a rather steep gradient to the river Aare from there.
5 For an overview over the Swiss Reformation see: Burnett and Campi (eds), *Die schweizerische Reformation*.

also meant celebrating the fact that it was possible to remain Catholic within the Confederation.[6] In sixteenth-century Switzerland, theatre performances were frequently linked to political gatherings or so-called 'friendship visits' by different towns or regions.[7] A celebration as important as that in Solothurn 1581 was unthinkable without the staging of a play. The idea to commission Hanns Wagner to direct the theatre performance was clearly fostered by the city notary Hans Jacob vom Staal, one of Wagner's former pupils: On 19 July, Hans Jacob vom Staal presented the order of the play to the City Council, who approved it within two days. Obviously, the play matched the city's interests very well.[8]

In what follows, I will briefly explain the tradition of the adoration of St Ursus as patron saint of Solothurn, and then demonstrate how the play argues in favour of the Roman Catholic faith as fundamental to the city and the Swiss Confederation. I am interested in both verbal and visual arguments and how they support each other.

St Ursus in Solothurn

In his *Passio Acaunensium martyrum* (dated 455), Eucherius of Lyon mentions Ursus and Victor as members of the Thebean legion who around AD 300 had followed Maximianus across the Alps to defeat revolting peasants,[9] and who were martyred in Agaunum [also: 'Acaunus'], when the soldiers and their general Maurice confessed their Christian faith and refused to persecute Christians. Ursus and Victor escaped the massacre and fled to Solothurn, where they were martyred soon afterwards.[10] The first *passio* of St Victor dates from the seventh century. It mentions the *translatio* of Victor's body from Solothurn to Geneva, initiated by Princess Sedeleuba of Burgundy (around AD 500).[11] The seventh-century chronicle by Pseudo-Fredegar also mentions the event, though Fredegar calls the Burgundian princess 'Theudeslinde'.[12] Finally in 870 a monastery of St Ursus is mentioned in Solothurn,[13] and around 900 the *Passio beatissimorum*

---

6 See R. Kully, 'Nachwort', p. 387.

7 See Greco-Kaufmann, *Zuo der Eere Gottes*, vol. I, pp. 222–23; Reinhardt, *Geschichte*, p. 165; Dietl and others, *Inszenierungen*, p. 20.

8 See R. Kully, 'Nachwort', p. 390; documentation: Wagner, *Sämtliche Werke*, ed. by Kully, vol. III, pp. 242 and 244.

9 For the historical background, Maximian's fight against the 'Bagaudes', see Widmer, 'Der Ursus- und Victorkult', p. 36.

10 Eucherius, *Passio*, ed. by Näf, § 14. See Widmer, 'Ursus- und Victor'.

11 See Widmer, 'Ursus und Victor'; Widmer, 'Der Ursus- und Victorkult', pp. 41–42.

12 *Fredegarii et aliorum Chronica*, ed. by Krusch, book IV, cap. 22, p. 129; Widmer, 'Der Ursus- und Victorkult', pp. 42–43.

13 See Widmer, 'Ursus und Victor'.

martyrum Victoris et Ursi was written for this monastery:[14] it narrates in detail how Victor and Ursus escape from Agaunum to Solothurn, where Hyrtacus, *praeses* of the province, has them imprisoned. Since they refuse to sacrifice to the heathen gods, they are tortured, until their torturers are struck by lightning and the Christians freed from prison. Hyrtacus claims that the saints use witchcraft and orders that they be burnt, but a sudden heavy downpour of rain extinguishes the fire. Now, Hyrtacus orders that the Christians be beheaded. They kneel down, pray, and accept the death stroke. Obviously influenced by the early ninth-century Zurich legend of Felix and Regula,[15] the legend narrates that the beheaded saints, whose bodies have been thrown into the river Aare, leave the river again, carrying their heads in their hands, and pray until they finally die. The *passio* ends with the *translatio* of Victor's relics to Geneva.[16]

While the *Passio beatissimorum martyrum* stands within the tradition of Geneva and thus concentrates on Victor, and while the trans-regional tradition (represented by Jacobus a Voragine's *Legenda Aurea*) concentrates on Maurice and only briefly mentions Ursus and Victor,[17] the local Solothurn tradition focusses on Ursus and on the foundation of the church of St Ursus. Around 1019 Berno, Abbot of Reichenau, writes to Henry, Bishop of Lausanne, announcing the *translatio* of Ursus' corpse to a new church in Solothurn, and asking for a copy of the legend.[18] From the eleventh century on, relics of St Ursus appear in other Swiss and Southern German churches,[19] indicating that the saint was honoured beyond Solothurn.

In the fifteenth and sixteenth century, the cult of St Ursus gained new popularity. In 1469 Solothurn's city notary Hans vom Staal mentions the bodies of Ursus' sixty-six comrades, newly-discovered in Solothurn.[20] Four years later, on 20 July 1473, Pope Alexander VI approves the sanctity of these relics in his bull *Alma Mater*. The bull also repeats and confirms the legend in its newest version, which combines traditions from Geneva and Solothurn. It states that Queen Bertha had founded a church in Solothurn at the spot where she had discovered seventeen Thebeans, and that thirty-seven further corpses were now found close to St Peter's

---

14 St Gall, Abbey Library, Cod. Sang. 569 (*Viten frühchristlicher Päpste und Märtyrer*), pp. 224–39, https://www.e-codices.unifr.ch/de/csg/0569/, ed. in Widmer, 'Der Ursus- und Victorkult', pp. 75–80.

15 Widmer, 'Der Ursus- und Victorkult', pp. 46–47.

16 See Kully's commentary, in Wagner, *Sämtliche Werke*, ed. by Kully, vol. II, pp. 151–52.

17 Jacobus, *Legenda Aurea*, ed. by Häuptli, vol. II, p. 1848.

18 Widmer, 'Der Ursus- und Victorkult', p. 53. The church of St Ursula, however, is mentioned for the first time in 1182. See ibid., p. 55. As late as mid-thirteenth-century a not specified queen 'Bertha' is mentioned as the founder of the church. See ibid., p. 53.

19 Widmer, 'Der Ursus- und Victorkult', p. 53.

20 Widmer, 'Der Ursus- und Victorkult', p. 57.

church.[21] Soon, however, on 8 February 1474, a second bull arrived in Solothurn, articulating the pope's serious doubts about the age of the bones, but still allowing the cult since the citizens of Solothurn reported miracles in connection with the relics.[22]

The status of the church and the cult of St Ursus changed again after the Reformation. When Berne and Basel embraced Reformation, the Protestant movement in Solothurn was strengthened. The City Council promised a public religious dispute in November 1530: however this debate was postponed, and finally never took place.[23] Solothurn tried to remain bi-confessional. One of the reasons that the City Council was hesitant to accept the new faith was Zwingli's critical attitude towards the mercenaries, who, however, were a large economical, social and political factor in Solothurn.[24] Since France was the most important client for mercenaries, the French Ambassador moved from Berne to Solothurn in 1530[25] — and gained influence in Solothurn's politics.[26] In 1531, after the defeat of the Protestant army at the War at Kappell, Solothurn finally decided to become Catholic[27] — and revived the cult of its patron, whose minster had been the centre of Catholicism during the bi-confessional years.

In his chronicle of Solothurn, dating from 1578, the patrician Anton Haffner stresses the importance of Ursus for the town. He starts the history of the town with the martyrdom of St Ursus and St Victor[28] and depicts Ursus as a most caring patron of his town. Haffner narrates, on the base of what he calls 'oral tradition', that during Leopold I of Hapsburg's siege of Solothurn in 1318 the citizens called upon their patron. At night, the Thebean legion became visible on the city walls and made Leopold withdraw his troops.[29]

St Maurice and *St Ursus* — A Secular Play?

In his *Chronica* Haffner reserves an extra chapter for Hanns Wagner's performance of his play about St Maurice and St Ursus on Sunday 27 and Monday 28 August 1581. This is remarkable insofar as Haffner's city history, which does not attempt to be comprehensive, does not generally

---

21 Widmer, 'Der Ursus- und Victorkult', p. 61.
22 Widmer, 'Der Ursus- und Victorkult', p. 62.
23 Haffner, *Chronica*, pp. 69–70. See Rüedy, 'Bauernkrieg', p. 80.
24 Zünd, *Gescheiterte Stadt- und Landreformationen*, p. 87; Koch, 'Kronenfresser', p. 175.
25 Koch, 'Kronenfresser', p. 153.
26 Dafflon, *Die Ambassadoren*, p. 31.
27 Haffner, *Chronica*, p. 71. See Rüedy, 'Bauernkrieg', p. 81.
28 Haffner, *Chronica*, pp. 6–7.
29 Haffner, *Chronica*, pp. 17–19. See Widmer, 'Der Ursus- und Victorkult', p. 57.

mention cultural events. He jumps from the early 1530s to 1581, not even mentioning the centenary celebration of Solothurn's membership of the Swiss Confederation. The play however seems to be important for him — and not only because he himself played the role of Hyrtacus: he is impressed by the incredible costs that the city accepted for the performance ('mit großen Kosten [...], daß schier ungläubig ist'), namely some 4000 gilders.[30] He also mentions the noble actors of the play. Among them were the city scribe Hans Jacob vom Staal and a remarkable number of *Hauptlüt*, i.e. of leaders of mercenary units, who wore their full armour on stage.[31] Haffner also mentions the enormous number of visitors who came to see the play, which might serve as a proof that the performance was indeed part of a large celebration: 'allein uß der Statt Bern ob den hundert Ingeseßenen Burgern alhie geweßen' ('there were alone some 100 citizen of Berne present for the performance'). He also highlights the short time that the amateur actors needed for learning the lines: 'nit länger dan zechen wochen' ('not more than ten weeks'): this underlines the high motivation of all participants in the production.[32]

Haffner does not mention any earlier performances of St Ursus plays in Solothurn. There is, however, a manuscript of an anonymous play about St Ursus in Solothurn, 1539.[33] Early research speculated that its author could be Johannes Aal, Hanns Wagner's uncle, the author of a famous play about St John the Baptist. However, this cannot be proven.[34] The anonymous *Play of St Ursus* is relatively short and combines the *passio* of St Maurice and the *passio* of Ursus and Victor in a one-day performance. Hanns Wagner extended the play twice, as is evident from its two autograph manuscript versions: a first from 1575,[35] dealing with the St Ursus and Victor only, and a second from 1581, consisting of two volumes: a *Play of St Maurice*[36] and a new *Play of St Ursus*.[37] The first manuscript contains so many corrections and additions to the first text that Wagner obviously saw the need to copy it again.[38] Rolf Max Kully's edition gives a detailed description of the manuscripts, and his apparatus points at the differences between Wagner's two versions of the *Play of St Ursus*.[39] He assumes that

---

30 Haffner, *Chronica*, p. 84.

31 Haffner, *Chronica*, pp. 84–85.

32 Haffner, *Chronica*, p. 85.

33 See E. Kully, 'Das ältere St Ursenspiel', p. 24.

34 See E. Kully, 'Das ältere St Ursenspiel', pp. 14–25.

35 Wagner, *Sant Vrsen Spiel*, Solothurn, Central Library, S I 81. See Wagner, *Sämtliche Werke*, ed. by Kully, vol. II, pp. 148–49.

36 Wagner, *St Mauritius-Spil*, Solothurn, Central Library, S I 101.

37 Wagner, *Tragoedia Ursina*, Solothurn, Central Library, S I 120.

38 See Wagner, *Sämtliche Werke*, ed. by Kully, vol. II, pp. 146–47.

39 In the following, I will use both his edition and the manuscripts. Since Wagner's manuscripts are paginated, I will refer to page numbers, not to folios, when using the manuscripts.

Wagner could have planned a performance of a play about St Ursus for the centenary of the papal bull *Alma Mater* in 1573, and then changed his plans and reworked the play for the feast in 1581.[40] However, the fact that there is no record of a performance in 1573/1575 does not necessarily mean that there was none.

The double play from 1581 starts with Maximian's army having just crossed the Southern rim of the Alps. The emperor is thankful to the Roman gods who have protected him and his army on the difficult route, and organizes a feast for them. Maurice and his legion of Christian soldiers agree that they will refuse to sacrifice to the Roman gods. They follow Vitalis's advice and move their camp to Agaunum (today: Saint-Maurice). At the end of the feast, which is most grandly celebrated, Maximian realizes that a part of his army is missing. Scouts have seen them in Agaunum: Maximian orders that they be arrested and forced to worship the Roman gods, on pain of death. While he and the larger part of the army are waiting for the operation in Agaunum to be completed, they perform sword dances and worship dances for the pagan gods Jupiter and Mars. These dances reflect the two options between which the Thebean legion is forced to choose. Now, the message arrives that 5000 soldiers have chosen to be put to death, while a smaller part of the legion (1000 soldiers) has escaped. Among them are Victor and Ursus, who have fled to Solothurn, and have started to preach and to baptise crowds of people there. Maximian has them persecuted. Here ends the first day.

At the beginning of the second day Hyrtacus, the Roman governor of Solothurn, tells his councillor Symbolus about a nightmare. Symbolus considers that the dream could refer to foreigners coming to town. The emperor's messenger arrives and demands that Hyrtacus imprisons the Christians who have come to Solothurn. We see Ursus and Victor preaching to the people and converting the masses. From now on, the play follows and expands the *passio*, including the miracle of the decapitated bodies of Ursus, Victor and four further leaders of their group leaving the river and praying until they finally die. Finally Hyrtacus has the juridical court convene and sentence the remaining Thebeans to death. Here the play ends with a very long epilogue retelling the history of Solothurn.

Rolf Max Kully claims that the *Play of St Maurice and St Ursus* should not be understood as a confessional play, since it forms the 'Höhepunkt einer Sekularfeier' ('the highlight of a secular feast').[41] In the following, a closer examination of Wagner's play, however, will reveal that there is no such thing as a secular feast of the Swiss Confederation without a religious component.

---

40 See Wagner, *Sämtliche Werke*, ed. by Kully, vol. II, pp. 4–6; R. Kully, 'Hanns Wagner', p. 124.
41 R. Kully, 'Nachwort', p. 391.

One of the central 'secular' problems discussed throughout the play is the status of mercenaries, i.e. the question as to whether their service is necessarily a confessional or political statement, and whether military service for a salary is morally acceptable at all. The Thebeans explicitly try to 'render unto Caesar the things which are Caesar's, and unto God the things that are God's' (Matthew 22. 21). Ursus explains:

> Zu Thebis in Aegypter Lannd/
> Da hår wir vnsern vrsprung hand/
> Erbôrn von gûtem stammen har/
> Der ritterschafft ergeben z'wâr
> Darinn wir vnsre Jugend gschlißen/
> Der Gotsforcht vnns darby geflißen/
> Der Tugend vnd der bscheidenheit/
> der mâßigkeit/ vnd grecchtigkeit.
> Da hår wir vnns verpflichtet hannd
> Ze bschrimen helffen Stett vnd Lannd
> Vor v̈bertrang/ vnd Fÿends gwallt. (ll. 889–99)

>> (In Thebe in Egypt, where we were born into noble families, we dedicated ourselves to knighthood, spent our youth acting it, and fearing God, exercised virtue, wisdom, measure, and justice, and obliged ourselves to help protect towns and countries against aggression and the violence of enemies.)

On this mission, he narrates, they came to Jerusalem:

> Z'Hierusalem wir vnderwegen
> Der heilgen ritterschafft gepflegen/:
> Da nach dem Touff vereinbart worden (ll. 903–05)

>> (When we were in Jerusalem, we served as 'holy knights'. Then we accepted baptism.)

The Thebean legion appears as a group of valiant knights who had already served the idea of knighthood until in Jerusalem, fighting for God, they learned about the *militia Christi*. In the first part of the play the allegory of the *militia Christi* (Ephesians 6. 13–17) is explained in detail: Fighting for justice and for the just cause in war reflects the proper Christian's fight on the side of God against Satan. With their baptism, the Thebean legion has gained the ideal state of Christian knights. In this role, they render to Caesar what is Caesar's, as long as the emperor's wars are just:

> Wir hand den Keisern z'Rôm bishar
> In kriegen g'dienet etlich Jar:
> Ihnn gholffen bhalten ire Lannd [...]
> Do aber wir in Wallis kommen/

Hat Maximian ihm fürgenommen
Vns z'zwingen/ bÿ den Gôttern z'schweeren:
Vnd sie mit vnser opfer eeren:
Z'veruolgen ouch die Christenlüt:
Das hand wir wôllen halten nüt:
Ist nie inn kriegen gar vnd gantz
Gwåsen vnser ordinantz. (ll. 914–40)

> (Until now, we have served the emperors in Rome in various wars for many years, and helped them to maintain their realms. [...] However, when we reached the Wallis, Maximilian intended to force us to swear on the Roman gods and to honour them with sacrifices, and also to persecute Christians. We did not want to do that. This has never been our rule in war.)

The Swiss Reformer Zwingli strictly criticised the mercenary career as a commercial deal with death, and voted for its prohibition: as a military priest, he had experienced the disastrous 1515 Battle of Marignano, where Swiss troops suffered huge losses partly due to mercenaries' unanimous reactions to French offers.[42] In *Ein göttlich Vermanung*[43] he claims that Christians may only kill others in defense of their own freedom, but not for money in the service of foreign lords. 'Hût dich Schwytz vor frômbden heren/ Sy bråchtend dich zů vneeren' ('Beware, Switzerland, of foreign lords, who will lead you to dishonour', Ciiijʳ), he warns his readers. Zurich banned mercenaries in 1522;[44] Solothurn, however, cooperating with France, kept and cultivated this important source of financial income. Contracts with the clients fixed the Swiss soldiers' right — and duty — to leave the army, if they were asked to fight against their home country, or if Switzerland was otherwise under threat and needed them. The contracts also forbade that Swiss mercenaries were used against the pope.[45]

When in Wagner's play Hyrtacus reproaches the Christians for fleeing war as cowards (l. 996), Ursus's words and the Swiss rule clearly state that they acted correctly when deserting from Maximian's army. Their exemplary correctness challenges Zwingli's argument against mercenaries. Though the question might be secular, the argument in the end is confessional.

---

42 See Campi, 'Die Reformation', p. 78. For Marignano see: Somm, *Marignano*; Meier, *Von Morgarten bis Marignano*, pp. 174–79.
43 Zwingli, *Ein göttlich vermanung*.
44 See Campi, 'Die Reformation', p. 94.
45 See Hitz, *Kämpfen um Sold*, pp. 42–43.

Theatrical Methods of Religious Persuasion

The plot of the play makes clear that the question of mercenaries is only a side-question of a more general religious debate. On the surface the play defends Christian faith against pagan persecution, but on a closer look, it defends the Catholic faith against political attempts to suppress it. The essence of Wagner's persuasive method is a doubled structure: Messages, dreams, arguments and divine promises are visibly mirrored in life and are thereby confirmed as true. Who, the play asks, would accept a tyrant suppressing the truth?

A Message Comes True: Ursus's Prayer and the Sacrament

At the end of the *Play of St Maurice*, a scout reports Ursus's sermons and the baptism of the people to Maximianus. They are seen as a threat to the pagan world (*M*, ll. 1764–89). When Ursus appears on stage for the first time in the *Play of St Ursus* (act II, scene 1), we in fact hear him preach, confirming the truth of the scout's message. Sermons arguing for the Christian faith are a traditional element of sixteenth-century drama, especially of Lutheran drama. Ursus's words at first sound very familiar to a possible Protestant audience: he promises God's grace to all those who turn away from sin and confess their faith (ll. 374–75), and excuses the audience which, by the devils' intrigues, has been imprisoned in heathendom, in *grusamliche Abgötterey* (l. 382), acting idolatry. Idols, however, cannot offer them any support, because they are made from wood and stone (l. 390). This is a classical argument used in the defense of Protestant iconoclasm, based on Deuteronomy 29. 17. Quickly, however, Ursus points at the differences between pagan Roman idols and Christian religious images: While Christian images of saints remember exemplary Christians (the Lutheran argument) and support their adoration (the Catholic argument), the pagan gods do not deserve any kind of honour:

> Wie man mag binn Poëten låsen:
> Die ir gspått ståts mit ihnen gtriben/
> Als sÿ ir bůbereÿ beschriben (ll. 419–21)

> (As you can read in the works of the poets who constantly mocked them when they wrote about their vices.)

Ursus claims that Classical literature (the canon of medieval and early modern learning) and also Greek and Roman philosophy suggest that the pagan gods are not respectable. Philosophy explains them as powers of nature, or of the planets (ll. 423–26). If, however, they are nothing but effects of nature, they cannot have existed before nature. And since everything in nature has a cause, there must be a creator of nature, who is beyond everything natural and thus is pure spirit (ll. 444–45, 489–90). This is the Aristotelian argument that there must be a first mover, which has traditionally has been used by scholastic theology to prove the existence of God.[46] Ursus uses it to convince the pagan inhabitants of Solothurn that there must be a first, purely spiritual god. Philosophy won't help him further to describe the god who cannot be discerned by natural means. He therefore changes to the matter of faith, and describes what God has revealed of himself: that he is merciful, promising eternal life to all who believe in him and confess their sins. Using scholastic philosophical arguments in addition to the Bible, and describing the idols in such a way that they could not be identified with images used in church, Ursus is discernable as Christian, but not as a Reformed Christian. Stressing the grace of God and the importance of faith, he certainly meets the consesus between the confessions.

When Gerontius, representing the people converted by Ursus's words, asks for further instruction in the Christian faith, Victor recites the Creed — and thereby seemingly chooses a typical element of Protestant drama.[47] When citing the Creed, Protestant plays normally use the *Apostles' Creed*. Victor, however, uses the more elaborate *Nicene Creed*, which is a product of early Christian theology stressing the church's unity against the wrong teaching of the Arians. Victor claims that his words are the common creed of all Christians, but in fact adds some details that are not part of the Creed.[48] He turns the sentence 'Et incarnatus est de Spiritu Sancto ex Maria Virgine, et homo factus est' ('and was incarnate by the Holy Spirit of the virgin Mary, and was made man') into:

[…] d'menscheit angnommen
Zůr Gottheit/ von einr Maget zart/
Maria gnennt/ von edler art
Die on Manns sâmen hat gebôren,
(Doch d'Jungfrowschafft keins wegs verlôren)
Vom heilgen Geist ihn hat empfangen (ll. 544–49)

> ([…] hast accepted human nature in addition to the divine nature from a meek virgin, called Mary, from noble family, who has born him without the sperm of a man and nevertheless has not at all lost her virginity, begotten by the Holy Spirit)

---

46 Burkhard, 'Beweger', p. 75.

47 See for example Daniel Walther's *Johannes Baptista*, Erfurt 1559, act v, scene 2; Balthasar Thamm's *Dorothea*, Leipzig 1594, act II, scene 5 (Thamm, *Dorothea*, ed. by Gold, ll. 1179–91).

48 See a very similar Mariological addition to the Creed in Hilger Gartzwiller's Catholic play *Chrysantus und Daria*, Münstereifel 1609, act I (Gartzwiller, *Chrysantus*, ed. by Freund, l. 600).

Stressing Mary's noble decent from David, and her virginity after the birth, Victor refers to the scholastic Mariological tradition, which was fixed in the *Catechismus Romanus* (1/2, 5) by the Council of Trent in 1566.[49] Similarly, Victor extends the sentence 'Et iterum venturus est cum gloria, judicare vivos et mortuos' ('He will come again in glory to judge the living and the dead') to a ten-line description of the Last Judgement, threatening the evil that they will remain in hell as Lucifer's comrades and suffer eternal fear and pain ('Da z'bliben Lucifers gesellen. | Da wird sin eewig angst vnd nôt', ll. 572–73), again following the *Roman Catechism* (1/2, 9). Finally he extends the sentence 'Confiteor unum baptisma in remissionem peccatorum' ('I acknowledge one baptism for the remission of sins') to:

[…] Die ouch den heiligen Touff bekennt/
Gibt den zů abwåschung der Sünnden
Durch rüw/ vnd glouben iren kinnden. (ll. 592–94)

([…] who also acknowledges the holy baptism, and offers it as purification from sin to all its members, if they confess and believe.)

Victor clearly stresses the sacramental character of baptism, which literally washes away sins and therefore needs to be done with water (see *Catechismus Romanus*, II, 4) and which needs to be based on a confession of sin and a confession of faith, as explained by the *Catechismus Romanus* (II, 9). Therefore he first teaches the people how to confess their sins (ll. 619–29) and adminsters the sacrament of repentance before he baptises the people with holy water and teaches them the two most important prayers: the Lord's Prayer and the *Ave Maria*. The latter prayer finally reveals that he has converted the people to Catholic faith.

The sacrament of bapstism extended to the converted through holy water sprinkled over them, and possibly over the bi-confessional audience, too (l. 624b), makes the aforementioned persuasiveness of Ursus's words visible and tangible. The impact of the teaching that the emperor's messenger described has quickly become a fact that cannot be denied.

A Dream Comes True: Ursus's and Victor's Invincibility

Just before the emperor's message arrives in Solothurn, the city governor Hyrtacus has a prophetic dream: He sees himself hunting. At a moment when his hunters have left him alone, a bear and other wild animals attack him. His hound fights the bear, and Hyrtacus calls for the hunters' support, but suddenly a lightning bolt strikes him, and he remains in a dead faint until his hunters find him and help him up (ll. 142–65). Symbulus's

---

49 *Römischer Catechismus*, trans. by Otto of Augsburg.

suggestion that the dream could mean foreigners coming to Solothurn is quickly confirmed by the emperor's messenger who informs them about Ursus ('bear') and the other Christians who have come to Solothurn.

The bear's attack on Hyrtacus does not only mean Ursus's and Victor's preaching to the people, but also their powerful argument against Hyrtacus himself. Discussing with the governor, Ursus does not use philosophical arguments as in the case of his sermon to the people. He rather adapts to the language that a ruler could understand. His arguments are legal (the mercenaries' right to leave the army if they are asked to fight against their own people), political (Christ as a lord mightier than the Roman emperor) and historical: God has been proven to punish his enemies, for example when Jerusalem fell after the Jews had crucified Christ (ll. 1011–14). Therfore, Ursus explains, God will also punish Hyrtacus, if he refuses to convert (ll. 1033–34). Hyrtacus, however, is not open to these arguments. The fall of Jerusalem could certainly also serve as a proof of the power of Rome, and the historical fact of the crucifixion of Christ does not speak for his power. The only arguments the Romans seem to accept are deeds that could be directly attributed to the Christian god. Therefore Symbulus wants to know what kind of miracles God could perform. When Constantius enumerates Christ's miracles as they are reported in the New Testament, but also tells of the miracles that God acts through his apostles and saints, Hyrtacus realizes his inferior position in the debate and is enraged, while Symbulus is convinced:

> Nach irer sag/ kan ich nit weeren
> Das sÿ nit Christum sôllind eeren.
> Die wÿl er würckt sôlch wunderthat/
> Als diser ietz erzellet hat:
> Welch' ie kein oug nie mee gesehen
> Von vnsern Gôttern/ darf ich iehen. (ll. 1199–204)

> (According to what they said, I cannot deny that they should honour Christ, if he works these miracles that this man has reported: Nobody has ever seen our gods performing miracles as great as these, I must say.)

While the audience knows the biblical and legendary reports, and while Symbulus trusts Constantius's words, for Hyrtacus the emperor's strict edict against the Christians still has more presence than a mere *narration* about divine miracles. 'Bôs ist's mit Herren Kirsi z'eßen' (l. 1221), he explains, using a popular proverb 'it is no fun to eat cherries with the powerful', meaning 'better do not provoke those in power'. He thus articulates a heavily discussed political problem of the sixteenth century, the so-called Augsburg peace that gave the rulers the right to decide upon their subjects' confession. He does not even see the chance to allow himself to reflect about matters of faith out of fear of the emperor's rage. This uncomforable situation is depicted by the bear attacking Hyrtacus in his dream.

The following scenes continue the confirmation of Hyrtacus's dream and at the same time present visible proofs of the sanctity of the Thebean soldiers — visible, however, at first only for Hyrtacus's soldiers (representing the hunting dog in his dream) and for the audience, not for Hyrtacus himself: Ursus and his comrades are tormented in prison, reflecting the flagellation of Christ (and thus stressing their sanctity through typology), until a lightning bolt strikes the torturers and an angel asks the Christians to leave the prison — reflecting the liberation of St Peter as reported in Acts 12. 6–9, and thereby comparing Ursus with the most important apostle. However, when the torturers report the miracle to Hyrtacus, he considers that the soldiers might not have bound the prisoners strong enough. A second and a third miracle are needed in order to convince him: Victor acts an exorcism, chasing the devil from a statue of Mercury, and the fire of the stake where the Thebeans should be burned, is extinguised by a thunderstorm, while the lightning strikes Hyrtacus. Only now, when a servant helps him up, does he accept:

> Symbûle/ du mir reccht hast gseit.
> Jetzt ist mir min troum worden waar/
> Der mir diß naccht ward offenbâr. (ll. 1768–70)

> (Symbulus, you were right. Now my dream has come true that was revealed to me at night.)

The dream has proven true, and it has proven that Hyrtacus is powerless against the bear. The dream stopped when Hyrtacus fainted. Thus, he now feels free to decide what to do afterwards, and he hopes to find revenge. It is however obvious that whatever happens, the true victory is on the side of the Thebean legion. Too many miracles have proven the power of the Christian god and the weak position of the pagan tyrant.

An Argument Comes True: Miracles

As stated above, the 'people' in the play are convinced by rational arguments. Symbulus is convinced by the proofs he had asked for: the narration of miracles which God performs either directly or through his saints. Constantius says:

> Ich gschwÿg/ das er den Jungern sin
> Sôlch krafft ouch hat gegoßen ín.
> Das wo Sant Pauls schweißtûchli bloß
> Die bseßnen b'rûrtend/ wurdend s'lôß.
> Wenn nur die krancken b'schritten hat

CATECHISM AND MIRACLES AS ARGUMENTS IN RELIGIOUS DEBATE

Vber die gaßen Petri schatt/
Sind s' früsch/ vnd gsund von dannen gangen.
Vergiffts tranck/ vnd schådliche schlangen/
Ouch grimme thier hand sie nit g'letzt.
Etlich in süttigs ôl gesetzt
Sind darûs gangen vnuerseert:
Im füwr ouch bliben nit verzeert.
Etlich so man s' enthouptet hat/
Trûgend ir hôupter selbs von statt: [...]
Noch hüttigs tags/ zeigt er grôß wunnder
Durch sine heiligen/ besunder
Die vesten glouben an ihn hannd. (ll. 1129–49)

> (I don't need to say that he has given his apostles the same power.
> Whenever people possessed by demons touched St Paul's *sudarium*,
> the demons left them [Acts 19. 12]. When only St Peter's shadow
> fell onto the sick in the street, they were relieved and healed [Acts
> 5. 15]. Poisoned drinks, poisonous snakes, and wild beasts have not
> hurt them. Many have been thrown into boiling oil and have left it
> unscathed. Fire could not burn them. Many who were decapitated
> carried their heads away by themselves [...]. Still today he reveals
> great miracles, especially through his saints, who have enduring
> faith in him.)

Miracles acted by God to protect his saints are a common element of
religious literature, and, though more frequent in Catholic literature, could
well be found in Lutheran plays, too.[50] God's lightning striking the perse-
cutors of Christians also appears in Valentin Boltz's *St Pauls Bekehrung*
in Basel, 1551.[51] Constantius, however, mentions not only this kind of
miracle, but also miracles performed by the saints. These are a matter
of inter-confessional debate. Miracles performed by the apostles that are
recorded in the Bible, however, could not really be criticized. Still, the
above mentioned reference to Paul's *sudarium* (l. 1131), the healing relic of
a saint, is a later addition to the text in manuscript S I 81. This might prove
that Wagner struggled with this passage, trying to make it as convincing
as possible. If Paul's shroud could exorcize devils, why shouldn't Victor be
able to do so, too?

The miracles that are subject to the fiercest disputes are non-biblical
postmortem miracles of saints, which could prove the saints' holiness.

---

50 E.g. in Arnold Quiting's *Petrus and Jacobus*, Dortmund, 1593, act IV, scene 7 (Quiting,
   Jacobus, ed. by Dietl) or in Wolfgang Waldung's *Catharinae Martyrium*, Nuremberg, 1602,
   act IV (Waldung, *Catharina*, ed. by Dietl).
51 Boltz, *Sant Pauls bekerung*, ed. by Christ-Kutter, act II, l. 1475a.

Wagner adds one postmortem miracle in the margins of S I 81, which is added to the text in the younger manuscript S I 120: the fact that some decapitated saints carried their heads away. While legends about the decapitation of St Paul report that he collected the blood from his throat during and after his decapitation, and that his dead body turned to the head and thereby identified it,[52] the miracle described here is typical for the stories of the Thebean legion. It is also contained in the legend of Felix and Regula, the patron saints of Zurich, with which the audience certainly was familiar. Constantius finally refers to post-biblical saints 'through whom' (l. 1148) God 'still today' (l. 1147) acts miracles: This is again a later addition to the text in manuscript S I 81. The first version said that God still today acts the miracles 'An sinen heiligen' (l. 1148): '(visible) at his saints'. The newer text clearly stresses the saints' power to perform those miracles.

The following plot will convince all those who doubt that this kind of miracle could be enacted by post-biblical saints. As soon as Ursus, Victor, Constantius and three further comrades have been decapitated and thrown into the river Aare, we hear Thaumantius's report that he has seen six beheaded men leaving the river with their heads in their hands, kneeling down and praying for a whole hour until they finally died (ll. 2047–64). Thaumantius shares the audience's impression that his report in incredible, yes, he can hardly believe it himself. Before he reports it to his friends, he speaks to himself:

> Was größen wunnders ist beschechen?
> Ich hab's min lebtag nie gsehen
> Es ist kein gspenst/ noch btrug gesin:
> Mir sind nit gblendt die ougen min (ll. 2030–34)

> (What a great miracle has occurred! Such a thing I have never seen in my life. It was neither a ghost nor a hallucination. My eyes are not blinded.)

Thaumantius guides his friends to the dead bodies, which all have their heads in their hands. For the Christians in the play these bodies are a sufficient proof of the truth of his observation. However, nothing would be easier than showing the observed scene on stage so that the audience would share Thaumantius's experience. The scene visibly proves Constantius's argument that God has the power to make his saints after their deaths perform miracles, for example the very visually arresting act of carrying

---

52 Jacobus, *Legenda aurea*, ed. by Häuptli, no. 90, pp. 1172–75.

their own heads. The play does not allow any doubt that Ursus and his comrades are saints in the Catholic understanding of sainthood and that the religion they preached is the 'proper' religion.

Christ's Promise Comes True: Solothurn Remains Catholic

The highest possible authority confirming the truth of Ursus's and his comrades' teaching is Christ himself appearing on stage. At the end of the last rescue miracle (the extinct fire), while Hyrtacus lies on the floor struck by lightning, an angel announces the near death of the saints and their upcoming coronation in heaven. In this moment Ursus kneels down and prays to God, asking for God's grace for his and his comrades' souls, and for the converted people. Using Christ's words, he also asks for mercy for his enemies — and for Solothurn:

> Laß Solothurn der Statt/ vnd Lannd
> Din heilgen namen werden bkannt.
> Din Geist/ frid/ gnad sennd diserm ôrt/
> Ze thûn allzÿt nach dinem wôrt.
> In recchtem waarem glouben z'bstân/
> Kein zÿt vom Gottsdienst ab ze lân.
> Statt/ Lannd erhallt in dienem segen:
> Gwår die ir's gbåtts von minet wegen.
> Wenn s' dich in nôten rûffend an/
> Wôllst s' in din schirm beuolhen han (ll. 1695–704).

> > (Let your holy name be known to the town and country of Solothurn. Send your spirit, your peace, your grace to this place so that the people will always follow your word and are steadfast in true faith and will never cease to celebrate the Mess. Hold the town and country in your blessing and grant all those their pleas who call upon you by my name in situations of urgent need.)

Ursus not only establishes his position as patron saint of Solothurn, but also clearly articulates a Catholic understanding of saints as mediators and advocates. Asking God to keep his people in 'recchtem waaren glouben' ('proper, true faith', l. 1699) and make them always celebrate Mass, he obviously asks God for protection against the Reformation. Christ himself promptly replies, proving visibly and audibly that Ursus has the correct understanding of sainthood and enjoys God's full support:

> Din trüw fürpitt will ich erhôren/
> Ja dinen namen, Vrse, meeren.
> Wer in dim namen etwas bgårt
> Dem sol es allzÿt werden gwårt. (ll. 1715–18).

(Your faithful plea I will hear, and I will raise your name, Ursus. Whoever asks for anything in your name, will always be granted it.)

Christ grants that a church will be built in Ursus's honour and that he will always hear the prayers of the people who ask God in the name of Ursus. He also promises to protect the town from all enemies:

> Vom Fÿnd wird d'Statt beschirmet zwaar
> Ob glÿch frömbd/ heimsch sich lågert dar.
> Dir wird diß Statt vergåbet werden
> So din g'bein wird erhebt vff erden:
> Hernach zů gantzer frÿheit kommen/
> So sÿ in bündtnus wird genommen.
> Min ståtes opfer wol nich hören/
> Ob glÿch nüw secten sich entbören:
> Min schöner roosgart sol rein blÿben/
> Die distlen/ dörn vmb sich vertrÿben. (ll. 1727–36)

> > (In truth, the town will be protected against the enemy, whether foreign or home troops besiege it. This town will be dedicated to you as soon as your relics are elevated. Thereafter it will come to complete freedom when it is accepted into the Confederation. My permanent sacrifice should not cease to be celebrated, even if new sects arise. My beautiful rosary shall remain pure and chase away all thistles and thorns that surround it.)

All the audience witnesses the promise given from the highest authority, which at the moment of the performance has already proven true: The relics of Ursus had been elevated by the legendary Bertha, who had the church of St Ursus built (in front of which the performance takes place) and made Ursus the patron saint of Solothurn. Ursus had protected the town against Leopold of Hapsburg in 1318, and in the confessional conflict in 1533. Solothurn joined the Swiss Confederation and made peace with its Protestant neighbours, but remained Catholic, with the Holy Mass constantly being celebrated at St Ursus minster. The highest authority who speaks these words, and the audience's knowledge that the promise has come true, support each other in a very explicit Counter-Reformation message, which refuses all possible intentions to turn the Swiss Confederation into a Protestant Confederation. Wagner suggests that God welcomes the Swiss Confederation as a peace treaty, but would never allow any doubt that Solothurn has decided for the right side in the confessional conflict.

Some 1000 lines or at least an hour later the epilogue confirms Christ's words. He retells the history of Solothurn and of the church of St Ursus, which was commissioned by Bertha, who had found the relics. The relics, we hear, had performed miracles, healing sick people, even before their elevation. The epilogue reminds the audience of the protective power of the saints, for example during the siege by Leopold, when the Thebean legion appeared on the walls of Solothurn, with their flag, which shows a white cross (l. 2976). The flag had been mentioned in the first act already (l. 303) as the sign by which the Christians could be identified.

Finally, the epilogue gives all citizens of Solothurn the advice:

Blÿb bestenndig in den glouben:
Nit laß dich disers kleinats b'rouben/
Noch verfürisch Secten rÿsen in:
Nit schütt die Berlin für die Schwÿn.
Ståts gevolg dinr Vordern weg (ll. 2953–57)

> (Remain steadfast in your faith, and let nobody steal this treasure from you, and do not allow seductive sects to gain land. Do not throw the pearls before the swine and always follow the way of your forefathers.)

Counter-Reformation and Diplomacy

Wagner's *Play of St Ursus* is clearly a Counter-Reformation play, defending the Catholic understanding of sainthood with saints as mediators and protectors, performing miracles after their death, transmitting healing power through their relics. It also defends in a more subtle way the role of Mary, the Catholic understanding of the Holy Mass and the sacraments of repentance and baptism. It portrays Protestantism as a dangerous sect that should be kept away from what Wagner calls 'the rosary of true faith': the enclosed garden of Marian devotion, the place of salvation, which in the end appears as a metaphor for the city of Solothurn. However, the play does not openly polemicize against Protestant teaching, and it does not call for active aggression against Protestants. Since the play clearly identifies Ursus, Victor and their comrades with the Catholic faith, one might be tempted to identify Hyrtacus and his soldiers with Protestantism. But they are clearly portrayed as pagans, and not as a Christian sect. The only *tertium comparationis* could be their aggression against the saints, claiming that all subjects have to accept the ruler's faith. However, idolatry would not fit as a description for the faith of the powerful Protestants.

There is only one scene that suggests that Hyrtacus's people could be understood as mirroring the Protestant members of the Swiss Confederation: When the Thebeans are arrested for the first time, one of the soldiers grabs the flag, with its cross design, from Constantius' hand with the words:

Du wirdst mir ietzt din Fennli lân/
Ich kan vil bas darmit vmbgân. (ll. 757–58)

(You must give me your flag. I know better how to deal with it.)

These words could simply mean that the soldier claims to be better at war than Constantius. However, in a revision in the younger manuscript S I 120 (**Fig. 6.2**), Wagner adds a fifth and a sixth soldier in this scene,[53] through whom he emphasises the quarrel about the flag. The fifth soldier also grabs it and says: 'Din fennli sol für hin sin in dem dienste min' (l. 772: 'Your flag shall from now on serve me'). Both statements of the soldiers ask the question who would best deserve the flag with the white cross. The characteristic red flag with a white cross, sign of the Thebean legion, is documented for the first time at the battle of Laupen in 1339, as the Bernese flag. It could have been designed as a counterpart to the flag of St George (the red cross on white ground) which the Habsburg army used,[54] or as a citation of the Savoyan cross of St Maurice.[55] In the sixteenth century, the white cross on red ground was used more frequently for armies uniting several Swiss regions. From the mid-sixteenth century it is mentioned as the 'cross of the Swiss Confederation',[56] as for example in Valentin Boltz' *Weltspiegel* (1550) where it is said to be a variant of the coat of arms of Schwyz (ll. 1341–44).[57] In fact, at that time, the Swiss cantons did not have a common coat of arms;[58] it is a mere war sign for common actions of mercenaries. This is exactly what the present scene is about: Soldiers and mercenaries quarrel about who has the right to carry the flag, i.e. to take the lead in military actions. The soldiers' act is most aggressive against the mercenaries from Solothurn.

A similarly subtle reference to the Protestant neighbouring towns is given in the aforementioned scene of Victor's exorcism. The columns visible at the entry to the churchyard of St Ursus in Fig. 6.1 are remnants of a Roman temple, dedicated to Mercury.[59] It is not totally clear when they were placed in front of the churchyard. We only know that between 1608 and 1612 they received new bases.[60] Wagner shows clear interest in the columns, which could mean that they were already at the indicated

---

53 The additional soldiers are also mentioned in a younger second column in the cast list on p. 2 of the manuscript.

54 See Kopp, 'Schweizerkreuz'; Marchal, 'Da la *Passion du Christ*', pp. 7 and 16.

55 Marchal, 'Da la *Passion du Christ*', p. 14.

56 Kopp, 'Schweizerkreuz'; Marchal, 'Da la *Passion du Christ*', p. 36.

57 Boltz, *Weltspiegel*, ed. by Christ Kutter; see Marchal, 'Da la *Passion du Christ*', p. 37.

58 Kopp, 'Schweizerkreuz'.

59 Blank, 'Zur Geschichte'.

60 Strübin/Zürcher, *Die Stadt Solothurn*, p. 34; Blank/Hochstrasser, 'Der Solothurner Stadtprospekt'.

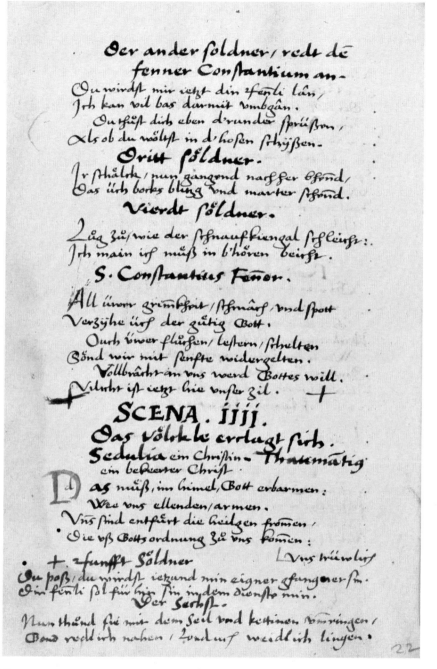

Figure 6.2. Hanns Wagner, *Tragoedia Ursina*, 1581, Solothurn, Central Library, ZBS S I 120, p. 34. Photo: Cora Dietl.

place, visible on the central stage. On the first day of the play, the columns could be used for the dance of adoration of Mars and Jupiter, which reflects the parallel action of the martyrdom of Maurice and the larger parts of the Thebean legion. On the second day, when Hyrtacus tries to force Victor to adore a statue of Mercury on a column, the use of the same scenery could underline the menace involved in Hyrtacus' request. The manuscripts show that Wagner repeatedly worked on this scene. He turned a short passage in the anonymous *Play of St Ursus* into a full scene. In the anonymous play, the idol does not have a god's name. In his older manuscript S I 81 Wagner corrected his stage direction on the bottom of p. 57: 'Beschweert den Abgott vff der Sûl, des Juppiters bild' ('he exocizes the idol on the column, Jupiter's image), by deleting 'Juppiters' and adding 'oder Mercurij bild' ('or Mercury's image'). The next leaf (pp. 58–59) is cut out, and a new leaf is glued to the remaining paper strip, which shows Wagner's hand. On the new page 58 we find Wagner's new version of the exorcism, and a drawing of a column with a statue on top (**Fig. 6.3**). Like the columns placed in front of the St Ursus churchyard, it does not have a capital, and it clearly does not have the elaborate new base that the columns received in the early seventeenth century. In the younger manuscript S I 120 Wagner slightly changed the stage direction again. It now says 'Beschweert den Götzen Mercurium' (l. 1408a). In the margins next to ll. 1405–07 Wagner added: 'Ad Mercurij Statuam' ('to the statue of Mercury'). It seems he gradually decided to refer to Mercury, not to Jupiter or any other idol, and thereby to stress the link with local history, or rather with the visible remnants of pagan history in Solothurn.

Victor enacts a formal exorcism. The wording is taken almost verbatim from the older anonymous play. The devil's reaction, however, is expanded: At first the devil laments in despair, running up and down 'uff der brügi' (l. 1420a: 'on the scaffolding') — most probably among the audience, but then he recovers and reveals his new plans — in long lines, which provide emphasis:

> Ich gloub/ ich wôlle louffen in ein andre Statt/
> Da man min falschen btrug noch nie vernommen hat/.
> Am selben ort will ich so gwaltig liegen/
> Das sich darab die balcken môchtind biegen.
> Ich mûß die Wellt noch lange zÿt betriegen (ll. 1423–27)

> > (I think I will run to another town, where my false fraud is not yet known. There I will lie through my teeth. I will continue betraying the world for ages.)

To which other town might he go? Bearing in mind that a remarkable proportion of the audience may have come from other Swiss towns, as suggested by the 100 recorded visitors from Berne, the devil's words could

CATECHISM AND MIRACLES AS ARGUMENTS IN RELIGIOUS DEBATE 183

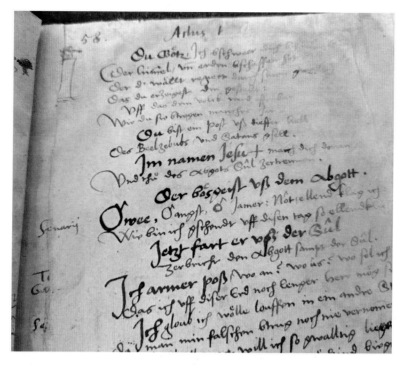

Figure 6.3. Hanns Wagner, *Sant Vrsen Spiel*, 1575, Solothurn: Central Library, S I 81, p. 58. Photo: Cora Dietl.

well be understood as a confessional commentary. He seems to claim that in the Reformed part of Switzerland he might not be recognized, and could continue to betray people for a very long time, while he has definitely left the city with the former sanctuary of Mercury.

A Play Celebrating the Swiss Confederation?

While Kully claims that, due to the political context of its performance, Hanns Wagner's *Play of St Maurice and St Ursus* could not be understood as a confessional play, I would rather question whether the clearly confessional play is apt for the celebration of the Swiss Confederation. Wagner serves the purpose of the performance when he explicitly celebrates the peace treaty and the Swiss Confederation in general as a divine gift, which should never be given up. At the same time, however, he also states that the Catholic faith is equally granted by Christ and needs to be conserved against all attacks of 'sects'. Thereby he is careful not to offend the partners openly by identifying the sects. He celebrates Christianity as a glorious achievement, which also means a triumph over tyrants like Hyrtacus and Maximianus. Visibly stylizing those who are responsible for that triumph as saints in the Catholic understanding of sainthood and as idealized mercenaries, and equating Christian teaching with Catholic teaching, he manages indirectly to identify all enemies of the cult of saints, and all those accepting a different teaching about the sacraments, with enemies of Christianity and supporters of the devil and tyranny. Stressing the links between the action on stage and the city history as well as the history of the Swiss Confederation, which is the object of the current celebration, he confirms the legend as part of his audience's identity, which should be local, Swiss, and Catholic.

Bibliography

Unedited Source Texts

Viten frühchristlicher Päpste und Märtyrer (St Gall: Abbey Library, Cod. Sang. 569)

Wagner, Hanns, *Sant Vrsen Spiel*, 1575 (Solothurn: Central Library, S I 81)

———, *St Mauritius-Spil*, 1581 (Solothurn: Central Library, S I 101)

———, Hanns, *Tragoedia Ursina*, 1581 (Solothurn: Central Library, S I 120)

Walther, Daniel, *Eyne Christliche vnd jnn heiliger Schrifft gegründte Historia/ von der entheuptung Johannis Baptistæ/ in ein Tragediam gestalt* [...] (Erfurt: Georg Baumann, 1559) (VD16 W 949)

Zwingli, Huldrych, *Ein göttlich vermanung an die Ersamen/ wysen/ eerenuesten/ eltisten Eydgnossen zů Schwytz das sy sich vor frömden herren huütind vnd entladind* (Zurich: Christoph Froschauer, 1522) (VD16 Z 856)

Edited Source Texts

Boltz, Valentin, *Sant Pauls bekerung*, in ders., *Bibeldramen, Gesprächsbüchlein*, ed. by Friederike Christ-Kutter, Schweizer Texte, 27 (Zurich: Chronos, 2009), pp. 13–141

———, *Der Weltspiegel*, ed. by Friederike Christ Kutter and others, Schweizer Texte, 37 (Zurich: Chronos, 2013.

Eucherius of Lyon, *Passio Arcaunensium martyrum*, ed. by Beat Näf (Zurich: text & bytes: 2015), https://passiones.textandbytes.com/impressum (accessed: 29 April 2022)

Fredegarii et aliorum Chronica. Vitae sanctorum, ed. by Bruno Krusch, MGH Scriptorum Rerum Merovingicarum, 2 (Munich: MGH, 1888)

Gartzwiller, Hilger, *Chrysantus und Daria*, ed. by Karolin Freund, Frühneuzeitliche Märtyrerdramen, 6 (Wiesbaden: Harrassowitz, 2019)

Haffner, Anton, *Chronica*, reprint of the edition Solothurn, 1577 (Solothurn: Franz Xaver Zepfel, 1849)

Jacobus a Voragine, *Legenda Aurea. Goldene Legende*, ed. and trans. by Bruno W. Häuptli, 2 vols (Freiburg i.Br.: Herder, 2014)

Quiting, Arnold, *Jacobus und Petrus*, ed. by Cora Dietl, Frühneuzeitliche Märtyrerdramen, 7 (Wiesbaden: Harrassowitz, 2021)

Römischer Catechismus Welcher auß beuelch Bäpstlicher Hayligkeit/ Pii des fünfften/ nach hieuor gegebner Ordnung des hailigen jungst zů Triendt gehalten Concilij [...] *im Truck außgangen ist*, transl. by Otto of Augsburg (Dillingen: Sebald Mayer, 1568)

Thamm, Balthasar, *Dorothea. Tragicocomoedia*, ed. by Julia Gold, Frühneuzeitliche Märtyrerdramen, 2 (Wiesbaden: Harrassowitz, 2019)

Wagner, Hanns (alias Ioannes Carpentarius), *Sämtliche Werke*, ed. by Rolf Max Kully, 3 vols (Berne: Peter Lang, 1982)

Waldung, Wolfgang, *Catharina*, ed. by Cora Dietl, Frühneuzeitliche Märtyrerdramen, 1 (Wiesbaden: Harrassowitz, 2019)

Secondary Material

Biermann, Heinrich, 'Nachwort', in Johannes Wagner, *Solothurner St Mauritius- und St Ursenspiel*, ed. by Heinrich Biermann, Schweizer Texte, 5 (Berne and Stuttgart: Haupt, 1980), pp. 207–61

Blank, Stefan, 'Zur Geschichte und Bedeutung der "Hermessäulen" in Solothurn', *Jurablätter*, 59 (1997), 185–88

Blank, Stefan and Markus Hochstrasser, 'Der Solothurner Stadtprospekt von Gregor Sickinger und Urs König – Versuch einer Datierung anhand des dargestellten Baubestandes', *Archäologie und Denkmalpflege im Kanton Solothurn*, 12 (2007), 133–35

Burkard, Franz Peter, 'Beweger, unbewegter', in *Metzler Lexikon Philosophie: Begriffe und Definitionen*, ed. by Peter Prechtl and Franz-Peter Burkard, 3rd edn (Stuttgart: Metzler, 2008), p. 75

Burnett, Amy N. and Emidio Campi (eds), *Die schweizerische Reformation. Ein Handbuch*, German version ed. by Martin E. Hirzel and Frank Mathwig (Zurich: Theologischer Verlag, 2016)

Campi, Emidio, 'Die Reformation in Zürich', in *Die schweizerische Reformation. Ein Handbuch*, ed. by Amy N. Burnett and Emidio Campi, German version by Martin E. Hirzel and Frank Mathwig (Zurich: Theologischer Verlag, 2016), pp. 71–133

Dafflon, Alexandre, *Die Ambassadoren des Königs und Solothurn. Ein 'vierzehnter Kanton' am Ufer der Aare. 16. bis 18. Jahrhundert*, Kleine Reihe, 3D (Solothurn: Zentralbibliothek, 2014)

Dietl, Cora and others, *Inszenierungen von Heiligkeit. Das schweizerische Heiligenspiel des 16. und frühen 17. Jahrhunderts im Kontext konfessioneller Auseinandersetzungen* (Berlin and Basel: Schwabe, 2023)

Fiala, Friedrich, 'Haffner, Anton', in *Allgemeine Deutsche Biographie*, vol. X (1879), pp. 317–18.

Greco-Kaufmann, Heidy, *Zuo der Eere Gottes, vfferbuwung dess mentschen vnd der statt Lucern lob. Theater und szenische Vorgänge in der Stadt Luzern im Spätmittelalter und in der Frühen Neuzeit*, 2 vols (Zurich: Chronos, 2009)

Hitz, Benjamin, *Kämpfen und Sold. Eine Alltags- und Sozialgeschichte schweizerischer Söldner in der Frühen Neuzeit* (Cologne: Böhlau, 2015)

Hochstrasser, Markus, 'Solothurn, "Hermessäulen"', *Archäologie und Denkmalpflege im Kanton Solothurn*, 3 (1998), 116–18

Koch, Bruno, 'Kronenfresser und deutsche Franzosen. Zur sozialgeschichte der Reisläuferei aus Bern, Solothurn und Biel zur Zeit der Mailänderkriege', *Schweizerische Zeitschrift für Geschichte*, 46/2 (1996), 151–84

Kopp, Peter F., 'Schweizerkreuz', in *Historisches Lexikon der Schweiz*, version: 18 November 2020, https://hls-dhs-dss.ch/de/articles/010104/2020-11-18/ (accessed: 4 August 2023)

Kully, Elisabeth, 'Das ältere St Ursenspiel', *Jahrbuch für Solothurnische Geschichte*, 55 (1982), 5–107

Kully, Rolf Max, 'Hanns Wagner und das Solothurner "Festspiel" vom Jahre 1581', *Jahrbuch für solothurnische Geschichte*, 55 (1982), 109–28

——, 'Wagner (Carpentarius), Hanns (Ioannes, Johannes)', in *Verfasserlexikon. Frühe Neuzeit in Deutschland 1520–1620*, ed. Wilhelm Kühlmann and others, vol. VI (Berlin: De Gruyter, 2017), coll. 419–23

——, 'Nachwort', in *Hanns Wagner alias Ioannes Carpentarius, Sämtliche Werke*, ed. by Rolf Max Kully, vol. 1 (Berne: Peter Lang, 1982), pp. 387–402

Marchal, Guy P., 'De la *Passion du Christ* à la "Croix Suisse". Quelques réflexions sur une enseigne suisse', *Itinera*, 9 (1989), 108–31

Meier, Bruno, *Von Morgarten bis Marignano. Was wir über die Entstehung der Eidgenossenschaft wissen* (Baden: Hier und Jetzt, 2015)

Reinhardt, Volker, *Die Geschichte der Schweiz. Von den Anfängen bis heute* (Munich: Beck, 2011)

Rüedy, Lukas, 'Bauernkrieg und Reformation in der solothurnischen Vogtei Thierstein', in *Jahrbuch für Solothurnische Geschichte*, 74 (2001), 51–189

Strübin, Johanna and Christine Zürcher, *Die Stadt Solothurn III, Sakralbauten*, Die Kunstdenkmäler der Schweiz, 134 (Berne: GSK, 2017)

Somm, Markus, *Marignano. Die Geschichte einer Niederlage*, 2nd edn (Berne: Stämpfli, 2015)

Widmer, Berthe, 'Ursus und Victor', in *Historisches Lexikon der Schweiz (HLS)*, Version 19 February 2013. Online: https://hls-dhs-dss.ch/de/articles/010199/2013-02-19/ (accessed: 29 April 2022)

——, 'Der Ursus- und Victorkult in Solothurn', in *Solothurn. Beiträge zur Entwicklung der Stadt im Mittelalter. Kolloquium vom 13./14. November 1987 in Solothurn* (Zurich: Verlag der Fachvereine, 1990), pp. 33–82

Zünd, André, *Gescheiterte Stadt- und Landreformationen des 16. und 17. Jahrhunderts in der Schweiz*, Basler Beiträge zur Geschichtswissenschaft, 170 (Basel: Schwabe, 1999)

PAMELA M. KING

George Buchanan, Dramatic Strategies, and Polemics in the Scottish Reformation

▼ **ABSTRACT** The paper reads George Buchanan's tragedy *Baptistes* (in the printed version, which is a palimpsest of the original version written in exile) as a companion-piece to his polemic dialogue *De Jure Regni apud Scotos*. Both texts are directed against contemporary 'tyrants' and false councillors, and the latter explicitly against the royal secretary William Maitland. The paper discusses the tensions between Calvinist critique against theatre and Buchanan's play that reveals an aggressive rhetoric far beyond the expectations of a school play. The fact that the Calvinist Reformation remained vitally adept in the deployment of dramatic device is finally realized in the highly dramatic dialogue *De Iure Regni apud Scotos*.

▼ **KEYWORDS:** George Buchanan, Scotland, neo-Latin drama, biblical plays, dialogue Reformation, polemics, tyranny, law, rhetoric.

Pamela M. King is Professor Emerita of Medieval Studies in the University of Glasgow. She previously held chairs in the Universities of Bristol and what is now the University of Cumbria, and spent her early career in the University of London. She is former president of SITM and is a specialist on medieval drama and religious festivals, especially on the York Mystery Cycle. For her publications she won the David Bevington prize and the Beatrice White prize. Her recent focus is on medieval Scots poetry and performance.

European Medieval Drama, 27 (2023), 189–214
BREPOLS ᛘ PUBLISHERS

10.1484/J.EMD.5.137683

George Buchanan's neo-Latin play, *Baptistes*, is a dramatization of the events leading up to the decapitation of John the Baptist. Though it was written in the 1540s in Guyenne, it was not published until 1576,[1] that edition being prefaced by an admonitory address to James VI of Scotland on the dangers of monarchical tyranny.[2] In the play, the descent of a monarch into tyranny is embodied in the character of Herod, and the nub of the debate within the play is the relationship between the monarch and the law, evidently considered sufficiently relevant by the author to be presented much later as an advice-piece for his former tutee, James.

The play can be read as a companion-piece to Buchanan's provocative *De Jure Regni apud Scotos*, his polemic dialogue addressing comparable issues and addressed to the same king. The dialogue was probably written and originally circulated in 1567 although it was not finally published until 1579.[3] The following paper will inevitably revisit Buchanan's major and highly controversial concerns about constitutional monarchy — a path well-trodden by other commentators on his work — but the chief project here is rather to consider Buchanan's rhetorical and stylistic strategies in the two works, and to propose that the effectiveness of those strategies in the treatise may in part be attributed to Buchanan's early work as a practised dramatist. Buchanan, considered the most dangerously eloquent of the Protestant partisans of his day, is not primarily remembered for his dramas, but we can see nonetheless how dramatic method and imagination in his hands becomes one of the most potent tools of Reformation ideology.

George Buchanan (1506–1582)'s long and eventful career is well known, and can only be summarized here.[4] Born into a Stirlingshire family, he was a native speaker of Gaelic, not Scots. His widowed mother's brother sent him to the University of Paris in 1520. On this uncle's death, he returned to Scotland and attended the University of St Andrews, but went back to Paris as a follower of the logician John Mair. It is from Mair that Buchanan inherited the radical scholasticism that is fundamental to both texts under consideration. Buchanan was to absorb new Humanist

---

1 See Buchanan, '*Baptistes*', ed. by Berkowitz, p. 7 for a full account of the original dating, and pp. 25–30 for a further account of how Buchanan's circle of friends wrestled his early works from him for printing.

2 Buchanan, *Tragedies*, ed. by Sharratt and Walsh, pp. 95–164. Translation of the dedicatory epistle only are mine (P.K.). All further page references refer to this text. When page numbers are given, they refer to the Latin text first and to the editors' translation second; line numbers refer to the Latin.

3 Buchanan, *De Jure Regni*, ed. and trans. by Mason and Smith, pp. XVI–XVII.

4 See, for example, McFarlane, *Buchanan* for the general details of the biographical information below; also the extended 'Introduction' in Buchanan, '*Baptistes*', ed. by Berkowitz, and the 'Introduction' in Buchanan, *De Iure Regni*, ed. by Mason and Smith. Buchanan's entry in *DNB* can be found at Macmillan, *George Buchanan*.

reactions against the scholastic methods of which Mair was an exponent, but Mair's conciliarism stayed with him: the belief that just as the pope should be guided by the Councils of the Church, so too should monarchs be accountable to assemblies of their people.

After his graduation in 1528, his rise in the University of Paris was meteoric, until he returned again to Scotland in 1537 with his then tutee, Gilbert Kennedy of Cassalis. He was, at this stage, probably best described as an Erasmian, but his attraction to radical ideas led him to have to flee back to France in 1539, as the Scottish crown, led by Cardinal Beaton of St Andrews, engaged in a purge of suspected Lutherans. When Beaton arrived in Paris, Buchanan removed to Bordeaux on the invitation of André de Gouvela, and became a tutor in the newly-founded College of Guyenne. He returned to Paris in 1544, but again the sojourn was brief as he was recruited by Gouvela to lecture in the Portuguese University of Coimbra. Whether by action of Gouvela's jealous brother, the posthumous influence of Beaton, or a Jesuit plot, Buchanan was investigated by the Lisbon Inquisition and committed to imprisonment in 1550 in the monastery of San Bento. Following his inexplicable release — he did not recant, — he returned to Paris, and, after a further decade, during which he formed connections with the French throne, he was prompted by the death of the young Francis II, first husband of Mary Queen of Scots to return to Scotland with the widowed queen. Despite his Protestant leanings, he became an intimate member of the (Roman Catholic) Queen's court, reading Livy with her. Consequently, when Mary made her second marriage to Henry Stewart, Lord Darnley, it was Buchanan who wrote the masques and poetic eulogies for the celebrations.[5] He also collaborated in scripting the celebrations in 1566 in Stirling for the baptism of the infant prince, James.[6]

Darnley's murder in 1567, Queen Mary's marriage to James Hepburn, Fourth Earl of Bothwell, and her subsequent forced 'abdication', caused Buchanan to break ties with the Queen forever and throw in his lot with the then regent, James Stewart, Earl of Moray. Buchanan had been for some years a member of a Catholic court and a Protestant church. With no inheritance and a hand to mouth existence based on patronage, he maintained a judicious inscrutability, but arrived at his eventual distinctive brand of Protestantism through intellectual consideration over time. His appointment by Moray to the Moderatorship of the Church of Scotland, though it is doubtful whether he had ever taken holy orders, testifies as much to his canny courting of safe patronage as to his doctrinal beliefs.

Buchanan accompanied Moray to England in his mission to expose the Queen's part in the murder of Darnley, and became an entrenched

---

5 See further Buchanan, 'Three Entertainments', ed. by Davidson, Montserrat, and Stevenson.
6 See further Lynch, 'Queen Mary's Triumph'.

member of the party opposed to the Queen. Moray's murder was a blow to Buchanan, but the Privy Council appointed him tutor to the infant James. Then the Duke of Lennox, Darnley's father, took over as regent and was, thus, a new ally. Buchanan was made Keeper of the Great Seal of Scotland, replacing John Maitland — of whom more later —, a post he held until 1579. He died in his Edinburgh apartment at the age of seventy-six.

Buchanan has long been acclaimed as one of the greatest thinkers Scotland produced, as one of Europe's most fluent Latinists, but he was also, evidently, a great survivor — of at least two bouts of mortal illness, of the Inquisition, and of the vicissitudes of one of the most turbulent periods of Scottish history — and a committed radical free-thinker. As one commentator reflects, Buchanan's Protestantism was hardened after the murder of Darnley in 1567, although his was always a blend of neo-Stoicism and Calvinism.[7] Though they were equally hard-line by the 1570s the distinction between Buchanan and Knox was that the former was educated on the Continent, whereas Knox was educated solely in Scotland. Buchanan was shaped by his years in Paris, associating with French poets and humanists during his formative years as a writer, and was never a native Scots speaker.

Baptistes is one of the suite of four Latin plays that survive originally written when Buchanan was in France in the 1540s. It has been deduced that that they were devised as school exercises, but their history is based on circumstantial evidence largely derived from Buchanan's correspondence with friends.[8] Their dramatic quality far exceeds the normal expectation of such exercises. Latin was Buchanan's primary language by this time, and one of the pupils at the school of Guyenne in Bordeaux, where they were probably performed, was Michel de Montaigne. Two of the four, *Medea* and *Alcestis*, are based on Greek originals. The other two, of more interest to us immediately, are the biblical plays *Baptistes* and *Jephthes*. According to Buchanan himself, he first translated *Medea* when he was learning Greek, so presumably in Paris, but he also stated that *Baptistes* was his first play. It is assumed, therefore, that all the plays were written, or rewritten, for performance purposes during his three years in Bordeaux, 1540–1543. Daniel Rogers, exiled son of martyred John Rogers, is known from the same sources to have read a manuscript copy of the play in Paris in 1566, but no copy from that date survives.[9] What began as an exemplar of classical style and moral education, appears to have held abiding interest specifically as a mirror for magistrates, a Renaissance disquisition on the dangers of tyranny in the tradition of Elyot's *The Governour* (1531). Berkowicz has argued, 'it was not necessary to revise the play to revise its function',

---

7 Blake, *William Maitland*, p. 8.

8 Buchanan, '*Baptistes*', ed. by Berkowitz, p. 7.

9 Buchanan, '*Baptistes*', ed. by Berkowitz, p. 119.

when the author-reader relationship changed from the education of several youths in Guyenne in the 1540s to one youthful monarch in Scotland.[10] Set against this argument, however, is the evidence that Buchanan's friends wrested his early works out of the hands of a procrastinating compulsive reviser for publication. In view of the author's known habits of fussiness, we can hardly imagine that the text of the play as produced in Guyenne in 1544, or read in Paris in 1566, was unaltered when finally published in 1577.[11]

First to be written, *Baptistes* was the last of the four plays to be published. *Medea* was published in 1544 by Michel Vascolin in Paris; *Jephthes* in 1554 by Gall Morel, *Alcestis* by Thomas Vautrollier both in London. Vautrollier of London also handled the publication of *Baptistes*, but not until 1577. Hence it can be accorded the status of an 'occasional' publication, presented as a warning to the young James VI, and with a long preamble to that effect:

GEORGIUS BUCHANANUS IACOBO SEXTO SCOTORUM REGI S. P. D.
Cum omnes mei libelli, postquam tibi erudiendo sum appositus, ad te familiariter accedunt salutant confabulantur et in tuae clientelae umbra conquiescunt, tum hic meus BAPTISTES pluribus de causis tui nominis patrocinium audentius sibi poscere videtur; quod meus quamquam abor-tivus tamen primus est foetus, et adulescentes a vulgari fabularum scaenicarum consuetudine ad imitationem antiquitatis provocet, et ad pietatis studium, quod tum ubique fere exagitabatur, animos excitare pro virili contendat. illud autem peculiarius ad te videri potest spectare, quod tyrannorum cruciatus et, cum florere maxime videntur, miserias dilucide exponat. quod te nunc intellegere non conducibile modo sed etiam necessarium existimo, ut mature odisse incipias quod tibi semper est fugiendum. volo etiam hunc libellum apud posteros testem fore, si quid aliquando pravis consultoribus impulsus vel regni licentia rectam educationem superante secus committas, non praeceptoribus sed tibi, qui eis recte monentibus non sis obsecutus, id vitio vertendum esse. det dominus meliora, et, quod est apud tuum Sallustium, tibi bene facere ex consuetudine in naturam vertat. quod equidem cum multis et spero et opto. vale.
Sterlino, ad Kalend. Novembres. 1576.

(George Buchanan to James the Sixth King of the Scots S.P.D.
As all my little books, since I was made responsible for your education, approach you familiarly, greet you, converse informally, and rest in the shade of your patronage, now here my BAPTISTES asks more boldly the patronage of your name for itself for several

---

10 Buchanan, *'Baptistes'*, ed. by Berkowitz, p. 120.
11 Buchanan, *'Baptistes'*, ed. by Berkowitz, pp. 25–39.

reasons; though it may seem to have been born prematurely, yet it represents my first foetal attempt to challenge boys by means of the vulgar custom of stage plays to imitate antiquity, and to study piety — which was at that time almost everywhere stirred up — and to strive to rouse their hearts to be manly. Although it may seem more specific to you, because it clearly sets forth the tortures of tyrants, and the miseries, when they seem most to flourish, I think that you should now understand that it is not only agreeable, but also necessary, that you should begin to hate early what you must always flee from. I also want this document to be a witness to posterity, that if you commit anything through bad advisers, or the permission of the kingdom, overriding your correct education, it is not because of the teachers, but because of you yourself, who, if you do not obey those who admonish you rightly, will turn your conduct into the vice that it is. May the Lord give you better things, and, as it is in Sallust, turn your habit of doing good into second nature, as I indeed, with many others, hope and wish. Farewell. At Stirling on the Kalends of November 1576.)[12]

Its editors note that there have been a number of 'candidates' for the identity of Herod and the Baptist in the play, including Henry VIII and Thomas More. Venerable mid-twentieth-century Scottish historian Hume Brown believed that *Baptistes* was a *piece a clef*, specifically directed against Francois I[er], represented as Herod, and Louis de Berquin, the Erasmian Humanist and Protestant reformer represented as John the Baptist. Other equivalences have been suggested. The very struggle to crack the perceived code of the play has largely ignored its original audience of citizens of Bordeaux. Surely like Orwell's *Animal Farm*, and all good political satire, the principles it enacts adapt to a number of interpretations which can be supplied by the audience. More to the point, at the period when it was printed, direct equivalences would have been suicidally seditious: religious and political debate in Scotland had already led to numerous executions, burnings, and murders on ideological grounds. The equivalences to the 1570s in Scotland are, perforce, more thematic than direct.

Here we treat *Baptistes* as a palimpsest, contextualizing the version that survives alongside the more well-known and contemporary text, the polemical prose dialogue, *De Iure Regni apud Scotos*. Our interest in the latter, to some degree taking its argument as a given, lies in exploring how it owes its power as much to the intuitive skills of the practised dramatist as to contemporary rhetorical theory, exploring Buchanan's writing strategies as he worked and reworked both pieces.

---

12 Translation my own.

The Prologue to the play establishes one of the major themes of both texts concerning the dangers in all spheres of influence of detecting those who are (virtuously) genuine, as against those who are (viciously) engaged in expedient role-play out of self-interest. Many men are Proteuses, the play's audience is warned by Buchanan *in propria persona*, 'who assume new features and turn themselves into every possible shape'. Initially Buchanan uses the comparison simply to deride theatrical critics and their slanders, elaborating on the fickleness of the tastes of theatre audiences. The play, however, will be an 'old story refurbished of how the Baptist of old was crushed by royal lust and the crafty calumnies of jealous people, and though innocent met an undeserved death'. The story is an old one, but 'as long as the human race lasts, new calumnies will always exist, and wicked spite will always oppress worthy men. Violence will prevail over right, deceit over innocence'.[13]

> nam quotquot homines video, tot me Proteos
> videre vultus credo qui sumant novos
> seseque vertant in figuras quaslibet,
> subiecta quorum maxime calumniis
> fortuna semper scaenici est spectaculi. (ll. 10–14)

> > (I believe that in all the men I see I behold as many Proteuses who assume new features and turn themselves into every possible shape; and the success of a stage-play always runs the gamut of their calumnies especially.)

As with theatre critics, so with the public world at large: here from the outset we have Buchanan's perennial agenda that all men are dissemblers and slanderers. It will, in exactly the same terms, be applied to the characters in the play who conspire to bring about the death of the Baptist. The essentially performative idea of dissembling, particularly when it involves political u-turns, and calumny, that is slanderous defamation confected from unfounded rumour, is not only the stock-in-trade of early sixteenth-century political morality plays, but forms the basis of all Buchanan's polemic, including his attack, as we shall see, on royal secretary William Maitland, *Chamaeleon*,[14] and directed at monarchy itself in *De Iure Regni Apud Scotos*.

The play's origins as a schoolroom piece are immediately recalled by the opening, which takes the form of a debate between the two rabbis Malchus and Gamaliel, each adeptly refuting the views of the other. John the Baptist's preaching is framed within this debate as one of the

---

13 Buchanan, *Tragedies*, ed. by Sharatt and Walsh. Translation of the Prologue at p. 134. All further in-text references are to this edition.
14 For an English translation see Buchanan, 'Chamaeleon', item III, pp. 97–116.

free-thinking Buchanan's lifelong preoccupations, that is the justification of punishing unorthodox views just because they are new.[15] As Dermot Cavenagh has observed, the play's operation as political theology is as 'a meditation on the consequences of defining religious heresy as a matter of public safety and the implications this has for understanding the scope of sovereign power', in the context of the rise in religious persecution in early sixteenth-century Europe. He notes that South West France was a particular site of sectarian violence during Buchanan's period at Guyenne.[16] The same was demonstrably true of the turbulence in Scotland in the 1570s. Hence the debate with which the play opens has traction in both cases.

Malchus argues for the need to conform to the conventions of one's generation, warning against ignoring anciently established practices. After he has left the scene, Gamaliel reflects aloud that Malchus has gone to make false claims to Herod that new sects are rising, ancient rites being challenged, royal authority exposed to mockery, while covering his wickedness behind honorable pretexts. The problem is that kings are peculiarly susceptible to empty fears and thus pay attention to gossip. The Chorus sums up the conventional problem with false counsellors:

CHORUS
occulit falsus pudor impudentem,
impium celat pietatis umbra,
turbidi vultu simulant quieta,
vera dolosi. (ll. 285–87)

> (An assumed modesty cloaks the shameless; the cover of piety conceals the impious. On their faces men who are disturbed feign tranquility, and deceivers feign truthfulness.)

Thus Buchanan reflects in this opening debate on the difficulty borne out by his own history, that new ideas become easily subject to paranoia and conspiracy theories, redounding on those who promote them.

The following debate introduces Herod's Queen, who, anticipating Lady Macbeth, feeds Herod's paranoia and taunts him with being mocked for excessive leniency. It is the Queen who is actually the dissembling counsellor, feeding her own fury that the Baptist condemned her marriage to Herod on the grounds that she was already married.

Herod warns the Baptist that he cannot protect him indefinitely, because, among other things,

---

15 See Buchanan, *Tragedies*, ed. by Sharratt and Walsh, pp. 102–3/136–37.
16 Cavenagh, 'Political Theology', pp. 91–92 and 96–97.

vulgusque veterum decipis legum rude
letale spargens dogmatis virus novi,
et turbulentis vocibus regni statum
tranquillitatemque labefactas publicam (ll. 418–21)

> ([...] and you deceive the common herd, ignorant of the old laws, by scattering abroad your deadly venom of new teaching. With your tempestuous words you confound the condition of the kingdom and the peace of the state.)

The attack on 'new teaching' purely for its newness, enters debate again. In his response, John warns Herod to set limits on his power which the application of law has imposed on him, precisely the point on the ideally voluntary constitutional constraint of monarchical power which Buchanan argues for in his own voice in *De Iure Regno*.

The audience then observes Herod, left on his own, reasoning what he must do. His soliloquy ventriloquizes Buchanan's projection of a kingly dilemma: people despise moderation but equally hate heavy-handedness. Kingship cannot, however, be solely a crowd-pleaser. He determines to impress the capricious mob with decisive action, in fact bloodshed, on the understanding that they can be appeased thereafter. He seizes opportunistically on his opponent's criticism of his marriage as the excuse to decide the Baptist is out of control and will eventually desire to rule rather than be ruled. (The comparison between sixteenth-century England and Scotland in which ill-judged royal marriages acted as tinder in ideological conflict need not be laboured here.)[17] To remove this threat may attract admiration, in which case the people can be rewarded for their support. If the people dislike the move, he can impose absolute power, impatient of the constraints of law. He thus talks himself into tyranny out of self-interest.

The rabbi Malchus is cast as the agent provocateur, determined to win personal advancement by feigning support for the Baptist while 'the rabbis mutter and the king winks'. Having thus revealed his intentions to the audience, he notices the Baptist nearby, and eavesdrops on the latter's celebration of God's order. The following speech is the first of two striking lyrical interventions in the voice of the Baptist which, after the audience knows that his fate is sealed, move the play's discourse into a different mode.

Without going into discussion of Buchanan's mastery of Latin metrics,[18] as the text with which we shall compare it is, of course, in prose,

---

17 Berkowicz points out (Buchanan, 'Baptistes', ed. by Berkowicz, p. 121) that both Heinrich Bullinger (1575), and Nicholas Grimald in *Archipropheta* (1548) 'show that the Queen's passionate nature urged her to plot John's execution'.
18 See Buchanan, *Tragedies*, ed. by Sharratt and Walsh, pp. 334–35, and Buchanan, 'Baptistes', ed. by Berkowitz, pp. 251–59, referencing Buchanan, *John the Baptist*, trans. by Mitchell.

we should note his observation chiefly of sapphics for the choral passages, and of iambic trimeters throughout the dialogue. Hence, metre plays no part in what I am describing as a mode-shift in these two interventions, but rather a stylistic shift into lyrical prayer, addressed to the Creator. This king is characterised in a series of epithets familiar in poetry from Boethius, through Old English, to the verse of George Herbert, as the munificent provider of all the earth's gifts, ordered according to day and night and the passage of the seasons, mustered according to the conventional high-style repetitions with variation, ordered in fours:

> O magne rerum rector auctor arbiter
> te quicquid aër continet laxo sinu,
> quaecumque tellus educat, quicquid suis
> fretum sub undis nutrit, agnoscit deum,
> sentit parentem, legibus semel datis
> obsequitur ultro tramite immutabili.
> iussu tuo ver pingit arva floribus,
> fruges dat aestas, fundit autumnus merum
> hiems pruinis vestit albicantibus
> montes; in aequor curva volvunt flumina
> moles aquarum, mare reciprocat vices,
> noctem Diana, Phoebus incendit diem
> et inquieta lustrat orbem lampade.
> nil denique usquam est sive caelo seu solo
> quod non libenter pareat regi suo,
> amet parentem et officiis quibus potest
> in conditorem studia declaret sua. (ll. 695–711)

> (Great ruler, creator, lord of the universe, all that the air contains in its yielding bosom, all that the earth brings forth, all that the sea nurtures beneath its waves acknowledges you as God, experiences you as parent, and follows your laws once given in unchangeable course. At your command the spring decks the fields with blossoms, summer proffers harvests, autumn pours forth wine, and winter clothes the mountains with whitening frosts. Winding rivers roll down to the sea masses of waters, the sea's tides ebb and flow, Diana fires the night and Phoebus the day as he traverses the world with his unresting torch. In short, there is nothing whatsoever in heaven or on earth, which does not gladly obey its king, love its father, and declare its zeal for its founder with all the functions which it can achieve.)

The rejoinder that follows, marked by *at solus* [only] identifies the ungrateful disrupter of this order as humanity, whose transgressions are again itemised in a list of five:

at solus homo, quem ceteris longe magis
gaudere decuit et obsequi iussis dei,
contemptor unus inter omnes maxime est.
praecepta spernit, frena legum reicit,
in omne praeceps facinus it; libidine
metitur aequum, ponderat ius viribus. (ll. 712–17)

> (Only man for whom much more than for the rest of creation it would be fitting to rejoice in and obey God's commands, amongst all supremely registers contempt. He spurns God's commands, rejects the reins of the laws, and rushes headlong into every crime. He measures justice by wantonness, and weighs law by violence.)

The two lyrical passages contribute nothing directly to the play's argument beyond affirming the status of the Baptist as victim. They do, however, underscore the narrative's status as biblical drama rather than purely secular debate, while providing a showcase for Buchanan's poetic élan and his pupils' vocal skills in delivery. John goes on to assert that the fault lies with the rulers, not with the people, and delivers a scorching diatribe against the priesthood, using not only 'rabbi', but 'sacerdotum sacrata dignitas | princepsque sacri pontifex collegii' (ll. 737–38: 'consecrated priests and bishop of the sacred College'), terms which, in the context of the play's publication are unavoidably contemporary. They, and presumably here we may read the Roman Catholic priesthood beloved of Queen Mary, are accused of tithing every vegetable — even nettles and grass — and as watchdogs of the teachings of the prophets, are significantly silent. No wonder they do not protect the flock from wolves; they are the wolves.

There follows another two-handed debate on the nature of authority, rights, privileges and duties between John and Malchus, in which the latter cross-questions the Baptist on who he is. Is he Christ – No – Is he the expected prophet – No — is he Elias – No. If none of these, on what authority does he preach. The Baptist replies with words adapted from Matthew 3. 1–12: 'Prepare ye the way, make straight your paths, for the Lord is nigh.' (l. 784).

The succeeding section, as the Baptist faces death, has remarkable resonance for a period in which a number of those with whom Buchanan was associated were martyred for their faith, be it at the hands of the Inquisition, or in the turbulent times of religious change in Scotland. The Chorus warns him of his approaching fate, begging him not to neglect his own safety but to 'soften the king's mind' just in the way that Christian martyrs, from Thomas More on the one hand to Scottish reformers Patrick Hamilton and George Wishart on the other were urged. The Baptist enacts the argument for refusing to recant:

> [...] Quid igitur mihi auctores? duo
> reges utrimque facere pugnantia iubent.
> caelestis alter, misericors clemens bonus;
> terrenus alter, impotens ferox malus.
> mortem minatur alter; alter me vetat
> mortem timere, pollicetur praemium
> vim non timenti. corpus alter perdere
> potest; at alter corpus una et spiritum
> torquere flamma poterit inevitabili
> hi cum repugnent, consule utri paream. (ll. 1024–33)

>> (What advice do you give me then? Two kings, one on each side,
>> bid me do opposing things. The one is in heaven, and is merciful,
>> kind, good; the other is earthly, and is uncontrolled, fierce, evil.
>> One threatens death, the other forbids me fear death and promises
>> a reward if I do not fear violence. One can destroy my body, but the
>> other will be able to torture body and spirit in flames unavoidable.
>> Since they are opposed to each other, advise me which I should
>> obey?)

The Chorus goes on, playing devil's advocate, as it were, to reproach him
for abandoning friends and family, but John responds that he is the one
being abandoned as he hastens towards what is the inevitable outcome
for everyone. This is followed by another meditative speech on death as
a haven, a disquisition offering a commentary on martyrdom for God
(pp. 125–27/157–58). Thus John loses the battle presented in the plot, but
wins the war of words, according to means that Buchanan will redeploy
in *De Iure Regni*, where again he stages debates in which one party is
constructed to hold all the cards.

The Chorus commends John for the constancy of his heart, reflecting
that 'nec toti morimur, sed merlior rogos | nostri pars avidos spernit'
(ll. 1121–22: 'We do not die in entirety, but the better part of us spurns
the greedy pyre'). The redolence of this whole section with fire imagery
— the fires of burning on earth, of seraphic burning in heaven, and of the
fires of hell — further emphasises the connotations of sixteenth-century
martyrdom, especially given that John will be beheaded, not burnt.

The play hereafter moves swiftly to its conclusion, as Salome makes
her request for the head of the Baptist on a platter, despite Herod's protes-
tations that the law enjoins limitations to what the king can command. Sa-
lome responds to this with 'Si principi quod placuit est ius, iam modum |
non regibus lex, legibus sed rex facit' (ll. 1207–08: 'If the law is what the
prince has decreed, the law does not limit kings, but the king the laws').
She is of course supported by the Queen who opines that once anyone has
a crown on their heads they need not attend to public opinion — anything
useful to the king is legitimate. Although this is presented as an unseemly

domestic brawl within the palace, it reiterates almost exactly the arguments on the limits of monarchical power rehearsed between the interlocutors in the *De Iure Regno*, and interestingly is in the female voice, a probable bonus in the light of Buchanan's animus against Queen Mary's personal rule at the period of publication. Herod is reluctant to the end, but of course the legendary sentence is carried out and the play winds to its close with conventional lamentation from the Chorus.

As a play, *Baptistes* may seem a little odd to the modern critic. It makes compelling reading and displays rhetorical and poetic flights well beyond the expectations of a school play. Its plethora of allusions to, and quotations from, classical authors is the stuff of footnotes to which I have not attended, nor has there been scope to analyse its structural principles and the development of the scenic division indicated by choric intervention. Although we know it was originally written for performance, the published version shows very little sign of any performative devices beyond verbal cut and thrust, generally between pairs of debating characters. Not only is the audience deprived of the main action, as the Baptist is beheaded off stage, and the audience learns of it by report of a Messenger, but the very sparse indicators of place and movement are crude in the extreme. For example, as Malchus plots to 'thrust torches beneath her [the Queen's] disturbed mind', he adds, 'Why, here she conveniently presents herself at the right moment' (pp. 121/53). The only other indicator that anyone moves at all is given us by the Chorus before its climactic encounter with the condemned man: 'Why, there he stands before the very doors of the prison' (pp. 124/56). There are some lively exchanges, notably between Herod, the Queen and Salome, but otherwise a very large number of speeches of more than three or four lines seem to forget the theatrical context and be delivered as address to audience, or soliloquy.

The play, we know, was originally written as a school-room piece, and expresses some concern for its critical reception as a real performance; even then it was certainly designed more for the display of rhetorical skills in Latin dialogue than for theatrical show.

The published version that has come down to us seems to be unconcerned with, or to have left behind, its performance potential, as all the marks of the sophistication of a mature writer lie within its dialogue and argument rather than its dramaturgy. The squeamishness of Calvinist ideologues for theatre is well known, and is the subject of continuing study. Freya Sierhuis and Adrian Streete, discussing the opposition to biblical drama, ask rhetorically, 'Do they not maintain bawdry, insinuate foolery, and renew the remembrance of heathen idolatry?'[19] Yet plays were written from a Calvinist point of view, even if, as is the case with John Bale's *God's*

---

19 Sierhuis and Streete, 'Calvinism', p. 123.

Promises, the audience is deprived of all the potential theatrical show of, for example, the building of Noah's ark. Under the influence of Calvinism, 'theatre' and 'drama' set off in determinedly different directions, as debate, influenced by the revival of Classical forms taught in the schoolroom, provided the substance of plays.

It is, then, perhaps not as paradoxical as may first appear that Buchanan's *De Iure Regni apud Scotos* displays the imaginative techniques of the mature dramaturge rather more acutely than the actual play *Baptistes*: a comparison of the two texts demonstrates that while the Calvinist Reformation may have disparaged theatre, it remained vitally adept in the deployment of dramatic device.

De Iure Regni apud Scotos was probably first written in 1567, the year of Darnley's murder, and evidence survives of manuscript circulation between 1569 and 1570.[20] Thomas Maitland, Buchanan's interlocutor in the text, wrote windily to Queen Mary in December 1570 that he had nothing to do with the tract, and that it was entirely Buchanan's invention. The editors suggest that there is evidence for very little change to the text between its initial appearance and its publication in 1579 as it preserves a number of references specific to the earlier date. Most obviously in 1567 Maitland was still an intellectual acolyte of Buchanan's not yet committed to the Marian cause, a cause which led to his premature death in 1572 on a mission to Rome to seek the pope's support for the deposed queen. The decade between writing and publication saw changes that would not have preserved the cordiality of Buchanan and Maitland's relationship as it is presented even had Maitland lived. Their dramatic dialogue is a piece of undisguised polemic directed against the evils of the self-indulgent rule of the 'bad' monarch, openly equated with Mary Queen of Scots. The other target, introduced for comparative purposes, is the Pope. The champion of constitutional monarchy, bounded by the law, is George Buchanan *in propria persona*, the other is a much younger 'Thomas Maitland', presented as sympathetic to Buchanan's opinions but naive. In order to understand the contemporary thrust of the piece fully, it is important that we now meet Maitland.

The real Thomas Maitland (*c.* 1545–1572) was the youngest surviving son of Sir Richard Maitland of Lethington near Haddington (1496–1586), privy councillor, Lord of Session, Keeper of the Great Seal of Scotland, and noted poet. John Knox, having dined at Lethington in 1542, said he was 'ever civil, albeit not persuaded in religion'. Sir Richard's significant strength was his commitment to keeping matters of religion and concerns of state firmly separate.[21]

---

20 Buchanan, *De Iure Regni*, ed. by Mason and Smith.
21 Blake, *William Maitland*, p. 2.

Despite his own position, Sir Richard and his family found themselves exiled from their country seat which was confiscated in 1571 because of the partisanship of his eldest son, and not restored to them until 1584. Richard's son and heir, William, was arraigned for treason, commuted to felony, for William was Mary Queen of Scots' sometime secretary.[22] Having initially deserted her on her marriage to Bothwell, William renewed his loyalty as soon as Bothwell was routed, attempting also to reconcile all parties to the new Regent Moray. He parted company with Moray, however, after the latter agreed that Mary should be tried at York for conspiring to murder Darnley. After the Regent was murdered, Maitland was finally no longer able to hold middle ground and became a partisan of the Queen's party in open warfare with what became the King's party, of which Buchanan was now an ardent supporter, as well as tutor to the king.[23] In 1570 William Maitland, already suffering from a debilitating disease, was implicated in the conspiracy to murder Darnley, confected from the notorious 'Casket Letters'. He died in prison of poisoning after the fall of Edinburgh Castle in 1573. William Maitland was the central target of a blizzard of anti-Marian, anti-Catholic propaganda. He endured satirical attack by Richard Bannatyne, who dubbed him 'Mitchell Wylie' (Machiavelli).[24] He was James Semple's *Bird in the Cage*.[25] His most dangerous, vociferous and eloquent opponent, who dubbed him the *Chamaeleon*, was George Buchanan.[26]

Richard Maitland's middle son, John, survived the family vicissitudes of fortune to became James VI's Lord Chancellor, but Thomas, the interlocutor in *De Iure Regni* and William's youngest brother by some twenty years, fell victim to his brother's partisanship. Thomas was an author in his own right, and despite his very short life, left some fine writing, including a *jeu d'esprit* of 1570, in which he made fun of the party supporting James VI in his minority and their charges of Machiavellianism against the Queen's supporters.[27] This was the same year in which he strove to distance himself from his part in *De Iure Regni*, because he was by then, one of the Queen's party. Buchanan's choice of him as fictional interlocutor, dates from the earlier period when the two had held each other in great regard, having met in Paris, where Thomas showed some enthusiasm for the reformed faith. Buchanan encouraged his 'perseverance in that career of glory which he had so happily begun'.[28] It is apparent that after the murder of Darnley

---

22 Skelton, *Maitland*, vol. I, pp. 322–24.
23 Blake, *William Maitland*, pp. 36–40.
24 Skelton, *Maitland*, vol. I, pp. 321–24.
25 Skelton, *Maitland*, vol. I, p. 230.
26 Buchanan, 'Chamaeleon', pp. 97–116.
27 Loughlin, 'The Dialogue', p. 237.
28 McKechnie, 'Thomas Maitland', p. 276.

he became embroiled in his eldest brother's affairs for reasons more political than ideological. He had been dead for seven years when the dialogue in which he is the fictional interlocutor was finally published.

The dialogue concerns what makes a good monarch, arguing forcefully in the voice of Buchanan for a constitutional monarchy, based on natural law and counselled, and where necessary vetoed, by the Estaits (the three constituents of the Scottish Parliament). As such, it is an exploration of what uses and abuses of power most affect the people of the nation, preoccupations that are current to its date but also familiar from Sir David Lindsay's earlier play *Ane Satyre of the Thrie Estaits*. Unlike the work of John Knox and Christopher Goodman, biblical literalists, the treatise is remarkably secular in spirit. Its only biblical reference is its refutation of the problematic texts in 1 Samuel and Romans decreeing that kings are ordained by God, to make the Humanist argument that it is the office, not the person, who is thus ordained. The political theory owes more to Mair, Erasmus, Elyot, Castiglione, and ultimately to Cicero and Aristotle, than it does to Calvin. Buchanan drills down into Aristotelian principles and definitions of natural law and of tyranny, justifying the people's right to depose, and even to kill, monarchs who rule according to principles of tyranny. 'Maitland' is set up as the dramatic voice of the sceptical pupil, perhaps even speculatively ventriloquizing James VI. The latter, far from taking his tutor's advice, moved further towards developing his own justification of the Divine Right of Kings, followed enthusiastically and with fatal results by his son, Charles I. Buchanan's ultimate influence was felt elsewhere, in Continental Europe, and may have included John Locke.

What has been less explored by commentators than the progress of the argument per se, is the suite of strategies by which Buchanan uses performative principles to shape it, so that his audience is eavesdropping on a debate between two interlocutors in real time. It is an incendiary polemical tract, with claims to be the first in modern Europe to propose and defend on entirely secular grounds the people's right to resist an oppressive monarch, and to justify the assassination of a tyrant. It was banned by the Scottish parliament in 1584. Yet the intuitions of a theatrical imagination present to its readers with delightful disingenuousness, something more like a fireside chat between two friends. Its 1689 translation into English, attributed to Philalethes, pays tribute throughout to Buchanan's 'Lofty Laconick stile of Latin'. The translation has its own history: a second issue was burned by the common hangman in 1680. It later became popular even in Jacobite circles.[29] In order to capture Buchanan's style fully for readers conversant with Latin, however, quotations in the following are

---

29 Buchanan, *De Jure Regni*, ed. Philalethes.

taken from the excellent standard edition of the Latin with facing page modern English translation by Roger Mason and Martin Smith.[30]

The book sets the (fictional) circumstances in which the debate arose: 'Maitland', just returned from France, asks about the troubled state of Scotland, while Buchanan wants to hear the latest news from France. Buchanan speaks of the love he bears for 'Maitland', adding that the latter in his modesty, spoke affectionately of him in return, but asks Buchanan why he seeks opinion from him on matters in which he is already well versed. Thus we have a performative encounter established, taking place in real time.

'Maitland' claims that the French are aghast at the deposition of Mary Queen of Scots, and equally at the murder of Lord Darnley. Buchanan points out that it makes no sense to deplore both, as the first was directly prompted by the second. He claims that three sorts of people defend the Queen: those who have given in to the 'lusts of tyrants' and believe in absolute monarchy; those whose self-interest dictates it to be the better path, and those who are unthinkingly conservative. The debate moves forward, into its core matter on what constitutes monarchy, how it can or should be constrained constitutionally, and what is the difference between a king and a tyrant, with blandly presented comparisons between Mary and Caligula. The arguments proposed by John in *Baptistes*, are here fully owned by Buchanan himself.

One of Buchanan's many confected methods for controlling the argument is the creation of the illusion that the debate is taking place in real time. For example:

> B. Sed recte an secus commodius alio loco expendemus; interea, si vis, hoc nobis sit positum, ea lege ut, nisi posterius satis confirmatum tibi videatur, tuo arbitrio id ipsum rectractare liceat. (pp. 11–12)

> B. Noli exspectare ut minima quaeque hic executiam. Neque enim temporis angustia id patitur nec ipsa res exigit. (pp. 22–23)

> (BUCHANAN: But we can more conveniently discuss elsewhere whether they are right or wrong hereafter at better conveniency. Meanwhile, if you will, let us take for granted our own point of view, on the understanding that, if you do not think it adequately proved later on, you will be free to withdraw your assent to it.)

> (BUCHANAN: Do not expect me to examine every tiny detail here. Time is too short for that, and the subject itself does not require it.)

and

---

30 Buchanan, *De Iure Regni*, ed. Mason and Smith. Page references to this edition follow all quotations.

M. Sed haec fortasse alias per otium; nunc vero, si quidem videtur, quod instituisti perge prosequi. (pp. 40–41)

> (MAITLAND: But perhaps we shall have leisure to deal with this on another occasion; for the present, if you will, go on with what you have begun.)

The frequent instances of *nunc* [now] and *nuper* [lately] in the text not only contribute to the argument by comparing the present with the past, but also draw attention to the specific moment in which the debate is taking place. The same applies to *iam* [already], which is used both for sequencing events within the narrative, and for referring backwards to previous points of argument. Equally *posterius* occurs both in the sense of 'the latter' in sequencing the points of argument, but as an adverb of time, 'later' referring to a future outside the text to which further discussion may be deferred.

Another aspect of the illusion of oral debating is Buchanan's insistence on reprising foregoing points, which offers the opportunity to reinforce them by putting them in different words. For example:

> B. Oblitus mihi videris quidnam inter nos nuper convenit. […] Dicam ergo apertius ut intellegas. (pp. 58–59)

> (BUCHANAN: You seem to have forgotten what we recently agreed. Then I shall put it more clearly to let you understand.)

and

> B. Visne igitur ut breviter quae dicta sunt colligamus? Ita maxime intelligemus quid sit praeteritum, et si quid temere sit concessum facillime retractabimus.
> M. Maxime. (pp. 40–41)

> (BUCHANAN: Would you like us then to summarise briefly what has been said? In this way we can best understand what has been omitted and most easily re-examine any point conceded unthinkingly. MAITLAND: Yes, that will be best.)

Each voice also adopts a range of responses to the other which serves to foreground the dramatic situation. Questions are used to prompt exchange of voice, such as

> B. Habesne aliquam in animo descriptam regis et tyranni imaginem? Nam si habes, magno labore me levabis.
> M. Ego profecto utriusque quam habeam in animo imaginem facile possem explicare, sed vereor ea ne sit impolita et informis. Itaque ne, dum tu me refutes, longior instituatur oratio, malo audire quid tu sentias, qui et aetate et rerum usu prior es, nec aliorum modo

STRATEGIES, AND POLEMICS IN THE SCOTTISH REFORMATION

sententias teneas sed ipse etiam 'multorum et mores et urbes videris'. (pp. 13–15)

> (BUCHANAN: Do you have some picture of a king or a tyrant sketched out in your mind? If you do, you will make my task much lighter. MAITLAND: I could easily explain what picture I have in mind of each of them, but I am afraid it is rough and shapeless. So rather than engage in a protracted discussion while you refute me I prefer to hear what your views are. You are older and more experienced and not only know the views of others, but have yourself 'observed the customs and the cities of many men.')

'Maitland' comes dangerously close to being set up as the stooge, but the performative balance will prove subtler than that as the younger voice changes his position. Buchanan praises his interlocutor's understanding a number of times including, 'Rem attigisti!' (pp. 32–33: 'You have hit the nail on the head'). He also uses his fabricated conversation to correct the impression that 'Maitland' has of him — presumably as an attempt at protection from real detractors. He has, for example, 'Maitland' accuse him of admiring ancient commonwealths, corrected as follows:

> B. Non to recte hic de me sentiebas. Neque enim ego apud Romanos, Massilienses, Venetos et si qui alii fuerunt apud quos potentiora fuerint legum quam hominum imperia, tam suspicio diversam civitatis administrandae rationem quam aequitatem; neque multum referre puto, rex, dux, imperator an consul vocetur qui praesit, modo illud teneatur, eum aequitatis tuendae causa in magistratu esse collocatum. (pp. 34–35)

> (BUCHANAN: You have not understood my views on this correctly. For I admire the Romans, the Massilians, the Venetians and any others for whom the authority of the laws was more powerful than that of men, not so much for their different method of administering the commonwealth but for their justice. I do not think it matters much whether the person who rules is called king, doge, emperor or consul, provided it is remembered that he is placed in office for the sake of maintaining justice.)

'Maitland' is given leave to resist the drift of argument here, as he suggests that Buchanan has disappointed him by reducing the office of kingship so far that no man in his right mind would want to hold it (pp. 36–37). This in turn prompts Buchanan to drive home his point further: 'B. Vide quaeso, quanto in errore veneris' (pp. 35–39: 'BUCHANAN: Consider, I pray you, in how wrong you are), which leads to the citing of a deluge of precedents. The brow-beaten 'Maitland' rejoins with:

M. Hic ego, si postules quid sentiam, vix audio fateri tibi vel meam inconstantiam vel timiditatem, vel si quo alio nomine tibi libeat id vitium apellare. (pp. 42–43)

> (MAITLAND: If you ask me what I think now, I hardly dare admit my uncertainty or timidity, or whatever other name you please to give to that fault.)

As the debate proceeds, 'Maitland' is increasingly given to admitting that he is beginning to understand what Buchanan is getting at. Faux conversational tags of encouragement praising his brave words, for example, become more frequent, as 'Maitland' shifts between confessions of inadequacy, assertions of rebelliousness, bamboozlement, and evasion. It would labour the point to quote more instances, though tellingly, just beyond the halfway point, Buchanan, who has called up various rather cliched analogies asks

> quid exspectabimus, aut potius quid non exspectabimus, ab eis principibus qui propinquitatibus et clientelis et vetustis opibus subnixi imperium accipiunt, qui in eam spem nati et educati sunt? Quantum autem eorum animos ad virtutem accendeere debet quod non unius diei laudem, ut histriones fabula bene acta, sperent, sed aetatis suae benevolentiam et admirationem in perpetuam et posteros celebritatem et honores divinis proximos sibi paratos esse intelligant? (pp. 74–75)

> > (what shall we expect of those princes — or rather what shall we not expect — of those princes who, born and bred in the hope of power, obtain it with the support of kinsmen, retainers and inherited wealth? What passion for virtue it must kindle in them that they are not simply hoping for a single day's fame, as with actors when a play has been well acted, but realise that they have the prospect of the good will and admiration of their own age, the everlasting esteem of posterity, and honours which are all but divine. If only I could put into words the picture I have in my mind of that honour.)

Buchanan uses this contrast as the starting point for his definition of the good king as one who is not playing a role:

> Haec est vera, nisi fallor, imago regis, non illa circumsaepti armis, semper metuentis aut metum facientis, ex odio de populum suo populi in se odium metientis. Hanc imaginem quam posuimus expressit pulcherrimus coloribus Seneca in Thyeste. Quod carmen, cum sit elegantissimum, tibi notum esse non ambigo. Ecquid tibi non humiliter et contemptim de rege sentire videor et eum (quod nuper dicebbas) oneratum compedibus in legem ergastulum compingere? (p. 76)

(This is, if I am not mistaken, the true picture of a king, not that picture of him with his armed retinue around him, always afraid or making others afraid, measuring the people's hatred of him by his hatred of them. This picture which we have given is painted in the most beautiful colours by Seneca in his *Thyestes*. That work is so fine that I have no doubt that you must know it. Do you really think now that my view of the king is disparaging and contemptuous, and that I am, as you put it a little while ago, loading him with fetters and locking him in a prison guarded by the laws?)

There follows the theatrical metaphor, recalling the Prologue to *Baptistes*. The king is not a performer seeking public admiration for outward show, but by his unimpeachable behaviour, aspiring to the role of God on earth:

Annon potius in lucem et himinum coetus et publicum humani generis theatrum eum produco, non superbo spiculatorum et μαχαιροΦορων coetu sericatisque nebulonibus stipatum sed sua tutum Innocentia, nec armorum terrore sed populi amore munitum, nec modo liberum et erectum sed honoratum, sed venerabilem, sacrosanctum et augustum, cum bonis omnibus et faustis acclamationibus prodeuntem, et, quocumque progrediatur, omnium ora oculos et anumos in se convertentem? Quae ovatio, quis triumphus cum hac pompa quotidiana comparari potest? Aut, si Deus humana specie delaberentur in terras, quis ab hominibus maior honos et haberi posset quam qui vero regi, hoc est, vivo Dei simulacro, exhiberetur? Hoc enim maiorem honorem nec amor largiri nex metus exprimere nec adulatio posset comminisci. Haec tibi regis imago ecquid videtur? (pp. 76–77)

(Or am I not rather bringing him into the light, into the company of men and the public theatre of the human race, not attended by an arrogant escort of body-guards and 'swordsmen' and by silk-clad scoundrels, but safe in his own innocence, protected not by the terror of arms but by the love of the people, not only independent and exalted but honoured and revered, sacred and majestic, proceeding amid auspicious omens and cries of joyful approbation, and attracting the gaze and attention of everyone wherever he goes? What ovation or triumph can be compared with this daily procession? Or, if God were to come down to earth in human shape, what greater honour could men pay to Him than that which would be shown to the true king, that is, the living image of God? No greater honour than this could be bestowed by love or extorted by fear or devised by flattery. What do you think of this picture of the king?)

This turning of the tables, by use of the theatrical analogy, to present ideal monarchy in substance, rather than in show, is used to push 'Maitland' into a position of scepticism, in which he refers to the corruption of the times, and the allurements to the contrary which mean that he fears real kings will never be persuaded to behave in the manner Buchanan describes.

The establishment of a definition of ideal kingship, which the interlocutors agree may prove unattainable, probably marks the point at which the discourse provoked greatest outrage. It also then prepares the way for an excursus into the definition of a tyrant. The negotiation of definition springs another of Buchanan's rhetorical traps, as he moves discussion into etymology and the consideration of how words do not carry essential meanings but how meanings change their nuances through context, custom and usage:

> Id certe in hoc vocabulo evenisse videtur quod in plerisque aliis contigit. Verborum enim per se naturam si consideres, noxia caret [...] tamen nihil omnino ex sese habent cur animos ad iram, odium aut hilaritatem, excitant aut alioqui voluptatem aut molestiam creent. Si quid autem tale nobis accidat, id non a verbo sed a consuetudine hominum [...] evenire solet. (pp. 80–81)

> > (Yes, the word seems to have had the same fate as a great many others. If you consider words in themselves they are blameless [...] they have no power in themselves to excite men's minds to anger, hatred or joy, or in some other way to produce pleasure or annoyance. If anything like this happens to us, it usually arises not from the word but from the way men use it [...].)

'Maitland' expresses some indignation at the assertion that the words 'tyrant' and 'king' are equally slippery, and the argument is allowed to run into the sand with Maitland's conclusion that they have moved off the point, whether the linguistic argument be true or false.

'Maitland' is then given his head to argue for born rather than elected monarchs, suggesting that accepting those given to the people accidentally is as good a method as any. He argues for the exercise of pragmatic forbearance with hereditary kings. This opens the way for the voice of Buchanan to suggest confining the review of the question to Scotland, to avoid further prolixity, and offers to set out how historically Scotland has been able to deal with bad kings.

These are just a number of instances of Buchanan's deployment of what we might call the devices of dramatic dialogue. There are colloquial idioms, a number of vocative addresses, tag questions, open and closed questions. Leech adds to the classic Gricean maxims, three relevant to conversation:[31] the approbation maxim, the modesty maxim, and the agreement maxim, all of which Buchanan deploys liberally. Without getting

---

31 See further in his classic work on pragmatics, Leech, *Principles*.

further into this, we can observe that Buchanan's polemic technique owes much to his adeptness in writing dramatic dialogue closely emulating real exchange.

Strict chronological sequencing suggests that Buchanan wrote no plays after the 1540s; the surviving, adapted, version of *Baptistes* was published, with its prefatory dedication to James VI, in 1577. There is no hard evidence of Buchanan's own active editing of the play for publication, but the evident dramatic strategies in the near-contemporary *De Iure Regni apud Scotos*, may offer covert evidence that the author revived, if he ever left, his flair as a dramaturge.

Bibliography

Edited Source texts

Buchanan, George, *'Baptistes' and its Anonymous Seventeenth-century Translation, Tyrannical Government Anatomised*, ed. by Steven Berkowitz (New York: Garland, 1992)

———, 'Chamaeleon or the Crafty Statesman', in *Miscellanea Scotica* (London: W. Taylor, 1710), pp. 95–119

———, *De Iure Regni apud Scotos Dialogus*, critical ed. and trans. by Roger A. Mason and Martin S. Smith (London: Ashgate, 2006, repr. London: Routledge, 2017)

———, *De Jure Regni apud Scotos, or a Dialogue Concerning the Due Priviledge of Government in the Kingdom of Scotland Betwixt George Buchanan and Thomas Maitland*, trans. by Philalethes (London: Richard Baldwin, 1689, repr. London: Forgotten Books, 2012)

———, *John the Baptist*, trans. by Gordon Mitchell (Paisley: Alexander Gardner, 1904)

———, 'Three Entertainments for the wedding of Mary Queen of Scots', ed. and trans. by Peter Davidson, Dominic Montserrat, and Jane Stevenson, *Scotlands*, 2 (1995), 1–10

———, *Tragedies*, ed. and trans. by Peter Sharratt and Patrick G. Walsh (Edinburgh: Scottish Academic Press, 1983)

Skelton, John, *Maitland of Lethington and the Scotland of Mary Stewart* (Edinburgh: Blackwood, 1887)

Secondary Material

Blake, William, *William Maitland of Lethington 1528–1573: A Study of Moderation in the Scottish Reformation* (Lampeter: Edward Mellen, 1990)

Cavenagh, Dermot, 'Political Theology in George Buchanan's *Baptistes*', in *Early Modern Drama and the Bible, Contexts and Readings 1570–1625*, ed. by Adrian Streete (London: Palgrave, 20212), pp. 89–104

Leech, Geoffrey N., *Principles of Pragmatics* (London: Longman, 1983)

Loughlin, Mark, '*The Dialogue of the Two Wyfis*: Maitland, Machiavelli and the Propaganda of the Scottish Civil War', in *The Renaissance in Scotland: Studies in Literature, Religion, History and Culture offered to John Durkin*, ed. by A. A. MacDonald, Michael Lynch, and Ian B. Cowan (Leiden: Brill, 1994), pp. 226–43

Lynch, Michael, 'Queen Mary's Triumph: the Baptismal Celebrations at Stirling in December 1566', *Scottish Historical Review*, 59 (1990), 1–21

Macmillan, D., *George Buchanan: A Biography* (London: Simpkin Marshall, 1906); *Oxford Dictionary of National Biography online* https://www-oxforddnb-com.ezproxy.lib.gla.ac.uk/view/10.1093/ref:odnb/9780198614128.001.0001/odnb-9780198614128-e-3837 (accessed: 21 August 2022)

McFarlane, Ian D., *Buchanan* (London: Duckworth, 1981)

McKechnie, William S., 'Thomas Maitland', *Scottish Historical Review*, 4 (1907), 274–93

Sierhuis, Freya, and Adrian Streete, 'Calvinism and Theater in Early Modern England and the Dutch Republic', in *Cultures of Calvinism in Early Modern Europe*, ed. by Crawford Gribben and Graeme Murdock (Oxford: Oxford University Press, 2020), pp. 123–37

SUSANNAH CROWDER _____

Staging Enmity

Performance Strategies in Wartime

▼ **ABSTRACT** This article explores local traditions of public performance during a period of political polarization, focusing on the independent francophone city of Metz, in what is now northeastern France. It examines a collection of contemporary texts created during the early fourteenth-century Guerre des Quatre Seigneurs, a war in which Metz faced devastating attacks from regional powers as well as an internal uprising of its own citizens. These works, when studied within their early, performed context, reveal a shared framework of performance practice within the city and an oral and embodied approach to public debate. This article details the distinct performance characteristics and conventions of the Metz pieces, and argues that theatre and drama scholars are well-positioned to illuminate the understudied performance aspects of urban environments and medieval urban history more generally.

▼ **KEYWORDS:** Guerre des Quatre Seigneurs, Metz, performance history, public sphere, urban history, cultural history, polarization, obscenity

Susannah Crowder is chair of the Department of Interdisciplinary Studies at John Jay College, CUNY. In addition to her award-winning monograph, *Performing Women: Gender, Self, and Representation in Late Medieval Metz*, she is the author of numerous articles on topics relating to gender, space, and performance culture. Her current project explores performance, political polarization, and 'extreme' speech in the later Middle Ages.

European Medieval Drama, 27 (2023), 215–234
BREPOLS ⚇ PUBLISHERS   10.1484/J.EMD.5.137684

Introduction

In the autumn of 1324, the people of Metz in northeastern France found themselves enmeshed in yet another regional war.[1] This particular conflict — the Guerre des Quatre Seigneurs, as it came to be known — quickly grew beyond the confines of other recent skirmishes; the Guerre was marked not only by constant battle raging across the countryside and attacks on the city itself, but also by a violent urban uprising. As these horrors unfolded over the next three years, how did the citizens of Metz react? With performance: whether staging an allegorical piece about filthy and foul-mouthed birds, or participating in a collective prayer that bemoaned the atrocities of war, the residents of Metz, the Messines, produced a dense body of performance practice that explicitly grappled with their perspectives on the hostilities.

Astonishingly, evidence for a small cluster of these performances has survived the centuries.[2] The Guerre performance pieces, as I term them, ranged across performance settings, moods and tones, literary genres, and political viewpoints. Their textual documentation shows that each original performance would have been relatively short and required little in the way of staging or props. Some dated to the early months of the war, while others celebrated the eventual arrival of peace. Although several constructed explicit cross-performance dialogues, most participated instead in an ongoing, larger conversation about the war. Taken together, the Guerre pieces offer a window into an adaptive, responsive mode of performance through which allies and enemies could communicate amid the acrimony and bloodshed.

Viewing this body of evidence in its original performance context permits us to deepen our understanding of late-medieval performance as an expressive medium that is both conversational and essential to public life. Scholars of drama and literature have long traced how theatrical and poetical works contribute to contemporary social and cultural debates. Yet often we lack the primary source evidence needed to study exchanges

---

1 Material in this article was presented at ASTR (2018 and 2022), SITM (2019 and 2022), MLA (2020), and the Medieval Club of New York (2019); I am grateful to the session organizers and participants, as well as to the anonymous readers of *EMD*, for their many helpful suggestions.

2 The Guerre performance texts have been the subject of sporadic study, with foundational studies first appearing in the late nineteenth century and a critical addition soon after: Jacques d'Esch, *La Guerre*, ed. by Bouteiller, and *Die Metzer Chronik*, ed. by Wolfram. More recently, Antoine Lazzari offers a long-overdue study of the full d'Esch chronicle in his 2020 Ph.D. thesis; in a 2021 book chapter, he also points to the importance of the Guerre texts as evidence of a unique contemporary literary tradition in Metz. See Lazzari, 'Die literarische Reaktion' and Lazzari, *Une histoire*. For a brief analysis of the poetic forms and traditions of the Guerre texts, based on the Bouteiller edition, see Seláf, 'La Guerre'.

among multiple kinds of embodied performance practice. The Guerre performance texts, however, document that overlapping public practices interacted in ways that developed fundamental systems of meaning.[3] Theories of the public sphere have demonstrated the importance of non-'literate' modes of communication to political and social critique in the Middle Ages.[4] The techniques and media of public exchange, in this framework, demonstrate a 'pervasive orality': they form audible and physical expressions and intrusions into the urban environment.[5] Performances such as these thus lie at the heart of medieval public life and communication: not simply through isolated interventions, but as systems. The original performances of the Guerre pieces in Metz — as urban, oral, and embodied events — illuminate a space for exchange and discussion that existed amid circumstances of violence and extremism. In this article, I explore the individual Guerre pieces within their early, performed context, and highlight how this remarkable collection points to a multivalent performance system operating within the hostile conditions of early fourteenth-century Metz.

Historical Overview

The Guerre pieces were originally created and performed during an intense period of internal and external conflict for the city of Metz. Over the course of the thirteenth century, a series of wars had enabled this francophone center to establish its independence from the Empire, and to expand its rule over a region that was to become known as the 'Pays Messin'. During the late thirteenth century, the influence of the bishops of Metz over civic matters diminished; by the early decades of the fourteenth century, control of the city rested in the hands of its citizens. This shift did not prove harmonious, however: even as the city continued to engage in sporadic warfare with neighbouring powers, the commons and patrician factions within Metz struggled to gain the upper hand internally. Then, in 1324, the Guerre des Quatre Seigneurs brought Metz into conflict with a coalition of regional forces.[6] The opposition comprised Ferry IV, duke of Lorraine; Edward I, count of Bar; Baudouin of Luxembourg, archbishop of

---

3 In this sense, I envision this wartime performance system as functioning similarly to the female performance networks that I detailed in Crowder, *Performing Women*.

4 These emerge from scholarly critiques of Habermasian theories; for the original theory and an overview of responses by medieval scholars, see: Habermas, *Strukturwandel*, transl. by Burger, and Symes, 'Out in the Open'.

5 Symes, 'Out in the Open', pp. 281 and 287.

6 The causes of the war are complex, but originate in a struggle over the large debts owed to Messine bankers by regional lords and Messine purchases of 'feudal' lands. For a nuanced picture of the social and political history of Metz in this period, see Schneider, *La Ville*, esp. pp. 464–71, and the sources in the bibliography.

Trier; and Jean I, count of Luxembourg, king of Bohemia, and nephew of Baudouin. Fighting began in September 1324, and Metz endured a lengthy siege, as well as suffering extreme devastation across the countryside. Although an official peace was concluded between the city and its external enemies in March 1326, severe internal clashes continued for a year over the taxes levied to pay for the war. These struggles were as disruptive as the war itself: in the summer of 1326, for example, the commons exiled the leaders of the patrician faction and demolished their homes. This party then established a short-lived commune, which governed Metz for several months before the patricians returned and seized control of the city, permanently. It is during these years — from the start of the war to the return of the patricians — that the Guerre performance pieces first were created and performed in and around Metz.

Guerre Performance Texts — Manuscript History and Performance Context

Evidence for the individual fourteenth-century performance events, originally produced separately during the period of the Guerre des Quatre Seigneurs for immediate purposes but nonetheless participating in an ongoing, shared conversation about the war, survives only in the form of a collection of short verse texts. As recently demonstrated by Antoine Lazzari, these texts had become associated by the fifteenth century and circulated as a group in at least two manuscript traditions, with as many as five copies existing by the early sixteenth century.[7] Within Metz, the Guerre performance texts were preserved in a mid-fifteenth-century 'chronicle': the manuscript Metz BM 831, created for a member of a local patrician family. This volume contained a collection of texts, written in a single hand around 1439. In addition to the fourteenth-century Guerre performance texts, it compiled other original material on the war with contemporary and later texts about the kings of Bohemia: legal agreements, treaties, Latin verses, and a lengthy verse history, known as the *Guerre de Metz*.[8] The performance texts are positioned within this manuscript amid a variety of other writings that tell a general history of the rulers of Bohemia —

---

7 Lazzari, 'Die literarische Reaktion', pp. 169–70. I do not distinguish between the manuscript traditions for the purposes of this performance analysis, since the texts show few variations and their record postdates the initial composition and/or performances by over a century.

8 For an introduction to this verse history of the war, which has been of much greater interest to scholars than the other contemporary materials in the collection, see Bouteiller, *La Guerre*. Seláf argues that this poem is unique within medieval French poetry, showing 'German poetical influence', see Seláf, 'La Guerre'. I do not include the *Guerre de Metz* piece within my analysis, as it does not contain clear markers of public performance beyond those demonstrated by contemporary French verse texts more generally.

who also held the title of count of Luxembourg, thus participating in the Guerre des Quatre Seigneurs — and their connections to Metz and the patrician d'Esch family. Within this context, the Guerre performance pieces functioned together with works across multiple genres to establish a history of noble alliance for the family who had Metz BM 831 made. Lazzari points to this change in purpose and use over time, as the textual record of the original works became integrated into a manuscript-based culture of remembrance in the fifteenth century.[9] Over time, the written artifact of the collected performance texts took on its own life in Metz.

A study of the original contexts for the Guerre pieces requires a navigation back through this transmission history, toward a reconstructed and imagined moment of performance. Naturally, this process is complicated by the vagaries of time, preservation, and scholarship. Metz BM 831 itself was destroyed during World War II, rendering its mise-en-page unavailable. This manuscript and other variants of the d'Esch chronicle are analyzed by Georg Wolfram in a rigorous 1906 edition; however, he did not include a Clervaux manuscript that had been rediscovered just decades earlier.[10] This is Clervaux, Luxembourg Klosterbibliothek MS 13, which dates to the late fifteenth or early sixteenth century and preserves only the *Guerre de Metz* and Guerre performance texts. This represents the second strand of textual transmission; an incomplete version of the manuscript is reproduced in an antiquarian edition by Ernest de Bouteiller.[11] Thus, what survives to our day are the late-nineteenth and early twentieth-century textual renderings of a mid-fifteenth to early sixteenth-century written record, which itself documents the textual repurposing of a lost, century-old written record. This evidence is far removed from the original, early fourteenth-century moment of creation, expression, and documentation of the Guerre performance pieces, yet it provides valuable traces of those initial performance events, nonetheless. Done with care, a reconsideration of this unusual material from a performance perspective offers a novel view of performance conventions and practice in Metz during the early decades of the fourteenth century.

Like much documentation of dramatic practice, the manuscript history of the Guerre performance pieces offers a complex lens on the past, filtered through many different perspectives and uses. When read through the disciplinary-specific approaches of history and literature, the dramatic, collective, and participatory aspects of these texts may easily be overlooked, especially given the form of their preservation. Existing

---

9 Lazzari, 'Die literarische Reaktion', pp. 167 and 172.

10 Wolfram, *Die Metzer Chronik*, pp. XI–XIX. Not all of the manuscript versions of this chronicle and the *Guerre de Metz* incorporate the Guerre performance texts; for example, Paris, Bibliothèque Nationale n.a.fr. 6706 does not.

11 Bouteiller, *La Guerre de Metz*, pp. 315–90.

research approaches the Guerre works as 'poems', even while acknowledging them as an oral medium; the result has been a focus on the textual aspects of the evidence. Lazzari, for example, refers to the texts as *Gelegenheitsgedichte* ('occasional poetry') and details their importance as evidence for a distinct contemporary tradition of poetical hybridity and satire in Metz, noting their oral adaption of existing forms.[12] Similarly, much of the earlier scholarship implicitly accepts the original performance nature of the Guerre texts, given the internal textual evidence showing that many of these works were created for sharing at specific events. Yet, despite a general recognition of the early oral and physical expression of these works, the specific mechanisms of that performance activity have gone unremarked and unstudied.

A performance-based approach, rooted in an expanded canon of performance texts, offers an additional perspective on how the Guerre pieces functioned in the early moments of their ongoing history. Drawing upon the work of Claire Sponsler and Carol Symes, I position these surviving texts in relation to public and civic modes of performance, through which the social and political life of the city transpired.[13] Although these original performed pieces shared an afterlife in which they circulated as a collection of texts — probably also shared orally — the early history of the Guerre pieces is rooted in their performance by an 'actor' at a specific moment and place, for a select audience.[14] Many of the works contain explicit references to performance elements and conventions, and are plainly 'occasional', in the sense that they were created for presentation at a distinct, collective event. In this framework, the Guerre texts need not have been staged with formal actors, costumes, and sets to have served a communicative function. Indeed, it appears that simple and varying modes of performance predominated: while one of the texts visualizes recent events through a dramatic narration for the political elite, for example, another creates a participatory devotional experience by intoning prayers that demand responses from the audience. Thus, rather than simply accepting the Guerre pieces as having 'circulated' in some abstract oral or written form, and continuing to centre the study of written texts and their authors, we must also foreground dramatic approaches by interrogating the performance aspect as well.

---

12 Lazzari, 'Die literarische Reaktion', p. 169.

13 Sponsler, *The Queen's Dumbshows* and Symes, *A Common Stage*.

14 Specialists in medieval French literature have demonstrated that contemporary oral representations of verse necessitated physical engagement and modulation of voice: in other words, performance techniques. See *Performing Medieval Narrative*, ed. by Vitz and others, and Vitz, 'Tales'. For a discussion of the possible process of creation of the Guerre texts, see my section on performance strategies and characteristics.

In addition to documenting a Metz-centred literary movement and the later shift to a memorial-based agenda, the surviving Guerre performance texts also provide valuable traces of an original performance framework. These pieces preserve a variety of potential stagings, performance and 'plot' settings, audiences, and socio-political perspectives. As well as the already-mentioned bird-centred narrative allegory (the *Sermon*) and the participatory *Paternoster*, the content of the performance texts includes a blessing to welcome a new bishop, a Metz-centred prophecy, explications of the bird allegory, and other participatory prayers. While some pieces are satirical, others create different and distinct emotional registers in response to special events. The blessing (the *Benedicite*), for example, functions on a practical level to sanctify a meal and its attendees, and the *Ave Maria* offers heartfelt, collective thanks for peace during a lull in the war. (Summaries and performance details of all the Guerre performance texts appear in the next section.) Considering these works from a performance perspective makes clear the many differences among them, while also underlining their participation in a shared conversation that took place through varied forms of oral, embodied performance.

Guerre Texts and Performance — Individual Overviews

[My citations reference the 1906 Wolfram edition and the manuscript paging recorded there; each text is discussed in the order it appeared in the manuscript.[15] While some of the pieces engage in explicit dialogue with each other, most of the works are connected through their design for interactive performance and the shared Guerre content.]

C'est le sermon du pappegay des Tresez de la guerre de Mets et de la commune, *originally 26 October 1325 and/or October 1326 (manuscript pages 139–42, pp. 214–21)*

The first short performance text recorded in Metz BM 831 and Clervaux MS 13 depicts an allegory of the Guerre des Quatre Seigneurs, voiced first by a human and then a parrot narrator.[16] The historical figures and

---

15 All translations are my own, based on the Wolfram edition. My summaries focus on the performance aspects of the works; for in-depth studies of the individual Guerre texts within the contemporary literary tradition, see Wolfram, *Die Metzer Chronik* and Lazzari, 'Die literarische Reaktion', pp. 166–69.

16 Satirical and parodic religious texts formed a lively tradition in the francophone world; these included sermons, *Paternosters*, *Credos*, *Ave Marias*, and other adaptations of popular prayers. A rich body of scholarship and critical editions examine these works: see, for

early events of the war are represented by different species of birds, who fight, squabble, and engage in deliberately coarse language and behaviour. While sympathetic to the Messine perspective, the work is simultaneously critical of internal conflict. Both narrators frequently employ direct address to the audience and physically implicate them in the 'low' actions of the avian characters. It is 140 lines, or about 7–10 minutes long, and could be dramatized by a single actor using multiple voices; internal and historical evidence indicates that the original audience was a mixed group of Messine citizens of varying political perspectives.

C'est l'exposicion du sarmont le pappegay, c. *26 October 1325 and/or October 1326 (143, pp. 222–23)*

The *Exposicion* follows the *Sermon* in the manuscripts and in its form and content. The stated goal of the *Exposicion* is to name and identify the historical figures represented by the allegorical birds of the *Sermon*, to ensure there is no obscurity. The narrator speaks in the same human voice as in the *Sermon* throughout and constructs a continuity of audience, pleading with the listeners to hear just one more word. Internal cues and content indicate its performance directly after the *Sermon*; it is 32 lines, or about 2–3 minutes long.

C'est la confirmacion le Jay d'Ingleterre, c. *26 October 1325 and/or October 1326 (144–45, pp. 224–27)*

The *Confirmacion* follows the *Exposicion* in the manuscripts. It also develops the same content, audience, and narrative structure of the *Sermon*. However, the human narrator introduces an English jay who offers further reflection on the dangers of internal strife and dissent. The narrator refers to having spoken the *Sermon*; a direct reference to the parrot's speech in the first line situates its performance directly after the *Sermon*, either before or after the *Exposicion*. It is 48 lines, or about 3–4 minutes long.

C'est la prophesie Maistre Lambelain de Cornualle, c. *December 1325 (146–48, pp. 226–31)*

The fourth short performance text, the *Prophesie*, departs from the *Sermon*'s allegorical and multiple-voice model, while continuing a critique of the progress of the war and the ongoing conflict among Messine groups.

---

example, Ilvonen, *Parodies*, and the essays in *La Tentation*, ed. by Gaucher especially Koopmans, 'La parodie'. For parrots and parody more generally, see Victorin, 'Du papegau au perroquet'.

Narrated by Lambelin of Cornouaille/Cornwall, who is named as the author, the piece draws upon local, contemporary events and antique sources to create a 'prophecy' that roughly translates to, 'When pigs fly, Metz will lose the war.'[17] The speaker opens by asking God to protect the audience from sin and criminal acts, before telling them to settle down for the new verses. The audience is identified as forming a single company or self-identified group; it is 76 lines, or 4–6 minutes long.

C'est li ABC maistre Asselin du Pont contre ceulx de Mets, c. *February 1325 (149–53, pp. 230–43)*

The *ABC* continues the format of first-person narration with direct address to the audience, but shifts to an anti-Metz perspective on the war in order to critique the Messine role in regional economics. The text identifies the author as Asselin du Pont, a notary; its verses are structured alphabetically, with the first letter of each stanza following in order.[18] The *ABC* alludes to a prophecy and thus perhaps to the *Prophesie*, but there is no narrative or structural continuity with the previous four performance texts, apart from the subject matter. Compared with the other surviving texts, the *ABC* contains fewer internal performance cues, suggesting that it may have originated and then circulated primarily in written form; a textual mode of transmission also makes sense given that the work reached Metz during the siege. The political standpoint and non-Messine details suggest a broad audience from the coalition attacking Metz; it is 178 lines, or 9–12 minutes long.

---

17 Among the handful of people named as performers, narrators, and/or authors in the Guerre texts, only Asselin du Pont (author of the *ABC*) can be connected with a known historical figure; see *Die Metzer Chronik*, ed. by Wolfram, p. LXII. Scholars have speculated that the names may be fictitious; in-depth analysis as to why these particular figures or names would have been chosen must await a future publication. For the *Prophecie* text, which is uniquely focused on events in Metz, the identification of Lambelin with Cornouaille/ Cornwall may represent a desire to align the work with the larger genre of prophecy, which often functioned as political polemic. For an introduction to the extensive literature of francophone prophecy, see Rayne-Michel, 'Introduction', and Daniel, *Les prophéties*. (It should be noted that, although the *Prophesie* is identified with the Tiburtine Sibyl tradition in the CNRS Jonas/IRHT database, this is not supported by the surviving manuscripts or scholarship.)

18 The *abécédaire* itself forms a well-known genre of medieval French poetry, examples of which vary greatly in content, lexicology, place of origin, and manuscript tradition. The research corpus is too great to cite here; for an introduction, see the articles in *Sur la 'sente' de l'ABC*, ed. by Radomme and Uhlig. For the authorship of the *ABC*, see the previous note.

C'est la rescripcion maistre Lambelin, recteur de Parix et d'Orliens, c. *October-December 1325 (154–58, pp. 242–55)*

The *Rescripcion* directly mirrors and responds to the content and structure of the *ABC* text, countering its claims while also stirring outrage against the people and viewpoints it represents. The narrator identifies himself as Lambelin, and frames his response to Asselin du Pont as being spoken aloud. The text of the *Rescripcion* directly foregrounds the oral and communal aspects of its performance — unlike the *ABC* — and integrates a public prayer at the end. Since internal evidence and content indicate a Messine audience for the *Rescripcion*, this suggests that the format of the *ABC* was deliberately adapted to fit local, performance-focused conventions of political dialogue. The *Rescripcion* is 186 lines, or 9–12 minutes long.

C'est une patenostre de la guerre de Mets que Robin de la Valee fist, *October 1325 (159–63, pp. 254–65)*

The *Patenostre* text records a collective prayer that elaborates upon the language and structure of the Lord's Prayer.[19] Each stanza begins with a word or phrase from the Latin, which is then developed in French verse. A rubric identifies the performer and/or author as Robin de la Valee. Situated within the context of the war, the speaker calls on God to aid and protect the suffering citizens of Metz, and verbally prompts the audience to listen and participate at various points. The participants are referred to as members of a company or other self-identified group; it is 189 lines, or 9–12 minutes long.

C'est le Credo Henris de Heix, c. *late February 1326 (164–70, pp. 264–79)*

The *Credo Henris de Heix* closely resembles the *Patenostre* in form, although it is based upon the first part of the *Apostles' Creed*. A rubric identifies the performer and/or author as Henris de Heix. Using first-person and direct address, the speaker details numerous events that have harmed the audience during a specific period of the war. The opening lines instruct the audience to be still and quiet; the text identifies them as a broad-based group of Metz citizens from varying professions and social groups. It is 234 lines, or 12–16 minutes long.

---

19 For the genre of The Lord's Prayer specifically, see Subrenat, 'Quatre Patrenostres', and Hirsch, 'La Patrenostre'.

C'est le Credo Michelet Petit Pain que maint devant les Repanties, *before 3 March 1326 (171–73, pp. 278–83)*

The *Credo Michelet Petit Pain* closely resembles the *Credo Henris de Heix* in form and content. It adapts the final lines of the *Apostles' Creed*, taking up the Latin text where the *Credo of Henris de Heix* ends. A rubric identifies the performer and/or author as Michelet Petit Pain. It concludes with a substantial element of audience participation; the point of view indicates an audience sympathetic to the Messine cause. It is 81 lines, or 4–6 minutes long.

C'est li Ave Maria Marguerite du Pont Rengmont, *after 3 March 1326 (174–75, pp. 282–87)*

The *Ave Maria Marguerite* takes the form of a collective prayer, similar in structure to the *Patenostre* and *Credo*s. It adapts and expands the first two lines of the *Ave Maria* to thank the Virgin for bringing peace and, relative to the other Metz-based performance texts, makes fewer local and immediate historical references. A rubric identifies the performer and/or author as Marguerite de Pont Rengmont.[20] The speaker addresses the audience as *seigneurs* and instructs them to take physical action or speaks on their behalf at several points; on the whole, it is less explicitly participatory than the other works, excepting the *ABC*. It is 72 lines, or 4–5 minutes long.

C'est ung Benedicite de Lowis de Pitie, evesque de Mets cui Dieu perdont, *soon after 3 March 1326 (176–78, pp. 288–93)*

The *Benedicite* is a communal prayer based upon the Latin blessing before a meal. Like the *Patenostre*, the two *Credo*s, and the *Ave Maria Marguerite*, it expands an original Latin verse to develop a theme; in this case, the redemption of the new bishop of Metz, Louis of Poitiers (1325–1327).[21] The *Benedicite* instructs its Messine audience to listen and make peace with the bishop, and outlines his good qualities. The audience is addressed as *seigneurs* and internal evidence indicates a pro-Messine perspective; the speaker also distinguishes the bishop's companions from the Metz audience. The function of the original Latin blessing suggests the performance of the *Benedicite* before the start of a collective meal at which both parties were present. It is 80 lines, or 4–6 minutes long.

---

20 The identification of a female performer and/or author for the *Ave Maria Marguerite* raises interesting questions about gender, women's history, and performance; I am exploring this topic in a separate study of the *Sermon*.

21 In this instance, the individual named in the rubric is neither the performer nor the author of the piece, but rather its subject.

Performance Strategies and Characteristics

Prior scholarship has shown the cohesiveness of the Guerre texts on both a literary and historical level; the performance features of these pieces reveal another layer of shared attributes, as well. In what follows, I delve into the potential mechanics of the original performance events, based on the surviving texts. I do not attempt to definitively answer the question of whether the individual Guerre works were first improvised and later written down, or initially were composed and then performed. The high level of performance detail in some of the texts suggests an origin in writing, with those details serving as cues to prompt the performer and audience at key moments. However, the documentation of and/or transformation of a dramatic work into written record often elides the evidence of ephemeral practices relating to body and voice. Given that the textual evidence for the Guerre pieces post-dates their initial creation by over a century, and that the pieces themselves originated separately over a period of several years, our evidence cannot demonstrate conclusively a single mode of creation. However, the surviving texts do testify to certain common practices, which include audience participation, timing and structural conventions, and site-specific design.

A basic analysis of the performance texts of the Guerre collection that originate in Metz indicates that they incorporate a comparatively large proportion of participatory elements. Some individual examples of these are detailed in the overviews, above. Other instances include moments when the texts require the performers to explicitly instruct their audiences on how to participate: the *Patenostre* directs its listeners about when and what they should speak, for example, stating 'Amen, dites, compaignons' (l. 174). In other pieces, the narrators instruct the audience to sit still, be quiet, and/or listen carefully at key points in the performance.[22] Viewed collectively, this evidence demonstrates that the Guerre pieces often make direct appeals to their audiences that engage them through aural, oral, and bodily spectatorship. Moreover, the performers straightforwardly name those listening, distinguishing among the potential audience members. To call a resident of Metz a *citain* versus a *seigneur* is to position them socially within contested local hierarchies; the word *compaignon*, on the other hand, frames the audience in collective terms.[23] Such performance-specific directives are commonplace throughout the Guerre texts, revealing a shared approach to the communicative process of these otherwise varied works. In performance, these techniques would have situated the audience

---

22 For example, *Patenostre*, l. 64.

23 Given the class-based conflict that dominated the contemporary history of Metz, these distinctions of terminology speak to the tailoring of the Guerre performance texts to target or address differing internal groups.

within the event, drawing them into the framework of the performance as active presences, if not also as contributors.

The Guerre pieces reveal the existence of other performance conventions that seem to have shaped the contemporary Metz performance environment, as well. Performance duration, for example: the pieces vary in length from roughly three to sixteen minutes, with the most frequent configurations being either five minutes or ten minutes long.[24] This suggests that systematic and customary practices shaped the length of the Guerre pieces, probably corresponding with the purpose and context of the initial individual performances. Interestingly, the longest piece is the *Credo Henris de Heix*, at twelve to sixteen minutes long, which adapts a portion of the Apostles' Creed; it is followed in the manuscript by the *Credo Michelet Petit Pain*, which picks up where the *Credo Henris de Heix* ends and is a more common four to six minutes long. In this instance, although the length of the source text seems to necessitate a single, comparatively long piece, the creators instead chose to divide it into two works. This division makes little sense for a piece intended purely or primarily for written consumption; instead, it suggests that performance considerations shaped the composition of the two *Credos*. In this instance, the division causes the texts — and thus their embodied performances — to correspond more closely with the standard duration of the other Guerre pieces. If we recall that the Guerre performances would have taken place within the concrete systems and rhythms of social and political life within Metz, then the need to meet practical considerations relating to timing makes sense. More fundamentally, just as the shared literary aspect of the texts suggests the functioning of a group of Messine authors in conversation, this performance evidence suggests that contemporary Messine creators also consciously participated in a collective, Metz-based performance practice, of which one aspect related to timing conventions.

The Guerre pieces often specify and envision the historical context and/or social settings of their performances, as well. This technique further cements the original occasional function of these works: as ad hoc pieces created for performance at particular moments, for specific settings and audiences that were intended to convey an immediate message. For example, the *Benedicite* takes the form of a participatory prayer before a meal, based upon the Latin blessing. Its explicit welcome of the bishop Louis of Poitiers and his companions, the short length, and the inherent ritual function suggest an initial performance at a ceremonial dinner attended by Louis of Poitiers and a group of Messine citizens, likely occurring in March or April 1326. Indeed, the initial performance of this text would have helped the elites of Metz to negotiate the metaphoric

---

24 I estimate the lengths of the performances through experimental practice, drawing a conservative conclusion based on minimal staging conventions.

and literal integration of Louis of Poitiers into Messine social and political life after a period of conflict. Many of the other works in the collection similarly express their intended settings, which range from large-scale participatory prayer events to intimate exhortations aimed at small companies of listeners.

The Guerre performance pieces create shared space in many other ways, as well; the local environment, and especially the natural world, feature heavily within these works. For example, the narrator of the *Sermon* employs the sound of storks honking to negatively characterize an opposing political party.[25] Storks then were native to the broader region, and this bird thrived in Metz in the later Middle Ages: hundreds of large nests perched atop the roofs and chimneys of the city, with the birds producing a tremendous noise.[26] The *Sermon*'s reference to the cacophony of storks thus evokes the immediate physical environment of Metz, while simultaneously drawing upon the lived experience of the Messine audience. The other Guerre performances also feature local aspects of the natural world: the *Prophesie* references the clarity of the water of the Seille river; some pieces make reference to the vineyards that dominated the countryside.[27] One performance even cites a recent, exceptionally destructive storm and its ecological impact.[28] On a basic level, the incorporation of these elements from the natural world anchors the individual performances within the immediate physical environment of the audience. Taken together, however, these details also connect the Guerre pieces by creating a shared space in which the city is envisioned as a setting for many intensely local, site-specific performances. Whether or not the performances share common perspectives or intents, they agree on the physical and cultural centrality of Metz to their endeavors.

The inclusion of singular historical elements, such as certain inhabitants or locations within the city, also contributes to the development of a shared context for the audiences of these works across performances. The *Sermon*, for example, characterizes a local patrician named Jacomin Boilawe as bravely standing up to the previously mentioned honking storks.[29] Archival evidence reveals that this figure, who was comparatively unimportant beyond the walls of Metz, was instrumental in the effort

---

25 'Lor se prannent a terteller | Come fait martel a marteller [Then they began to honk, like a hammer pounding]', *Sermon*, ll. 59–60.

26 For some of the early references to storks in Metz, see Serdeczny, 'Le Bec de la cigogne'. The later draining of wetlands and swamps throughout the region led to a sharp decline in stork numbers.

27 *Prophesie*, ll. 54 and 62. The Seille reference is perhaps ironic, given the location of many tanneries along its lower course in the later Middle Ages.

28 *Credo Henris de Heix*, l. 152.

29 *Sermon*, l. 137. I previously have discussed this incident in detail, as part of my larger project (see note 1).

to establish the 1326 commune. Unlike the other patrician leaders of Metz, who were well-connected regionally and might be recognizable to a non-Messine audience, the inclusion of the Boilawe character in the *Sermon* creates a performance context in which only insiders — specifically, residents of Metz — can recognize all the figures depicted. Other individual Guerre performances echo this practice: the *Benedicite* for Louis of Poitiers, newly appointed as bishop, endeavours to rehabilitate him in the eyes of the Messine populace. As a performance, the *Benedicite* only makes sense when viewed from the perspective of a long-term Metz audience, as Louis of Poitiers had not been in conflict with the other populations and leaders of the larger war. In both of these examples, the figures depicted in their respective performances were locally controversial. Thus the changing 'cast' of the shared backdrop could be highly contentious, even as the composition of the different audiences was dictated by a tight focus on Metz. Moreover, the representation of a shared and contested performance context reinforces the centrality of Messine practice as a forum for difficult conversations about and amid the conflict.

Lastly, the Guerre performance pieces create discourse through performance, producing dialogues that operate across perspectives and viewpoints. The *ABC* and *Rescripcion* speak to each other directly, for example; they reveal a responsive mode of performance that is rooted in structure as well as content. The *ABC* was created first, and gives voice to an anti-Messine perspective on the Guerre des Quatre Seigneurs. It lacks the extensive local detail and participatory elements present in most of the Metz-based Guerre performances, and seems to address a broad coalition on the opposing side. As such, it offers the unusual example of a non-Messine perspective within the collection, created outside of Metz. Although the *ABC* seems to have circulated within Metz in some form, it does not target a focused audience through the same performance methods as outlined above.

By contrast, the performance techniques of the *Rescripcion* more closely resemble those of the other Guerre performances, employing direct address both to audiences aligned with and against Metz. Moreover, the *Rescripcion* explicitly frames itself as an oral work, with the narrator emphasizing that his speech will contradict the *noise* and *hault parler* of Metz's enemies.[30] On the whole, the *Rescripcion* displays an open antagonism toward the people and viewpoints depicted in the *ABC*. Yet, despite this deliberate differentiation, the *Rescripcion* very closely mirrors the *ABC*: it adapts the alphabetical structure to connect with the *ABC* intimately. The *Rescripcion* speaks directly to the *ABC*'s act of hostility through mimicry: this permits a point-by-point rebuttal of its content,

---

30 *Rescripcion*, ll. 5–6.

while simultaneously reworking the *ABC*'s genre as a performance and claiming it for Metz. In essence, the *Rescripcion* creates a discourse with the *ABC* in order to communicate the superiority of the Messine position and the dominance of its performance practice.

Thus, despite the differences among them, many of the Guerre pieces share a common framework of performance practice. Most preserve a high proportion of textual material that centres on participatory behaviour among the audience. Performance conventions relating to timing and structure also link the works. Other characteristics reveal the site-specific nature of the original performances: the individual pieces situate themselves within spatially and temporally distinct performance contexts through similar tactics. They employ references to concrete, regionally specialized information and hyper-local historical figures and events; they also accentuate environmental features and/or an immediate ceremonial context. These shared performance elements embed the individual works within a public debate about the war that took place in Metz by means of performance; although this discussion was surely buttressed by other communicative modes — such as writing — the crass humour, poignant supplications, and extreme speech of these works initially operated in an oral, embodied context. As such, the Guerre texts testify to a mode of wartime exchange within this particular urban environment that expressed contention through the collective medium of performance.

Conclusions

The Guerre performance texts are exciting for the sheer density of performance practice that they preserve: a relatively rich sampling of the often-ephemeral public debates generated by a community at war. Each of the Guerre pieces is linked to a specific local perspective, frequently at odds or contradictory. These competing narrations, recitations, and prayers bubbled up throughout the years of the war, offering performed expressions of political doctrine and dissent. From a historical perspective, this evidence provides a window into competing perspectives on the war in early fourteenth-century Metz, beyond the battlefield. A literary analysis of the material reveals the creators' adaptation of genre and form, and the adoption of the Guerre texts by later generations, who were eager to claim the works for their own purposes. Yet drama also has something to add: a methodology which reveals that a cohesive body of performance practice was essential to the unfolding of this particular urban conversation.

As performances, the Guerre pieces create a seemingly contradictory space: a shared meeting ground, where disparate and competing narratives could overlap and interconnect, where individuals could hate and grieve and be reconciled, and where hostile factions could speak to each other and be heard. In early fourteenth-century Metz, residents employed the shared mechanisms of performance to work through the ongoing rupture to daily and civic life that the war had entailed. This framework created a forum in which individual performance moments could engage in conversation, adapting and responding to each other as well as to the larger events of the war and the commune. These performances both provoked and soothed internal strife: they could weaponize the aural cityscape by linking the natural sounds of storks honking to political vilification, and rehabilitate and reintegrate controversial individuals after an interval of animosity. Despite polarizing circumstances, the people of Metz found a way to communicate — not always in service of peace or the greater good — but using performance to engage with each other nonetheless.

As such, the Guerre pieces testify to the essential role that drama studies must play in the wider study of medieval urban history. To fully understand the historical processes of public debate, we must incorporate the methodologies of performance. These approaches allow us to integrate and contextualize texts — as well as other forms of evidence — that show local systems of information functioning within physical spaces, with embodied 'actors' and audiences, at specific historical moments. In the case of Metz, the Guerre evidence reveals the audible and physical expressions that operated across the spaces of the city. By insisting on the primacy of Messine performance practice and the immediate environment, the residents of Metz positioned themselves at the heart of a larger dramatic narrative, casting themselves as the main characters in a series of episodes set in their communal, urban sphere. Yet Metz is not unique in its internal focus and shared mode of communication: other cities used performance to develop complex forums for public life and debate, as well. As scholars of theatre and performance, we have an essential role to play in exploring this phenomenon; if we work collectively to span the geography of the late medieval world, perhaps we might find that urban performance culture *is* medieval urban culture.

Bibliography

Edited Source Texts

La Guerre de Metz en 1324: Poème du XIVe siècle, ed. by Ernest de Bouteiller (Paris: Firmin-Didot et Cie, 1875)

Die Metzer Chronik des Jaique Dex (Jacques d'Esch) über die Kaiser und Könige aus dem Luxemburger Hause, ed. by Georg Wolfram, Quellen zur lothringischen Geschichte, 4 (Metz: G. Scriba, 1906)

Secondary Material

Crowder, Susannah, *Performing women: Gender, self, and representation in late medieval Metz*, Manchester Medieval Literature and Culture, 22 (Manchester: Manchester University Press, 2018)

Daniel, Catherine, *Les prophéties de Merlin et la culture politique, XIIe–XVIe siècle*, Culture et société médiévales, 11 (Turnhout: Brepols, 2007)

Habermas, Jürgen, *Strukturwandel der Öffentlichkeit: Untersuchungen zu einer Kategorie der bürgerlichen Gesellschaft* (Neuwied and Berlin: Luchterhand, 1962), trans. by Thomas Burger as *The Structural Transformation of the Public Sphere: An Inquiry into a Category of Bourgeois Society* (Cambridge: Polity Press, 1989)

Hirsch, Ilan, 'La Patrenostre de Lombardie: désordre divin et désordre social', *Médiévales*, 4 (1983), 148–65

Ilvonen, Eero, *Parodies de thèmes pieux dans la poésie française du Moyen Âge: Paternoster-Credo-Ave Maria-Laetabundus* (Paris: Honoré Champion, 1914)

Koopmans, Jelle, 'La parodie en situation. Approches du texte festif de la fin du Moyen Âge', *Cahiers de Recherches Médiévales*, 15 (2008), 87–98

Lazzari, Antoine, 'Die literarische Reaktion auf den Angriff Johanns von Luxemburg auf Metz (1324) und deren Rezeption durch die lokale Geschichtsschreibung – Überlegungen zum Funktionalitätswandel spätmittelalterlicher Gelegenheitsdichtung', in *Über den Hof und am Hofe: Literatur und Geschichtsschreibung im Mittelalter*, ed. by Dana Dvořáčková-Malá, Kristyna Solomon, and Michel Margue (Dresden: Thelem, 2021), pp. 163–74

———, 'Une histoire messine de la dynastie impériale des Luxembourg: les Chroniques de Jacques Dex (vers 1439)' (Ph.D. Thesis, University of Luxembourg, 2020)

Margue, Michel, 'L'histoire impériale au service de la bourgeoisie: les Chroniques de Jacques d'Esch et la maison impériale de Luxembourg', in *Écrire l'histoire à Metz au Moyen Âge*, ed. by Mireille Chazan and Gérard Nauroy (Bern: Lang, 2011), pp. 281–312

Omont, Henri, 'Anonyme auteur d'un poème de Metz en 1324', in *Histoire littéraire de la France*, vol. XXXV, ed. by Charles-Victor Langlois (Paris: Imprimerie Nationale, 1921), pp. 580–97

——, 'Rimeurs de Metz', in *Histoire littéraire de la France*, vol. XXXV, ed. by Charles-Victor Langlois (Paris: Imprimerie Nationale, 1921), pp. 592–97

Performing Medieval Narrative, ed. by Evelyn Birge Vitz and others (Woodbridge: Boydell & Brewer, 2005)

Rayne-Michel, Servane, 'Introduction: La prophétie médiévale: Théologie et fiction, politique et langage', *Questes*, 28 (2014), 3–28

Schneider, Jean, *La Ville de Metz aux XIIe et XIVe siècles* (Nancy: Imprimerie Thomas, 1950)

Seláf, Levente, '*La Guerre de Metz*: un hapax formel de la littérature française médiévale', in *Sens, Rhétorique et Musique: Études réunies en hommage à Jacqueline Cerquiglini-Toulet*, ed. by Sophie Albert and others, Colloques, congrès et conférences sur le Moyen Âge, 21 (Paris: Honoré Champion, 2015), pp. 381–89

Serdeczny, Anton, 'Le Bec de la cigogne: Déchiffrement de l'héritage d'un mythe', *Études Rurales*, 187 (2011/12), 205–21

Sponsler, Claire, *The Queen's Dumbshows: John Lydgate and the Making of Early Theater* (Philadelphia: University of Pennsylvania Press, 2014)

Subrenat, Jean, 'Quatre Patrenostres parodiques', *Senefiance*, 10 (1981), 515–47

Sur la 'sente' de l'ABC: les poèmes abécédaires en français (XIIIe–XVe siècles), ed. by Thibaut Radomme and Marion Uhlig = *French Studies* 75/3 (2021)

Symes, Carol, *A Common Stage: Theater and Public Life in Medieval Arras* (Ithaca: Cornell University Press, 2007)

——, 'Out in the Open, in Arras: Sightlines, Soundscapes, and the Shaping of a Medieval Public Sphere', in *Cities, Texts, and Social Networks, 400–1500*, ed. by Anne E. Lester, Carol Symes, and Caroline Goodson (London: Ashgate, 2012), pp. 278–302

La Tentation du parodique dans la littérature médiévale, ed. by Elisabeth Gaucher = *Cahiers de Recherches Médiévales*, 15 (2008)

Victorin, Patricia, 'Du papegau au perroquet. Antonomase et parodie', *Cahiers de Recherches Médiévales*, 15 (2008), 145–66

Vitz, Evelyn Birge, 'Tales with Guts: A "Rasic" Aesthetic in Medieval French Storytelling', *The Drama Review*, 52/4 (2008), 145–73

Wolfram, Georg, and F. Bonnardot, 'Les Voeux de l'épervier: Kaiser Heinrichs VII. Romfahrt', *Annuaire de la société d'histoire et d'archéologie de la Lorraine*, 6 (1894), 177–257

Online Resources

Jonas. Répertoire des textes et des manuscrits médiévaux d'oc et d'oïl (CNRS Jonas/IRHT), https://jonas.irht.cnrs.fr/ (accessed: 5 February 2024)

THEODORE K. LERUD

MS Bodley 175, William Bedford's 1604 Copy and the Antiquarian Afterlife of the Chester Plays

▼ **ABSTRACT** This essay takes as its topic the late, post-performance copying of the manuscripts of the Chester plays, arguing that, in particular, William Bedford's apparently hastily-copied 1604 version (MS Bodley 175) is neither a production text nor a clandestine exercise in Catholic recusancy, but instead a contribution to the larger movement in *antiquarianism and historiography* prevalent in the early seventeenth century. Taking as a point of departure David Mills' assessment of the Bedford manuscript as a 'personal copy', the essay argues, that the purpose of the hurried copy was almost certainly to preserve the manuscript for later refinement and bestowal (for potential remuneration) on some wealthy Cestrian patron with an interest in drama and a developing library. A likely candidate for such a presentation copy would be Lord William Stanley, the sixth Earl of Derby (1594–1642).

▼ **KEYWORDS:** Chester, Whitsun plays, libraries, manuscripts, scribes, collectors, Bedford, Earls of Derby

Theodore K. Lerud is Emeritus Professor of English at Elmhurst University and is currently teaching in the Department of English Communication at Payap University International College in Chiang Mai, Thailand. His research interests centre around medieval and early modern English drama. Previous publications include *Memory, Images, and the English Corpus Christi Drama* (Palgrave Macmillan, 2008) and, with Kretzschmar and others, *Handbook of the Linguistic Atlas of the Middle and South Atlantic States* (University of Chicago, 1994).

European Medieval Drama, 27 (2023), 235–258
BREPOLS ❧ PUBLISHERS

10.1484/J.EMD.5.137685

One of the puzzling aspects of the history of the Chester Whitsun plays has always been that, aside from two fragmentary texts, which may represent acting texts, all of the surviving manuscripts date from the period between 1591 and 1607, significantly after the last production of the plays, apparently at Midsummer, in 1575.

Table 9.1. Post-Reformation copying of the Chester Whitsun plays: Five substantially complete manuscripts.

Year	Document reference number (Scribe and location)
1591	Huntington 2 (Edward Gregorie – Huntington Library)
1592	Additional 10305 (George Bellin – British Library)
1600	Harley 2013 (George Bellin – British Library)
1604	**Bodley 175 (William Bedford – Bodleian Library)**
1607	Harley 2124 (James Miller et al. – British Library)

This creates a different situation, in terms of what the texts represent, than that of York, where our single manuscript of the whole cycle, apparently a Register of the official performance text, was copied somewhere between 1463 and 1477, in the full flourish of the plays' production.[1] To complicate matters further, two of the full Chester manuscripts, Additional 10305 (1592) and Harley 2013 (1600), were copied by the same scribe, George Bellin, who, according to Lumiansky and Mills, 'served for nearly thirty years as scribe of the Coopers' Guild in Chester';[2] in fact, Bellin also completed a copy of the of the Coopers Guild's play, 'The Trial and Flagellation', which has apparently remained in the Guild's records since 1599. As can be seen even from the black-and-white reproductions in the frontispiece of Lumiansky and Mills' EETS edition of the plays,[3] two of the remaining manuscripts, Huntington 2 (copied 1591 by Edward Gregorie), originally from the collection of the Duke of Devonshire; and BL Harley 2124 (copied 1607 by James Miller and others) were, like Bellin's, executed with considerable care — including ruled pages, clear speech divisions and attributions, indentations or linings (generally to indicate quatrains), and, in the case of Harley 2124, the use of rubrication at selected points.

While Bellin, then, was clearly the 'go-to' scribe for work concerning the Whitsun plays, as Lumiansky and Mills note, it is unclear why Bellin 'chose to prepare a second full version of the cycle'.[4] Or a first, one might add, given that the heyday of the plays was long past even by 1592, with

---

1 Beadle, *The York Plays*, pp. 10–11.
2 *The Chester Mystery Cycle*, ed. by Lumiansky and Mills, vol. I, p. xv.
3 *The Chester Mystery Cycle*, ed. by Lumiansky and Mills, vol. I, S.S.3.
4 *The Chester Mystery Cycle*, ed. by Lumiansky and Mills, vol. I, p. xx.

the impact of the Reformation having long been felt in Chester, and even the final 1572 and 1575 productions proving controversial.[5] It is not the purpose of this essay to analyse all of these manuscripts at length, but instead to take as a case study the even more mysterious, single, rough copy of the 'pageantes or playes' of the City of Chester[6] completed by William Bedford, in 1604. These could not have been production texts. What, then, could have been the purpose of Bedford's hastily-done orphan 1604 copy of the plays?

For context, the last, controversial production of the 'Whitson playes' had taken place under mayor John Savage in 1575, on the eve of the construction of the Theatre in Shoreditch, just north of the London boundary. Having been moved to Midsummer, this production could hardly have been a full production of the Whitsun plays, but instead must have been incorporated into the longstanding 'midsummer watch', which even in contemporary reconstructions mixes less 'offensive' aspects of the Whitsun plays with long popular elements (**Figs 9.1–9.3**).[7] According to the 1619 version of David Rogers' *Breviary* (an important contemporary account of Chester's history and customs which we will treat at greater length later),[8] as transcribed by the Records of Early English Drama (REED) editors, the 'midsomer show' had been performed from 'antiquitie', and more recently 'reformed by the Instance of worthy Preachers'.[9]

---

5 See Mills' illuminating discussion of the controversy surrounding the two final productions in 1572 and 1575, in the face of Reformation objections, in Mills, *Recycling*, pp. 146–52. Mills notes that Chester's Assembly voted to stage the plays again in 1575 'with such correction and amendement as shalbe thaughte Convenient by the saide Maior' at Midsummer, rather than during the Whitsun holiday; he considers this change 'a further recycling of the cycle' (p. 149).

6 Oxford, Bodleian Library, Bodley 175, inside front cover.

7 We know that the final 1575 production of the Whitsun plays was moved to Midsummer, likely being combined with the longstanding Chester Midsummer Watch. Although the tradition of the Midsummer Watch in Chester has not continued unbroken since early modern times, it was revived in 1989 and currently takes place each year on the Saturday and Sunday nearest the summer solstice. The parade regularly includes a recreated family of Chester giants, as well as green men, angel and devil figures, and a hellmouth. The photos included here (my own) are from the 2019 celebration, reproduced courtesy of Chester Midsummer Watch; Production: Chester West and Chester Council; Artistic Director: Russell Kirk.

8 Not long after William Bedford completed his copy of the Chester Whitsun Plays in 1604, a similar exercise in historical preservation was undertaken by David Rogers, son of Chester Cathedral's Archdeacon Robert Rogers, who died in 1595. It appears that Archdeacon Rogers had made a hobby of collecting numerous records and documents relating to Chester's history and customs, and his son David began, in 1609, in the first of series of five versions of his *Breviary*, to bring order to this collection by organizing it in a series of ten (sometimes eleven) chapters.

9 *Cheshire*, ed. by Baldwin and others (see also note 53, below), vol. I, p. 440.

Figure 9.1. Chester Midsummer Watch 2019. Photo: Theodore K. Lerud.

Meanwhile, in London, by 1604, the year of Bedford's copy, James was in the second year of his reign (in fact, Bedford mentions this in the postscript to his copy of the Chester plays, fol. 176^r), creating a new mood at court and expectations for a more sophisticated theatre. For example, the Globe had long since been built (in 1599), and Shakespeare was at the height of his career, having completed *Othello*, and at work on *Macbeth*, in deference to the new sovereign's interest in things Scottish, and in witchcraft. Marlowe had been dead eleven years, and taste, at least at court, had turned away from his strutting overreachers to the subtleties and nuances of the indoor theatre. Shakespeare's company, the King's Men, was frequently called upon to perform at court, where tastes turned to a new, highly artificial theatrical form, the masque. Rival playwrights such as John Marston, Ben Jonson and, at times, Thomas Dekker, wrote for the 'boys' — the Children of the Queen's Revels — who performed plays indoors at Blackfriars for an audience of witty gallants from the Inns of Court. Their plays were filled with theatrical and political in-jokes, and satirical jabs at

Figure 9.2. Chester Midsummer Watch 2019: Hellmouth with other figures. Photo: Theodore K. Lerud.

one another, though by 1604 the so-called 'War of the Theaters'[10] had come to a truce, signified by the fact of Jonson and Marston working together on *Eastward Ho!*, a play first performed in 1605.

In contrast, locally, in the northwest in Chester, the mood was quite different. Certainly, some were aware of the trends in London: after all, Chester had been sending members to parliament since 1543, and, as Sally-Beth MacLean and others have shown, local families such as the Stanleys, as Earls of Derby (about whom more later), had sponsored traveling troupes of players in Chester.[11] In his 1609 *Breviary*, Rogers alludes more than once to the 'wittes' of London in his account of Chester's

---

10 On the 'War of the Theaters' in the late fifteenth and very early sixteenth centuries, see, for example, Bednarz, *Shakespeare*.
11 See MacLean, 'A Family Tradition'.

Figure 9.3. Chester Midsummer Watch 2019: The giants. Photo: Theodore K. Lerud.

Whitson playes. Early in this manuscript's[12] copying of the Late Banes, or announcement of the plays, Rogers states apologetically that if the plays

> [...] be lykeinge to the commons all,
> Then oure desyre is satisfied; for that is all oure gayne.
> If noe matter or shewe thereof enye thinge speciall
> Doe not please but mislycke the moste of the trayne
> Goe backe againe to the firste tyme, I saye.
> Then shall yow finde the fine witte, at this daye aboundinge,
> At that daye and that age had verye smale beinge. (fol. 19ʳ)

Similarly, in a paradoxical statement at the conclusion of the Banes, Rogers warns the reader (viewer?) 'of one thinge':

---

12 Chester, Cheshire Archives and Local Studies [CALS], ZCX 3.

That not possible it is those matters to be contryved
In such sorte and cunninge and by suche players of price
As at this daye good players and fine wittes coulde devise. (fol. 21ᵛ)[13]

Rogers seems to ask his 1609 reader, who may well have never seen these ancient *Whitsone playes*, to imagine a less sophisticated production than they might have been accustomed to from visiting London, or watching traveling troupes.

As in the loss of its Whitsun plays, which had lapsed into obscurity, so by 1604 Chester more broadly had fallen on hard times. For by then, Chester had for all practical purposes been forced to relinquish its special Palatine relationship to the crown, along with its accompanying privileges and independence. Though the Earl of Chester was still nominally the Prince of Wales, and heir to the throne (James' eldest son Henry Frederick in 1604, before Charles succeeded him upon his untimely death in 1612), Cheshire since 1543 was no longer exempt from paying its Parliamentary subsidy, and sending members to Parliament, thus ending its special status among English counties.[14] Moreover, since the Tudors had traced their lineage in part from Wales, there was no longer the present and imminent danger from Wales that had given Chester its unique defensive role as a buffer in earlier times. In fact, though Elizabeth had initially renewed Chester's special charter, and agreed to a 'co-governing' arrangement,[15] it was unclear how the new sovereign would view this. Indeed, in that very year (1604), Mayor Dutton went down to London to confirm what was left of Chester's Palatine Charter.[16] Further, the silting of the Dee had turned Chester into a nautical backwater, with most port trade now going through Liverpool.[17] In addition to the natural exigencies of a tidal river, this longstanding problem had been complicated by the building by Hugh Lupus, first Norman Earl of Chester, of the weir just outside of town (still visible just upriver from the Dee Bridge), to promote the milling trade (**Fig. 9.4**).[18]

---

13 Chester, CALS, ZCX 3, my transcription. For similar but slightly varying versions, see also Lumiansky and Mills' transcriptions of these passages in The Chster Mystery Cycle. *Essays*, ed. by Lumiansky and Mills, pp. 287 and 294 — as well as those in *Cheshire*, ed. by Baldwin and others, vol. I, pp. 334 and 340.

14 See *A History*, ed. by Harris and others, vol. v, part 1, p. 58.

15 Ormerod, *History of Cheshire*, Vol. I, pp. 127–28, provides a transcription of Elizabeth's 1568 'Confirmation of the Liberties of the County Palatine.' Elizabeth's confirmation states: 'we have been informed, that the jurisdiction and authority of our county palatine of Chester, hath been of late years impeached.' Reaffirming Henry VII's ancient charter, she seeks 'to have our said county preserved in the ancient right thereof.'

16 Fenwick, *A History*, p. 179.

17 *A History*, ed. by Harris and others, vol. v, part 1, p. 7.

18 *A History*, ed. by Harris and others, vol. I, concludes based on the evidence that this 'man-made causeway or weir [was] constructed just upstream from the Dee Bridge no later

Figure 9.4. Chester's weir, just above the Dee Bridge. Photo: Theodore K. Lerud.

Past charters, including that of Henry VII in 1506, had acknowledged Chester's problems through successive reductions in the annual farm fee owed by Chester to the Crown in exchange for its Palatinate status (in fact, under Henry VII this fee had dropped to 20 GBP 'in perpetuity').[19] Although Chester had been able to sustain modest population growth throughout much of the sixteenth century (in 1586 Chester reached its highest population of the century, at 6130),[20] in the latter decade, population growth had fallen off due to economic decline, and by 1600 it fell to nil.[21]

---

than the 1090s' (p. 3). The corn mills were located just west of the Dee Bridge: 'Earls Hugh I and Richard apparently intended that they should include a mill for Chester Abbey' (*A History*, ed. by Harris and others, vol. II, p. 104). For a fuller account of the history of the corn mills and the weir, see pp. 104–10.

19 *A History*, ed. by Harris and others, vol. V, part 1, p. 58.
20 *A History*, ed. by Harris and others, vol. V, part 1, p. 91.
21 *A History*, ed. by Harris and others, vol. V, part 1, p. 91.

Then, to make matters worse, in 1603 the bubonic plague struck. In fact, Bedford's 1604 copying of the Chester plays was sandwiched in between two severe outbreaks of the plague in Chester, first in 1603, and a more virulent second wave in 1605. As recounted in the *Victoria County History of Chester*, the first, which began in August 1603, was longer and less severe, while the 1605 outbreak, though shorter, was more deadly, costing the lives of over 1000 Cestrians.[22]

In addition, factors intrinsic to the manuscripts' history also obscure the status of Bedford's copy. The *REED Cheshire* editors note that the evidence 'calls into question whether the extant versions of the plays can safely be dated before the 1560s',[23] well after the effects of the Reformation had been felt across England. Indeed, the case of Chester, and Bedford's hasty version, is even further complicated by the apparent loss of the 'Regenall' (or Original) in 1568, making it unclear exactly what Bedford was copying (or reconstructing?). The disappearance occurred under rather mysterious circumstances. According to the Mayors' Books, on 30 April in the tenth year of Elizabeth's reign, one Randall Trever, 'gentleman', was called before the mayor and 'was demaunded for the original booke of the whydson plaies of the said Citie'.[24] Trever admitted that he had had the 'regenall' (though it is unclear what for, since as a 'gentleman' he was not likely performing in the plays, nor copying out an acting text) and swears upon 'the holy evangelist of god' that he returned it — though oddly he cannot say 'to whom he deliuered the same book'.[25] The record abruptly ends here, without any indication of punishment for the gentleman, or apparent concern over the recovery of the 'regenall', which presumably was essential to earlier productions of the plays.

One wonders what Trever, 'a gentleman', wanted with this text, which he mysteriously lost. At any rate, after this date the state of any full text may be fragmentary, and is thrown in doubt until the creation of Huntington 2 in 1591. The editors describe the origins of this manuscript as 'uncertain', though possibly in the collection of the Egertons, 'an important Cheshire family' in the sixteenth and seventeenth centuries.[26] It is true, as the REED editors note, that at least the Painters and Smiths paid sums toward copying the 'orygenall'[27] or in the case of the Smiths 'the makinge of a new booke',[28] but it is unclear whether this copying refers just to a routine periodic recopying of their own play, or to some broader effort at the time

---

22 *A History*, ed. by Harris and others, vol. v, part 1, pp. 92–95.
23 *Cheshire*, ed. by Baldwin and others, vol. II, p. 893.
24 *Cheshire*, ed. by Baldwin and others, vol. I, p. 118.
25 *Cheshire*, ed. by Baldwin and others, vol. I, p. 118.
26 *The Chester Mystery Cycle*, ed. by Lumiansky and Mills, vol. I, p. XIII.
27 *Cheshire*, ed. by Baldwin and others, vol. I, p. 122.
28 *Cheshire*, ed. by Baldwin and others, vol. I, p. 126.

to reconstruct the lost original. In the case of the Painters, for example, they pay both for paper 'to coppye the orrygenall'[29] and, significantly, for 'Coppyng of *oure* orygenall',[30] whereas the Smiths seem to be giving money to the mayor towards the copying. Nowhere in the records do we find reference to a broader, collaborative effort to recover and recopy the mysteriously lost original, casting radical uncertainty on the nature and purpose of the extant texts. Thus the plays as we have them are at best a (late) Tudor, if not a Jacobean, reconstruction, despite being customarily referred to as 'medieval drama'.

And yet, in this context, William Bedford chose to make a copy of Chester's 'ancient' Whitson playes, which had not been performed in nearly three decades. And unlike Bellin's more ornate 'presentation copies', such as that commissioned by the Coopers, Bedford's copy appears hasty, and is riddled with cross-outs, corrections and some marginal insertions (**Fig. 9.5**).[31]

Bedford's copy begins abruptly, eliminating the (more critical, 'post-Reformation') beginning parts of the Banes, as well as, inexplicably, the opening Tanners play's description, and starts instead with the Drapers (the second play in the series). The top of the first page is cut off (**Fig. 9.6**) — though as F. M. Salter notes there seems to be enough room left to include at least some of any part of the Banes that had been copied.[32]

In addition, any front pages which might have contained the usual dedication or note to the reader have also disappeared here. All that appears in the current manuscript before the beginning of the Banes' description of the Drapers play is a notation inside the front cover, in a much later hand: 'Wm. Bedford's twenty-four pageantes or playes played by the twenty-four craftseller [sic] of the City of Chester.'

As Lumiansky and Mills observe, 'the manuscript is bound in a vellum wrapper, much repaired' which 'contains 179 paper folios measuring approximately 7 ½ by 11 ½ inches'.[33] They note that 'the manuscript is

---

29 *Cheshire*, ed. by Baldwin and others, vol. I, p. 122.

30 *Cheshire*, ed. by Baldwin and others, vol. I, p. 122 (my italics).

31 Permission for sharing of images in Figs 9.5 and 9.6 (my photos) from MS Bodley 175 is granted according to the terms of the Creative Commons Non-Commercial Licence (https://creativecommons.org/licenses/by-nc/4.0/deed.en), Bodleian Libraries, Special Collections.

32 Salter, 'The Banns', pp. 435–36. F. M. Salter suggests that Bedford may have deliberately eliminated the more critical beginning parts of the Banes (p. 436), though if so it is hard to say why he would also eliminate the opening Tanners play's description, and begin instead with the Drapers (the second play in the series). Further, Salter argues that the **Late** Banns were written for the 1575 production (pp. 444–49), but as this production at Midsummer seems to have been partial or incomplete, it may be equally possible that the Banns in this form were never read for a production.

33 *The Chester Mystery Cycle*, ed. by Lumiansky and Mills, vol. I, p. XXI.

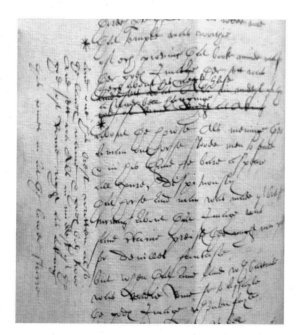

Figure 9.5. A characteristic page of William Bedford's manuscript of the Chester Whitsun Plays. Oxford, Bodleian Library, MS Bodley 175, fol. 48ᵛ. Photo: Theodore K. Lerud.

written in black ink, in one hand',[34] with very few notable decorations. Further, they conclude, as intimated above, that:

> The pages were apparently unruled and the handwriting is hasty, often with blots, cancellations, intersecting letters which make readings difficult, and scrawls which make many forms in final position — especially -st and -e — doubtful.[35]

Indeed, in their facsimile edition of the manuscript, they count 'over 380 cancellations, ranging in extent from a single downstroke to a four-line sequence, and over 60 alterations and insertions [...]'.[36] Not surprisingly, then, the key editors of the Chester plays characterize Bedford's copy as 'not a presentation copy',[37] and Mills concludes that it 'must have been a personal copy'.[38]

---

34 *The Chester Mystery Cycle*, ed. by Lumiansky and Mills, vol. I, p. XXII.
35 *The Chester Mystery Cycle*, ed. by Lumiansky and Mills, vol. I, p. XXII.
36 *The Chester Mystery Cycle. A Facsimile*, ed. by Lumiansky and Mills, p. XI.
37 *The Chester Mystery Cycle*, ed. by Lumiansky and Mills, vol. I, p. XXIII.
38 Mills, *Recycling*, p. 183.

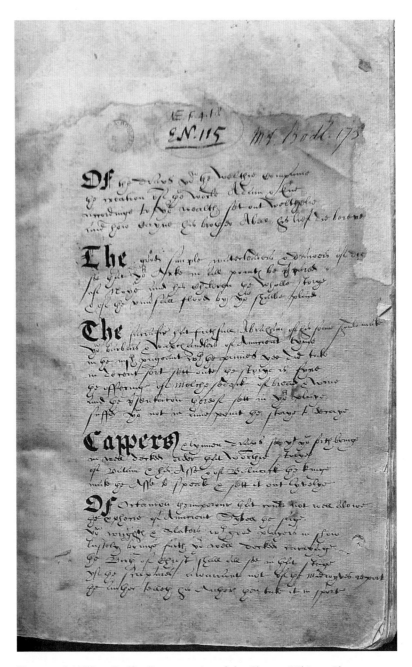

Figure 9.6. William Bedford's manuscript of the Chester Whitsun Plays, Oxford, Bodleian Library, MS Bodley 175, first page. Note partial restoration at top. Photo: Theodore K. Lerud.

So we know what it likely was not, but the idea that it was a 'personal copy' really begs the question of what such a personal copy would be for. Light reading before bed?

What little we know of Bedford himself can be pieced together from the Chester records. He is not mentioned in any of the lists of prominent Chester families, either noble or mercantile, who, according to Rogers, assumed the offices of mayor and sheriff — the Duttons, Stanleys, Hattons, Savages, Goodmans — or even the Masseys, who donated this copy of the plays to the Bodleian in 1710.[39] No Bedford associated with Chester or its environs appears in the *Dictionary of National Biography* prior to the 1800s.[40] Salter notes that William Bedford was clerk for a time to the Brewers guild 'at a salary of four shillings per annum for some years after 1606',[41] also finding that he did other records work in Chester in 1613. David Mills says he was parish clerk (i.e., scrivener or record keeper) of St Peter's,[42] but he must not have been in orders, as no record of him appears in the Clergy of the Church of England Database. During the mayoralty of the Puritan zealot Henry Hardware, according to the Chester Mayor's Book (1599–60),[43] Bedford, 'clerk of the parish church of St Peter's in Chester', receives a charge 'for repairing and keeping in order the chimes of St Peter's for a year in return for 26s 8d wages' (fol. 123^r).[44] Unlike George Bellin, who seems to have had special commission to produce multiple (as we have seen he completed three of the existing six post-1590 copies) more decorative copies of the plays, using for example rubrication for speech headings and stage directions, multiple rulings, and more elaborate finials,[45] Bedford's single rougher copy remains an anomaly.

Bedford's association with Henry Hardware implies Anglican respectability, and, as Mills suggests, removes the likelihood of any kind of Catholic recusancy as a motivation for his copying the plays. Hardware banned many elements of the Midsummer Watch, including the popular giants, and his *Mayor's Book* (fols 1–124) is filled with citations of citizens

---

39 See *A History*, ed. by Harris and others, vol. v, part 1, p. 99, for an account of the prominent families in early modern Chester; a list of the Mayors and Sheriffs of Chester in the late sixteenth and early seventeenth century may also be found in the vol. v, part 2, 'Culture, Buildings, Institutions'.

40 *DNB*, ed. by Stephen and others. The first mention of a Bedford in the electronic *ODNB* is a John Bedford (1810–1879), a clergyman born near Wakefield.

41 Salter, 'The Banns', pp. 435–36.

42 Mills, 'Recycling', p. 91.

43 Chester, CALS, M/B/28a (Hardware, *Mayor's Book*).

44 Earlier in Hardware's *Mayor's Book* (fol. 71^v), Christopher Conway and John Ratcliffe, 'Leavelookers', are accused before the Mayor of 'not maintaining the chymes of St Peter's in sufficient repair'; although the matter is presented as still under examination, it may well be that Bedford, as more competent, was chosen to replace them.

45 *The Chester Mystery Cycle*, ed. by Lumiansky and Mills, vol. I, p. xx.

for unlawful games ('ludi illicit')[46] — e.g., fol. 65[r] alone cites Hugh Case and William Shurlock for playing at 'le footeball' at an inappropriate time, a [James] Smith for keeping 'unlawful games in his house', and one John Wade for maintaining in his house tables to play at 'le shofleboard'. Although succeeding mayors restored the giants, the first decade of the seventeenth century was an uncertain time for Cestrians, and there appears to have been a major antiquarian effort to preserve and document their customs, as evidence of a glorious and singular past which seemed to be slipping away. As Mills suggests, Bedford, along with Bellin and Archdeacon Robert Rogers and his son David, seem to have been part of a group of mainstream Protestant antiquarians, particularly intent on preserving Chester's distinctive past.[47]

So what evidence we do have of Bedford suggests that he was literate and educated, though evidently not a wealthy man among Cestrians — and we can also conclude that he seems to have been a practical man, earning and expecting appropriate pay for his clerical labours. As we have seen, he was appropriately compensated for his clerical work for the Brewers, as well as St Peter's; he was also paid for an inventory he completed on behalf of the waitman William Maddock.[48] Similarly the Chester Treasurer's accounts record a payment for 'dustinge of the [city] records' in 1613,[49] most likely a task he took on at the Pentice, or centre of city government, which was literally an extension of St Peter's. Again, as clerk of St Peter's, the central church in Chester, and also more or less the seat of the city's governance, his religious views must have been beyond reproach.

Rather than a performance text, then, or a clandestine effort to preserve 'Catholic' texts, it is important to see Bedford's 1604 copying of the plays as *an exercise in antiquarianism and historiography*, part of a larger movement not only in Chester, but throughout England. Chester, with the impending loss of its special privileges, seems to have been particularly impacted by what Peter Clark refers to as a general 'transformation' of historical writing throughout England in the sixteenth and seventeenth centuries.[50] Clark speculates that this transformation occurred as England caught up with the Italian renaissance, but an equally strong motivation,

---

46 For further examples of Hardware's citations for illicit games, see fol. 75[r] where, among others, Gruff Lawrens is cited for illicit gaming with 'globis' (bowls) and, once again, James Smith, for maintaining a 'common [bowling] alley' and a 'common gaming house' for his own gain. Further, on fol. 79[v], beside the margin note 'ludi illicit', we encounter, among others, one James Broster cited for illegally keeping 'le gamminge' in his dwelling place, and, yet again, James Smith (who seems to have been a hard case) for 'the like.'

47 Mills, *Recycling*, p. 192.

48 Chester, CALS, WS 1604.

49 Salter, 'The Banns', p. 436.

50 Clark, 'Visions', p. 109.

particularly in the provinces and in the North, would have been the sense of loss resulting from the deprivation of the monasteries — the most important locus of copying and record keeping prior to the Reformation — creating a cultural anxiety about the preservation of the past. Certainly, Chester had witnessed this destruction, both at the Abbey of St Werburgh and St John's church.

The city of Chester was clearly participating in this new historiography, whose first fruits were urban chronicles and annals, such as Aldersey's Chester chronicle from approximately 1580–1609. Indeed, the civic annal became a popular genre — Clark identifies over thirty such efforts from regional and county towns from the 1570s onward.[51] As Frank S. Fussner notes, 'antiquaries and historians *made transcripts* of records and took notes on all kinds of documents which held traces of the past', and such 'notes, transcripts [...], and written copies of manuscript treatises were as important to scholars seeking knowledge of the past as original manuscripts'.[52]

Perhaps a clue to Bedford's motivation, then, can be found in his payment for 'dustinge of the records', seen in the wider context of the transformation of historical writing described by Clark above. Indeed, the efforts of Robert Rogers' collections, organized in his son David's *Breviary*, are particularly emblematic of Chester's participation in this contemporary revolution in historiography. David 'reduced', starting in 1609, the collections of his father, Archdeacon Robert († 1595) into ten or eleven 'chapters' concerning the 'the Aunchant and ffamous Cittie of Chester' (fol. 1ʳ).[53] Roger's *Breviary*, almost certainly influenced by Stowe's popular 1598 *Survey of London*, exists in five manuscripts (none published), with Rogers' authorial influence becoming increasingly apparent in each.

---

51 Clark, 'Visions', p. 110.

52 Fussner, *The Historical Revolution*, p. 34 and 62 (my italics).

53 Chester, CALS, ZCX3. For a good contextualized comparative study of the five versions of Rogers' *Breviary*, see Hart and Knapp, '*The Aunchant and Famous Cittie*'. The authors note that the (10- or 11-) chapter structure of the 5 versions remains quite consistent, as follows: 1. Names of the City of Chester; 2. The history of the layout and first building of the city; 3. Memorable things done in or near the city of Chester; 4. Building of the parish churches of Chester, and laudable exercises and playes; 5. Erection of a monastery, and a history of Abbots and Deans; 6. A succession of the Bishops of Chester; 7. The Earls of Chester, pre- and post-Conquest; 8. Governance of the city, naming the Mayors and Sheriffs; 9. Magistrates and officers of the City, along with their oaths of office; 10. Commendable deeds done for the city; 11. (sometimes included) miscellaneous items not found in the earlier chapters. References to the Whitsun plays appear as a small part of the 'laudable exercises' mentioned in Chapter 4; Chapters 7 on the Earls of Chester are among the most extensive and colorful (with illustrated coats of arms) of the various versions of the *Breviary*. Hart and Knapp note that David's authorial presence (as opposed to mere editing) increases in subsequent editions.

250 THEODORE K. LERUD

Table 9.2. The Five Versions of David Rogers' *Breviary*.

Document reference #	Year and manuscript location
ZCX 3	1609 Cheshire Archives and Local Studies (CALS)
DCC/19	*c.* 1619 Cheshire Archives and Local Studies (CALS)
BL Harley MS 1944	*c.* 1619 British Library
BL Harley MS 1948	*c.* 1624 British Library
LUL MS 128	*c.* 1637 Liverpool University Sydney Jones Library

This 'collection', the first version of which was copied in 1609, five years after Bedford's edition of the plays, is well-known to historians of the theatre as it contains, in Chapter 4 on the 'lawdable exercises' (or worthy historical customs) of Chester, the well-known description of pageant wagons and 'true processional' production which for many years was considered the norm for medieval drama production:

> these pagiantes or carige was a highe place made like a howse with two rowmes beinge open on the tope, the lower rowme they apparalled and dressed them selves. and the higher rowme[s] they played. and thei stoode vpon vj wheeles, and when the had donne with one cariage in one place theie wheled the same from one streete to another, firste from the Abbaye gate, to the pentise [...] through the lanes & so to the estegatestreete (fol. 18ʳ)[54]

However, despite the influence of this description on generations of theatre scholars, Rogers makes no claims to be an historian of the theatre, *identifying the plays as only one of many customs*, and instead taking the larger view of Chester's history in writing his *Breviary*. For the new historiography also gave rise to interest in family history, and genealogy — and these are reflected in the decorative coats of arms which adorn the most interesting and lengthy chapter, number 7, on the Earls of Chester in the various versions of the *Breviary* (the coats of arms are particularly striking and colourful in the first [1609] version, ZCX 3 in the Cheshire Archives and Local Studies office, but are included in all five versions of the *Breviary*) (**Fig. 9.7** and **9.8**).

Seen in the context of Roger's *Breviary* and other artifacts of this new era of historiography, the transcript of the *Chester playes* made by William

---

54 Chester, CALS, ZCX3.

55 Images from David Rogers' 1609 *Breviary*, Cheshire Archives and Local Studies, ZCX 3, are reproduced with the permission of Cheshire Archives and Local Studies and the owner/ depositor to whom copyright is reserved.

Figure 9.7. *Arma Civitatis*, Arms of Chester, David Roger's *Breviary* (1609), Cheshire Archives and Local Studies (CALS) ZCX 3, fol. 89ʳ.[55] Photo: Theodore K. Lerud.

Figure 9.8. Coat of arms of Richard Lupus, David Roger's *Breviary* (1609), Cheshire Archives and Local Studies (CALS) ZCX 3, fol. 52ʳ. Photo: Theodore K. Lerud.

Bedford in 1604 was almost certainly an antiquarian exercise in copying, intended for some developing collection of an influential Cestrian. For this was also the era of collectors, and the beginnings of the great private libraries, such as those of Robert Cotton and Robert Harley, which subsequently formed the foundations of the British Library, the Bodleian, and others. As such, Bedford's copy should not be viewed as a production text. It seems likely that Bedford saw the value of quickly copying, for later use, a manuscript that might be lost in the prohibitions of the Henry Hardware years. Bedford worked for money: there is no evidence that he was a collector himself, nor that he was particularly interested in plays per se. But there were, in Chester, other influential citizens who were, and also had the resources for and interest in building private libraries, such as the Earls of Derby (already mentioned above).

As we have already seen, Lord William Stanley, the sixth Earl of Derby (1594–1642) and Earl during the time of Bedford's copying, who owned a home in Chester and is buried there, was a patron of theatre, with connections in London as well as the northwest. In fact, ever since the ascendancy of the Stanley family in Chester based on the generous grants of Henry VII, the Stanleys,[56] as Earls of Derby, had dominated the social and cultural life of Chester. Patronage and support of players and their companies had, in fact, become a family tradition for the Earls (as mentioned above) — and one which crossed the boundaries by which we conventionally distinguish 'medieval drama' from early modern drama. According to John J. Bagley, even as early as the beginnings of the sixteenth century, Thomas († 1521), the second Earl, patronized 'the Chester players', who at that time 'were chiefly concerned in performing the cycle of mystery plays sponsored by the trade guilds'.[57] Corroborating evidence for the Earls' support of the Chester plays can be found in 1572, when Edward, the third Earl of Derby († October 1572), intervened in a dispute over one of the final productions of the Chester (or Whitson) Plays. The Puritan divine Christopher Goodman, who was determined to stamp out the 'absurdities' of the Whitsun plays, complains in a June 1572 letter to the Archbishop of York that despite the latter's directive that the Mayor (whom Mills identifies as John Hanky)[58] 'surcease from further preparation for setting forth the said [Whitson] plays, & utterly to forbear the playing thereof', the Mayor 'would not be stayed from his determination in setting forth the plays'.[59] In his defense, says Goodman, the Mayor ('as it is reported')

---

56 Coward, *The Stanleys*, notes, 'After the grants they received from a grateful Henry VII, the Stanleys of Knowsley and Lathom were the largest landowners in Lancashire and Chester and no longer shared the rule of those counties' (p. 112).

57 Bagley, *The Earls*, p. 71.

58 Mills, *Recycling*, p. 146.

59 *Cheshire*, ed. by Baldwin, vol. I, pp. 144–45.

had directed letters to his Council as well as 'one to my Lord of Derby chief of her Majesties commission for Cheshire and Lancashire', by whose authority, to Goodman's dismay, Mayor Hanky sees himself as freed from the Archbishop's Commission.[60]

According to the *Dictionary of National Biography* subsequent Earls of Derby continued the patronage of theatre and the arts. Henry Stanley, the fourth Earl (1572–1593), invited actors and poets to perform at his house in Chester.[61] Mills recounts that Henry and his son Ferdinando paid a private visit to Chester in 1577, when, in addition to a comedy by Terence, they saw what might have been one of the final performances of a Chester mystery play:

> The Shepheards playe played at the hie crosse [i.e., the centre of the city] with other Triumphes upon the Rode eye [the parade ground and current horse racecourse just outside the city walls].[62]

It was also the fourth Earl who became patron of the company of actors known as 'Derby's Men' who became even more famous under the patronage of the fifth Earl. The company, known under Ferdinando, the fifth Earl of Derby, as 'Strange's Men' (Ferdinando, like other heirs to the Earldom of Derby, styled himself as 'Lord Strange' until his brief ascendancy to the Earldom in 1593) became the leading company in England. Without attempting to enter the discussion about which acting troupe or troupes Shakespeare might have joined in his early years, we can nonetheless conclude that Lord Strange's men were in residence at Henslowe's Rose Theatre, on the south bank of the Thames, during much of 1592, where they performed plays by Marlowe and Greene, as well as at least the first part of Shakespeare's *Henry VI*.[63] When plague closed the London theatres in the summer of 1592, Strange's men went on tour, performing in a number of northern cities, including, not surprisingly, Chester.[64] It is here that we find the legacy of the Earls of Derby intersecting not only with the medieval Chester plays but also with Shakespeare and his company, several of whom were likely members of the Lord Strange's company,[65] which played at court, in the public theatres, and also toured the provinces during plague years.

Upon Ferdinando's premature and suspicious death in 1594, his younger brother William became the sixth Earl of Derby († 1642). His

---

60 *Cheshire*, ed. by Baldwin, vol. I, pp. 145.

61 Knafla 'Stanley, Henry', says of Henry: 'Plays were given in his honor in the 1570s, and several writers of prose and verse dedicated their works to him.'

62 Chester, CCA CR 60/83 f. 13ᵛ, qtd. in Mills, *Recycling*, p. 134.

63 Bagley, *The Earls*, p. 73.

64 Bagley, *The Earls*, p. 73.

65 Holland, 'Shakespeare'.

much longer earldom spans the period of the copying of most of the Chester manuscripts, including that of Bedford. According to Leo Daugherty, he continued and expanded his predecessors' interest in theatre:

> He patronized his own troupe of players, Derby's Men, who mainly toured the provinces but also played in London during the same years he himself was busily (and scandalously) writing comedies for the public theatres (*c.* 1599–1601); he may have written for them, though no plays attributed to him have survived.[66]

In fact, such was William's reputation that he was seen by some (though groundlessly) as a 'rival claimant'[67] for authorship of the works of Shakespeare.

Stanley, friend of John Donne, Thomas Middleton, and other London wits,[68] had been at Lincoln's Inn, and apparently helped in 1599 to finance the revival of the Children of Paul's, along with John Marston.[69] William's players also performed in London at the Curtain during the winters of 1599 and 1600 — and it seems likely that he was involved in or at least supportive of the construction of the first purpose-built theatre outside London, in Prescot, just outside his Knowsley estate.[70] In 1605, Richard Grosvenor, major benefactor of Chester, whose family is even today memorialized in a statue in Chester's Grosvenor Park,[71] dedicated a history of the house of Stanley to William. Given these connections, there is every reason to suspect that Derby's Men would have performed in Chester in those first years of the seventeenth century, thus further exposing Cestrians to the 'good players & fine wittes' of London.

Although the early years of William's earldom were marred by an inheritance dispute with Ferdinando's widow and her entire family, who tried to keep his inheritance from him,[72] by 1601 'his financial affairs stood

---

66 Daugherty, 'Stanley, William'.

67 Daugherty, 'Stanley, William'.

68 According Daugherty, 'Stanley, William': 'As Thomas Middleton and the earl's friend William Percy (younger brother of the ninth earl of Northumberland, another friend) also wrote for the Paul's boys at this time, Derby would necessarily have worked in association with them. The young John Donne seems to have accompanied Stanley on his unlicensed foreign travels of 1585–7, and he is almost certainly the addressee of the epistolary sonnet that Donne titled "To E. of D. with Six Holy Sonnets", now thought to date from about 1594, when both were at Lincoln's Inn.'

69 Daugherty, 'Stanley, William'.

70 Bagley, *The Earls*, p. 76, notes that this *theatrum* was probably built around 1596 and was actively used until *c.* 1609, when it was converted by its new owner into a 'dwelling house.'

71 For the Grosvenors as patrons of Chester, developing parks, public works, and more while also maintaining important London connections in Belgravia and Mayfair, see *A History*, ed. by Harris and others, vol. v, part 1, p. 4.

72 See Coward, *The Stanleys*, chapter 4, 'The Disputed Inheritance', pp. 41–55.

on a fairly firm footing', and by 1603 he was on the privy council.[73] This allowed him to consolidate and increase his estates, and perhaps also, as Barry Coward speculates, to 'spen[d] most of his time [at Chester and Bidston] … perhaps also on theatrical and literary projects'.[74] Although, given the inheritance dispute, the members of Ferdinando's (Lord Strange's) company might not have immediately transferred to William's troupe, Derby's Men, his players were nonetheless on tour in the midlands and East Anglia within six months of Ferdinando's death.[75]

While there is no evidence that Bedford, as a paid scribe, was a collector of books and manuscripts, there can be little doubt that the Earls of Derby maintained a library among their lavish collections (the current library at Knowsley Hall was reconstituted in 1954–1955, and contains about 5000 volumes[76]). Although the current collection has changed substantially, in accordance with the tastes of the more recent Earls, Stephen Lloyd notes that four major auctions of books, manuscripts, and other items from the Knowsley collection were held in 1953–1954, both at Knowsley and in London; at the same time, the University of Liverpool acquired around 1400 books and 3400 pamphlets, now indexed in Special Collections, from the Earls' library.[77]

That Earl William, along with his two predecessors, was also a collector can be amply demonstrated by the inventory contained in a probate document following the funeral of the fourth Earl, Henry, in 1593. According to Lloyd, this probate document contains a list of all the mourners who attended the funeral, followed by an inventory of the Earl's property. Along with an account of weapons and armour, elaborate arrases and tapestries, and portraits of leading sixteenth- and seventeenth-century figures — including Henry VIII, Queen Elizabeth, and the King of France — contained at Lathom and Knowsley, the document also makes provision for a library (unfortunately without any accompanying list of books and manuscripts). Lloyd states that 'a library is known to have been at Lathom in 1594 for the use of the 4th, 5th, and 6th earls'.[78] Even if we do not accept the specious case for William, the sixth Earl, as an (or *the*) author of Shakespeare's plays, his interest in theatre and patronage of players cannot be in doubt, and we can assume that such a library would provide source material for one who, according to George Fenner in 1599, was 'busye in penning comedyes for the common players'.[79]

---

73 Daugherty, 'Stanley, William'.
74 Coward, *The Stanleys*, p. 57.
75 Bagley, *The Earls*, p. 76.
76 See Lloyd, 'Patronage', p. 341.
77 Lloyd, 'Patronage', p. 340.
78 Lloyd, 'Patronage', p. 340.
79 Coward, *The Stanleys*, p. 64, n. 6.

While we cannot be certain that Bedford had a specific patron in mind when he made his hurried copy of the Chester plays in 1604, it would not be surprising if his aim was to have available the texts of the plays, in preparation for making a fair copy for presentation to Earl William, sixth Earl of Derby, and the Stanleys, the most prominent family in Chester, and longstanding patrons of the theatre. Certainly, Lord Stanley, patron of the theatre in London and the provinces, might wish to add to his library a fair copy of the Chester Whitsun plays attended and defended by his ancestors.

Bibliography

Manuscripts

Chester, Cheshire Archives and Local Studies (CALS) DCC/19 (1619) (David Roger's *Breviary*)
——, M/B/28a (Henry Hardware, *Mayor's Book*)
——,WS 1604 (William Maddock inventories)
——, ZCX 3 (1609) (David Roger's *Breviary*)
London, British Library, Additional 10305 George Bellin (1592) (Chester Whitsun plays)
——, Harley MS 1944 (1619) (David Roger's *Breviary*)
——, Harley MS 1948 (1624) (David Roger's *Breviary*)
Liverpool, Sydney Jones Library LUL MS 128 (*c.* 1637) (David Roger's *Breviary*)
Oxford, Bodleian Library: Bodley 175 William Bedford (1604) (Chester Whistun plays)

Edited Source Texts

Cheshire, including Chester, 2 vols, ed. by Elizabeth Baldwin and others, Records of Early English Drama (REED) (Toronto: University of Toronto Press, 2007)
The Chester Mystery Cycle, ed. by R. M. Lumiansky and David Mills, 2 vols, EETS, S.S. 3, 9 (London: Oxford University Press, 1974 and 1986)
The Chester Mystery Cycle. A Facsimile of MS Bodley 175, ed. by R. M. Lumiansky and David Mills, Leeds Texts as Monographs (Leeds: The University of Leeds, 1973)
The Chester Mystery Cycle. Essays and Documents, ed. by R. M. Lumiansky and David Mills (Chapel Hill: University of North Carolina Press, 1983)
A History of the County of Chester, 5 vols, ed. by B. E. Harris and others, Victoria History of the Counties of England (Oxford: Oxford University Press for the Institute of Historical Research, 1979–2005)
The York Plays, ed. by Richard Beadle (London: Edward Arnold, 1982)

Secondary Material

Bagley, John J., *The Earls of Derby, 1485–1985* (London, Sidgwick and Jackson, 1985)
Bednarz, James, *Shakespeare and the Poets' War* (New York: Columbia University Press, 2001)
Clark, Peter, 'Visions of the Urban Community: Antiquarians and the English City before 1800', in *The Pursuit of Urban History*, ed. by Derek Fraser and Anthony Sutcliffe (London: Edward Arnold, 1983), pp. 105–14

Coward, Barry, *The Stanleys, Lords Stanley and Earls of Derby, 1385–1672* (Manchester: Chetham Society, 1983)

Daugherty, Leo, 'Stanley, William, sixth earl of Derby', *ODNB*, version 14 November 2018 (accessed: 5 February 2024)

Dictionary of National Biography (*DNB*), ed. by Leslie Stephen and others, 63 vols (London: Smith, Elder & Co., 1876–1996)

Fenwick, George Lee, *A History of the Ancient City of Chester* (Chester: Phillipson and Golder, 1896)

Fussner, Frank S., *The Historical Revolution: English Historical Writing and Thought, 1580–1640* (New York: Columbia University Press, 1962)

Hart, Steven E., and Margaret M. Knapp, *'The Aunchant and Famous Cittie': David Rogers and the Chester Mystery Plays* (New York: Peter Lang, 1988)

Holland, Peter, 'Shakespeare, William (1564–1616)', *ODNB*, version 12 August 2021 (accessed: 5 February 2024)

Knafla, Louis A., 'Stanley, Henry, fourth earl of Derby (1531–1593)', *ODNB*, version 28 May 2015, (accessed: 5 February 2024)

Lerud, Theodore, review of *Cheshire, including Chester*, REED, ed. by Elizabeth Baldwin and others (Toronto, 2007), *Modern Philology*, 108/2 (2010), 79–84

Lloyd, Stephen, 'Patronage, Performance, and Memory at Lathom and Knowsley: Curated Artworks, Books, and Archives relating to Shakespeare and the Earls of Derby', *Shakespeare Bulletin*, 38/3 (2020), 333–53

MacLean, Sally-Beth, 'A Family Tradition: Dramatic Patronage by the Earls of Derby', in *Region, Religion and Patronage: Lancastrian Shakespeare*. ed. by Richard Dutton and others (Manchester: Manchester University Press, 2003), pp. 205–26

Mills, David, 'Recycling the Cycle: The Chester Mystery Plays', *Manchester Memoirs*, 131 (1991–1993), 75–95

——, *Recycling the Cycle: The City of Chester and Its Whitsun Plays*, Studies in Early English Drama, 4 (Toronto: University of Toronto Press, 1998)

Ormerod, George, *History of Cheshire*, vol. 1 (London: George Rutland and Sons, 1882)

Salter, Frederick M., 'The Banns of the Chester Plays', *Review of English Studies*, 15 (1939), 432–57

Online Resources

Oxford Dictionary of National Biography (*ODNB*), ed. by David Cannadine and others, https://www.oxforddnb.com (accessed: 5 February 2024)

Reviews

Barbara Sasse, *Zwischen Tugend und Laster. Weibliche Rollenbilder in den Tragedi und Comedi des Hans Sachs*, Imagines medii aevi, 50 (Wiesbaden: Reichert, 2020), 409 pp. ISBN: 978-3-95490-403-7.

The impressively rich book deals with Hans Sachs's fifty-three tragedies and comedies that have female main characters, either as single protagonists, or within a pair. The texts are listed in an appendix of the book, sorted in chronological order, and indicating the primary literary or biblical sources used by Hans Sachs.

Sasse pleads for a new understanding of Sachs's plays, which have traditionally been regarded as an uncritical promotion of Luther's teaching about marriage and family. In her view, these dramas give space to a critical discussion of the role of women in society, and of the fractures between Lutheran teaching and the lived reality of an early modern craftsman's family. She structures her book according to the different evaluations of the female protagonists, and thereby proofs that pure misogyny is rare in Sachs's tragedies and comedies: The chapter about virtuous women deals with the heroines of ten plays: Lucretia, Virginia, Daphne, Pura, Genura, the anonymous exiled empress, Esther, Griselda, Abigail, and Bathsheba, while the chapter about vicious women only comprises four examples: Clytemnestra, Rosamunde, Cleopatra, and Isolde. In addition, there are two pairs of plays mirroring positive and negative female protagonists: Lisabeta and Violanta, and the anonymous innocent empress and the false empress. Finally, there are several 'hybrid women', which are treated in the last chapter: Jocasta, Melusina, Marina, Aretaphia (compared with Judith), and Arsinue. The analysis of the individual plays, however, suggests that most protagonists of the previous chapters could as well be included in this category. The final *moralisatio* of the plays might rate the women as positive or negative examples, the plot, however, opens other perspectives.

The text interpreting chapters follow a largely parallel structure: After a short summary of the plot and a description of the structure of the individual play, Sasse compares the biblical and literary source texts used

European Medieval Drama, 27 (2023), 259–266
BREPOLS ❧ PUBLISHERS   10.1484/J.EMD.5.137686

(and normally also mentioned) by Sachs with his adaptation; she contrasts the plays with other early modern dramatizations or narrative versions of the same topic, as well as representations in the depictive arts, and she asks how Sachs re-uses the same topic in various literary genres (*Meisterlieder*, *Spruchdichtung*, narrative poems, or drama). Her focus thereby is strictly the characterization and evaluation of women, their capacity to take an active role, their conflicts with patriarchal structures, and the various concepts of marriage or chastity presented and defended by the figures in the plays. Sasse identifies two central techniques of representation in Sachs's dramas: he contrasts figures and thereby highlights their specific positive or negative exemplary qualities, and he designs his female figures as parallels or even citations of the protagonists in his other plays, and thereby directs the audience's attention to the typical and to the extraordinary aspects of the individual figure. Sasse is convinced that the repeating structure of the plays (which are normally divided in five acts, when based on a novella by Boccaccio, and structured in seven acts, when based on a prose narrative), the recurring motifs, and the similarity between the characters, not regarding whether they are biblical, ancient, or medieval characters, should be understood as a matter of theatrical didactics. The new and often unknown plots can easier be comprehended by an unlearned audience, if they all follow a common pattern. The audience may thereby spare its cognitive capacity to realize the fine differences and grading of the protagonist's exemplary qualities, that do not only refer to the current gender and family discourse, but also to social, political, and religious discourses. Figures might fail in their traditional gender role, but succeed in their social, political, or religious role, or vice-versa. By crossing the different discourses in his plays (not in his songs), Sasse claims, Sachs questions the patriarchal structures of church and society, and presents himself as a dramatist standing in the middle of basic changes in early modern society.

The book is convincing through the overwhelming mass of material used — I certainly excuse that Sasse has overseen my article about Pura in EMD 18 (2014) — and the rigor by which she follows her line of argumentation, while mirroring the seriality of Sachs's plays in the seriality of her chapters. A critical reader might wish to learn more about the other discourses crossing the gender and family discourse, which are frequently alluded to in the book and form part of the conclusion. With regard of the readability of the book, however, Sasse's decision to follow her priorities and to concentrate on the gender discourse has proven right.

Cora Dietl
University of Giessen
cora.dietl@germanistik.uni-giessen.de

REVIEWS 261

Neidhartspiele. Edition und Kommentar, ed. by Meike Katharina Gallina, Editio Bavarica, 9 (Regensburg: Pustet, 2021), 889 pp. ISBN 978-3-7917-3271-8

The book provides a new edition of those Neidhart plays that John Margetts has edited in 1982,[1] i.e. *Kleines (Nürnberger) Neidhartspiel, St Pauler (schwäbisches) Neidhartspiel, Großes Neidhartspiel, Mittleres (Sterzinger) Neidhartspiel, Sterziner Szenar*, with an extensive commentary, which is inspired by Wolf's commentary to the *Alsfeld Passion Play*[2] and Janota's synoptic edition of the Hessian Passion play group.[3]

All the plays in this volume are preserved in only one manuscript. The edition (part I) closely follows the manuscript's spelling, with only a few instances of normalization. Gallina manages to correct several reading mistakes made by Margetts. However, her edition provides new mistakes, mostly due to Word's auto-correction. The line numbering of the edition is odd: Gallina treats the stage directions and the speakers' names as verse lines, and even keeps the original line break of the prose paratexts. Consequently, she mentions Margetts's different line numbers in the margins, and the different line breaks of the stage directions in Margetts's edition, in the apparatus, together with his misreadings. Apart from Margetts's, she does not use any other older edition of the texts.

The commentary (part II) starts with a general introduction to the genre of Neidhart plays. Without any further discussion, Gallina treats them as Carnival plays. She explains the early modern genre of Carnival plays by comparing it with twelfth/thirteenth-century courtly romance, assuming that her readership would know these texts best. She does not compare them with other theatrical genres, such as religious plays, processions, dialogues, etc.

The individual commentaries of the plays comprise a description of the manuscript in which the play is preserved, and a scene-by-scene explanation: at first a linguistic analysis of the dialect, some short considerations concerning the audience and the stage, lexical annotations. Thereafter follows a very long parallel edition of sequences of the play text facing other texts that might have served as sources, or simply describe similar situations, use similar phrases, the same rarely used vocabulary, or the same rhyme. Each scene commentary concludes with a résumé of the scene and its setting, as it might be imagined for a reenactment of the play.

---

1 *Neidhartspiele*, ed. by John Margetts, Wiener Neudrucke, 7 (Graz: LIT, 1982).

2 Wolf, Klaus, *Kommentar zur 'Frankfurter Dirigierrolle' und zum 'Frankfurter Passionsspiel'*, Die Hessische Passionsspielgruppe, Suppl., 1 (Tübingen: Niemeyer, 2002).

3 *Die Hessische Passionsspielgruppe. Edition im Paralleldruck*, ed. by Johannes Janota, 3+2 vols (Tübingen: Niemeyer, 1997–2004).

Gallina tries to proof that the tradition of Neidhart plays might rather have started in Vienna than in Tyrol. Her linguistic analysis (which is irritating in its phrasing, and is not always correct in details) manages to proof that the plays' dialect (except for the oldest play, which clearly is Swabian) is rather common Bavarian/Austrian and not specifically Tyrolean, except perhaps for the Sterzing play. However, she cannot proof that Neidhart plays in general or only one of them originates from Vienna.

Concerning the audiences and stages, she does not dare to speculate anything concerning the shorter plays, but regarding the *Große Neidhart-spiel* she starts another attempt to proof its Viennese origin. She can identify the territories *Strůmpüechl* and *kayser tal*, which are given to Neidhart by the Duke of Austria in the *Große Neidhartspiel* (l. 1135), with two Hapsburg territories Sturmbichel and Kaiserthal. Not considering that the Hapsburg monarchy still was a wandering monarchy and that Maximilian I often was welcomed to imperial or Hapsburg cities with theatre performances, she takes the named territories and the resulting reference of the figure of the Duke to the Hapsburg family, as a proof that the play was staged in Vienna. She manages to find both inhabitants of Vienna and members of the Faculty of Arts at Vienna University in fifteenth and sixteenth century who had the same names as some figures in the play and concludes that the play refers to these historical persons. However, by chronology, the proof is not convincing, since the persons lived at very different times, and some of them lived later than the date of the manuscript. Thus, again, she cannot proof that the play is from Vienna, though it might certainly be possible.

A major part of the commentary consists of the already mentioned synoptic edition of passages of the plays and passages from other texts. Since Gallina does not explain why she finds the texts comparable with the play texts, even though they might be from very different regions, different times, different literary genres (romances, chronicles, didactic literature, religious and secular plays, medieval and nineteenth-century poetry), the collection overwhelms and puzzles the reader. The same is true for other collections of documents in the book: on pp. 250–53, for example, Gallina lists various documents that proof the existence of female actors and performers in fifteenth-century German speaking countries. This is a most valuable collection, but it does not serve the intended purpose — here: the proof that the *St Pauler Neidhartspiel* was staged by professionals.

Gallina's book is of unquestioned value as a collection of various material. It is a helpful new edition of Neidhart plays, which is better than Margetts's in some instances, and worse in others. It is, however, not convincing in its arguments, and it is confusing to read, with many disturbing features, such as an absurd numbering and hierarchy of the chapters, frequent verbatim repetitions of phrases or whole text blocks, many mistakes in the layout, the non-consistent use of a stylesheet, an often-wrong use of terminology or misleading phrasing, lacking bibliographical references. Gallina's poor understanding for medieval stage settings, finally is expressed in a very strange reconstruction of the stage of the *Große Neidhartspiel*. Unfortunately, I must conclude that the book desperately needs to be re-written.

Cora Dietl
Justus-Liebig-University Giessen
cora.dietl@germanistik.uni-giessen.de

Carlotta Posth, *Persuasionsstrategien im vormodernen Theater (14.–16. Jh.). Eine semiotische Analyse religiöser Spiele im deutschen und französischen Sprachraum*, Trends in Medieval Philology, 41 (Berlin: De Gruyter, 2022), 419 pp. ISBN 978-3-11-073727-5.

Having observed that monographies about medieval theatre history tend to concentrate on single language areas and refer to other languages only by reconstructing possible influences, Posth suggests a new approach to comparative studies in theatre history. She identifies several common fundaments of European medieval plays: the canonical narrative or biblical sources, the traditional use of Ciceronian rhetoric, and the use of theatre as a persuasive form of literature. Posth's main interest are the persuasive strategies used in late medieval and early modern religious theatre. As the corpus of analysis she chooses four German and four French Passion Plays, and ten German and three French eschatological plays.

In chapter II Posth defines the terms 'Spiel' (play), 'Drama' (drama) and 'Theater' (theatre) and discusses the relationship between text and performance, as well as the possibility to distinguish manuscripts used for performances from reading manuscripts. Finally, she lays the foundation for her analysis by discussing modern theories of multimodality and communication theory, and by defining a vocabulary, which she will use for the description of the persuasive strategies of the texts.

Chapter III identifies the topos of 'threat' as one of the major strategies used in religious plays, both to justify the staging of them, and to support their character. If the Christian values or the Christian community are imagined as threatened by some kind of enemy, an instructive play is needed as a defensive tool. Posth observes that in medieval Passion and Antichrist plays the assumed 'enemies' are normally painted as Jews, no matter whether the towns where the plays were staged had a Jewish community or not. The topos of a (Jewish) 'threat' produces further topoi: a topos of 'competition' is mostly visible in scenes of dispute between the high priests or Pharisees and Christ, or in allegorical disputes between Synagoga and Ecclesia. In Doomsday plays this topos is further developed to a topos of a 'looser', when the Jewish competitor must realize that he cannot win a dispute against the judging God. In Antichrist plays, the losing competitor could also substitute the Antichrist himself; Posth speaks about the topos of a 'representative', when the Antichrist stands for all Jews who ignore the true Messiah. Part of the topos of 'threat' could also be the topos of a 'tool': The threatening forces are painted as devil's tools, with no respectable intention on their own. Finally, Posth identifies the topos of 'nature', which tends to combine anti-Judaism with antisemitism. Reactivating old literary and iconographic patterns, the plays depict Jews as boorish, cruel, stubborn, and greedy. Post-Reformation Catholic plays, she observes, transfer the topos of 'Jewish nature' to the Protestants, characterizing them as equally boorish — and lusty. Posth also speaks of the topos of 'equality', meaning that Protestants could be identified with the Antichrist both in their teaching and in their habits.

The following chapter IV deals with the topos of 'authority'. Posth points out that religious plays faced a frequent change of permission and prohibition. This is why they needed not only to stress their own value as means of religious instruction in their prologues, but also used the topos of authority in their main text, supporting their claim of authenticity. Posth identifies various figures of authority on stage: the Church Fathers (especially Augustine and Gergory), the prophets, and the patriarchs of the Old Testament. An even more effective version of the mentioned topos could be the use of direct quotations from the Bible or from liturgy, preferably in Latin, and direct references to chapters of the Gospels. In addition, the use of familiar iconography could serve as topos of authority. When several competing authorities appear on stage, the 'wrong' authority normally is identified either by not referring to the Scriptures at all, or by misinterpreting or incorrectly citing the Bible, or by speaking bad Latin.

Chapter V deals with stereotypes as an emotive strategy of evaluation and persuasion. Distancing herself from nineteenth century scholarship's critique of the use of stereotypes as a sign of 'mean literary quality', Posth regards the use of stereotypes as very effective for pursuing the plays' aims. She observes a frequent use of linguistic methods of forming stereotypes. Most plays address the audience in the first person 'we', stylizing the audience to a homogeneous in-group, while the others, referred to in the third person, 'the Jews', are defined as out-group. By addressing the Jews as a group and not as individuals, they can be given stereotypical attributes. Using demonstrative pronouns, both groups indicate distance to the other: 'this Jesus', or 'these Jews'. Finally, stereotypes are also created and supported by multimodality. Posth observes that all the plays she analyses use a rather homogeneous repertoire of signs to indicate good and evil, such as harmonious music vs. disharmonious noise, or bright and beautiful angels vs. dark, ugly, and partly monstrous devils. The use of space (above vs. below, centre vs. periphery, etc.) also signals good and evil.

In her concluding chapter VI, Posth does not only give a brilliant resume of the book, but she also addresses the question of a difference between late medieval and early modern religious plays. For the Catholic plays she states that the continuity is far stronger than the changes. The old medium 'theatre' continued to be used flanking the new printed media. Old topoi were adapted to the new circumstances, as in the case of the new 'threat' called 'Reformation'. As an effect of new lay interest in the Scriptures, Catholic plays of the sixteenth century augment the number of direct Bible quotations, in addition to the traditional integration of the audience by ritualized prayers and songs.

Taken individually, many of Posth's observations might not be surprising. It is, however, of enormous value for scholarship to have all these strategies of persuasion collected and systematized, and to have a convincing proof that they are an international phenomenon. Posth's concept of a new comparative approach to medieval religious play works well for her study. The German and the French plays display striking similarities. Her argument is easy to follow due to a very clear language, a thoroughly defined terminology, facing translations accompanying all quotations, tables inserted into the chapters displaying the distribution of the discussed phenomena, and a brilliant overview of all the analyzed texts in the appendix.

Certainly, a dissertation treating twenty-one plays in two different languages cannot consider all secondary material about each individual play. However, this is not an encyclopedia, but a fine piece of comparative literature study, very well founded in modern theory, and most pleasant and rewarding to read.

Cora Dietl
University of Giessen
cora.dietl@germanistik.uni-giessen.de